How To Create Strong Institutions In Developing Economies

(Re-Uploaded August 28, 2020)
(After Minor Editing)

How To Create Strong Institutions In Developing Economies

Gabriel Zowam

<u>Copyright/Indemnity</u>

<u>Remarkable Quotes</u>

- *"" ... It has become obvious in the 1990s that neither good policies nor good investments are likely to emerge and be sustainable in an environment with dysfunctional institutions and poor governance""*

  - The World Bank in its Strategy for Reforming Public Institutions & Strengthening Governance (November 2000)

- *"...Every generation must discover its mission and either fulfil it or betray it. To fail to build institutions that support growth and stability is to betray the mission of this generation"*

  - Nigeria's Pat Utomi invoking Franz fanon's "rebuke "on the pathetic state of the nation's governance institutions (Sep 9, 2012)

- *"Africa doesn't need strongmen, it needs strong institutions"*

  Barack Obama, as the President of the United States of America, in his speech to the Ghanaian Parliament (July 2009)

- *"... I state here that what Nigeria needs is both a strong leader and strong institutions."*

  Nigerian Presidential candidate, Muhammadu Buhari, during Nigeria's 2011 Presidential campaigns debate

- *"... To achieve our sustainable development goals we need institutions at all levels that are effective, transparent, accountable and democratic"*

  The United Nations Conference on Sustainable Development, Rio de Janeiro, June 2012

Table Of Contents

Acknowledgements

I wish to start by acknowledging the Divine support of our God Almighty, in Whose guidance and care, my family thrives.

I owe enormous debts to a large number of persons, who have given depth to my life, and from whose support and inspiration this work benefitted immensely. First is an important person in my life, my brother Fabian, for all that my interactions with him over our lives, have taught me about becoming a better human being! Fabian's influence on my life, especially on the right attitude to life, has been truly immense.

I also owe a somewhat similar debt to Charles Onyeador, former Finance Director at Nigeria's Tertiary Education Trust Fund, for how his infectious enthusiasm for God has influenced me.

In terms of my intellectual debts, my benefactors are simply too many to fully enumerate! First are those I regard as my early "reform mentors", David Osborne, Ted Gaebler, Michel Hammer and James Champy. Their seminal works gave enormous depth to my own thinking about reengineering and governance reform; and awakened me not only to begin to ask questions that challenged traditions, but also to become open to whatever alternatives the answers could inspire.

I also owe important dues to Geoff Colvin, Fortune's Senior editor-at-large, whose writings on diverse subjects exposed me to new realms of scholarship and literary quality. The same goes for Kevin Roose!

The very rich materials that the World Bank, UNDP and the U.K.'s Department for Business, Innovation and Skills (DBIS) put in the public domain, were a very helpful resource for this book. The same goes to Douglass North, Daron Acemoglu, James Robinson, Simon Johnson, Christopher Carrigan, and Lindsey Poole, whose great works really enhanced my understanding of institutions, and have been quoted generously in this book. I can also mention the various works of Ngozi Okonjo-Iweala, Peter Drucker, John Chubb, and Pat Utomi. The list continues! This book was a lot easier because of the insights they provided.

I thank Tony Obioha, T. Garnvwa, Clara Fejokwu, St Peter CMO, Sakar, Christopher Okafor and my other social media platform friends. Their steady streams of materials significantly lightened the drudge of this work!

Lastly, let me appreciate the Zowams, starting with our wonderful sons, Ogadi, Vincent, Samuel, and Fabian – for being such a bundle of joy and inspiration! I cannot thank God enough for them! And then, my beautiful wife! I always smile, when people compliment her beauty, because unknown to them, her great looks actually veil an extraordinary treasure of strength, maternal care, and kind-heartedness. She has been a great pillar of support! The best way to appreciate them all is probably what I like to do every day – committing them to God in prayer!

Gabriel Zowam

Preface

The weak, dysfunctional governance institutions prevalent in the developing countries (DCs) have been accepted as a fundamental cause of the vast disparities these DCs suffer relative to other nations, in economic development. It is remarkable how many of these poor countries are wasting away in hopeless poverty and underdevelopment, at a time many other economies are bustling, innovating and progressing. Now, if "strong institutions" have become the answer, how exactly can a nation with weak institutions, go about strengthening them? What practical guidance can policymakers find, when they want to embark on that critical journey to strong institutions? The first goal of this book is to attempt to provide such guidance!

The second goal is also very interesting! It has been decades since reform experts (in the league of David Osborne, Ted Gaebler, Michel Hammer and James Champy) unveiled a flurry of basic (but profound) principles that should guide the structuring of systems and institutional programs. Most of these principles remain as relevant today as ever. However, it is remarkable how the systems, processes and institutional programs one encounters in the DCs tend to be structured almost in total ignorance of them! This book seeks to correct that, by using an extensive range of real-life case-examples to explain these violations, and how they may be corrected.

The book has also tried to provide generous guidance to policymakers on various trending issues that can affect institutional quality today – such as technology issues (including globalization and the digital economy), private-sector integration into governance, regulation, benchmarking, performance measurement, leadership, accountability, and more. A very important feature of this book is its extensive use of real life cases (over 170 of them) that show how various on-going programs of the DCs uphold or violate specific institutional principles, and how any violations may be corrected. These cases also show many low-hanging opportunities for achieving very effective governance reforms, even within the constraints of existing political arrangements. All these issues are expected to be relevant to policymakers not just at the national, regional, and local councils levels, but also even at the levels of government ministries, departments and agencies (MDAs) and individual public programs. The author has tried to present the issues not like an academic paper, but with policymakers in mind.

For ease of reference, this book is set out under the following distinct sections that I have chosen to call "Slices":

- *Slice A* looks at the concept of institutions, and how they seem to explain successfully the disparities in development across nations.

- *Slice B* looks at the challenges of institutional reform, and the compelling need for such reform in the DCs, leveraging the authoritative works of Douglass North, Daron Acemoglu, James Robinson, Simon Johnson and others. It then suggests some key structures that a DC can set up, to drive such a reform process. An important school of thought (to which Nigeria's Muhammadu Buhari belongs) argues that it would take strong leaders to create strong institutions. That is why this Slice also looks at the issue leadership, and attempts to situate "strong" leadership in the context of institution building today.

- *Slice C* is where we start the actual reform of institutions. It presents a very important basket of principles and techniques for transforming institutional performances, by restructuring the incentives that drive behaviors of public agents. These tools leverage extensively the great works of reform godfathers such as David Osborne, Ted Gaebler, Michel Hammer and James Champy. Some of these tools offer us the means of replicating in governance, the kind of conditions that propel vibrancy in the private sector. The tools, and indeed this entire book, emphasize the "diagnostic" approach, in contrast to any one-size-fits-all notion of blindly copying a "best practice".

- *Slice D* is similar to Slice C, and presents some tools for improving organizational performance as a way of improving overall institutional performance. While Slice C focuses on processes, the focus of Slice D is on organizations.

- *Slice E* looks at technology, which offers an exciting window of opportunity to the DCs for leapfrogging their weak institutions, by cutting off the institutional learning curves that the developed economies had to pass through. The DCs also need to begin to pay serious attention to the profound impact that technology is making on governance, including the very unsettling (but largely stealth) impact of globalization and the digital economy on the DCs; and the new dangers that any DC will face, if it should fail to become seriously proactive with technology.

- *Slice F* explains the pivotal role that "Regulation" can play in each DC in strengthening institutions; and provides specific suggestions on how to go about this.

- *Slice G* finally explains how each DC can leverage the private sector to strengthen institutions. Contrary to the thinking of many policymakers, privatization is not always an automatic solution to the corruption and inefficiencies in government services. Moreover, even when privatization has the potential to help, it is often handled very poorly, leading to disappointing outcomes! This Slice explains how private-sector integration (or PSI) must be done properly, in terms of both conceptualisation and execution, so that it does not end up worsening the institutional problems it is supposed to solve.

Going forward, the author hopes that this work will deepen ongoing conversations on the institutions challenge in the DCs – especially now that the global community (including the developed nations) is bracing up for the potentially unprecedented disruptions that the surging advances in technology are set to unleash on governance and national economies – the consequences of which will be devastating to any DCs that fail to shape up right away.

This work has been a big challenge in another way. It was exciting to be able to take advantage of the new technology-driven process of self-publishing, through Amazon-KDP. However, it was somehow sobering to discover that putting the book together (including all the research, compilation and editing) in MS-Word was just the first part of the challenge! Thereafter came a second (and hitherto unanticipated) challenge of making the work upload properly to the Amazon-KDP publishing platform! This eventually required practically rewriting the entire work, to remove all the embedded tables and other features that had been used with great efforts to structure the book and boost its esthetics. Even at that, the MS-Word version (the source) is so much better esthetically, than the converted version. But we are continuing to work on it.

Gabriel Zowam

Table Of Cases

(Practical, Real-Life Illustrations of the Concepts Presented in This Book)

Slice A: Getting Started: Institutions, Economic Growth & Development

Because this book is about the reform of institutions, this first Slice highlights what the experts are telling us about institutions, its role in national development, and why our DCs should treat the reform of governance institutions with a sense of urgency.

Chapter 1

1. Institutions & Economic Development

"The main determinants of cross-country differences in income per capita are differences in economic institutions ... As a result, understanding underdevelopment implies understanding why different countries get stuck in political equilibria that result in bad economic institutions."

(Institution experts, Daron Acemoglu & James Robinson in "The Role of Institutions in Growth & Development", Review of Economics and Institutions, Fall 2010)

The Topics Covered in This Chapter

- Introduction
- Institutions and economic growth & development
- What it all means for our DCs
- The Obama tonic & Buhari's garnish
- Strong institutions must subordinate everybody
- President Muhammadu Buhari & the twist of fate

Introduction

On gaining independence in 1965, Singapore faced an uncertain future that included inter-ethnic tensions among its diverse groups, tension with its neighbors, skeptic international media, potential instability from high unemployment, and a hopeless lack of natural resources. However, the young nation paid a surprisingly early attention to what was obviously "institutions building". We can get some insight from Gundy Cahyadi and team, and their *"Singapore Metropolitan Economic Strategy Report"* for Global Urban Development:

Case 1:   Singapore's Early Embrace of Development Institutions

Soon after gaining independence, the Singapore government asked the United Nations to send economic advisors who had worked in similar countries, especially in terms of size and economic stage. As explained by Gundy Cahyadi etal, the United Nations team was led by Dr. Albert Winsemius, a Dutch industrialist who had previously advised Portugal and Greece.

One of their first initiatives was to establish an institution that would facilitate easy foreign investment in the island, including a one-stop center for general and procedural information, about investing in Singapore that could ease the transfer of investment into the country and allow foreign investors to bypass a lot of government bureaucracies.

(For more details, please see Singapore's Economic Transformation, by Gundy Cahyadi, Barbara Kursten, Marc Weiss, & Guang Yang)

To appreciate just how remarkable this early foresight by the founding fathers of Singapore must have been, we can consider that it took Singapore's contemporary, Nigeria (another nation that became independent at about the same time, in 1960), several decades to embark on a similar initiative!

Case 2:   <u>Singapore's 30-Year Gap Over Nigeria</u>

It was not until 1995 (30 years later) that Nigeria created its own special agency, the Nigerian Investment Promotion Commission (NIPC) for facilitating foreign investment in the country. By that time, Singapore's GDP per capita (according to the World Bank) was already $24,937, compared to $263 for Nigeria, despite Nigeria's huge comparative advantage in natural resources:

- Singapore: $24,937
- Nigeria: 263

It took 11 more years for Nigeria's NIPC to establish (in March 2006) a "One Stop Investment Center" (OSIC) for the country! By this time, Singapore's GDP per capita (according to the World Bank) had reached $33,579, compared to $1,015 for Nigeria:

- Singapore: $33,579
- Nigeria: 1,015

While some other economic, social, cultural and geographic factors might have contributed to Singapore's phenomenal development, its early attention to development institutions was certainly an important "plus" – attesting to the remarkable foresight of the founding fathers!

Institutions, Economic Growth & Development

Economists and development practitioners are today bluntly telling us that good policies even when backed with good budgets, investments (and even knowledge transfer), are not likely to lead to sustainable national development and economic prosperity, if the institutional environment is very dysfunctional.

Institutions as a factor in economic development have come a long way! Up to the 1960s and 1970s, the standard model that economists used to plot national economic development revolved around the factors of technology, human capital, and efficient economic organization – especially the rate of adoption of new technologies. Then, came the pivotal works of Douglass North, and the compelling body of work that they inspired (for example, from Daron Acemoglu, James Robinson, John Wallis, Barry

Weingast, Simon Johnson, Ronald Coase, Joseph John, Oliver Williamson, and others). These started to create a profound new perspective on economic development, incontrovertibly linking institutional differences across nations to their vast differences in prosperity.

Today, we can say that institutions have earned an eminent place in the global development agenda. The World Bank, in an important recognition of this, published a major report in 2000, on reforming public institutions and strengthening governance, as a key component of its work of helping its client countries build well-functioning and accountable governments. According to the Bank:

> "The critical importance of well-performing public institutions and good governance for development and poverty reduction has come to the forefront in the 1990s. Just as it was increasingly recognized in the 1980s that individual investment projects are less likely to succeed in a distorted policy environment, so it has become obvious in the 1990s that neither good policies nor good investments are likely to emerge and be sustainable in an environment with dysfunctional institutions and poor governance."

Economists often cite the case of North Korea (NK) and South Korea (SK), the two nations that came out of what used to be one homogenous Korea

Case 3:   Acemoglu & Robinson's Case of The Two Koreas

As pointed out by Acemoglu and Robinson, the two Koreas used to be one country, economically and culturally, and were ethnically homogeneous until their separation following the World War II. Thereafter, NK adopted a very centralized command economy, where institutions had no room for private property ownership. On the other hand, SK under another dictatorship of its own, pursued a capitalist policy, where institutions allowed the private ownership of the means of production, and legal protection of private property. Under these two contrasting institutional arrangements, the two economies diverged! While the SK's approach was generally supportive of private local and foreign investment (leading to rapid growth and development), NK experienced minimal growth since the 1950s, because of its own form of institutions and policies.

(Source: For more details, please see Daron Acemoglu & James Robinson: The Role of Institutions in Growth & Development, Review of Economics and Institutions, Vol. 1 – No. 2, Fall 2010)

In their compelling book, Why Nations Fail, Daron Acemoglu and James Robinson similarly used the example of the two Nogales to illustrate how institutional differences can make dramatic differences in growth and development, even for societies with similar cultures that are separated by a mere fenced boarder!

Case 4:   Acemoglu & Robinson's Case of The 2 Nogales

According to Acemoglu and Robinson (2012), Nogales, Sonora (in Mexico) and Nogales, Arizona on the United States side of the boarder, are literally two adjacent cities separated by a fenced boarder. In Nogales on the American side, roads are better, life expectancy is higher, and there is democracy. However, just across the border, on the Mexican side, it is the complete opposite!

The authors explain that Nogales, Arizona is so much richer than Nogales, Mexico because of the sharply different "institutions" at work on the two sides of the boarder, which create different incentives for the inhabitants of Nogales, Arizona versus those of Nogales, Mexico.

(Source: Again, for a more interesting rendition, please see Acenoglu, Daron & Robinson, James A: Why Nations Fail, Profile Books Ltd, London 2012)

The United Nations Conference on Sustainable Development held in Rio de Janeiro in June 2012, reached a global consensus on the importance of institutions for national development:

"… To achieve our sustainable development goals we need institutions at all levels that are effective, transparent, accountable and democratic".

The OECD in its High-Level Panel Report on the Post-2015 Development Agenda, reached a similar conclusion:

"While no single "one-size-fits-all" model of governance can be held up as the gold standard, there is a strong consensus around the role and significance of effective, accountable, and inclusive institutions in promoting sustainable and equitable development."

The United Nation's High-Level Report on the Post-2015 (HLP, 2013) Development Agenda has called for a *"fundamental shift to recognize the significant role of institutions in contributing to citizens' well-being"*. In fact, Goal 16 of the UN's universal call for actions to end poverty, protect the planet and ensure that all people enjoy peace and prosperity – the global Sustainable Development Goals (SDGs) – focuses on peace, justice, and *"strong institutions"*.

More recently, in its 2017 *World Development Report*, the World Bank has highlighted the need for paying attention not just to the forms of institutions, but also to how they function – citing China's stunning four decades of double-digit economic growth, which (according to the bank), lifted over 700 million Chinese out of poverty):

"…China's experience highlights the need to pay more attention to how institutions function and less to the specific form they take".

In this book, we shall not only pay very close attention to the "forms" of institutions, but also seek to influence how institutions function.

What It All Means for Our DCs

From Daron Acemoglu, we get some unpalatable numbers about our DCs:

- The income per capita in sub-Saharan African countries such as Mali, Zaire, and Ethiopia range around 3% of that of the United States!

The question is, "why?" What can be responsible? In anticipation of the standard economic answers – physical capital differences (DCs do not save enough), human capital differences (DCs do not invest enough in education and skills), and technology differences (DCs do not invest enough in technology adoption, and cannot organize their productions efficiently) – Daron is ready with some follow-up posers:

- Why do some countries invest less in physical and human capital?
- Why do some countries fail to adopt new technologies and to organize production efficiency?

The consensus is that beneath all these problems are dysfunctional institutions that are creating perverse economic incentives, and driving the DCs' persisting poverty and underdevelopment! For example, the development community including donor agencies has realized that their injection of technology and individual investment projects into poor countries fail to make the right impact, once the institutions of governance continue to be dysfunctional. Mark Wentling, a seasoned development and humanitarian relief specialist, put it this way:

> "Some low-income countries have received funding on a per capita basis that is the equivalent of providing several Marshall Plans over the past decades but few, if any, countries have much to show for this assistance largesse. Too much funding has achieved temporary and poor results because strong institutions were not in place to carry on the work started with donor funds"

Our DCs must therefore recognize that they will not find enduring solutions in their mantra of attracting more foreign aid, foreign technology, foreign capital or foreign investments – as long as their dysfunctional institutions continue to create perverse economic incentives! In other words, our DCs must urgently start looking into their dysfunctional institutions, including in most cases, the balance of political forces that have created (and are sustaining) them. Luckily, the awareness is growing. For example, as Pat Utomi put it (based on Franz fanon's "rebuke"):

> "…every generation must discover its mission and either fulfill it or betray it. To fail to build institutions that support growth and stability is to betray the mission of this generation"

The Obama Tonic & Buhari's Garnish

Across Africa and other DCs, two recent events seemed to catapult the *institutions* discourse from the realm of development economists and reformers, to the center of the political space. First, was the charge of Barack Obama (as the President of the United States of America) to the Ghanaian Parliament in July 2009, which dwelt significantly on putting the continent's democracies on firmer footings.

Case 5: Barack Obama's Charge To Ghanaian Parliament

> "…No person wants to live in a society where the rule of law gives way to the rule of brutality and bribery. (Applause.) That is not democracy, that is tyranny, even if occasionally you sprinkle an election in there.

"…Now, time and again, Ghanaians have chosen constitutional rule over autocracy, and shown a democratic spirit that allows the energy of your people to break through. (Applause.) We see that in leaders who accept defeat graciously -- the fact that President Mills' opponents were standing beside him last night to greet me when I came off the plane spoke volumes about Ghana -- (applause); victors who resist calls to wield power against the opposition in unfair ways.

"…Across Africa, we've seen countless examples of people taking control of their destiny, and making change from the bottom up. We saw it in Kenya, where civil society and business came together to help stop post-election violence. We saw it in South Africa, where over three-quarters of the country voted in the recent election -- the fourth since the end of Apartheid … Now, make no mistake: History is on the side of these brave Africans, not with those who use coups or change constitutions to stay in power. (Applause). "Africa doesn't need strongmen, it needs strong institutions. (Applause.)"!

(Source: The White House, Office of the Press Secretary, July 2009)

The part of the remarks declaring that Africa didn't need strong men but "strong institutions" particularly resonated across Africa and other DCs! President Obama would later underscore this point in July 2015, when he again addressed the people of Africa at the African Union Headquarters, Addis Ababa, Ethiopia.

Case 6: President Obama At The African Union HQ

"…I have to also say that Africa's democratic progress is also at risk when leaders refuse to step aside when their terms end. (Applause.) Now, let me be honest with you -- I do not understand this. (Laughter.) I am in my second term. It has been an extraordinary privilege for me to serve as President of the United States. I cannot imagine a greater honor or a more interesting job. I love my work. But under our Constitution, I cannot run again. (Laughter and applause.) I can't run again. I actually think I'm a pretty good President -- I think if I ran I could win. (Laughter and applause.) But I can't. So there's a lot that I'd like to do to keep America moving, but the law is the law. (Applause.) And no one person is above the law. Not even the President. (Applause.)

"…When a leader tries to change the rules in the middle of the game just to stay in office, it risks instability and strife -- as we've seen in Burundi. (Applause.) And this is often just a first step down a perilous path.

"And sometimes you'll hear leaders say, well, I'm the only person who can hold this nation together. (Laughter.) If that's true, then that leader has failed to truly build their nation. (Applause.)"

-Source: The White House, Office of the Press Secretary, July 2015

The second event, which in itself was an evidence of how Obama's charge was resonating across the DCs, was the modification that a major Nigerian Presidential candidate, Muhammadu Buhari, brought to the development discourse during his

Presidential campaigns. According to Muhammadu Buhari, Nigeria did not JUST need strong institutions but also strong men to create those strong institutions! Max Amuchie, a member of the editorial board of *BusinessDay*, recalls this Buhari twist:

> "…At the presidential debate last Friday, Buhari asserted: 'While in Ghana, Obama stated that what Nigeria needs is not strong individuals but strong institutions, but I state here that what Nigeria needs is both a strong leader and strong institutions.'"

Muhammadu Buhari's modification was also very interesting! Even if he had a vested interest in that argument (considering that one of the political selling points of his candidacy, was his stereotype as a strong, "no nonsense" leader), many analysts have nevertheless agreed that it represented a sensible accompaniment to the Obama's thesis. According to Ventures Africa:

> "A way to look at this is that the principles of modern democracy such as social justice, equality, rule of law, human rights and so on were championed at one point or another by men and women such as George Washington, Abraham Lincoln, Mahatma Gandhi, Martin Luther King Jr., Nelson Mandela, and Aung San Suu Kyi. The institutions of democracy were built, and continue to develop, on a foundation enshrined by the principles championed by these leaders. This supports the view that strong leaders are needed to strengthen institutions."

There is another factor that makes Muhammadu Buhari's submission relevant: A nation's institutions are often related (as we shall see in the next Slice) to the nation's balance of political forces. As Acemoglu and Robinson have argued very strongly, behind every dysfunctional economic institution are usually some powerful political forces that are sustaining them – forces that may be feeding from the dysfunction.

Therefore comprehensive institutions reform will ultimately tinker with the balance of the political forces in a DC – something that definitely calls for political will (or strong leadership, however defined). We have devoted two full Chapters in this Slice to explore the political nature of institutions and the challenges of reforming them; and a third Chapter to explore the issue of strong leadership in today's DCs.

Strong Institutions & Power Of Subordination

Finally, note that governance institutions cannot quite be described as "strong", if they are functioning well merely because of the benevolence of the current rulers, who have "graciously" allowed them to function well! Institutions become truly "strong", when they become invested with so much legitimacy that they can on their own, subordinate all citizens (including the political leaders) to their boundaries! In that case, they become sustained by that political and bureaucratic capacity to create uproar and outrage, whose consequences may even become unpredictable, if leaders dare to mess with them.

Imagine a President of the United States trying to scheme for another term of office beyond the constitutionally allowed two terms! An unprecedented outrage will simply ensue, which may even consume the President! Barack Obama put it this way (in his Ethiopia speech):

Muhammadu Buhari (Nigeria's President) & The Twist of Fate

The task of strengthening institutions may even be providential for Nigeria today! Muhammadu Buhari made his submission as a Presidential candidate, during Nigeria's Presidential campaigns of 2011, which he lost. He had lost two such elections before then; and he always contested every loss in court, claiming that he had been rigged out (a case of weak electoral institution).

Now, Muhammadu Buhari, in an interesting twist of fate, has (since May 29 2015) become the President and Head of State of the Federal Republic of Nigeria, and Commander-In-Chief of the armed forces, following his 4th shot at the Presidency. This means that the man, who has a reputation for "strong" and "no nonsense" leadership (and who had argued while campaigning for the job that it would take such a strong leader to create strong institutions) is now face-to-face with a golden opportunity to do just that! He is in a position to etch his name on the board of fame of other legendary leaders, who when they similarly came face-to-face with history, showed patriotism, as well as decisive and transformational leadership. We can remind ourselves of:

- Singapore's Lee Kuan Yew (1959 –1990)
- Malaysia's Mahathir Mohamad (1981 to 2003)
- South Korea's Park Chung Hee (1960-79) and Kim Dae Jung (1998-2003)
- Dubai's Sheikh Rashid bin Saeed Al Maktoum (1958 – 1990) and Sheikh Mohammed Rashid Al Maktoum (since 2006)

For this vital national assignment, Muhammadu Buhari is remarkably complemented by a Vice President, Prof Yemi Osinbajo, who has also come to office with a very high level of academic achievement. Together, they have inherited a nation that is unusually rich in human and material resources, but tragically trapped in worsening poverty, underdevelopment, and instability, all of which are being attributed to weak governance institutions. In other words, Pat Utomi's adaptation of Franz Fanon's "rebuke" cannot apply to a better setting:

"…Every generation must discover its mission and either fulfill it or betray it. To fail to build institutions that support growth and stability is to betray the mission of this generation"

Chapter 2

2. Institutions 101: The Basics (For Policymakers)

"Institutions have and follow rules, strong men have friends and follow whims. The outcome from one is calculable probability of outcomes; from the other uncertainty. Uncertainty makes decision making problematic and often results in either the avoidance of economic engagement or the high cost of hedging against undesired outcomes. These high transaction costs translate to un-competitiveness for the economy."

(Prof Pat Utomi, September 2012)

Topics Covered in This Chapter:

- Introduction
- Understanding institutions
- Institutions & organizations
- Types of institutions
  - Formal & informal institutions;
  - Political & economic institutions
  - Contracting & property-rights institutions
  - Horizontal & vertical institutions
  - Social & cultural institutions
  - Good & bad, strong & weak institutions
  - Extractive & inclusive institutions
- How Good Economic Institutions Drive Prosperity
- Institutions, governance, government & the State

Introduction

In the last Chapter, we looked at the critical role of strong institutions for national development; and how institutional differences seem to explain the vast differences in prosperity observed across nations.

Because this book is about institutions reform, let us step back in this Chapter to appreciate the fundamentals of institutions – what they are, their types and characteristics – for the benefits of leaders and policymakers.

Understanding Institutions

It is almost inevitable that when discussing institutions, one would start with Douglass North, regarded as the godfather of institutional economics. North, together with John Joseph Wallis and Barry R. Weingast (2009) have explained institutions as:

> "the 'rules of the game', the patterns of interaction that govern and constrain the relationships of individuals … Institutions include formal rules, written laws, formal social conventions, informal norms of behavior, and shared beliefs about the world, as well as the means of enforcement. The most common way of thinking about institutions is that they are constraints on the behavior of individuals as individuals."

The World Bank (2000) similarly defines institutions as:

> The "rules of the game" that emerge from formal laws, informal norms and practices, and organizational structures in a given setting

The DFID (2010) also defines institutions as:

> The formal and informal 'rules of the game' that shape, but do not determine human behavior in economic, social and political life

A very helpful explanation of institutions that policymakers will easily relate to, comes from the OECD's High-Level Panel (HLP) of eminent persons on the Post-2015 Development Agenda: HLP uses the term "institution" to cover:

> "rules, laws and government entities, as well as the informal rules of social interactions … [which] in essence define how power is managed and used, how states and societies arrive at decisions, and how they implement those decisions and measure and account for the results …"Effective institutions can take many forms: robust legal frameworks and representative parliaments with strong capacity for oversight; adept civil services and the timely and quality delivery of public services; efficient judiciaries that uphold the rule of law; vibrant and actively engaged civil societies; and free and independent media."

Institutions & organizations

The DFID (2010) has made a very noteworthy distinction between institutions and organizations. Organizations, according to North, Wallis and Weingast (2009), are best understood as

> The formally or informally co-ordinated vehicles for the promotion or protection of a mix of individual and shared interests and ideas. In other words, they are players of the game

The DFID (2010) explains that like institutions (as we shall see shortly), organizations may be *formal* or *informal* and may operate within, across or outside economic, political or social institutional arrangements.

The DFID lists the following examples of formal and informal organizations:

1. *Formal Organizations*: Companies, trades unions, political movements or parties, churches, news media, banks and businesses, public bureaucracies and ministries, security services, professional and business associations

2. *Informal Organizations*: The mafia, secret societies, criminal gangs, cabals, political factions or cliques within parties and organizations and some forms of both social movements

Informal organizations tend to have less or no public profile, no formal constitution and operate behind the public space.

The following is an adaptation of a very helpful football (World Cup) analogy that the DFID has used to differentiate institutions from organizations, and also show how institutions work.

<u>Case 7:</u> **Institutions vs. Organizations: DFID's Football Analogy**

In a World Cup tournament, national teams converge from different countries, divided by language, religion, culture and politics – with some countries rich, and others poor.

The DFID has used this tournament in the following institutional analogy:

- *Institution*: This game of football can be understood as an 'institution', the 'rules of the game' of football are clearly known and agreed by various stakeholders, such as the teams, players, and fans. That's what an institution is and what it does. As the DFID puts it, "It shapes, without determining, human behavior in different spheres of life, whether the 'game' is football or stable and predictable patterns of economic, political or social interactions … Because people in China and Chile understand and accept football rules, they can play the game with or without each other."

- *Organizations*: The various teams from different countries represent the organizations. Notice the differentiation of the "rules" of the game (the institution) from the "players" of the game (the organizations).

- *Enforcement of the rules of the game*: The players, individually and in their teams, are expected to operate within the rules of the game, which they understand (the imposition of "form"). Other stakeholders, including the fans, have over time, become familiar with the rules, and expect the teams (the organizations) to play according to the rules (making it easier "to anticipate behavior").

  To enforce these rules, there are referees, who represent FIFA, the international organization that upholds and implements the game of football (the institution).

- Transgressions: When rules are transgressed, the stakeholders expect some punishment on the lawbreaker; otherwise, an understandable outrage can ensue. As an example of this outrage, the DFID cites the outburst of Irish fury at Thierry Henry's "hand-ball" infringement in the pre-World Cup qualifying match between Ireland and France.

Finally, because some organizations may seek to change the rules of the game, there need to be rules for changing the rules! Of course institutions can be more complex than this simplification, but the analogy captures the basic essence.

For details, see the DFID-funded (IPPG) Research, Beyond Institutions. Institutions & Organizations In The Politics & Economics Of Poverty Reduction - A Thematic Synthesis Of Research Evidence (September 2010)

The terms "institutions" and "organizations" sometimes overlap, but as we can see from the foregoing, they are certainly not synonymous.

Types Of Institutions

To deepen our appreciation of institutions, let us peep into the common names and classifications of institutions that are often highlighted in connection with economic outcomes. In trying to distinguish between these institutions, let us bear in mind that they tend to be connected, and that real-world societies usually combine them.

Formal & Informal Institutions

1. *Formal institutions*: John M. Carey explains "formal" institutions as the written laws, regulations, legal agreements, statutes, contracts and constitutions, which are enforceable by third parties. They are sometimes called "parchment" institutions.

2. *Informal institutions*, on the other hand, are the (usually un-written) norms, customary practices, procedures, and traditions, which influence how the formal institutions are used. As pointed out by the DFID (2010), using the caste system in India for illustration, informal institutions are often embedded in the people's culture and its associated ideology. They also explain that although there are, increasingly, formal institutions governing social interaction and (especially) public behaviors, cultural and social institutions are usually informal.

Daron Acemoglu explains that even when formal institutions are similar in two nations, there can be important differences in how those formal institutions function, if there are differences in informal institutions between the nations. We can use Nigeria and the United States to illustrate this. Both nations operate the Presidential system of government. In fact, Nigeria copied its system from the United States. Yet the practice of politics (particularly, the constraints on Presidents and the elites) is dramatically different in both countries, because of the differences in the distribution and exercise of political power!

This also brings out the danger in trying to implement the so-called global best practices in the DCs: those best practices will have to operate under informal institutions that may be alien to them!

Political Institutions

As explained by the DFID (2010), political institutions define how power is obtained, used and controlled, and by whom; and how authoritative decisions are made – including decisions about economic institutions, the respective rights and obligations of states and citizens, and the distribution of resources. They define things like the form of government (military, presidential democracy, parliamentary democracy, socialism, monarchy, and so on); the powers of various political offices; the citizens that can ascend to them and how; the checks, balances and other constraints on politicians, and so on.

In particular, political institutions regulate what Elias Braunfels calls the bottom-up influence of citizens in the state – how citizens may participate in politics, and importantly, the extent to which the executive branch is subject to checks and balances. In this way, political institutions tend to regulate accountability in political decision-making, which can lead to policies that are in the common interest and conducive to long-term economic development.

Political institutions have a very important relationship with economic institutions: It is the nature of political institutions and the distribution of political power in a society that determine the kind of the economic institutions the society will have. This is the argument that Acemoglu & Robinson (2010) have made very strongly. They have also found out that the quality of political institutions has a large effect on cross-country income differences.

Economic Institutions

These have to do with the environment under which businesses can operate in a state. As explained by Wiggins and Davis (2006), economic institutions facilitate exchange, define and protect property-rights, determine the ease of starting a business, and the length of time this takes; promote and regulate competition, and so on. According to Elias Braunfels, economic institutions protect property-rights of private citizens and businesses, against powerful elites and political actors. They regulate the top down relation by protecting citizens' property from various powerful elites. In short, they shape business incentives.

The DFID (2010) makes some useful distinction between formal and informal economic institutions:

1. *Formal economic institutions* define and protect property-rights, determine the ease and length of time it takes to start a business, facilitate exchange, and so on;

2. *Informal economic institutions* refer to those informal norms and traditions that might govern access to opportunities – such as gender issues, caste system, and so on.

   Acemoglu and Robinson (2012) have found that the differences in economic institutions are the main determinant of the differences in prosperity across countries; and that the quality of the economic institutions of each nation influences whether the nation will be poor or prosperous.

Contracting & Property-Rights Institutions

These terminologies refer to two important classes of economic institutions, the contracting and property-rights institutions.

1. *Contracting institutions*: Acemoglu and Johnson (2005) define these as the rules and regulations governing contracting between ordinary citizens, for example, between a creditor and a debtor or a supplier and its customers. They regard the functioning of a nation's legal system as the most important component of contracting institutions. Differences in both laws and the implementation of laws across countries introduce significant differences in the costs of enforcing contracts. Notice from this that contracting institutions have to do with transactions taking place at the level of firms and ordinary citizens.

   According to Acemoglu and Johnson (2005), weak contracting institutions can be very costly; but citizens also tend to have certain recourses: Citizens can change the terms of the contracts or the nature of their activities to protect themselves from the worst type of opportunistic behavior.

   - This seems to be supported by the experience in Nigeria. Prior to the introduction of cashless program by the Central bank of Nigeria, many businesses preferred their transactions to be in cash, even transactions involving huge amounts of money! Nigerians seemed no longer to trust personal checks, company checks, and even certified bank checks, following rampant cases of frauds involving such checks!

   The World Bank also seems to substantiate such recourses in its *Doing Business* report for 2016:

   > "If resolving a commercial dispute takes too much time—such as the 1,402 days in Guatemala—it can reduce the number of potential clients and suppliers for a company. Where courts are inefficient, firms are more likely to do business only with people they know."

   Acemoglu and Johnson (2005) believe that although weak contracting institutions can be very costly, they tend to have limited impact on growth and investment; and that economies can function in the face of weak contracting institutions without disastrous consequences. This is probably attributable to the recourses that citizens tend to have in the face weak contracting institutions.

   On the other hand, Elias Braunfels argues that good contracting institutions can support economic development through efficient contract enforcement and the reduction of transaction costs.

2. *Property-rights institutions*: Whereas contracting institutions drive the business transactions taking place at the level of firms and ordinary citizens, property-rights institutions regulate the state's interactions with firms and ordinary citizens. Acemoglu and Johnson (2005) define property-rights institutions as:

   > "The rules and regulations protecting citizens against the power of the government and elites ... Property-rights institutions relate to the relationship between the state and citizens. When there are no checks on the state, on

politicians, and on elites, private citizens do not have the security of property-rights necessary for investment … The most obvious example of these types of institutions is those protecting (or failing to protect) investors against government expropriation. Another example would be regulations that create a non-level playing field in favor of large firms with close relationships with the government"

Acemoglu and Johnson also contend that while outright government expropriation is deemed virtually impossible in many countries, it is judged very likely in many sub-Saharan African and Central American countries.

We should also note that expropriation can take many different forms in the DCs, including the following:

a. The rampant practice of some DCs' Central Banks of sacking the management of some of the commercial banks they regulate (sometimes under disputed excuses), and sending caretaker officials to take over the banks. Prof Pat Utomi talks about this in the case of Nigeria, and the institutional implications:

> "What is even more bothersome is that those who have come to manage banks as caretakers with no long-term commitment of ownership and whose agency functions are not superintended by owners, use the positions to abuse and to abuse on behalf of those who sent them. As they service their friends and those who sent them and fight the perceived enemies of those for whom they serve as surrogates, they further fracture the system and set up the environment for the next systemic crisis. Ironically, they themselves are often the victims on the next round. But theirs is a mindset of momentary advantage, which dulls effort at building institutions to make the playing field level, and removed from what I called the 'predatory acts of public officials' in my 1998 book "Managing Uncertainty".

b. Slamming outrageous fines and penalties on private firms, which are out of proportion to their infractions, with the ulterior goals of:

i. Forcing the firms to the dark negotiating alley, where they will be coerced into parting with large sums of bribes, or forfeiting some equity shares to state elites;

ii. Eroding the firms' going-concern values, so that predatory elites can cheaply acquire interests in the firms; or simply

iii. Raising revenue for a government that may be cash-strapped

Case 8:   Nigeria's NCC'S Fine On MTN

In October 2015, Nigeria's telecoms regulator, the NCC, slammed a titanic fine of \$5.2 billion (N1.04 trillion) on the Nigerian operations of the international telecoms operator, MTN, for failing to deactivate about 5 million unregistered subscribers on its Nigerian network, after several grace periods. NCC, which seemed to have used a rate of N200,000 (or \$1,000) approximately for each unregistered subscriber, later announced a 25% reduction on the fine, following the uproar that trailed it.

The fine (unfortunately, for a DC gasping for foreign investors) attracted very negative interpretations from the global community: For example:

- Pete Guest of Forbes: "… even those who remain positive about Nigeria's long-term potential admit it has added volume to an already noisy chorus of negative views on the country"!

- Gareth Brickman of ETM Analytics: "Turning the screws on a multinational company … sort of holding them to ransom with an incredible fine … it's the kind of thing that will raise red flags for foreign operators."

- Toby Shapshak editor-in-chief and publisher of Stuff magazine: "the fine … is almost 40 times larger than the next-biggest fine imposed anywhere in the world on a telecoms operator ($100-million on America's AT&T)".

- Chris Spillane, James Batty, & Paul Wallace of Bloomberg: "the full payment of the penalty will amount to half the on-going value of [MTN's] operations in the country."

(Notes: Pete Guest: Forbes, Oct 30, 2015; Toby Shapshak: Forbes, Dec 4, 2015; and Gareth Brickman: Bloomberg, October 29, 2015)

Note from these comments that the global investment community regarded the fine as "almost 40 times larger than the next-biggest fine ever imposed anywhere in the world on a telecoms operator (which was the $100-million on America's AT&T"). Why on earth was a DC setting that kind of record? Note also that the global investment community assessed the fine as about "half the on-going value of [MTN's] operations in the country". What then could be on the mind of the regulator that imposed such a fine? To run the company down? Imagine this kind of global uproar at a time the nation seemed desperate to attract foreign investments!

While not holding brief for the company (and while recognizing the obligation of investors to comply with the laws and regulations of their host nations) too many things appeared wrong with this particular fine!

c. Sudden policy changes targeted at businesses (for example, new exchange control policies that make the repatriation of funds difficult for foreign investors)

Acemoglu and Johnson have established that property-rights institutions determine the security of private property, capture differences in state-society relations, and have a major influence on long-run economic growth and investment. Countries with greater constraints on politicians and elites (and so have more protection against the predatory tendencies of these powerful groups) have substantially greater long-run investment and growth rates.

Acemoglu and Johnson have also found that the impact of contracting institutions on these factors appear to be more limited. These findings suggest that economies can function in the face of weak contracting institutions without disastrous consequences, but not in the presence of significantly weak property-rights institutions.

Horizontal & Vertical Institutions

The terms "horizontal" and "vertical" institutions are simpler (and somewhat more intuitive) names that Acemoglu and Johnson (2005) have coined for "contracting" and "property-rights" institutions. Notice that the name "horizontal" intuitively brings out the important fact that these institutions regulate interactions at the level of ordinary citizens, while the term "vertical" intuitively shows that those institutions have to do with the relations between citizens and the state.

Social & Cultural Institutions

As explained by the DFID (2010), these institutions shape the areas of largely private and communal behaviors, relations and interactions between individuals and amongst many social groups, including those defined by age, gender, and religion. The DFID also points out that although there are, increasingly, formal institutions governing social interaction and (especially) public behaviors, most cultural and social institutions will pass as "informal" institutions discussed earlier.

Good & Bad Institutions

According to Daron Acemoglu, good institutions will encourage investment in physical and human capital, and in technology, while bad institutions can be expected to do the opposite. Good institutions will on their own, subordinate all citizens (including the leaders) to their boundaries. As explained by the OECD's Secretary-General's High-Level Panel (HLP), good institutions enable people to work together effectively and peacefully; ensure that all people have equal rights and chance to improve their lives, and access to justice when they are wronged. In a democratic context, they will usually have the following attributes:

1. Adept civil services and the timely and quality delivery of public services;
2. Efficient judiciary that upholds the rule of law;
3. Vibrant and actively engaged civil societies;
4. Free and independent media; and
5. Robust legal frameworks and representative parliaments with strong capacity for oversight

Good institutions are invested with legitimacy, and sustained by strong political and bureaucratic capacity, such that any attempt by a leader to manipulate them can easily lead to uproar and outrage, whose ultimate outcome may be unpredictable even for the leader!

Strong & Weak Institutions

We shall use "good institutions" interchangeably with "strong institutions", and "bad institutions" interchangeably with "weak institutions". For example, if the property-rights institutions in a DC are not protecting citizens, and there are no serious checks on the use of political power by the government and elites, then we can describe property-rights institutions to be weak (bad, poor) in the DC. However, if the reverse is the case, and property-rights institutions protect citizens and exercise serious checks on the use of political power by government and elites, then we can describe the property-rights institutions in the DC as strong or good. We shall regard state institutions that facilitate economic growth and development as "strong" (or "good" or "effective") institutions. On the other hand, we shall regard state institutions that facilitate vices such as corruption, extortion and nepotism as "weak" (or "bad" or "dysfunctional") institutions.

Extractive & Inclusive Institutions

Acemoglu and Robinson (2012) have popularized the terms "extractive" and "inclusive" institutions. The term, "extractive" applies to institutions that limit citizens' access (participation), while inclusive institutions level the playing field and provide all citizens with opportunities to participate in shaping public policy. Notice that institutions that are truly "good" will be "inclusive", while "extractive" institutions would tend to belong to the "bad" category.

In the case of DCs, factors such as tribalism, nepotism and corruption in politics and policymaking, will tend to make state institutions anything but "inclusive"! As duly noted by OECD (in the Post-2015 Reflections), when state institutions are unduly and non-transparently influenced by private interests, the result is "state capture" – a form of political corruption, which will lead to vices such as inequitable distribution of resources, disproportionate allocation of political power, and limited accountability and transparency.

Good Economic Institutions Drive Prosperity

According to Acemoglu and Robinson, while economic institutions shape economic incentives in a state, the quality of economic institutions is itself determined by politics and the political institutions of the state:

> "While economic institutions are critical for determining whether a country
> is poor or prosperous, it is politics and political institutions that determine
> what economic institutions a country has".

This provides important insight on the frustrations often experienced in reforming institutions: if we reform economic institutions without reforming the political forces that create (and sustain) them, those forces will tend to recreate in other ways, whatever benefits and rents they lose to the reform – including even manipulating the reform to frustrate its goals.

Institutions, Governance, Government & The State

Let us also try to differentiate between <u>institutions</u>, <u>governance</u>, <u>government</u>, and <u>the state</u>:

1. *Institutions*: As we have seen, we can regard institutions as the "rules, laws and government entities, as well as the informal rules of social interactions which in essence define how power is managed and used, how states and societies arrive at decisions, and how they implement those decisions and measure and account for the results.". In this way for example, the Parliament, Presidency and the Federal Executive Council can all be components of Nigeria's formal political institutions.

2. *Governance*: The United Nations Committee of Experts on Public Administration defines governance as follows:

> "The exercise of political and administrative authority at all levels to manage a country's affairs. It comprises the mechanisms, processes and institutions, through which citizens and groups articulate their interests, exercise their legal rights, meet their obligations and mediate their differences"

The World Bank (2000) gives a similar definition as "the manner in which power is exercised in the management of a country's economic and social resources." In its 2017 World Development Report, the Bank essentially maintains the definition of governance:

> "the process through which state and non-state actors interact to design and implement policies within a given set of formal and informal rules that shape and are shaped by power"

The Bank explains the characteristics of "good" governance as follows:

> "predictable, open, and enlightened policymaking (that is, transparent processes); a bureaucracy imbued with a professional ethos; an executive arm of government accountable for its actions; and a strong civil society participating in public affairs; and all behaving under the rule of law."

3. *Government & The State*: The World Bank in its 2017 World Development Report, defines a government as a set of formal state institutions that enforce and implement policies

Susanna Seltzer of the Potomac Institute for Policy Studies, differentiates "the state" from "government":

- "<u>The state</u> is the entity itself, as in its land, people, etc.

- <u>The government</u> is the political/bureaucratic system that runs the state. So for example, I love the State of Israel, but I do not love the government of Israel"

Slice B: Getting Set For Institutions Reform

Chapter 3

3. The Political Nature of Institutions

"Institutions are what they are because the political actors in any given society have an interest in keeping them that way ... Many development agencies act as if leaders in developing countries want to do the right thing, if only they knew how, and that development assistance should therefore consist of sending smart people from places like Washington out to teach them, perhaps accompanied by some structural adjustment arm-twisting"

- Daron Acemoglu & James Robinson in Why Nations Fail,
(See the review by Francis Fukuyama)

The Topics Covered in This Chapter:

- Introduction
- How political institutions emerge
- How dysfunctional economic Institutions can emerge
- The self-Centeredness of dysfunctional institutions
- The insatiability of the forces behind dysfunctional institutions
- Every DC can take its destiny in its hands

Introduction

As we saw in the last Slice, the political institutions of a nation refer to the nation's form of government, how citizens may participate in politics, the powers of various political officeholders, the specific citizens that can ascend to them and how; the checks, balances and other constraints on politicians; and so on. To help us appreciate the nature of institutions, and the challenges of reforming dysfunctional institutions, it will be useful to start by appreciating how a nation's political and economic institutions can possibly emerge, and how dysfunctional institutions tend to arise.

How Political Institutions Emerge

The kind of political institution a nation adopts is the product of the balance of political forces in the nation. As Thelen (2004) puts it, institutions are *"the object of on-going political contestation; and the changes in the political coalitions on which institutions rest, are what drives changes in the form that institutions take and the functions they perform in politics and society"*

If the various groups in the nation have political powers that are largely at par, with no group having absolute powers to impose its interests on others, then the political institution that will emerge will likely be progressive.

This will be even more likely if the following conditions additionally prevail:

1. When, as Daron Acemoglu has noted, there are relatively no natural resources to be extracted or exploited using military or political power;

2. When, as we shall see in the next Chapter, the political demand for economic improvement (the demand for what DFID calls "pro-poor" institutional change) is strong; or there is a sizable coalition, mounting a strong, bottom-up pressure for effective institutions – enough pressure to threaten the existing balance of power;

On the other hand, if one or more groups are able to impose their interests on others, the political institution that will emerge will likely be skewed and dysfunctional, as the dominant groups skew things for their narrower interests. In understanding political powers, Acemoglu and Robinson have made a very useful distinction between *"de jure"* political power and *"de facto"* political power:

1. *De jure political power*: This refers to the powers that originate from the political institutions of the nation – for example, the powers of the President, Governor, legislature, and so on.

2. *De facto political power*: This refers to the unofficial powers that a group of individuals may have, which it can use to influence government policies. It can arise from a group's military power, economic power, propensity for violence, capacity to create social unrest, control of the media, control of the legal system, and so on.

<u>**Case 9:**</u>   <u>**Examples Of "De Facto" Political Powers**</u>

Some examples of "de facto" political powers, using Nigeria to illustrate, can include the following:

- <u>Nigerian club of retired generals</u>: they are extremely rich and from among them have already emerged two Presidents since democracy returned in 1999; they are very influential, and may even have the capacity to destabilize governments

- <u>The Federal public servants</u> (especially the top echelon of the service): They are considered very corrupt and over-bloated. Quoting Alh. Ahmed Al-Gazali, former Chairman of the Federal Civil Service Commission (FCSC):

  > "… They [government agencies] have … become a cesspit of corruption, resulting in the over-bloating of contracts, loss of value for money and vandalisation of public property."

- <u>The civil service</u> is reputed to have powerful influence on the nation's politics, including the capacity to frustrate (perhaps, even bring down) the political officeholders. The Rivers State governor, and former federal Minister of Education, Chief Nyesom Wike, put it this way:

  > "No matter how sound your policies are, they depend on the drivers and implementers – the civil servants. I was Chairman of Council; I

> was Chief of Staff to a Governor. I do know how civil servants can
> make you not move an inch. That is the truth of the matter"

- **The Kaduna Mafia**, which the Punch newspaper (February 26, 2017) describes as "legendary" and "an influential group of … northern Nigerian intellectuals, civil servants, business tycoons and military officers residing or conducting business in the former northern capital city of Kaduna". According to Akin Osuntokun, members of the group are known for their intelligence, commitment to the traditional values and socio political interests of northern Nigeria. Although rumored members of the group deny its existence, it is alleged to have a pronounced influence on Nigeria's national politics.

- **The Niger Delta region of Nigeria**, because Nigeria's oil wealth, which is sustaining the entire country, comes from there; and they have the capacity to disrupt oil industry activities

- **The southwest zone of Nigeria**, because of their (relatively) high-literacy level and enlightenment; the region also boasts of the commercial nerve center of the country (Lagos), as well as a large proportion of the nation's most influential legal personalities. In addition, many of the nation's media outfits operate from the zone.

[For Al-Gazali (BusinessDay, 8-Jun-11); Osuntokun (Thisday 23-May-2012); Punch newspaper (February 26, 2017)]

It is possible for a group in a DC to have "de jure" political power, while some other groups have significant "de facto" powers. The balance of all those forces will shape the nation's political institutions.

How Dysfunctional Economic Institutions Emerge

According to Acemoglu and Robinson, various factors can play a role in shaping a nation's economic institutions, including history and chance; but at the end of the day, the relative political powers of the different constituents of the nation will be the deciding factor. According to Acemoglu and Robinson (2012):

> "… While economic institutions are critical for determining whether a country is poor or prosperous, it is politics and political institutions that determine what economic institutions a country has"

In a nation, the ultimate trophy for a group's political powers – whether "de jure" or "de facto" – is the economic benefits the group can use such powers to engineer for itself. Behind every DC's dysfunctional institution, are often some significant selfish benefits (sometimes in the form of economic rents) for its politically powerful groups! That is why we often find non-level-playing fields in a typical DC's economy – usually engineered and sustained by politically powerful groups for their own benefits, irrespective of the adverse effects of the dysfunction on national development.

Typically, groups use their "de facto" political powers to advance their immediate economic interests. However, considering that "de facto" political powers can be transient (since any number of things can suddenly alter the balance of forces in a nation) Acemoglu and Robinson submit that an astute group can more wisely leverage such powers to re-engineer the political institution to its favor. This will make their gains more durable through future "de jure" political powers, with which they can continue to skew economic institutions, and create even more perverse incentives for their benefits.

Dysfunctional Institutions Tend To Be Self-Centered

As we have seen above, bad institutions persist because some powerful forces are interested in keeping them that way; and that is always because those forces are profiting selfishly from the dysfunction, at the expense of the larger society. For example, Nigerians have been accusing its federal public service of being very self-centered. The Kaduna State Governor, and former Chairman of Nigeria's Public Service Reform Team (2005-2007), Mallam Nasir El-Rufai, put it this way:

> "The public service has been short-term in its vision, self-centered in policy formulation and corrupt in program implementation. Instead, it has focused on taking care of itself and interests to the detriment of the nation and system which sustains it."

Even the President of the country, Olusegun Obasanjo, has made the same point.

Case 10: **President Olusegun Obasanjo & The Self-Centeredness of The Civil Service**

In August, 2005 at a national Presidential Retreat on Public Sector Reforms and Public Private Partnership, the Nigerian President, Olusegun Obasanjo, in his vote of thanks to the Chairman of the Plenary Sessions, said the following of Dr. Mahmud Yayale Ahmed, the Head of the Civil Service of the Federation (HOSF) at the time:

- "As a Civil Servant, the Head of the Civil Service is often caught between loyalty to the Civil Service, his constituency and national interest; but I am happy to say that more often than not he has stood on the part of national interest"

Ironically, the audience, incidentally mostly civil servants, responded with a rousing applause – ostensibly in gratitude and solidarity with their HOSF! It was very noteworthy that the civil servants applauded their HOSF who apparently had to manage their interests *against national interests*! These civil servants appeared oblivious of the subtle implications of the President of the country saying that the interests of the nation's civil service were now in conflict with national interests!

As Goke Adegoroye, former Director-General of the BPSR, put it:

- "Are the loyalties to the Civil Service and national interest mutually opposing? Isn't the bureaucracy the traditional guardian of national interests? At what point was the bureaucracy overtaken in this sacred duty by the short-timers? Outside national interests, what other interests do Civil Servants pursue? … I believe, and very strongly too, that when political leaders, particularly the President of a nation, begin to think that Civil Service's interests are outside national interests then there is a crisis of confidence."

We can also see this self-Centeredness in the budgeting priorities of many Nigerian government agencies. Let us use the nation's education ministry as an example.

Case 11:   Nigeria's Education Needs vs. Budgets

From Funmi Ogundare, we can get some insight on the Nigerian education system as at 2006:

- It was graduating about 1.5 million secondary school students every year. Out of these, 800,000 to 1,000,000 would typically apply for admission into higher institutions. Only about 140,000 would find places in the university system, because of capacity constraints. Another 180,000 would be squeezed into the available polytechnics and colleges of education; and (perhaps) up to 30,000 would additionally be able to find their ways to study abroad.

- The big question then is: what then was happening to the rest?

  One would expect this kind of situation to create panic and trigger alarm bells in the education ministry! However, consider the following breakdown of the budget of the Ministry of Education for 2006: The ministry's 2006 budget, according to Nigeria's Appropriation Act 2006, was N166.6 billion. Out of this, the Ministry planned to spend 78% as recurrent expenditure (roughly what the ministry would spend on its officials, and on some other overheads); while proposing a mere 22% as capital expenditure (the component of the budget earmarked for developmental projects)!

    - Total Budget (N'billions): N166.6
    - Capital's share: 22%
    - Recurrent share: 78%

The focus of this kind of budget appeared to be on the internal needs of the ministry, rather than on the social crisis in the sector, which the general public was relying on the ministry to solve!

It may be unfair to single out the education ministry for what was apparently the general pattern for the entire Nigerian federal bureaucracy. For example, the table below provides some insight on the "recurrent" and "capital" expenditure budgets of Nigeria's federal government, in 2014.

<u>**Case 12:**</u>   <u>**Nigeria's Capital & Recurrent Budgets (For 2014)**</u>

- Total Budget (N'billions):   <u>4,695.2</u>
- *Capital (N'billions):*   *1,119.6*
- *Recurrent (N'billions):*   *3,575.6*

- Capital's share: 23.8%
- Recurrent share   76.2%

(Source: Budget figures from Nigeria's National Assembly
(Please, note that budgeted figures, as appropriated by the National Assembly, are usually
different from the actual expenditure)

This budget means that the federal government was spending over 70% of its revenue, as cost of governance (for the welfare of the public officials and some other overheads). This is interesting not just because the public officials comprise less than 1% of the nation's population, but also because the entire nation was relying on these public officials to tackle the raging social problems of poverty, poor infrastructure (such as roads, housing and electricity), health, education, and so on! It is also these public officials that should be striving to launch the country into the global economy!

The Insatiability Of The Forces Behind Dysfunctional Institutions

It is not just that the forces behind dysfunctional institutions can be savagely self-centered as we have seen above, they can also be very insatiable. We can again use the education ministry to illustrate this.

<u>**Case 13:**</u>   <u>**The Insatiable Appetite of The Forces of Dysfunction**</u>

If we considered the 78% "recurrent expenditure" of the 2006 budget of Nigeria's education ministry as very unresponsive to the social crisis facing its sector, it was very interesting that the bureaucracy was not even done yet! By 2014, government's allocation to education had more than doubled to N424.3 billion (increasing by a whopping 155%) according to Nigeria's Appropriation Act for 2014. Did this increase serve as an opportunity for the ministry to tackle the infrastructural crisis bedeviling the sector? The answer was "NO"!

The Ministry's response to this increase, was to explode its recurrent expenditure to N373.5 billion (a whopping 189.0% increase) which now represented 88.0% of the total education budget for 2014, leaving only a paltry 12% for capital projects in that year! In other words, even when the Ministry got more money, it seemed to have largely used it for further nourishing itself (more recurrent expenditure), not minding the alarming social crisis in the sector it was overseeing!

(Source: Budget figures from Nigeria's National Assembly. Note that budgeted figures (as
appropriated by the National Assembly) could differ from actual expenditures)

We should note that the recurrent budget of the education ministry (or any ministry at all) might not have been entirely within the control of the ministry, because many of the factors that built up costs (such as personnel size) could have resulted from political demands. We should also note that this exploding recurrent expenditure reflects the pattern for the entire Nigeria's federal bureaucracy. For example, the table below compares the recurrent and capital budgets of the federal government for 2014 with what they had been in 2001.

<u>Case 14:</u>   **Nigeria's Capital Vs. Recurrent Expenditure Trend**

	2001	**2014**
• Total Budget (N'billions	894.2	4,695.20
• Capital (N'billions)	496.4	1,119.60
• Recurrent (N'billions)	397.9	3,575.60
• Capital %	55.5%	23.8%
• Recurrent %	44%	76.2%
• Increase in Recurrent (from 2001-2014): 798.7%		

- Source: Budget figures from Nigeria's National Assembly.

It may be useful to highlight the following points that have emerged from the foregoing analysis:

1. We are referring to 2001 because the nation's current democracy started in 1999, and we can assume that by 2001, all the required structures for democratic governance had come in place.

2. Note that the federal budget for that year, 2001 (by the Appropriation Act 8 of the National Assembly) was only N894.2 billion, out of which about 56% was budgeted for capital projects.

3. Government required only about N397.9 billion (about 44%) in that year for recurrent expenditure (which was approximately the cost of governance).

4. It is very remarkable that by the 2014 budget, the recurrent component had ballooned to N3.6 trillion, growing by a gigantic 798.7%!

5. This Recurrent budget also took up a much higher portion of the entire government budget (76% from only 44% in 2011)!

6. Apparently, as more money started coming to government, perhaps from its increasing oil revenue, the appetite of the forces driving the dysfunction expanded, and they started swallowing more and more of the additional revenue, at the expense of capital (development) projects.

7. This also meant that the public officials comprising less than 1% of the population, used up something close to 76% of the entire budget for themselves, leaving the paltry balance for development (capital) projects for the rest of the country!

If Nigeria's education system is in tatters, the health system is even in a worse state, with the nation recording one of the worst child mortality rates in the world! Yet, a 2008 event in the nation's health ministry, can serve as another illustration of how self-centered some public institutions can really be. Let us use an account of that event by Ihekweazu and Anya, to conclude this discussion of how self-centered the forces of dysfunction can be!

Case 15:   Self-Centeredness in The Health Ministry

In 2008, Nigeria's President, Umaru Musa Yar'Adua, sacked some top officials of his health Ministry, including the health minister, Prof Adenike Grange, and the Minister of State for Health, Arc. Gabriel Aduku; and some others. Their offence (as reported by Ihekweazu and Anya), could be regarded as the epitome of self-centeredness: They allegedly shared a part of the ministry's 2007 budget among themselves, claiming it was the unspent funds from the budget. Even if it was truly unspent funds, too many questions would still call for answers! For example:

- Why was the health ministry recording unspent budgets – in a nation with one of the worst health indices in the world?

- What was the mindset of the officials that put such "unspent" budget in their private pockets, not minding the deplorable state of the nation's healthcare facilities?

(Ihekweazu, Chikwe and Anya, Ike: Prof Grange: Villain or Victim, Nigeria Health Watch, 14 April 2008)

Every DC Can Take Its Destiny in Its Hands

Case 16:   Back to Those Underdevelopment Posers

Let us return to the questions we looked at in Chapter 1, which were inspired by Acemoglu, Robinson and Johnson (2010):

- Why should one economy be innovating and progressing, while another comparably endowed economy is breeding poverty and underdevelopment?

- Why should the income per capita in sub-Saharan African countries such as Mali, Zaire, and Ethiopia (as reported by Daron Acemoglu) range around 3% of that of the United States?

- If it is because of physical capital differences (DCs don't save enough), human capital differences (DCs don't invest enough in education and skills), technology differences (DCs don't invest enough in technology adoption, and cannot organize their productions efficiently) then

- Why do some countries invest less in physical and human capital?

- Why do some countries fail to adopt new technologies and to organize production efficiency?

- If institutions have such a profound effect on economic riches, why do some societies end up with, and remain with these dysfunctional institutions?

- In short, why are some countries stuck in political equilibriums that result in bad economic institutions (again, borrowing the words of Acemoglu and Robinson)?

The answers are in what we have just discussed! Many DCs are aware of their dysfunctional economic institutions, and why they need to be better; but the political forces with enough clout to change these institutions, are often the beneficiaries of the dysfunction. Acemoglu, Johnson and Robinson put it this way, using Nigeria as an illustration:

- *"Bad institutions are the product of political systems that create private gains for elites in developing countries, even if by doing so they impoverish the broader society. ... Think of Nigeria, which has many multimillionaires while 70% of the population lives below the poverty line. ... Doing the "right thing" would take away the rents they receive, which is why no amount of hectoring or threats to withhold the next loan tranche has much effect on their behavior. Institutions are what they are because the political actors in any given society have an interest in keeping them that way"*

This also explains why crusades against corruption and electoral reforms are hardly ever pursued with sincerity in the DCs, notwithstanding official pronouncements. The political officeholders, who are in a position to drive the reform, are the main beneficiaries, who are often even relying on the dysfunctionalities to remain politically relevant. As they say, only a foolish rat will invite a snake into its hole! Fortunately, as we shall appreciate later (Sections C to G), there are often important low-hanging opportunities for very effective institutional reforms, even within the constraints of the existing political arrangements.

In all, if Mali and any other poor sub-Saharan African countries think that geography has consigned them to eternal poverty, they should only look at Botswana! As pointed out by Acemoglu and Robinson, Botswana is a small tropical and landlocked country in sub-Saharan Africa; but it has had the fastest average rate of economic growth in the entire world in the last 35 years! Parsons and Robinson (2006) have also established that Botswana compares with the Western European countries in terms of the indices of governance and corruption. The reason for all these is not a concealed mystery – Botswana's political equilibrium facilitates good economic institutions that places firm checks and balances on the political elites; which does not sacrifice the society's larger interests, for any narrower elite interests! No wonder, as Acemoglu and Robinson conclude:

"There is no intrinsic reason why Mali is poor and it is [similarly] possible to make its citizens rich ..."

Chapter 4

4. The Challenges of Reforming Institutions

"Rather than focus on layoffs of a certain number of civil servants, as was common in our early adjustment lending, it is increasingly helping build long-term systems for efficient employment and career incentives in the civil service. And rather than focus on the direct supply of physical infrastructure or social services, it is increasingly helping build the institutions that allow public or private actors to enter the market and that encourage them to provide services efficiently and equitably"

(World Bank in its strategy for Reforming Public Institutions & Strengthening Governance, 2000)

Topics Covered in This Chapter:

- Underscoring why bad institutions persist in the DCs
- The frustrations of institutional reform
- Other challenges of institutional reforms
- The important inspirations for reform (despite the challenges)

Introduction

The purpose of this Chapter is to prepare us for the difficulties inherent in institutional reforms. A useful way to start may be to underscore why bad institutions persist. Francis Fukuyama explains it in reference to Afghanistan:

"Institutions are what they are because the political actors in any given society have an interest in keeping them that way. ... Many development agencies act as if leaders in developing countries want to do the right thing, if only they knew how, and that development assistance should therefore consist of sending smart people from places like Washington out to teach them, perhaps accompanied by some structural adjustment arm-twisting. ... As the American nation-building efforts in Afghanistan and Iraq have indicated ... bad institutions exist because it is in the interests of powerful political forces within the poor country itself to keep things this way. Hamid Karzai [Afghanistan's President] understands perfectly well how clean government is supposed to work; it's just that he has no interest in seeing that happen in Afghanistan. Unless the outsiders can figure out a way to change this political calculus, aid is largely useless."

According to the World Bank (in its 2000 strategy for Reforming Public Institutions and Strengthening Governance):

> "At the extreme are countries locked into a dysfunctional political equilibrium, where powerful interests block any actions with the potential to promote development"

According to Mustapha Nabli, the World Bank Chief Economist:

> "Institutional reform is deeply political – it affects the balance of power between actors in society, and challenges the entrenched practices and economic privilege that some have enjoyed for generations. It should be no surprise then that worldwide, successful institutional change has proven difficult"

We can gather from all these that an important reason why bad institutions persist in the DCs is that some powerful political forces in those DCs want to keep them that way.

The Frustrations Of Institutional Reforms

We can therefore expect that the powerful 'vested interests' highlighted above would resist institutional reforms, and at least, make them very difficult. This is a major source of the frustration in institutional reforms. The vested interests are usually well organized and highly influential; and because they understandably include the bureaucracy (especially, senior civil servants), they are also very well informed. They will typically strive to frustrate any meaningful reforms, and have any of the following outcomes:

1. The reform is discredited; which can happen in several different ways:

    a. Misinformation (including even media propaganda) and against the reform;

    b. Efforts to compromise or discredit the reformers;

    c. Deliberately heightening the initial disruptions, hardships and negative fallouts, to discredit the reform;

    d. Mobilizing the general public (including organized labor) in other ways against the reform, not minding that successful reform would be in their ultimate interests; and so on;

2. They can create an illusion of progress in the form of motions and activities, but without meaningful movement: Here, the public can be inundated with the usual <u>workshops</u>, <u>seminars</u>, <u>committees</u>, <u>studies</u>, <u>capacity building</u>, at the end of which we get things like <u>strategic frameworks</u>, <u>strategic plans</u>, <u>roadmaps</u>, <u>mission statements</u>, <u>service-delivery brochures</u>, which are thereafter locked up in cupboards! Unfortunately, these outputs in themselves (however useful they may be) can at best only represent the "means to" rather than the institutional reform that we want! Rotimi Lawrence Oyekanmi talks about it in respect of Nigeria's education sector reforms:

> "Another strategic plan, put together by the Federal Ministry of Education,
> but which has not been made public, was presented to President Goodluck
> Jonathan on September 5, by Education Minister. This was done because the
> President had asked the ministers to explain what they intend to do over the
> next four years. It is still unclear if the plan is a fresh one or the same as the
> so-called Roadmap, launched with fanfare by former Education Minister, Dr.
> Sam Egwu, but which has largely remained on paper. While the problems
> and practical solutions of the education sector are well known and begging
> for implementation, Nigerians have continually been saddled with a plethora
> of strategic plans, which have been given various names since the advent of
> democracy in 1999"

(See The Guardian newspaper, 13 October 2011)

3. The reform is overwhelmed by corruption, or fails to live up to its potential: We can also use Nigeria's cost of governance reforms as an illustration.

Case 17:   **Nigeria's Intractable Cost of Governance**

During the administration of President Olusegun Obasanjo (1999-2007) a key goal of the federal government was to reduce governance costs, particularly the "recurrent" expenditure – understood roughly as what the government was spending on its officials and other overheads, rather than on development projects.

Government applied several measures towards this. For example, it informed the government's privatization and concessioning programs, which were extensive (and highly disruptive) and caused many public-sector workers to lose their jobs and means of livelihood. It also largely informed the administration's "monetization" program, by which government decided to start paying cash instead of continuing to bear the expensive responsibility of the various fringe benefits it provided to its ballooning senior public officers. These benefits included residential accommodation, furniture, utility, domestic servants, motor vehicles, purchase, fuelling and maintenance of staff cars, medical treatment, canteens for meals and tea/coffee, and so on. The goal of the policy was to relieve government of the burden (and corruption) associated with providing these basic amenities to public officers. What overall impact did all these programs have on governance costs? Let us try to find out from the federal government's actual recurrent expenditure, as published by the Central Bank of Nigeria (CBN)

According to the CBN:

	Year	Recurrent Expenditure (N Billions)
•	1999	449.66
•	2000	461.60
•	2001	579.30
•	2002	696.80
•	2003	984.30
•	2004	1,032.70
•	2005	1,223.70
•	2006	1,290.20
•	2007	1,589.27
•	2008	2,117.36
•	2009	2,300.19
•	2010	3,310.34

(Source: The Federal Government Recurrent Expenditure, 1961-2010, as published by the Central Bank of Nigeria (CBN))

From these figures, which refer to actual expenditure (and which can usually be different from budgeted expenditure) we can note the following:

- Despite the reforms (and all the disruptions they caused) the recurrent expenditure in 2007 of N1,589.27 billion was still 253% higher than that of 1999!

- By 2010, it had exploded to N3,310.34 billion, which was 636.2% higher than the 1999 figure!

- There was practically, no single year that the recurrent expenditure did not increase!

What then can we say was the overall impact of the reforms on government's recurrent expenditure?

4. There can also be situations in which the reform is overwhelmed by corruption, and so fails to live up to its potential! There could have been some elements of this in the cost of governance reforms highlighted above.

5. There are also situations in which changes are achieved, but those changes again get reversed – perhaps, in what Acemoglu et al dubbed the "see-saw" effect (whereby the underlying forces restore their rent, or simply replace one form of rent instrument with another)! After all, as Acemoglu and Robinson (2010) have pointed out, there are usually many different ways and a multitude of instruments that such powerful interests can use to achieve any specific economic goal.

<u>**Case 18:**</u>   <u>**Goke & Nigeria's Reforms That Seem To Go In Circles**</u>

Goke Adegoroye, on being appointed the pioneer Director-General of Nigeria's Bureau of Public Service Reform (BPSR) during the administration of President Olusegun Obasanjo, remarkably lamented Nigeria's history of reforms that seemed to lead nowhere, and wondered whether BPSR's efforts would ultimately end the same way! As Goke put it:

> "The recommendations of the Udoji Commission of 1972 and several of the Dotun Philips report of 1988 were so profound that they are still in the domain of public debates to solve contemporary problems of the public service ... The Dotun Philips recommendation that were implemented and even backed by a Decree had to be abrogated ... "Many of the strategies in our current Action Plan of Reform are basic elements in the Recommendations of Udoji (1972) and Dotun Philips (1988) ... How am I sure that efforts of the journey I am now to embark upon, by my appointment as Director-General of the Bureau of Public Service Reforms, would not come to naught at the end of the day? What is it in the system that seems to make the Service go in circles and leading nowhere?"

(Dr. Goke Adegoroye, Director-General, BPSR, 2004)

Ironically, Goke might have been very prophetic, if indeed we look back at what became of many of the reforms of that era – anti-corruption, monetization, SERVICOM, and so on! For example, consider the issue of Nigeria's elaborate program of right-sizing the federal workforce, which the BPSR championed, as a key policy of that era. Kaduna State governor, Nasir Ahmad El-Rufai (who incidentally was the Chairman of the federal Public Service Reform Team at the time, and Minister of the Federal Capital Territory in that administration), talks about that program and what become of it:

> "An initial batch of 36,843 officers were put through pre-retirement training, disengaged and paid about N24 billion as their severance entitlements. Unfortunately, about 20,000 of these severed civil servants have found their ways back into the civil service, thereby defeating the clean-up exercise"

(See El-Rufai: Reforming Our Dysfunctional Public Service, 2011)

Factors such as these are inevitable when reforms fail to speak to the source or fountain of the problems. According to Matt Andrews of the Harvard University Center for International Development, the evaluations carried out by some multilateral and bilateral organizations sponsoring reforms across the developing nations, showed that as many as 70% of the reforms produced muted outcomes! As Matt put it:

> "Billions of dollars are spent each year on institutional reforms in development, aimed ostensibly at improving the functionality of governments in developing countries. However, ... success is often limited ... They produce new laws that are not implemented, or new budgets that are not executed, or new units and agencies

that go unstaffed and unfunded. In short, new forms may emerge but they frequently lack functionality: what you see is not what you get!"

Various experts have used this phenomenon to explain why poverty has persisted in the DCs, despite all the aids pouring into these poor countries. According to Mark Wentling, a seasoned American development and humanitarian relief specialist:

"Some low-income countries have received funding on a per capita basis that is the equivalent of providing several Marshall Plans over the past decades but few, if any, countries have much to show for this assistance largesse. Too much funding has achieved temporary and poor results because strong institutions were not in place to carry on the work started with donor funds"

The World Bank (2012) similarly warns that even when a DC's leader is showing enthusiasm, it can sometimes not be deep-rooted:

"Apparent reform 'championing' may owe more to the need to keep aid flowing and relationships with donors positive, than to any deeper determination to drive change!"

We can also recall the point made by Francis Fukuyama, which is again very relevant here:

"If growth is a by-product not just of good policies like trade liberalization, which can in theory be turned on like a light switch, but rather of basic institutions, then the prospects of foreign aid look dim. Bad governments can waste huge amounts of well-intentioned outside resources; indeed, the flow of aid dollars into poor countries can undermine governance by undercutting accountability, thereby leaving societies worse off than they would otherwise be. As the American nation-building efforts in Afghanistan and Iraq have indicated, moreover, foreign efforts to help construct basic institutions are an uphill struggle. Bad institutions exist because it is in the interests of powerful political forces within the poor country itself to keep things this way".

All these are in line with the profound submission of Acemoglu and Robinson (2010):

"… direct institutional reform in itself is unlikely to be effective … it might be more useful to focus on understanding and reforming the forces that keep bad institutions in place. It is therefore important to focus on political institutions and the distribution of political power as well as the nature of economic institutions in thinking about potential institutional reform or institution building."

Indeed, successful institutional reforms are often triggered by circumstances that disrupt the entrenched interests – circumstances that the political forces cannot ignore nor contain. Such circumstances create pressure coalitions within and outside the nation that begin to press (and build the clamor and momentum) for reform, which can become overwhelming to the political leadership. Sometimes, in that state of the nation, a deeply patriotic person can emerge (perhaps even from among the elites) who has a strong liver to champion the reform.

But as the World Bank (2012) points out, even for such a leader, it will not be easy! For example, such a leader will inevitably have to wrestle with strong issues that will often even come from well-meaning sources:

- *"Why be the first leader to stop the patronage that we have enjoyed for several generations?"*

- *"Why betray the patronage system without which you could never have attained what you are?" And so on!*

Other Challenges Of Institutional Reforms

We should also be aware of the following other challenges that come up in institutional reforms:

1. *Issues of institutional clarity*: Despite the significant progress that institution economists and development practitioners have made on the role of institutions in development, there seems not to be full clarity on the key issue of how exactly institutions boost or retard development.

> **Case 19:**   **Some Verdicts On The Inadequate Understanding Of Institutional Reforms**

- Acemoglu and Robinson (2010*):*

   "Our state of knowledge does not yet enable us to make specific statements about how institutions can be improved (in order to promote further economic growth)... As yet, we only have a highly preliminary understanding of the factors that lead a society into a political equilibrium which supports good economic institutions".

- The World Bank (2012):

   "There have been many important advances in practitioner and academic understanding of institutional reform in recent years. But PSM reform remains a distinctively difficult policy area … There is relatively little explicit evidence about what matters most in improving public sector performance. The connection between strong PSM and social and economic development is evident to any experienced government official or practitioner – but hard to pin down precisely"

- Mustapha Nabli, 2006):

   "Thus, I think it would be fair to say that in the vast study of institutions and growth over the last two decades, as much of the vastness comes not from the answers we have reached, but the questions which remain … As Jeffrey Sachs has pointed out, institutions matter, but they are not the only things that matter,

> and those other factors may have an overriding effect on the
> success with implementing institutional reform"

If there was full clarity on how institutions precisely boost or retard development, it would have strengthened practitioner's hands in designing good institutions.

2. *Issues of methodology*: Perhaps as a consequence of the foregoing, there also does not seem to be a universally agreed path to institutional reform – i.e. a gold standard on how precisely to go about improving bad institutions for development. Again, Mustapha Nabli of the World Bank explains:

> "… juxtaposed to our increasing appreciation for the importance of institutions – be they market systems, legal systems, political systems or civil society – is a sincere dearth of knowledge on how to transfer this to a successful plan for implementing institutional reform at the country level … [Institutional reform] is not a well charted path. Successful institutional reform has followed many paths. For many countries, reform has come as the result of political or financial crisis. But other countries have approached reform with gradualism. In some cases, institutional change has come from the bottom up, with greater demand for better institutions. In some cases it has come from the top down

3. *Behavioral change*: As pointed out by the World Bank (2012), it can be very tough trying to change the actual behaviors of public agents – the decisions that thousands of public servants make in their day-to-day activities. Yet, this is what institutional reform must achieve, because successful outcome hinges on changing the incentives behind the daily official behaviors of these agents.

The Inspirations For Reform

Against the possible frustrations of the foregoing challenges are also some important incentives, which serve as inspirations to strive for reform:

1. *No other option*: What other option really does a DC have, if it is still poor and underdeveloped in today's rapidly globalizing world? For such a nation, the first inspiration for reform should be an impatience to change things – because something needs to be done, and very urgently too!

2. *Success stories*: Despite the challenges of institutional reform, some countries have actually successfully reformed their institutions, and transitioned into the paths of true development. Acemoglu and Robinson put it this way:

> "… Countries do reform their institutions and move onto different
> development paths. Obvious examples that come to mind from the
> post–World War II development experience include Taiwan, China in
> the late 1950s; Singapore, the Republic of Korea, and Botswana in the
> 1960s; and Chile, Mauritius, and China in the 1970s"

3. *Easy wins*: There are often many low-hanging opportunities for carrying out very effective institution reforms even within the constraints of existing political arrangements. For

example, it is often possible (even within the existing balance of political forces) to restructure the incentives behind individual programs, organizations and systems, to make them begin to deliver desired outcomes.

4. *Once there is leadership*: Public officials in the DCs are not inherently evil people that are bent on subjecting their nations and citizens to poverty for their own selfish benefits! Rather, many of them are merely acting in accordance with the incentive structures of their environment, and would respond positively to a political leadership that is genuinely and firmly committed to change, for nation building. Nick Manning put it thus:

> "Public officials are not inherently rapacious rent-seekers; they respond to the incentive structure they face. There is ample evidence, both theoretical and empirical, to suggest that the performance of public officials is greatly determined by the institutional environment that they find themselves in."

5. Finally, any nation that sincerely wants to embark on institutional reform can count on the assistance of many international sources – the World Bank, OECD, UNDP, DFID, ADB, AfDB, and so on. These organizations are supporting various countries (developed and developing) in building institutions that are more effective.

Chapter 5

5. Role of Leadership in Reforming Institutions

*"My grandfather rode a camel, my father rode a camel, I drive a Mercedes,
my son drives a Land Rover, his son will drive a Land Rover, but his son will ride
a camel"*

(The famous line of Sheikh Rashid bin Saeed Al Maktoum, credited for transforming Dubai from a small cluster of settlements to a modern port city and commercial hub. He was concerned that Dubai's oil, which was discovered in 1966, would run out within a few generations; and this drove him to develop the economy of Dubai so that it could survive beyond the oil era. [Source: See Wikipedia, the free encyclopedia (downloaded, October 2015), for much more])

Topics Covered in This Chapter:

- Introduction
- The legends of old
- The changing dynamics of power
- Leadership tips for driving successful institutional reforms

---

Introduction

As we saw earlier, some people, such as President Muhammadu Buhari of Nigeria, have opined very credibly that it would take strong leaders to create strong institutions. The question now is who can be a "strong" leader? What leadership attributes does institutional reform call for?

This Slice looks at the issue of leadership, and attempts to situate "strong" leadership in the context of institution strengthening – especially in this era of globalization and rapid technological developments. The author hopes that this will provoke robust debate on the kind of leaders (and leadership attributes) that can engineer successful institutional reforms in the DCs, to navigate these DCs out of the precarious situations in which they happen to be, at a time that technology and globalization are set to worsen their plights.

The Legends of Old

Because we are focusing on the developing economies, let us start by acknowledging some leaders that engineered some of the most phenomenal third-world national transformations of recent times:

<u>**Case 20:**</u>　　　　<u>**Some Past Transformational DC Leaders**</u>

- *<u>Singapore's Lee Kuan Yew (1959 –1990):</u>* one of the most revered and admired Asian visionaries and leaders, who even in the absence of any significant natural resources, was able to transition his country from the 3rd world to the 1st world in a single generation. Singapore's development model has fascinated leaders and visionaries across the world.

- *<u>Dubai's Sheikh Rashid bin Saeed Al Maktoum (1958 - 1990)</u>* the visionary leader, who sensibly and with a sense of urgency, used his country's oil wealth (production started in 1969) to develop the economy so that his people could survive even if oil production ended. He reflected his fear of his people being left in the cold if measures were not immediately put in place for "life after the oil boom"

> "My grandfather rode a camel, my father rode a camel, I drive a Mercedes, my son drives a Land Rover, his son will drive a Land Rover, but his son will ride a camel"

He kick-started a development program which has become the envy of other oil-producing DCs.

- *<u>Dubai's Sheikh Mohammed Rashid Al Maktoum (since 2006)</u>* has not wavered from his father's vision. Instead, he has expanded it, dramatically turning Dubai into a global city and "one of the best countries in the world" – with numerous visionary projects and development milestones that are fascinating world leaders, rich and poor alike.

- *<u>South Korea's Park Chung Hee (1960-1979),</u>* under whose guidance South Korea launched into what it is today. For many years, commentators regarded the economic growth he engineered as unprecedented in human history, which put South Korea in a position clearly superior to North Korea.

- *<u>South Korea's Kim Dae Jung (1998-2003)</u>* the architect of South Korea's democratization turning point (a political watershed), and other legacies including successfully leading South Korea out of the Asian Financial Crisis, and implementing a ground-breaking policy of "nordpolitik" towards North Korea

- *<u>Malaysia's Mahathir Mohamad (1981 to 2003)</u>* credited with shifting Malaysia's economy from agriculture and natural resources to manufacturing and exporting – using wide-scale privatization of government enterprises, massive infrastructure projects (including the North-South Expressway running from the Thai border to Singapore) and rapid economic growth. Malaysia's GDP (according to World Bank figures) rose by over 330% from $25.5 billion in 1981 to $110.2 billion in 2003 (current US$).

These leaders (the list is not exhaustive) seemed to have stood out from their contemporaries in at least one important respect – they allowed larger national interests to override their narrower personal, family, ethnic or religious interests; and the results they achieved were spectacular! Consider the following comparative GDP per capita figures:

<u>Case 21:</u>   <u>**Some Comparative GDP Per Capita Figures (In Current US$)**</u>

	Country	GDP/capita (2014)
•	Qatar	97,518.6
•	Singapore	56,286.8
•	Hong Kong	40,169.6
•	South Korea	27,970.5

<u>Compare:</u>

	Country	GDP/capita
•	Congo, Dem Rep.	440.2
•	Liberia	461.0
•	Uganda	696.4
•	Nepal	696.9
•	Tanzania	998.1
•	Kenya	1,358.3
•	Cameroon	1,429.3
•	Ghana	1,442.8
•	Cote d'Ivoire	1,545.9
•	Nicaragua	1,963.1
•	Honduras	2,434.8
•	Morocco	3,103.2
•	Nigeria	3,203.3

(Source (GDP/capita figures): The World Bank)

These legends apparently belonged to the school of thought of Calvin Coolidge, the former President of the United States, who once described *patriotism* as:

- *"Looking out for yourself by looking out for your country"!*

Notice indeed that because they focused on larger national interests, the national prosperity that ensued would certainly have equally benefited their narrower interests; because their families, tribes and regions would all equally have prospered in the tide of the national prosperity boom!

The Sense in Buhari's Declaration

Today, our DCs are thirsting for leaders that can similarly imbibe Calvin Coolidge's *patriotism*, of looking out for themselves by looking out for their countries! When we remember that behind every dysfunctional institution, are usually some powerful political forces that are sacrificing larger societal interests for their narrower interests, then any leader that wants to reform state institutions must have enough liver (what the DCs like to call "political will") to step on powerful toes.

Such a leader can emerge from among the privileged groups. For example, some of the elites can realize that everybody in a DC (including the elites) will ultimately be better off in a peaceful, stable and prosperous nation. This will contrast with Shishir Srivastava's *islands of opulence in an ocean of poverty,* which tends to characterize the corrupt wealth of the elites, side-by-side with the abject poverty of the rest of the people – and the tensions and instabilities that this brings.

The Changing Dynamics of Power

Let us note that the strong leaders needed here are not necessarily new dictators that will want to stay in power for life, jail political opponents, or muzzle up the press. A key attribute required is patriotism – Calvin Coolidge's patriotism of *"looking out for yourself by looking out for your country"!*

Besides, it is also important to note that the kind of brute, coercive or tyrannical power, which many of the legends (profiled earlier) exercised so successfully in their days, may not be very successful today – because of the very significant changing dynamics of power.

Joseph Nye of Harvard's Kennedy School of Government describes "power" as "*the ability to obtain the outcomes one wants.*" That description of power is still valid. However, for present-day leaders, that "ability" can no longer be equated automatically to brute, coercive or tyrannical power! This is one major phenomenon that is reshaping leadership today across the world, as the world becomes radically more open and more connected, and national boundaries continue to be fuzzier and fuzzier.

Today, as explained by Gordon M Goldstein, brute, tyrannical power is dramatically losing its value, because power is becoming increasingly *"easier to disrupt and harder to consolidate"* (using the words of Moisés Naím)! Actors that would once have been considered inconsequential are increasingly emerging to disrupt and undermine hitherto uncontested leaders in politics, warfare, business, government, and religion! A good illustration used by Gordon was the terrorist attack on the United States in September 2011 – now popularly referred to as "9/11".

> **Case 22:**   **The Disruptive Significance of 9/11**
>
> The United States has been the world's most powerful nation for many decades. But a hitherto inconsequential terrorist group known as Al-Qaida attacked the United States, leveraging the resources and technologies available in the United States, to inflict unprecedented havoc on the country – perhaps creating more fatalities than the nation ever endured in any previous single battle. And it happened in one single, hitherto peaceful day! On that fateful day, the awesome military might of the United States proved helpless before a rag-tag, hitherto inconsequential Al-Qaida group, which spent only about $500,000 to produce 9/11, whereas the direct losses of that day's destruction plus the costs of the American response to the attacks were in the order of $3.3 trillion!

This Al-Qaida case is an example of how power has dramatically become *"easier to disrupt and harder to consolidate"*! Geoff Colvin, senior editor at Fortune, calls this the growing *powerlessness of power*! Another factor feeding this growing powerlessness is that the solutions to today's leadership challenges are increasingly requiring the participation of ever more diverse parties. Perhaps, nothing illustrates the changing concept of leadership better than Fortune's recent choices for the *World's Greatest Leaders*. In the past, the highly respected magazine used to focus on tough, macho power, as Geoff Colvin, senior editor at Fortune explains:

> *"In the 1980s Fortune used to run articles on America's ten toughest bosses. These guys (they were all guys) were the masters of hot power. They intimidated, humiliated, and threatened. Robert Malott, chief of the big Chicago manufacturer, FMC, spoke for many of them when he declared, 'Leadership is demonstrated when the ability to inflict pain is confirmed.'*

- We can be confident that such a sentence would horrify today's leadership experts, but it won Malott quite a few fans".

(Source: Please see Fortune, March 26, 2015)

In fact, Fortune's 50 greatest leaders for 2015 did not include Hong Kong's leader, Leung Chun-ying, but included Joshua Wong, his teenage citizen, who led Hong Kong's "umbrella revolution" of 2014! While Leung was in charge, it was apparently the teenage Joshua that pulled the leadership! Geoff Colvin explains why:

- "Leung Chun-ying is the leader of Hong Kong. As chief executive, he signs bills into law, issues executive orders, appoints and removes judges and other public officials, and pardons convicted criminals. He's the leader—except that last fall well over 100,000 Hong Kongers chose dramatically not to follow him. When they learned that the 2017 election for Leung's position would not be free and democratic, as authorities had previously suggested, they poured into the streets and followed Joshua Wong, then 17, who had started a pro-democracy student group.

- "Leung, 60, commanded a vast city administration, including police wielding pepper spray and truncheons. Wong had a cell phone. Yet the protesters paralyzed Hong Kong for three months! Leung's already low approval ratings plunged to their lowest ever, and Wong landed on the cover of Time's Asia edition, which called him the 'Voice of a Generation'.

- "So who's the real leader? The answer is obvious: Leung has the leader's job, but he doesn't have leadership. Wong is the one who demonstrated that—which is why he's the one on our 2015 roster of the World's 50 Greatest Leaders."

(Source: Geoff Colvin, Fortune's Senior Editor-At-Large, March 2015)

Clearly, "being in charge" is no longer what it used to be! The world has simply become radically more open and more connected, with collapsing boundaries – thanks to the surging advances in technology. In Geoff's words, everyone is getting to know everything, and *"can communicate with everyone else at any time"*!

Technology has transformed the concept of broadcasting and mass-replication of information. It has given citizens the power not only to bypass the traditional media (including increasingly, the government-controlled media), but even to create their own content – thanks in particular to the growing power of blogs and social media!

Technology has also rendered political activity far more convenient, by dismantling those traditional barriers of physical mass mobilization (such as time, distance, and organizational requirements); and by proliferating web forums that create anonymity, and allow individuals to escape the limitations of prejudice, timidity, disability, and poor finances.

That is what the case of Leung Chun-ying and 17-year-old Joshua Wong illustrates; and why the old order is losing ground, in every continent (including the DCs) and across every sector of human activity!

In a remarkable illustration of the growing powerlessness of power, we can note that the Russian President, Vladimir Putin, the commander-in-chief of one of the world's most powerful armed forces (perhaps second only to those of the United States), was not included in Fortune's list of the *World's 50 Greatest Leaders* for 2015!

<u>**Case 23:**</u>   <u>**How Russia's Vladimir Putin Missed The List**</u>

Moisés Naím gives some insight into the factors that might have been at play:

- "Until recently [Russian President] Vladimir Putin was customarily included in lists of the world's most powerful people.

- "… Putin continues to wield immense power, but less than before, and betting that his power will increase would be a long shot. The Russian President is clearly more constrained than he has been at any time since he took office, as multiple changes overtaking the country make his grip on power less secure. Unlike the Russia of the early 2000s, when Putin ushered in a transformative and economically uplifting era, the country today is spiraling downward. The economy teeters on the brink of recession, battered by falling oil prices (50% of government revenue comes from the sale of oil and gas), onerous economic sanctions, massive capital flight, and disappearing foreign investment.

- "Last year alone, the rubble lost half its value, food prices rose 23%, and inflation accelerated to 16.7%. The Kremlin has had to deploy massive resources to bail out some of the nation's largest companies and banks. Standard & Poor's in January cut the country's credit rating to junk. The continuing conflict with Ukraine may lead to more sanctions and isolation from the international community. And Russia's corruption is notorious: In a 2014 survey Transparency International ranked it 137th out of 172 countries, tied with Iran, Nigeria, and Lebanon".

(Source: Leadership expert, Moisés Naim; March, 2015)

Although I do not expect Fortune's list of the world's 50 most powerful *persons* today to leave out Vladimir Putin, the point here is that we are in a world of increasing difficulty of consolidating power!

<u>**Case 24:**</u> <u>**More Examples Of The Increasing Difficulty Of Consolidating Power**</u>

The following examples illustrate the increasing difficulty of consolidating power and the growing ease of disrupting it!

- Terrorists are striving with growing sophistication to acquire the capability to bring down passenger flights. Think of how much damage they will wreck on the world other if they should succeed – in terms of not just the loss of lives and property, but also the impact that success would have on the aviation industry!

- Moisés Naím also reminds us of Edward Snowden, a lone hacker that successfully downloaded millions of pages of highly sensitive documents belonging to the United States government. Think of how much disruption and damage he wrecked on the US government and intelligence community – even just as a lone hacker!

The new dynamics of power is not limited to the national and international scenes, but cuts across every sector of the human endeavor. In particular, today's business leaders cannot get good sleep because of the increasing difficulty of consolidating power, and growing threat of disrupting it. Geoff Colvin gives some examples:

<u>**Case 25:**</u> <u>**Geoff Colvin's Examples Of The Growing Ease of Disrupting Power in Business**</u>

- "With 90% market shares in operating systems and applications, Microsoft could once use its dominance to crush competitors or simply buy them. But what happens when competing products like Linux can't be economically destroyed because they're free, and are created by thousands of volunteers instead of by a company that can be bought?

- "… When John D. Rockefeller ran Standard Oil, he destroyed competitors not just by under-pricing them until they failed but also by getting railroads to refuse to serve them. Today that kind of hot power is becoming irrelevant. Partly that's because in an information economy, start-up costs and fixed costs are so low that new competitors can spring up anywhere there's an opportunity. Online banks, brokerages, and others have taken billions of dollars of revenue from once-almighty firms."

Geoff Colvin, Fortune's Senior Editor-At-Large (March, 2015)

Leadership Tips for Driving Successful Institutional Reforms

What the foregoing illustrations suggest is that for the "strong" leader of today to succeed in reforming state institutions, leadership styles different from the brute, tyrannical approach of old, are becoming increasingly valuable!

Below is an attempt to profile some *"success tips"* that today's DC leader (who truly wants to reform institutions and put their nation on a firm path of development) is likely to find helpful:

1. *The 1st tip* is to recognize that even though digital technology has reduced their ability to exert the kind of tight control that used to be possible some decades ago, today's leaders still have opportunities to be effective. In fact, Geoff suggests that the leaders' opportunities to be effective are greater than ever:

   - "They can gather more information more easily than their predecessors would have dreamed possible, and they can communicate with their many constituencies in more ways and more often."

2. *The 2nd tip* is to pay attention to the new notion of "soft power", which Joseph Nye has been championing. He explains "soft" power (sometimes called "cool" or "smart" power) as the ability to get what you want by attracting others to your cause, in contrast to trying to use brute force to coerce them (the latter is the "hard" or "hot" power approach). Soft power has become highly important! It exerts its considerable influence through intellect and inspiration, and as Joseph Nye explains, brings people to "share our values and help us pursue common goals". That was what teenager Joshua Wong used to torment his President, Leung Chun-ying! Geoff Colvin also uses the charity, Médecins Sans Frontières (Doctors Without Borders) to illustrate the kind of inspiration and traction that good leaders can generate from leveraging shared values and common goals:

   "Consider … the situation of Joanne Liu, the International President of Médecins Sans Frontières (Doctors without Borders). She controls practically no one. The organization's office staff is modestly paid, but the tens of thousands of doctors, nurses, and others who deliver relief in many of the world's most dangerous places are volunteers. Governments can keep them out. Local people sometimes attack or kidnap them. Only a vast, easily disrupted network of voluntary cooperation enables anything good to happen—and yet it happens".

   (Source: Geoff Colvin: Fortune's World's Greatest Leaders: 50 Intrepid Guides For a Messy World, March 26, 2015)

3. *The 3rd tip* is to carefully seek out the best brains available in the country, very dispassionately, and leverage them! Future prosperity of nations lies in the knowledge economy, where staggering successes are arising more from the quality of human capital, than from budgets sizes or investments. Any DC leader, who is so parochial that they are unwilling to leverage their nation's very best hands, is not yet ready to move that nation out of poverty and misery, in the unfolding global economy!

   Perhaps, Geoff Colvin's private-sector examples will provide some insight on the preeminent role that human capital has assumed in national development:

   "It has become possible in recent years to create staggering amounts of shareholder wealth with business models that use very little financial capital but tons of human capital. For example, Microsoft has used about $30 billion of financial capital from all sources over its corporate lifetime, and it has created about $221 billion of shareholder wealth. By contrast, Procter & Gamble, one of the best managed and most admired companies in the world, has used far more capital than Microsoft, about $83 billion, yet has created much less shareholder wealth—about $126 billion. Even more dramatically, Google has used only about $5 billion of capital but has created about $124 billion of shareholder wealth. Contrast that with, say, PepsiCo, another superbly managed company built on a business model from an earlier age; using much more financial capital than Google, about $34 billion, it has created much less shareholder wealth, about $73 billion.

"Microsoft and Google understand perfectly well that their success is built on human capital. Both companies are famous for the scorching intelligence of the people they hire and for the brutally rigorous tests they impose on job applicants. Bill Gates has said that if you took the twenty smartest people out of Microsoft, it would be an insignificant company, and if you ask around the company what its core competency is, they don't say anything about software. They say it's hiring. They know what the scarce resource is."

(Quoting Geoff Colvin in his Talent Is Overrated)

Unfortunately, this phenomenon is completely lost on the DCs, where one of the greatest causes of retardation, is the obsession with self, family, tribe and (sometimes) even religion. Critics accuse leaders at different levels in the DCs of not only treating their best brains with scorn, but even nurturing poverty and illiteracy in their constituencies so that only they and their children (and descendants) can be the future contenders for leadership. Local kingmakers allegedly often reject government appointment quotas for their communities, if they do not immediately have qualified family members to take them up! They would rather miss such opportunities, than allow them to go to non-family persons – so that those non-family members will not become empowered, and future leadership contenders.

It is even worse at the inter-tribal level, where leaders routinely use second-rate persons from their tribes for government programs, rather than well-qualified professionals of other tribes. Some leaders even go to the extent of quietly supporting other nationals for positions in multilateral agencies, rather than see such positions come into their countries, and go to persons of other tribes!

It is important to note that by the dynamics of the present global knowledge economy, any DC that wants to see development and prosperity must aggressively seek out and leverage its very best minds. Leaders, who are ignoring their best brains (or treating them with scorn) because of tribalism or similar vices, do not have what it takes to create strong institutions, nor what it takes to move their DCs out of poverty.

4. *The 4th tip* is to pay attention to the "eternals" (borrowing this term that Geoff Colvin used in a slightly different context) – i.e. some old leadership attributes that have continued to remain relevant! Today's leaders, in trying to manage the bewildering new order, can take solace in the fact that the following age-old attributes are still as relevant as ever:

a. *Patriotism*: Former U.S President, Calvin Coolidge, explained this as *"looking out for yourself by looking out for your country"*. The institutional change agent must be mentally ready for this. Incidentally, people will tend to be far more united behind a leader whose actions portray a genuine passion for what is best for the nation – rather than one seen for example, as pursuing narrow personal, ethnic, or zealous religious interests.

b.   *Courage*: This refers to the political will to take the difficult decisions that institutional reforms usually demand. For a start, it should be clear that reforms are supported and driven at the highest levels of government.

There must also be courage to let reform run its course. The World Bank has highlighted in its World Development report (WDR97), the importance of "Internal rules and restraints" in promoting public sector effectiveness and good governance. Courage in that respect will involve the leader's political will to allow reforms that will for example, ensure the independence of the judiciary, the central bank, the ombudsmen and other internal watchdog bodies that often report to Parliament – which will tend to water down the Executive's grip on power.

c.   *Values*: Values are especially very important because the choices that the leader will face in carrying out institution reform will usually be hard – very hard. Leadership Expert, Prof Gautam Mukunda of the Harvard Business School, explains that a leader's values are the beliefs that guide their actions, when the choices are hard:

> "Leaders' values aren't judged just by the everyday choices they make. They're measured most importantly by what they do when every option seems like a bad one … If you don't want to make hard choices, don't try to become a leader. Once you've got the job, 'it's hard' is no excuse for failing to live by the values you claim to hold … because values are what you do when the choice is hard … The difference between beliefs and values is simple. Your values are the beliefs that guide your actions; in particular, they're the beliefs that guide your actions when the choices are hard …"

(Source: See Harvard Business Review, July 27, 2016)

d.   *Integrity*: People everywhere still want leaders who will speak to them honestly about their real goals, and the challenges they face together.

e.   *Vision*: People will be inspired if they see a clear vision of the future, and how the leadership is taking them there;

f.   *Strategy*: Successful leaders are increasingly those that can influence even the people they cannot control with money or force – who can galvanize the entire nation towards a vision;

g.   *Humility*: to admit and learn from errors, and leverage all good hands, including even opposition hands.

Our 21st century leaders in the DCs will find that these age-old attributes are still highly relevant to effective leadership!

5. *The 5th and final tip* is to recognize that people still want to be led – and will tend to gravitate around a leader, especially in crises. However, as Geoff Colvin put it:

> "What's strikingly new is that in a radically more open, more connected world, that leader could be the designated authority—or it could be a 17-year-old kid with a cell phone!"

Chapter 6

6. Setting Up The Reform Implementation Structures

"An overly large proportion of assistance funds is used to pay for the administrative overhead of implementation agencies and high-paid technical advisors and consultants. The portion of total available assistance funding that trickles down for use in addressing the essential needs of poor people at the grassroots level is therefore smaller than it could be. This is something that needs to change…"

(Seasoned development and humanitarian relief specialist, Mark Wentling, 2015)

The Topics Covered in This Chapter:

- Introduction
- The Reform Steering Committee (RSC)
- The Crack Reform Team (CRT)

Introduction

This Chapter describes two critical vehicles of reform that a DC interested in reforming its institutions, can consider, for driving the reform process. These two structures can go by any names; what matters is their functions, as described in this Chapter. The two vehicles of reform are:

1. The Reform Steering Committee (RSC), and
2. The Crack Reform Team (CRT),

The Reform Steering Committee (RSC)

The RSC will serve as the decision-making organ for the reform process. It should be sufficiently high-level, so that:

1. It can have the authority to quickly resolve the many cross-party, inter-agency and inter-departmental issues that will usually arise during in the course of the reform; and

2. When it takes a decision, it will be sufficiently representative of Management, and won't have to embark on the potentially frustrating process of applying and waiting for approval.

In general, we can expect the basic functions of the RSC to include the following:
1. To set out the overall goals of institutional reform;
3. To provide overall direction for the reform process;

4. To allocate resources (including budgets) to the reform program;
5. To initiate strategic ideas for the reform;

6. To review any reform proposals that may come from the CRT (discussed shortly), or from other sources, such as labor and civil society organizations (CSOs), private and corporate citizens;

7. To manage the reform process, including coordinating implementation, monitoring progress, and resolving issues that may come up;

Once a decision has been made to embark on this kind of reform (whether at the national or sub-national level), it will be useful to co-opt into the RSC, those that will help realize the goals. For example, at the national level, it will be helpful to have the following persons on the Committee:

1. The Vice President, as well as other selected members of the Cabinet, such as those responsible for national planning, finance, and legal;

2. The Chair of the CRT (which is the 2nd vehicle of the reform, as explained later);

3. An international expert – if possible, from multilateral aid agencies, such as the World Bank, UNDP, IMF, OECD, and DFID; or regional development bodies such as the AuDB, and ADB – who will bring the cross-country experience;

4. A local consultant (for local perspectives, and to build future local expertise);

5. Representative of the organized private sector; and

6. Representative of organized labor

A similar arrangement will also do for other levels, such as at the level of a state government, local council, or a government agency. For example, at the level of a government agency, it will be helpful to have the following persons as members of the RSC:

1. The CEO or better, the equivalent of the Chief Operating Officer;
2. About 3 other senior members of Management, including Planning, Finance, and Legal;
3. The Chair and Secretary of the CRT, who should also serve as the Secretary to this RSC;
4. An external consultant;
5. Representatives of the major stakeholders; and
6. Representative of labor

It is very useful to bring into the RSC those that can help to drive the reform. Notice for example, the rationale behind the foregoing choices of members:

1. *The President or Vice President*, because institutional reform can be politically very sensitive, and the political leadership needs to be actively aware of what is going on in the reform process;

2. *The Chair of the CRT*, because the RSC provides overall direction to the CRT, and also needs feedstock from (as well as thorough briefings on) the activities of the CRT;

3. *The international expert* – because the international development agencies have extensive cross-country experience on institutional reform, which a DC can leverage; and also because they are usually willing to provide assistance to the developing nations. In any case, if aids from donors are a significant share of the DC's budget, the aid agencies will be an important stakeholder that should be carried along (as explained shortly)

4. *Important stakeholders*: It is important to involve an agency's key stakeholders (or customers, for example, if the agency is involved in service delivery), to show that the agency is really serious about improving! For example, any agency that wants to transform its service delivery must get the customers' perspective. The customers who are at the receiving end of the agency services know the shortcomings of the agency (perhaps even more than the agency itself); and so will have an important contribution to make!

5. *The local consultant* will be useful for knowledge transfer to the DC, because they will be better positioned than government officials to pick up useful tips from the international consultant.

   The local consultant will also help the RSC to look at problems with some freshness, and be inclined to challenge existing traditions. The consultant will also bring in vital local perspective and expertise, as the government officials will tend require extended "hand holding", especially as the international consultant will not always be around.

6. *The representative of organized labor* will help to bring organized labor very early into the process. For example:

   a. The presence of organized labor will help to carry labor along, and make it an ally rather than adversary of reform;
   b. It will give labor the opportunity to present its positions at the RSC, which should be studied carefully and debated; and then adopted or convincingly defeated;
   c. The presence of labor will also help in managing the "wild" rumors within the workforce; and in reassuring workers that it is not an "us" versus "them" affair

   The worst that labor can be is a "deviant". But the truth, as people often say, is that every Committee needs a deviant – if not for sound critic, at least for the nuisance value!
Besides, responsible union leadership, from experience, often has no problem with properly focused reforms that are for the general good. For example:

   a. In the private sector, the experience of re-engineering teams over the years, often puts middle managers (rather than unions) as the toughest obstacles to change!

   b. Public sector unions have actually been known to even be a leading advocate of reforms! We can recall the late Albert Shanker as a good example:

   <u>Case 26:</u>   <u>Organized Labor In Support Of Reform</u>

   The movement for charter schools in the United States received a great boost, when Albert Shanker, the then president of the American Federation of Teachers, threw his weight behind it. As Kahlenberg & Potter (2014) explain, Shanker, a visionary union leader, was looking for a bold way to respond to the escalating demand in the United States for radical school improvement. "Charters" were Shanker's way of saying that the union recognized the virtue of a more market-like education system, in which teachers would be granted charters to run public schools, free from the regulations that seemed to frustrate teachers, but subject to strict accountability requirements!

Overall, when it is a reform at the level of a government agency, a member of the top management as the head of an agency's RSC will provide some very important benefits:

1. It will give the RSC enough clout to be able to resolve any inter-functional issues that may arise in the course of the reform;

2. It will underscore Top Management's commitment to the reform program.

In some situations, it may not be appropriate for the CEO to head the RSC, such as when the CEO is too busy to have time for the RSC, or when the CEO is about to retire. In such cases, another highly placed official, who has the "big picture" perspective (typically the equivalent of the Chief Operating Officer), should head the RSC. This person should have a passion for change and improvement.

The Crack Reform team (CRT)

Most of the RSC members will be part-time members who are ordinarily very busy, with other sensitive responsibilities. They will be meeting, perhaps only once in a month. That is where this CRT comes in. Members of the CRT will be full-time, reform-minded staff, who would have been re-deployed from their previous schedules to this new CRT.

This unit will functionally report to the RSC, while its duties will include (for example, at the national level) the following:

1. To serve as a secretariat to the RSC, feed ideas to it, and drive the implementations of the RSC's policies;

2. To drive the reform both directly and through central cross-cutting agencies [such as (in Nigeria) SERVICOM, EFCC, ICPC, etc]; and also through other intervention and regulatory agencies;

3. To develop templates for the reform;

4. To carry out necessary spade work for the RSC, such as research, scenario analysis; benchmarking, developing templates for approval; and so on;

5. To liaise with members of the international community for ideas and suggestions for the reform;

6. To serve as a central contact point for diverse officials and citizens that may have ideas and suggestions for the reform. The CRT, when it receives such ideas, can utilize them directly, or pass them to the relevant organs of government; and then try to follow up on those ideas it considers potentially useful.

    The alternative to this central contact point will be for citizens to inundate the Presidency (or governor, in the case of state government reform) with their ideas, which such office will not have the capacity to pore through!

    Another alternative can be to expect people to take their reform ideas directly to the MDAs that will implement them. This may not be wise because:

    a. It will put the MDAs, which are not enthusiastic about reform, in a position to quietly kill the reform ideas. We must not forget that in the institutional environment of the DCs, many officials in the MDAs may be complicit in the vices we are trying to reform!

    b. It is also not wise to subject members of the public (who have ideas for reform) to the ordeal of searching for which arm of government would be interested in the ideas! Such people will simply get bounced about, and will (most likely) give up in frustration!

7. One of the tasks of the CRT will be to help wake up the numerous regulatory agencies in the DC, sharpen their instincts for reform, and put them in a position to replicate CRT's reform templates in their sectors.

8. Another duty of the CRT will be to disseminate information about the reform, give visibility to the program, and provide a liaison point for central agencies and lower reform organs.

9. The CRT will also carry out any other assignments that may come from Management and the RSC.

Chapter 7

7. A Broad Framework For Successful Institutional Reform

> "There is nothing more difficult to plan, more doubtful of success, nor more dangerous to manage than the creation of a new system. For the initiator has the enmity of all who would profit by preservation of the old system and merely lukewarm defenders in those who would gain by the new one"
>
> *(Niccolo Machiavelli (1469-1527) in his work, "The Prince")*

The Topics Covered in This Chapter:

- Introduction
- The suggested path for the reform

Introduction

The goal of this Chapter is to suggest a broad framework for the reform, which can have a chance of circumventing the explosive minefields inherent in institutions reform. We shall set out the broad framework here, and progressively expand it in the subsequent Sections.

Suggested Path For The Reform

Here are some general suggestions that can help a DC achieve successful institutional reform outcomes:

1. *Reform structure*: The first step must be to set up the structure that will drive the reform. In the previous Chapter, we looked at the Reform Steering Committee (RSC) and the Crack Reform Team (CRT).

2. *Inventory taking*: The first task of the CRT must always be to understand what is on ground (i.e. to take an inventory). While it is always very useful to benchmark as much as possible, and be guided by what has worked in other jurisdictions, a thorough understanding of what is on ground will enable the CRT to structure a "good fit", based on the DC's peculiar circumstances. Why are we stuck with this bad institution? What forces, if any, are sustaining it? What groups, if any, are benefiting from the situation? And so on. This book prefers that approach, to blindly adopting any "best practice", as an automatic solution.

The World Bank (2000) puts it this way:

> "… we need to work with our partners to understand and address the broad range of incentives and pressures – both inside and outside of government – that

affect public sector performance … We need to start with a thorough understanding of what exists on the ground and emphasize good fit rather than any one-size-fits-all notion of best practice. And we need to work with our clients and other partners to develop and apply analytic tools effectively."

We shall look at "Inventory Taking" in more details in the next Chapter, while "Benchmarking" comes up in Slice D.

3. *Strive for some "quick wins"*: It is always wiser to start an institutional reform from the areas that can lead to early and inspiring results. Quick wins will boost the confidence of both the reform team and the political leadership, and also generate public support for the reform program!

> **Case 27:** **The Inspiration From Nigeria's Telecoms Reform**
>
> - The reformers in Nigeria flaunted the phenomenal impact of the nation's deregulation of its telecoms sector, as an inspiration for pushing for the reform of other sectors such as oil and power, where the entrenched-interests were far more formidable. Even at that, it took government nearly 14 years from the successful telecoms reform in 2001, to achieve the more difficult power-sector deregulation (achieved only in 2014). So far, the opposition to the petroleum sector deregulation has remained insurmountable.
>
> - Incidentally, the impact of the power sector deregulation, at least from the point of view of the energy consumers (even after three years, post-deregulation) has not been inspiring – certainly not anything like that of the telecoms reform. It would therefore have been disastrous in terms of the overall enthusiasm for further reform, if government had started with the power sector, instead of the telecoms sector.

Note that some other factors (in addition to prospects of quick wins) can influence the sequencing of the reform program. They include the following:

a. The ultimate benefits (business, social or political) that stand to be reaped from the reform; as well as the extent of disruptions and chaos that the reform can create

b. The cost implications (financial, social, and political costs);

c. The processes in deepest trouble (there will be pressure to reform them);

d. The potential of reforms to reinforce each other;

e. The enthusiasms of specific ministers for the reform: For example, it will usually be helpful to start a reform from those ministries headed by cabinet members that are enthusiastic about the reform; and then move from there to other ministries); and so on

4. *The 1ˢᵗ Generation reforms*: These are some initial steps that fall into what Mustapha Nabli calls "levers for change", which will help to create the right climate, as well as build up the "pressure coalition" and momentum for institutional reform.

This pressure coalition is vital in weakening the resistance to reform, which is always very strong:

a. The job of even a reform-minded leader becomes a lot easier, when there is a loud clamor for change! We must not forget that such a leader wrestles with issues such as *"why be the one to cause us to forfeit the benefits we have enjoyed for generations?"* *"Why make enemies that will last into even your unborn generations?"* And so on.

b. Indeed, successful institutional reforms are often triggered by problems or pressures that leaders cannot ignore – including political crisis, bottom-up pressure to close a loophole or punish an elite; severe economic crisis, desperation to access donor funds; and so on.

The 1st Generation reforms, which can often be undertaken by a relatively small number of policymakers and public managers, can include the following kinds of policies:

a. **Greater trade openness,** such as the usual exchange rate reforms and trade liberalization; and they come with the following important benefits:

    i. External agreements on trade and investment allow countries to leapfrog some of the domestic resistance and political inertia encountered in driving policy reform.

    ii. Greater trade openness, as pointed out by Mustapha Nabli, will also spur competition, which will expand the role of non-rent-dependent export sectors – which are the more productive and efficient segment of the economy. These sectors demand better institutions across the board, and provide the feedback mechanisms for other areas of reform. As examples, Mustapha Nabli cites the following cases:

        • *Mexico, whose trade liberalization (through NAFTA) opened its economy to more competition, which in turn induced local business associations to lobby the government for reductions in the regulatory burden to help them compete;*

        • *Hungary, the Czech Republic and Poland, which recorded remarkable successes following the Accession Agreements they had with the EU.*

    iii. Greater trade openness will also expose the work force to new skills and knowledge, creating another effective coalition for reform, as this workforce begins to demand the skills and services needed to compete in the new economic environment.

    All these contribute to the pressure coalitions that can begin to press (and create the momentum) for further institutional reforms. Mustapha Nabli calls this "virtuous circles" – i.e. building those coalitions within the economy which need quality institutions, thus building the demand on institutions to respond.

b. *__Improved accountability__:* With the corruption and impunity that ravage most DCs, no reform can gain meaningful traction, if there is no simultaneous effort to improve accountability. Here, what matters most is the actual "body language" of the political leaders, rather than their official pronouncements. Sometimes the leaders will be singing "reform", integrity, and "zero tolerance for corruption", while they and their inner "kitchen" officials are quietly involved in the same corruption that they are condemning.

This "body language" is very critical, because it provides the first signpost on the seriousness of the political leadership with the reform program. The civil servants, who process vouchers and contract documents (and therefore see the transactions involving the political leaders) will be among the first to see the real "body language" of the leaders. If they observe that the leaders do not mean what they are mouthing, they will just smile, and can even put their superior knowledge of the bureaucracy at the disposal of the corrupt leaders, and guide them to accomplish their bad desires. But that means that the reform will amount to "all noise and no movement".

On the other hand, if the bureaucracy sees that the political leadership is genuinely committed to change, it will panic and quickly key in. Indeed, if the civil servants in the DCs are corrupt, it is often because they are acting in line with the "body language" of the political leadership! We shall look at the important role of accountability in institutional reform, in more details, in Slice D.

- *The World Bank in its WDR (2017) attributes China's phenomenal development to the nation's profound changes to its mechanisms of accountability and collective leadership.*

c. <u>*Information openness*</u>: Information is another vital tool for creating the coalition for better institutions. People can only agitate for change based on what they know! According to Mustapha Nabli:

i. Information helps to expose the sources of economic rents in the economy, increasing the pressure to dismantle them;
ii. It also helps to expose institutional weaknesses and to provide alternatives to the status quo – thus helping to create the demand for change.

Incidentally, freedom of information (FOI), which is a vital tool for mobilization, and also taken for granted in the advanced economies, is a very scarce commodity in the DCs! We shall have a separate Chapter on the vital role of information (the "Sunlight") in Slice C. For now, we can compare Hong Kong's 2014 "Umbrella Revolution" (particularly, the role that information played in the mobilization) with the restrictions citizens face in the DCs.

<u>Case 28:</u>   <u>Hong Kong's Umbrella Revolution Vs. The DCs' Lid On Information</u>

In 2014, Leung Chun-ying was the leader of Hong Kong. But when citizens of Hong Kong learned that their upcoming 2017 election for the leader's position would not be free and democratic (as authorities had previously suggested), over 100,000 Hong Kongers poured into the streets and followed Joshua Wong, then 17, who had started a pro-democracy student group. As Geoff Colvin, Fortune's Senior Editor-At-Large, put it:

"Leung, 60, commanded a vast city administration, including police
wielding pepper spray and truncheons. Wong had a cell phone. Yet the
protesters paralyzed Hong Kong for three months! Leung's already low

> approval ratings plunged to their lowest ever, and Wong landed on the
> cover of Time's Asia edition, which called him the 'Voice of a
> Generation'".

This mobilization was possible because of the social media, and Hong Kong's relative freedom of information, which is a very scarce commodity in many DCs. Mustapha Nabli uses the Arab region to illustrate:

> "The Arab world has much to do to create openness in terms of
> information. Little government information is accessible by the public (a
> few countries have recently began to publish some government statistics).
> Freedom of the press is carefully monitored and circumscribed in most
> countries. Use of the internet is often controlled. There are, of course, a
> multitude of restrictions on citizens from mobilizing for change, in terms
> of restrictions on civil society and the like. These are symptomatic of the
> institutional challenges facing the region. But without the information, few
> demands can be mobilized for change. Information is the first step in
> creating the groups interested in better institutions".

-----

5. **Reforming the incentives that drive behavior**: A successful institutional reform is one that is able to change the deep-rooted incentives driving the everyday-decisions of thousands of public servants. According to the World Bank (2012):

> "Sustainable institutional change often requires that thousands of public
> agents alter their behavior ... Public management changes are implemented
> through the day- to-day decisions of thousands of administrators and
> managers. Improving results hinges on changing the daily transactions they
> make – yet finding effective entry points for changing engrained behaviors
> and values is hard."

Unlike the 1st generation reforms, which relatively can (at least in theory) be "turned on like a light switch" (borrowing an expression that Francis Fukuyama used in a different context), changing the incentives of thousands of public servants, takes more time. The various tools that can help in reforming incentives are the subjects of Sections C, D, E, F, and G.

6. *Reforming organizations*: According to the DFID (2010), the way organizations interact with each other and with the institutional context are the essence of the politics and political economy of growth and poverty reduction, because organizations and informally organized interests play a key role in the politics of institutional formation, implementation and change. We shall indeed use the tools set out in Sections C to G, to seek to improve the ways that organizations work, especially the ways that they interact with the public, and with each other, in the institutional context.

Any DC interested in driving institutional reform will find the 1st generation reforms to be a very useful starting point. Even if a DC's leadership is not enthusiastic about them, donor agencies should press for them, because they are usually largely within the powers of the executive arm of government; and they will also work in the long-term interests of wider institutional reforms.

Chapter 8

8. The Central Role Of "Inventory Taking" (Diagnostic Review)

"We need to start with a thorough understanding of what exists on the ground and emphasize "good fit" rather than any one-size-fits-all notion of "best practice." And we need to work with our clients and other partners to develop and apply analytic tools to do this effectively"

(World Bank in its report, Reforming Public Institutions & Strengthening Governance, A World Bank Strategy, November 2000)

Topics Covered in This Chapter:

- What is inventory taking?
- Inventory-taking at the agency level
- Inventory taking at the ministerial level
- Other benefits of inventory taking

Introduction To Inventory-Taking

The most sensible starting point for institutional reform is to have clarity on what is on ground, by taking an inventory. It is also the most sensible first-step for anybody that is taking up leadership of any kind.

For the CRT, inventory-taking means carrying out a diagnostic review of what is on ground. It is the most sensible starting point for institutional reform, and indeed for anyone that wants to fix any problem – to have clarity on the problem. It is also the first of several data-driven governance practices that we shall emphasize in this book. It will require inspections and interactions with the internal and external stakeholders. We can take an inventory of any program or project, or of government ministry, department, or agency (MDA).

Inventory Taking At The Agency Level

As an illustration, inventory-taking at the agency level, will review the agency's functions, structures, people and other resources, to fully situate the agency and provide clarity on issues such as:

The basic organizational details, including:
1. The mandate of the agency (what it was set up to do);

2. The present operational focus of the agency;
3. Office locations;
4. Organization structure – the units, departments, divisions, etc
5. Functions of the units, departments, divisions, etc;
6. Use of ICT;

Staffing & capacity issues
7. Availability of qualified staff for core mandate;
8. Staff profile (by grades, gender, etc);
9. Staff distribution by departments, divisions, units, etc;
10. Staff distribution by functions, programs, services;
11. Staff distribution (by tribes, states, regions, etc);

Functional activities & overlaps
12. All the present functional activities
13. Any intra-agency functional overlaps (within the agency);
14. Any inter-agency overlaps (overlaps with other agencies);
15. Any functional activities that are regulatory;

Functional activities that are potentially commercial
16. The financial position:
17. Annual budgets (revenues & expenditures)
18. Revenue structure (such as subvention, donors, self-generation)
19. Self-generated revenue (by units, programs, services);
20. Overall expenditure profile (such as by capital, recurrent)
21. Expenditure profile, by units/departments/divisions, etc;
22. Expenditure profile, by functions, services, programs;
23. Distribution of the agency's assets and liabilities;
24. Financial performance

Organizational performance
25. The performance standards if any;
26. Assessment of organizational performance by Management
27. Assessment of organizational performance by other stakeholders
28. Fulfillment of agency goals
29. Any gaps in agency goals (mandates not yet being addressed);
30. Potential obstacles to closing the gaps

Possible strengths and weaknesses
31. Functional & organizational strengths
32. Opportunities from political trends;
33. Opportunities from business & other trends
34. Possible challenges & threats
35. Budgetary threats,
36. Threats of outsourcing, privatization, closures, mergers, etc;
37. Any other pressures for reform;

Institutional forces
38. Possible beneficiaries from the current arrangements
39. Possible losers from the current arrangements
40. Capacity of these losers to influence a change

41. Incentives for reform
42. Incentives for reform (donor pressures, foreign investments, etc)
43. Pressures for reform (scarcities, unemployment, social unrest, etc);
44. Political support for reform (some of these can be silent notes);
45. Political enthusiasm for reform
46. Possible "no go" areas
47. Possible obstacles to reform; and so on

These are just general guidelines. The specific issues of interest will vary from case to case. The ultimate goal is to establish the present state of the agency (we can denote this as "*where we are*"), which we can then compare with what the state of the agency should be ("*where we should be*").

Inventory Taking at The Ministerial Level

In the same way, inventory-taking at the level of a government Ministry (which oversees agencies) will provide equivalent information on the ministry at that level – including all the agencies under it.

As an example along this line, we can cite what Mrs. Oby Ezekwesili did for Nigeria's education sector in 2006, when she became the Minister of Education.

Case 29:   **Diagnostic Review of Nigeria's Education Ministry**

Nigeria's education ministry oversees the nation's education needs in the following areas:
- Early child education,
- Basic education,
- Secondary education,
- Tertiary education (universities, polytechnics, and so on),
- Adult non-formal education, and
- Special needs education

When Mrs. Oby Ezekwesili became the Minister of Education in 2006, one of the useful things she did was to undertake some basic review of the state of education in the country. Her findings were wide-ranging and very revealing. Here are some highlights from Chinedu Bosah, Secretary of Nigeria's Education Rights Campaign:

- There were only about 102 Unity Schools, out of 11,000 secondary schools in the country (the Unity Schools were secondary schools, owned and managed directly by the federal government through its ministry of education). This figure meant that the Unity Schools represented less than 1% of all the secondary schools in the country].

- Only about 6.4 million Nigerian children were enrolled in the nation's public and private secondary schools, out of a total of 33.9 million children of secondary schools age;

- The Unity Schools accounted for only about 122,000 out of the nation's 6.4 million students in secondary schools;

- However, the education ministry was spending 70-80% of its total yearly budget on Unity Schools!

- Between 2000 and 2004, only seven Unity Schools (out of the 65 schools that made reports) recorded 50% and above in the West Africa School Certificate examinations;

- Only about 15% of the Unity Schools students passed up to five credits in the same examinations for the previous five years, even in the face of increase in funding to the schools in the same period;

The findings formed the basis for the reform program that the Minister and her team subsequently articulated for the sector. Although some aspects of the reform became highly controversial, they took nothing away from the useful insight that came out of the diagnostic review.

Other Benefits of Inventory Taking

In conclusion, let us also note the following other potential benefits of inventory taking (or diagnostic review):

1. *Clarity*: It helps to produce clarity of what exists on the ground, including (as explained above) where we are, where we should be, and hopefully, why we are where we are.

2. *Balance of political forces*: We have already seen that behind every dysfunctional institution are usually some powerful forces that are sustaining it. A good diagnostic review will help to uncover the real incentives and interests that may be at play.

3. *Good fit*: In articulating the reform program that can to take us from *where we are* to *where we should be*, this clarity will put the CRT in a position to take context into account, and emphasize "good fit" rather than any one-size-fits-all notion of "best practice." While the insight from benchmarking is extremely helpful, we should be very wary about automatically importing a solution that works very well in another country, even when the formal institutions in the two nations may be similar. As we saw before, even when the formal institutions are similar in two nations, their informal institutions can be quite different, leading to dramatic differences in the outputs of the formal institutions. Mark Wentling, a seasoned development and humanitarian relief specialist, put it this way:

> "The strengthening of any institution will require an in-depth knowledge of the sector(s) it covers. Gaining this knowledge will entail sector analyses that provide the information needed to elaborate the institutional capacity building framework and program action plan that describes the role and tasks of the institution and the objectives of its operation"

Slice C: Strengthening Institutions By Restructuring Incentives

This Slice unveils a basket of tools for restructuring institutional behaviors (including those of public-sector officials) to ensure that institutional processes and programs deliver desired outcomes. This basket includes tools that the CRT can use to replicate in the public sector, the kind of factors that drive vibrancy in the private sector.

These tools also provide many low-hanging opportunities for carrying out very effective institutional reforms, even within the constraints of the existing political arrangements. This is important because even a corrupt leader will like to see national programs working fine, at least within the existing political arrangements. For example, a corrupt leader, despite indulging in corruption, may still not want airplanes crashing all the time in their DC, because of corruption in the aviation sector; or widespread deaths in hospitals because medical staff are looting the drugs supplied to hospitals; and so on.

Notice that we are now about to commence the real task of this book, which is the actual reform of institutions, to strengthen them

9. Leverage The Lessons Of The "GI Bill" In Structuring Public Programs

"The GIs were appreciated, and more than that, the country realized that education was important to the country, and that education paid for itself ten-fold, if not more"

(82-year old Jerome Kohlberg, who enrolled in the US Navy when he was 17, and subsequently (after the war ended) became a beneficiary of the GI Bill)

Topics Covered in This Chapter:

- Introduction To The GI Bill
- The Phenomenal Impact of The Bill
  - The impact of the GI Bill on the education sector
  - The impact of the GI Bill on the overall national economy
  - The socio-political impacts impact of the GI Bill
- Why Every DC Should Look Again At The Bill
- Lessons from the GI Bill's education scheme
- Lessons from the GI Bill's housing loan scheme
- Putting A Program's Funding In Users' Hands
- How This Principle Differentiates Public & Private Sectors
- A Tool For Making Governance Institutions Sensitive To Us
- Various Opportunities For Applying The Principle In The DCs
- Good Fit, Not Just Best Practice
- Reform Within Existing Political Constraints

Introduction To The GI Bill

When World War II (WW2) ended in 1944, it was time for the United States soldiers stationed in different parts of the world (the war veterans, or simply the "vets") to start returning home. They were many – about 16 million young men and women, who (according to the figures by Thalia Assuras of CBS news), amounted to over 10% of the entire US population at the time.

They had also tasted war, and were mostly of little education, as they largely belonged to the ordinary, blue-collar segment of the society. The US government was therefore understandably anxious about the impending influx into its labor market, of these 16 million young men and women! The labor market had itself changed in character in the course of the war, because while the men were away fighting, a large number of women had entered the workforce, taking over the jobs vacated by the men!

Government was also eager to avoid a repeat of its agonizing experience with the vets of WW1, who in 1932, during the Great Depression, had to march to the seat of government in Washington, to protest their unfair treatment. As recounted by Thalia Assuras, the standoff that ensued prompted the federal government to call in troops and disperse them by force, in what became a sad chapter in the nation's history.

In answer to all these challenges, the government of President Franklin D. Roosevelt came up with the "Servicemen's Readjustment Act" of 1944 (popularly known as the GI Bill). The term "GIs" was a very popular nickname for the returning vets, coined from their "*General Issue* uniforms". The three basic programs of the GI Bill, according to the US government's Veteran Administration (VA), were:

1. *Free scholarships* for higher education, to hopefully, drain off a substantial proportion of the vets away from the labor market and into educational programs: It gave each vet up to $500 per year for tuition (which was very adequate), as well as a living monthly stipend that depended on whether the vet was single, or had a family to support while schooling

2. *Loan guarantee*, by which government backed the veterans' borrowing for the purchase or construction of homes, farms, or business properties: This made it easy for the GIs to get low-interest credit that did not require down-payment. It created further incentives for new construction as opposed to existing housing.

3. *Weekly unemployment benefits*, which placed the GIs that opted to look for work on a weekly unemployment stipend that could last, if necessary, for up to one year.

The overall cost of the program, according to the Khan Academy, was about $14.5 billion, which was a very hefty figure for that period.

The Phenomenal Impact of The GI Bill

The GI Bill turned out an unprecedented success, and what the US Veteran Administration (VA), described as one of the most significant pieces of legislation ever produced by the United States government. As we shall see shortly, the principle that propelled this phenomenal success is something that policymakers across the world (especially the DCs) need to begin to replicate in day-to-day policymaking! But first, the impacts:

The impact of the Bill on the education sector

1. First, it defied the initial concerns and apprehensions about the influx of millions of vets belonging mostly to the ordinary, blue-collar segment of the society, into the American higher education system, which up to that point, had been elitist! For example, the highly publicised gripe by Robert Hutchins, the innovative President of the University of Chicago, that the program was going to turn the campuses into "hobo jungles", failed to materialise!

2. Instead, the Bill extended college education, which had been elitist for the most part, to the average American. For example, according to Jerome Kohlberg, a GI Bill beneficiary, now 82 and a billionaire businessman, who had enrolled in the Navy when he was 17:

3. According to the VA, in the peak year of 1947, veterans accounted for 49% of college admissions. And by the time the original GI Bill ended on July 25, 1956, about 8 million WW2 vets had participated in an education or training program, completely reinventing American higher education – and becoming, as Historian James T. Patterson, put it

4. As pointed out by the Khan Academy, the GI Bill also expanded American university curriculum from sole focus on the liberal arts, to one encompassing a range of career paths, including science, business, and engineering;

5. For the nation's colleges and universities, it provided a long and profitable boom. For example, according to William Celis 3D (quoting the Education Department) by March 1991, 23.2% of the US population had attended college for four years or more, compared to only 4.6% in 1940 before the GI Bill!

The impact of the Bill on the overall national economy

1. First, it helped government to avert the economic depression that policymakers had feared would hit the country, with the end of WW2, just as had been the case with WW1. About 8 million vets that would have flooded the job market opted for education, saving the economy from a potential unemployment crisis.

2. Instead it spurred economic activities by creating an education boom! Colleges sprang up overnight all across the United States, including those described by Wikipedia as "fly-by-night" "for-profit" colleges, in a scramble to collect veterans' education grants! They created jobs and other ancillary economic activities.

3. It boosted government's tax revenue! According to the Khan Academy, the veterans who took advantage of the educational subsidy earned, on average, $10,000-15,000 more per year than those who did not, generating ten times the cost of the program in tax revenue – and prompting some analysts to call the GI Bill the best investment the US government had ever made!

4. The impact of the GI Bill's housing program was similarly phenomenal! Before WW2, homeownership was elitist – "unreachable dreams for the average American", according to the VA. But the GI Bill's guaranty for home and business loans made homeownership available to ordinary folks, and ignited an economic boom of its own, financing the construction of thousands of new homes, and propelling the development of suburban America.

5. The GI Bill's housing program also propelled a new mortgage industry for the US economy, which Americans take for granted today!

6. In all, experts agree that the GI Bill was a major factor driving the American post-war prosperity, which created what Khan Academy has described as "the gift that kept on giving" – helping to fuel an economic prosperity that characterized the post-war era. As

more Americans took advantage of higher education, they earned higher wages, and could therefore pump more money into the economy by buying homes and consumer goods. William Celis 3D, quoting Jerome Kohlberg, put it this way:

> "… The country realized that education was important to the country; and that education paid for itself ten-fold, if not more."

7. Even beyond that, many experts are today tracing back many of America's national achievements, to the GI Bill! Speaking about the huge educated manpower that the Bill pumped into the economy, Ed Humes, author and Pulitzer Prize-winning journalist, put it this way:

> "Really, the cold warriors were educated on the GI Bill. They used different weapons. They had the drafting table instead of the draft board. They used their new skills to later on take us to the moon. GI Bill guys were behind that. Same with the Internet, with the invention of computers. You can trace back much of what's good in America today, to the skills and the prosperity that the GI Bill brought to this generation."

The socio-political impacts impact of the Bill

1. The Bill enabled Americans through their government, to truly appreciate their heroic GIs! In fact, according to William Celis 3D, the years immediately after WW2 were government at its best, for a wide swath of American society!

2. The Bill also made a huge impact on patriotism and national pride in Americans. As Jerome Kohlberg put it:

> " … The GIs were appreciated, and more than that, the country realized that education was important to the country."

Why Every DC Should Look Again At The Bill

There are some important reasons for taking all these pains to review the GI Bill:

1. The underlying principle that propelled the Bill's success is by no means limited to the rehabilitation of war veterans. As we shall see shortly, the principle is a tool that policymakers need for their day-to-day social programs; because it can give similar success to numerous other kinds of institutional programs in the DCs.

2. Even in terms of the rehabilitation of war veterans, it is remarkable that despite the Bill's legendary impact and how it has been admired across the world, policymakers in our DCs appear to be completely oblivious of it! Even those DCs that have since come out of major wars – such Nigeria from its civil war, Sudan from its civil war, and Liberia from its civil war – were not known to have crafted any similar post-war programs, even when funding was not a barrier, and even when huge international post-war aids poured into such DCs.

Therefore, the reason for taking all these pains to review the GI Bill, is to make our DCs aware of the basic principle behind its phenomenal impact, and the numerous opportunities our DCs have even today, for replicating that impact in different public programs.

Lessons from the Bill's education scheme

Note that instead of government embarking on the construction of hundreds of new schools for the GIs, it simply gave the GIs the money, and allowed them to select by themselves any schools that they wanted! In other words, the Bill put the funding of the education program in the hands of the GIs, and allowed the money to follow each GI to whatever schools they selected!

In contrast, note that even today (and even in its environment of corruption, tribalism and other vices), the typical DC will opt to award contracts for the construction of new, free higher institutions; and the following consequences will be inevitable:

1. The DC's scheme will lose the kind of massive injection of third-party (private-sector) funds that the GI Bill generated for the economy;

2. Awarding contracts for the construction of new schools will also open the scheme's doors to the usual corruption, patronage politics, outright embezzlement, and similar vices prevalent in the DCs!

3. It will also lose that scramble by third parties for the GIs' funds, and the kind of "*quality competition*" that the scramble created. Let us particularly appreciate this was a quality competition

    -   It was a quality competition because each school had to scramble to impress and attract the GIs, instead of, for example, looking for which government official to bribe or induce!

4. Notice also that the US government did not ask any of its agencies (any government agency) to take up the task of posting the GIs to schools: The bill simply gave each GI their money, and allowed that money to follow them to whatever school they selected!

    This again contrasts with what the typical DC would have done! Notice that even today (and even in its environment of widespread corruption, tribalism and other vices), our typical DC will simply mandate one of its agencies to take up the task of assigning the GIs to schools! That will open the scheme's doors to the usual corruption, tribalism, rent seeking, nepotism, missing files and the delays and frustrations that all these create!

    -   In general, putting the funding of a public program in the hands of the people the program is designed to serve, will usually drive the program to great success!

This is the profound lesson we need to learn from the GI Bill, which as argued by Osborne and Gaebler, was the principle behind its phenomenal success!

Lessons from the Bill's housing loan scheme

Notice similarly that the Bill did not award contracts for the constructions of new government estates for the GIs, nor even give the vets the loans! It simply provided guarantees for the loans, which empowered the GIs to go and negotiate individually with their preferred commercial and financial institutions, for the best deals they could get!

This again contrasts with what the typical DC would have done! The typical DC would have:

1. Embarked on building housing estates itself for the GIs; or

2. Insisted (if it chose to provide loans to the DCs) on administering the loans directly to the GIs (starting of course, with the setting up of a new agency to administer the loans); or

3. Alternatively (in the case of loans) possibly negotiating some lending terms with a few (typically favored) financial institutions, and requiring the GIs to go to only those favored institutions for their loans!

What would have been the impact if a DC had followed these alternative approaches? The following possibilities immediately come to mind:

1. The scheme would have lost the kind of massive injection of private-sector funds that the GI Bill's approach attracted to the housing sector. The project's funding would have been limited to government's own budget, which would have severely limited the impact.

2. The economy would also have lost the vibrancy and multiplier effects that the scheme created through its effect on the construction and finance industries.

4. The economy would have lost the new mortgage industry, to which the GI Bill gave impetus!

5. If a DC chose to administer the loans directly, it would have needed to set up an enforcement structure for ensuring that beneficiaries paid back punctually – something that the GI Bill's allowed the private sector to handle!

6. Above all, each of these options would have opened the scheme's doors to the usual vices associated with public programs in the DCs – corruption, nepotism, patronage politics, and perhaps, even outright embezzlement of the program's budget!

   - Again a profound strategy should always be to strive to put the funding of each public program in the hands of the people the program is designed to serve! This remains the enduring institutional lesson from the GI Bill.

Putting A Program's Funding In The Users' Hands

This principle calls for putting the funding of an institution's program in the hands of those the program is designed to serve, in such a way that if the people do not pay, the program will not get funded.

To do this effectively, three things need to be present: <u>choice</u>, <u>exit</u>, and <u>payment</u> (the <u>CEP</u>).

1. *Choice*: We as the service receivers must have different sources of the service, and the freedom to decide whom we receive the service from (this includes the right environment that enables us make informed decisions that can drive competitive outcomes)!
    - Note that the GI Bill's education approach achieved this because each GI had the freedom to patronize any school they wanted. Several schools emerged to try and grab some of the funds, and the fund followed each GI to whatever school they patronized.

2. *Exit*: Each service receiver must have the freedom to change their service provider at will;

    - Again note that the GI Bill's education approach achieved this because if a GI left any college they did not like, the funding would follow them to whatever alternative school they chose. So the college had a vital reason to strive to serve the GI well, so they would not exit!

3. *Payment*: It is also important that the payment that a service receiver makes, goes to only the precise service provider that has delivered the service.

    - Again note that the GI Bill's education approach achieved this because only the school selected by the GI, received the scholarship funds of the GI.

How This Principle Differentiates Public & Private Sectors

Whenever we put the funding of an institution's program in the hands of the people the program is designed to serve, it will compel the service providers to make efforts to access the funds (similar to what the private sector goes through), and will tend to navigate the program towards the vibrancy and efficiency of the private-sector!

Indeed, one of the key differences between the private and public sectors, as noted by Osborne and Gaebler, is that the funding for the services we receive from the private sector is usually in our hands; while the funding for the services we receive from government is usually <u>not</u> in our hands!

Case 30:   Nigeria's Public vs. Private Schools

Like Osborne and Gaebler, let use the public and private school systems as an illustration:

- A private school tends to perform better than public schools, not because it necessarily has better qualified teachers, but mostly because of the institutional environment it faces: Its funding is in the hands of the people it serves! Each private school knows that if parents are not satisfied, they can readily pull out their children to other competing private schools; and money will stop flowing in! This tends to make private schools very sensitive to the people they serve!

- On the other hand, the funding of a public school in a typical DC comes from government, rather than from the people the school serves. Even when the school is not doing well, it does not stop its funding from government; and it does not stop its teachers from being paid. It may even not stop the pupils from continuing to flow in, especially pupils from the poor and economically disadvantaged families that cannot afford the higher cost of private education! In this way, such a public school can get away with poor and unsatisfactory performance; and can continue to perform unsatisfactorily!

We can now appreciate why the typical private firm searches profusely for ways to please us – because the funding it must get to remain in business, is in our hands! Any private firm that cannot find ways to extract this money from our hands, will simply go out of business! That indeed, is why we have the following paradox noted by Osborne and Gaebler:

- The goal of the public service is to serve us, while the goal of the private sector is to make profit. Yet it is the private sector that is always searching profusely for ways to please us!

Note also that the following corollary is true:

- Any private firm or program, whose funding is not in the hands of the public it serves (according to the CEP explained above), is unlikely to produce the famed "private-sector" performance!

A Tool To Make Governance Institutions Serve Us

We can already begin to see from this concept, a potentially powerful tool for strengthening institutions – a tool that can make institutions sensitive to the people they serve! For if we firmly put the funding of a public program in the hands of the public that the program is designed to serve – so firmly that if people do not pay, the program will not get funded – then the program (and all those associated with it) will step up their game! The officials in charge will spring to life, and become service-oriented!

As noted by the World Bank in its 2000-2001 World Development Report, the key to reducing poverty in the DCs is to facilitate the empowerment of poor people, by making state and social institutions more responsive to them.

Now, based on what we have discussed so far, we have just seen a powerful tool for making state and social institutions more responsive to the people they serve! Just strive whenever feasible, to structure an institution's programs in such a way that each program's funding will be in the hands of the public the program is designed to serve! If we can do this very firmly, the program and its officials will become very service-oriented; and the World Bank's "responsiveness", which is vital for poverty reduction, can be taken for granted!

From the foregoing discussions, we can already guess that a typical DC will have numerous opportunities to apply this principle to its social and governance programs, not only to strengthen institutions, but also to create economic vibrancy.

Example#1: Some countries and localities use some forms of "school voucher" system, which we can regard as another indirect way of trying to put education funding in the hands of the schoolchildren and their parents.

Case 31:   The School Voucher System

In a typical application, government defines the voucher value every year, which each school child is entitled to; and which is usually enough to cover the school fees in public schools.

A DC can use the voucher system to ignite life into its schools, if the level of funding that each school gets (for teachers' salaries and other projects) depends on the amount of voucher funds it receives (the number of children it is able to attract). Parents will tend to keep away from schools that are performing poorly, which will tend to dry up funds from such schools; while the schools performing well will attract children – and the funds that follow them! In this way, the voucher system has the effect of putting school funding in the hands of the schoolchildren and their parents.

If a family opts to send their child to a school, whose fees exceed the face amount of the voucher (such as an expensive private school), the family can be required to pay the difference.

Example#2: This next example has to do with Nigeria's SERVICOM initiative and the challenges it has faced!

Case 32:   Nigeria's SERVICOM Charter!

The SERVICOM Charter was an initiative that Nigeria's President Olusegun Obasanjo flagged off with a lot of pomp, on March 21, 2004, during which Mr. President and his Ministers dedicated themselves, on behalf of the government ministries, departments, and agencies (MDAs) to:

- "Providing the basic services to which each citizen is entitled, in a timely, fair, honest, effective, and transparent manner".

Government had preceded the flag-off with a Special Presidential Retreat on Service Delivery in Nigeria. It was a very important initiative expected for example, to make all government officials to start treating the public in a "timely, fair, honest, effective, and transparent" manner; and stop them from trying to extract bribes. For example, it would make those in government's lands offices to begin to allocate lands strictly on "first-come, first-served" basis; prevent clerical officers across the public service from "hiding" case files; and so on! To underscore its importance, government even located the SERVICOM office within the Presidency, ostensibly to ensure that "government's commitments under SERVICOM to the people of Nigeria were faithfully performed".

What has been the impact of SERVICOM on the quality of public service in Nigeria? Can we truly say that the nation's public servants have become less corrupt? In Nigeria's institutional environment, we can already guess one reason why the scheme was doomed to have problems: There was no institution-propelled force driving it – just mere policy pronouncement (or official directive to public servants to begin to behave well) in an institutional environment riddled with vices such as impunity, corruption, tribalism, rent-seeking, nepotism, and so on! As we go through this Slice, we shall appreciate the superiority of institution-propelled drivers of change, over mere policy directives.

Later, when we look at operations measurement (OM), we shall suggest a more institution-propelled strategy for realizing the noble objectives of SERVICOM.

Example#3: Nigeria's Pension Reform Act (PRA) 2004 complied with this principle <u>to some extent</u>, which is a great credit of the designers of the scheme.

<u>Case 33:</u>   <u>Nigeria's Pension Reform Act</u>
Nigeria's Pension Reform Act (PRA) 2004 created one of the nation's landmark reforms, which rescued the federal government from the trauma of its mismanaged pension system, and accumulated and mounting pension arrears.

The PRA created some private-sector Pension Fund Administrators (PFAs) that manage the pension fund – arising principally from the monthly pension deductions from the workers and the matching contributions by their employers.

The PRA puts the funding of the PFAs significantly in the hands of the workers, by giving each worker the freedom to choose which PFA they want to save their pension money with. Also the contribution of each worker to the scheme goes to the PFA the worker has selected.

Notice the power that this "choice" has given to the worker, to influence the quality of service – because it means that workers can keep away from any PFA that is not performing well. The functioning of the system would have been traumatic if this feature was not there!

However, the workers' empowerment is not complete, because the system restricts the power of workers to change their PFAs, should they desire to do so – a rather unnecessary restriction! According to Part 1, Section 11(2) of the PRA 2004:

- The employee may not more than once a year, transfer the retirement savings account (RSA) from one PFA to another, without adducing any reason for such transfer

> Although it wisely shields the employee from having to adduce "any reason for such transfer", we should nevertheless note the restriction to employees from changing their PFA "more than once a year".
>
> Incidentally, PENCOM, the agency regulating the pension system, does not (so far) even allow any mobility at all, not even the "once a year" movement that the law prescribes!

It is indeed an irony that PENCOM does not even allow the "once a year" movement that the law authorizes! This PENCOM-made restriction is unnecessary for the following reasons:

1. It is weakening the institutional quality by inadvertently inhibiting the workers' ability to drive the quality of service of the nation's pension system! For example, it shields the PFAs that are not performing well, by denying workers the opportunity to identify and dump them – thereby allowing such PFAs to continue to perform poorly.

2. There is also no plausible technical reason to justify the restriction. The PFAs belong to the same finance industry as Nigeria's banks. In fact, it was mostly Nigerian banks that set up the PFAs. Now, Nigerians maintain different accounts with their banks – far more complex accounts than the straightforward retirement benefit accounts (RBAs) they maintain with their PFAs. For example, bank customers can open multiple accounts of different features with the same bank! Yet customers are not restricted from moving from one bank to the other! Why then the restriction on the RBAs?

3. Clearly, the Nigerian finance industry, to which the PFAs belong, is already used to customer mobility! There is therefore no plausible technical reason for this PENCOM's institution-weakening restriction!

Example#4: We can also use Nigeria's National Health Insurance Scheme (NHIS) as another example. The scheme, the way Nigeria is currently operating it, has many useful features. Unfortunately, however, it does not put the scheme's funding in the hands of the service receivers (i.e. the patients, called the "enrollees").

<u>Case 34:</u>   <u>**Nigeria's NHIS & Its Empowerment of Service Receivers**</u>

> As in the pension system, NHIS is funded by monthly deductions from the workers and the matching contributions by their employers. Some licensed health management organizations (HMOs) manage the workers (the enrollees) and pay the hospitals that render the services (provide treatments) to them.
>
> In a typical Nigerian workplace, it is the employers of labor that select the HMOs on behalf of their workers. Each employee in the workplace can thereafter choose a hospital from the list of hospitals covered by the selected HMO. An employee can only select a hospital from that list. If a hospital that an employee wants is not in that list (not covered by the HMO), then too bad!
>
> This arrangement is a major structural defect, because it prevents the scheme's funding from being firmly in the hands of the workers (service

receivers)! Unlike in the GI Bill, where the schools run after the GIs, the HMOs have no incentive to waste time on the workers, since the relevant decisions on the patronage they want, are made by organizations' chief executives (CEOs), and possibly human resources managers (HRMs).

The nation's NHIS arrangement may have other structural defects. However, our concern here is with the definite violation of the CEP empowerment principle of this Chapter. This violation may appear inconsequential, but its institutional implications can be profound!

In Nigeria's weak institutional environment, this arrangement will tend to focus the NHIS on the business (rather than the "service quality") aspect of healthcare! For example:

1. If the workers (the service receivers) had been empowered to select their HMOs by themselves, they would have based their choices on "*quality of service*", which would have become the driver of the scheme! The present arrangement has downplayed "*quality of service*"; and instead, entices the HMOs to start using bribery and material inducements to win the CEOs and HRMs, to whom "*quality of service*" is not paramount! The tragic irony is that in the nation's weak institutional environment, the HMOs that focus on material inducement are likely to sign up more organizations than the HMOs that try to compete by striving to improve service quality!

2. The implication is that the NHIS funds (the monthly deductions from workers and the matching contributions by their employers) will become the engine and driver of corruption in the healthcare industry, instead of helping to develop it.

3. This corruption will prevent the healthcare institution from producing private-sector performance despite being dominated by private parties (the HMOs and most of the hospitals in the scheme are of the private sector).

4. In other words, the failure to put the funding of the NHIS in the hands of the service receivers, has turned a scheme, which was created to develop healthcare, into a potential impediment to healthcare development!

In view of this, it should not be surprising that the scheme has been attracting scathing criticisms from stakeholders, for corruption, fraud and poor performance.

<u>**Case 35:**</u>   <u>**Nigeria's NHIS & The Scathing Criticisms**</u>

Some examples of the scathing stakeholders' criticisms of the NHIS:
- In June 2010, the National Chairman, Association of Community Pharmacists of Nigeria (ACPN), Mrs. Ejiro Foyibo, described the NHIS as a fraud, and requested that its participants and Nigerians at large should demand their right to qualitative healthcare. According to her, the scheme was with good intentions, but the implementation had become faulty and fraudulent:

> "I boldly say that NHIS is a fraud ... Nigerians, who are enrollees of the NHIS, should rise and ask questions on the functionality of the NHIS"

- Even Nigeria's National Assembly has been blasting the Scheme. For example, in November, 2011, the House of Representatives, while mandating its Committee on Health to investigate the scheme's "haphazard implementation" thundered:

> [The NHIS is] "a national embarrassment, disaster and colossal failure,"

- As recently as June 2017, the House of Representatives held a public hearing on what it described as *"Inhuman Treatment of the NHIS Enrollees and Urgent Need to Investigate the Activities of HMOs and Healthcare Providers in Nigeria"*. During the hearing the Executive Secretary of the NHIS, Prof. Yusuf Usman, addressed the HMOs in these words:

> "We are fixing the mistakes and you [pointing at HMOs] are the big mistake, we are going to fix … Today, I am exposing everything from our inadequacies as regulator, the fraud by HMOs and the recklessness of service providers"

- Similarly at the hearing, the National Presidents of the Nigerian Labor Congress (NLC), Ayuba Wabba, described the HMOs as an impediment to enrollees getting first-class service.

(For more details, please see The Nation, 15/06/2010; Nigerian Tribune, 21/11/2011; MetroNews NG, June 28, 2017; The Sun, July 4, 2017)

When a public program generates huge funds in a weak institutional environment, with the kind of corruption-inducing loophole that this NHIS has created, the funds become a powerful driver of corruption, which in turn makes it a disastrous impediment to development!

Incidentally, this is similar to the impediment that corruption (particularly the corruption associated with the nation's "fuel subsidy" system) is also thought to be creating in Nigeria's oil sector. Nigeria's oil industry is so underdeveloped, even after more than 50 years of existence, that the nation still does not have functional refineries (and so imports most of the fuel consumed domestically)!

For Nigeria's NHIS to have any real chance of driving true healthcare development (in the nation's present institutional environment), the starting point must be to rejig its implementation so as to fully put its funding in the hands of the enrollees. Then, the corresponding role of each of the other stakeholders of the scheme can be reverse-derived. This means that the enrollees should as a minimum, be able to:

1. Select their HMOs freely, just the way they also select their pension fund administrators (PFAs), instead of their employers doing the selection on their behalf;

2. Change their HMOs at will, without having to give explanation to anybody, just the way they can change their banks and salary accounts; or even best of all,

3. Select the hospitals they want, so that the HMOs managing those hospitals will then receive the funds associated with the respective enrolees. In this way, the level of funding each

hospital gets will depend on the number of enrollees it is able to attract (which itself will now depend on its quality of service). This will cause the hospitals to compete for the enrollees' funds, while the HMOs compete for the most patronized hospitals (which will be those providing the most attractive services).

Good Fit, Not Just Best Practice

The problem of Nigeria's NHIS may be because the arrangement has emphasized a "best practice" model, rather than one that appreciates the nation's institutional environment! Even if a similar model is working well in another nation, it is clearly not working the same way in Nigeria – because of Nigeria's unique institutional environment! Let us again remember the World Bank (2000) emphasizes this "good fit" approach:

> "We must work with our clients to find reforms that fit local conditions while also reflecting broad fundamental principles of efficiency, equity, and poverty orientation. While broad end goals may be similar, "best practice" in achieving them is not uniform across countries; rather "good fit" that builds on basic principles is in essence "best practice"

Indeed, the various principles we are taking time to treat in this section represent powerful tools for creating such *"good fits"*, because they create behavior-changing incentives, in the institutional environments of the DCs.

As a rule, especially in the institutional environments of the DCs, something intrinsic to a system will always be necessary to propel service quality; and putting the funding of that service in the hands of the service receivers, always creates that propulsion. Our DCs' CRTs need to take this profound principle to heart.

Helps To Achieve Reform Within Existing Political Constraints

Finally, observe again that the technique of this Chapter (structuring a program that delivers services in such a way as to fully put the program's funding in the hands of the service receivers) will often allow us to improve overall institutional performance, without necessarily starting a fight on the DC's balance of political forces. In other words, it can help us to achieve improvements in institutional services, even within the constraints of the prevailing political arrangements.

The same thing applies to most of the other tools and techniques reviewed in this Slice. They will often allow us to get desired outcomes from targeted institutional processes and programs, even without having to confront the prevailing political forces.

Chapter 10

10. Making Governance Systems Self-Propelling

*"I believe that for us to get to where we want to go, as a nation, we have to
build strong institutions and when we build strong institutions, these institutions
will drive the process."*

*(Nigeria's President Goodluck Jonathan, speaking at the 51st Independence Anniversary Lecture in
Abuja; October 27, 2011)*

Topics Covered in This Chapter:

- Introduction To Institution-Driven Incentives
- Benefits of Institution-Driven incentives
- Many Ways To Apply This To Institutional Processes
- Reform Within Existing Political Constraints
- Creating Negative Incentives
- How to Create Institution-Driven Incentives

Introduction To Institution-Driven Incentives

Sustainable institutional change, as aptly noted by the World Bank (2012), often requires that thousands of public agents alter their behaviors. Incidentally, one of the most effective ways of altering the behavior of people is to restructure the incentives they face, in such a way that the incentives the institution creates, can begin to propel them in the direction that government wants them to go.

For example, the reform godfathers, Osborne & Gaebler, have described *"self-propelling"* system as one that creates its own internal incentives for improvement and automatic consequences for failure to improve. If a system is self-propelling, it means that the system itself is creating the kind of incentives that will draw people in the direction that government wants.

As an example, consider the bottle-deposit initiative of the United States government, cited by Osborne & Gaebler:

Case 36:   The US Bottle-Deposit Policy

Many years ago, the United States government was faced with the menace of used beverage bottles, which littered its streets, as Americans simply "drank and dropped"! Instead of trying to create a new law, and setting up a special agency and infrastructure for apprehending and punishing violators, government simply restructured the system: it put a 5-

cent deposit on each bottle, to be refunded to the buyer whenever the bottle was returned.

The result was dramatic! The empty bottles disappeared! It was not just that people no longer wanted to lose their bottles, but that some persons might actually have started gathering empty litters, so as to collect refunds on them! According to the website of the Iowa State Department of Natural Resources:

- The scheme in the State currently recycles 82,352 tons of material per year.

- Energy savings from the scheme in the State could heat 42,845 average Iowa households (because it takes more energy to make a bottle from fresh materials than from recycled items)

Although the bottle-deposit system has become commonplace today, it was a very interesting initiative when it was first crafted, and an example of a policy that the incentives of the people concerned.

(Data on Iowa downloaded from the website of the State of Iowa Department of Natural Resources, as at 16-Jul-2015)

Observe that the bottle-deposit initiative creates its own internal incentives that propel people to start enthusiastically to do on their own, what government would want them to be doing. It is an example of "institution-driven" incentives, because what is driving compliance is the incentive that the institution itself has created – not necessarily the directive of government!

In a self-propelling system, the parties concerned will be behaving in line with what government wants, not necessarily because of a government "directive" requiring them to do so, but because they themselves have now become interested in doing so (the system itself has cleverly incentivized them to begin to do so).

Case 37: A Workers' Suggestion Scheme

Suppose government in a DC with corrupt officials puts in place a new policy that encourages public servants to start making suggestions on how to save money in their workplaces – with the proviso that such public servants will get a pre-agreed percentage of any savings that result from their suggestions. People can work in teams. Each team will be encouraged to report whatever it can find in its workplace (or anywhere else in government operations) that can enable government save money, by reducing wastes, closing a loophole, changing an operating procedure, and so on.

Note that if a loophole gets closed in this way, government will save the money it has been losing to that loophole, and only use a fraction of what it has saved to compensate the team concerned. Therefore, government will be gaining! More importantly, this kind of scheme can transform government employees into teams of auditors and cost analysts, who instead of resisting changes, will now be the ones advancing them! People may even start working overtime, looking for loopholes to bring up!

Not minding that this example is hypothetical, it does bring out many interesting things:

1. With the restructured incentives, it is now the public that will themselves be bringing up initiatives for change, instead of resisting change. They will be doing so not necessarily because of the directive of government, but simply because they now want to do so; it serves their own interests! In other words, we have changed their behavior by restructuring the incentives they face!

2. We can compare the expected enthusiasm of the public workers for this initiative against what their attitude would be towards an alternative (and more coercive) approach of inviting a consultant to come to detect the loopholes. In this latter case, the staff and officials may become quietly uncooperative, and may even be inclined to suppress valuable information from the consultant!

In the DC environment, where corruption, connivance, nepotism, and similar vices tend to be very widespread, institutions will work better whenever the CRT can structure some internal, institution-driven incentives to propel people in the direction that government wants – rather than government merely issuing directives and relying solely on its coercive power to achieve compliance. In the DC environment, the effectiveness of coercive power wears out very quickly under constant battering from the prevalent vices of corruption, nepotism, tribalism, impunity, and others.

To further differentiate this internal, institution-driven incentives from the usual coercive approach of governments in the DCs – what people variously call the "Rules & Enforcement" (R&E) approach, or "command & control" (C&C) approach – let us examine the following additional examples:

Case 38:   Coercive Vs. Institution-Driven Incentives

Some examples of the usual coercive approach of governments, as opposed to internal, institution-driven incentives:

- On 15 Jan 2012, Thisday newspaper carried a story on how Nigerian port operators were striving to comply with government's directive to commence 24-hour operations. Apparently as a way of coping with the congestions at the ports, and long delays in clearing goods, the federal government had directed the private-sector port operators (who had taken over the management of the ports from the Nigerian Ports Authority) to commence 24-hour operations in all the nation's seaports.

    – *Compare this C&C approach with an arrangement that could have seen the port operators themselves initiating the 24-hour operations – since each operator's income should depend on the cargoes processed!*

- As a way of keeping the environment clean, the Lagos State government (in Nigeria) requires all markets and shops not to open on Thursdays until after 10am. The state government wants these business owners to use the period before 10am for cleaning their environment. It has enforcement teams across the state that patrol and apprehend violators.

> *– Compare this C&C approach with an arrangement that could see the markets and shops themselves eagerly keeping their environments clean, every day of the week!*

- On Nov 25, 2014, the Leadership newspaper carried a story on the warning by Nigeria's Minister of Power, Prof. Chinedu Nebo, to the nation's private-sector power distribution companies (Discos) to desist from rejecting power allocated to them from the national grid – or risk the cancellation of their licenses. Note that the Discos were expected to make their money by distributing the power they received from the transmission segment, to consumers, and billing the consumers accordingly. Was it then not absurd that at a time consumers were experiencing acute shortage of power, government could still be threatening the Discos to stop rejecting power wheeled to them by the transmission segment?

> *– Compare this C&C approach with an arrangement that could see the Discos scrambling for as much power as they could get from the transmission system, which they would promptly distribute to consumers, to bill them and make money!*

(See Thisday, 15 Jan 2012 & Leadership, 25 Nov 2014)

Benefits of Institution-Driven incentives

Let us now look at some of the potential benefits of the "self-propelling" approach, relative to the usual coercive approach of government:

1. *It reduces the efforts and resources required for enforcement:* This is a basic benefit of the institutional processes that propel themselves. Once we can structure the incentives created by an institution to begin navigate people towards the direction that government wants them to go, government goals can be achieved with minimal enforcement efforts, because enforcement efforts will only be needed for the deviants! Therefore, institution-driven incentives tremendously reduce the level of enforcement resources that will be required. Sometimes, it may even be difficult for government to attain its goals if there is no help from system-driven incentives!

Case 39:   The Overwhelming Odds Against Nigeria's EFCC

In Nigeria, the Economics and Financial Commission (EFCC) is the government's primary agency for fighting corruption, which is expected to convict and jail all persons found to be corrupt.

However, the truth is that the hundreds of cases pouring into the agency would be overwhelming to even 100 EFCCs! How many investigations does the agency truly have the resources to undertake effectively? How many cases does it have the capacity to prosecute? What is EFCC's annual budget? Can the nation even afford the cost of the meticulous investigations expected of the agency in all these cases, and the cost of meticulous prosecution?

The EFCC will be far more successful when government develops the culture of structuring internal, institution-driven incentives to propel its programs – so that institutional activities and energy will basically be flowing in line with the desired outcomes. That way, the EFCC can now focus on any deviants that arise – rather than having to chase practically everybody in the system!

The coercive force of enforcement will always be necessary, because not every institutional process can be self-propelling; and even those that are, will themselves occasionally feature deviant behaviors!

2. *It helps to overcome the notorious vices of the DCs*: In the DC environment, where corruption, connivance, nepotism, and similar vices tend to be very widespread, institutional processes that propel themselves, work far better than those relying merely on the force of government's coercive power, because the effectiveness of coercive power wears out very quickly under constant battering from these vices.

3. *It undercuts the forces sustaining institutions dysfunctions*: It is relatively easy for powerful interests in a DC to frustrate the institutional policies or processes that they do not want, if the implementation relies on the coercive force of government. They will try to influence, corrupt or even intimidate those implementing the policy; and the latter usually cave in eventually. But any policy or process that propels itself will not be so easy to quench, because everybody concerned will seem to be enjoying it!

4. *It can lead to continuous improvement*: According to the reform godfathers, Osborne & Gaebler, "self-propelling" systems tend to create their own internal incentives for improvement and automatic consequences for failure to improve.

    Indeed, when people are doing something because they like it, they are likely to be more innovative, than when they are being compelled to do it. For example, if the Nigerian government directs its private-sector port operators to commence 24-hour operations in the nation's seaports, they (the operators) may comply for the sake of compliance; but it cannot be the same as when we restructure the operators' incentives, so that they themselves become enthusiastic about 24-hour operations. In fact, under coercion, the operators can even comply on the surface, but devise other ways to frustrate the policy, once it is a policy they do not want.

    Similarly, in the "workers suggestion" scheme discussed before, there can be no limit to how far the workers can go in looking for loopholes to improve! Some can even start doing overtime, searching for loopholes to bring up! Compare this to the coercive case of inviting a consultant to come and detect the loopholes. In the latter case, the staff and officials may be quietly even hiding valuable information from the consultant!

5. *Institution-driven incentives will often create consequences for "failure to improve"*: We can use the workers suggestion scheme to illustrate Osborne & Gaebler's automatic consequences for failure to improve. For example, if the official overseeing a functional process with a given loophole (and perhaps benefitting from that loophole) fails to bring it up, some other people will ultimately become aware of the loophole, and not only take the reward from the official's domain, but possibly even cause questions to be asked about the official's competence! There is therefore some "consequence" for failure to improve!

6. *It is cheaper to implement*: Consider the US bottle-deposit initiative: If government had used the coercive approach, it would have needed to set up an enforcement structure; and this would have needed to be nationwide! Think of the costs of assembling and maintaining the enforcement officers, plus their nationwide offices, regional offices, and

of course a befitting head office! Rather, the bottle-deposit initiative is propelling itself towards government goal!

The 2001 telecoms roll-out by Nigeria's federal government can be a good example of how government can structure an institutional program to become self-propelling:

Case 40: Nigeria's Self-propelling Telecoms Reform

At the time that the Nigerian government through its telecoms industry regulator, the Nigerian Communications Commission (NCC), deregulated the nation's telecoms industry in 2001, the country could only boast of about 250,000 functional telephone lines, for a population of over 120 million!

Nigerians were truly denied decent telecoms services, despite the fact that the government-owned telecoms monopoly, Nitel, had been in existence for many decades. Thousands of Nigerians were in the queue to get telephone lines, which were not forthcoming, even with outrageous deposits. Those who had phone lines were equally groaning from their inability to get their calls through! This continued even when neighboring countries started to implement mobile telephony!

Therefore, one of the goals of the NCC was to increase teledensity in the country, through a rapid telecoms rollout nationwide. NCC started by deregulating the sector, and by licensing international telecoms firms to come into the country, through a competitive bidding process. Here were some of the key factors that tended to make the program self-propelling:

- *The auctioning process*: After two international operators (MTN and Econet Wireless) won the GSM licenses in a very competitive and transparent bidding process, and paid a whopping competitively-derived $285 million as license fee each, nobody needed to push them to be serious with building their networks! They on their own, needed to work hard to protect the huge investments they had made!

  Notice that if government had given its agency (Nitel) money to execute the project, or if the licenses had been awarded to the "friends" of government at ridiculous prices, this self-propelling incentive to get serious would not have been there!

- *The business reward*: The 2nd factor was the reward that awaited any of the GSM operators that was able to roll out lines quickly. Such an operator stood to reap huge profits from jumbo pricing that would progressively thin down, as the market matured. We can recall that a GSM line, which is practically free today, cost as much as N20,000 in those early days; and that call rates which today can be below N7/minute were as high as N50/minute.

- *Limited Exclusivity*: Related to the business reward was the awareness of the GSM operators that they only had a limited exclusivity period, after which government would throw open the market. So they needed to move fast.

With all these factors playing out, the industry had acquired its own incentives to urgently roll out, as well as obvious consequences for failure to do so! Imagine the hectic board meetings and strategy sessions that must have taken place across the world, by investors, operators and telecoms equipment suppliers, on how to roll out in Nigeria – on how to accomplish the precise outcome that the Nigerian government wanted for its telecoms sector!

In particular, notice that it was not government convening the rollout meetings and strategy sessions! The industry itself was doing so in its eagerness to rollout – the precise thing that government wanted! Government had effectively structured the system so that the operators would be falling over themselves, producing exactly the outcome that government wanted, in an enthusiastic pursuit of their own interests!

Somebody may wonder if it was not the mere injection of the private sector into the telecoms industry that made the difference. Yes, the basic government policy of deregulation was the critical seed that led to the transformation of the sector. However, we should also note that other privatization initiatives in the country (such as the concessioning of the Nigerian seaports, and the privatization of the electricity-sector) have not been anywhere as successful as that of telecoms. In fact, many others (such as the privatization of the steel, fertilizer and paper companies, and petroleum refineries) were outright failures! Therefore, it was not just the injection of the private sector into the telecoms industry that made the difference, the in-built institution-driven incentives also made the big difference.

We can also compare this telecoms process with the alternative of giving the government-owned telecoms company (Nitel) money to carry out the telecoms expansion! The competitive spirit would also not have been there! More importantly, government would have had to worry about implementation fidelity, and would probably have looked for an "outstanding" person to drive it (somebody who would not steal the money, or succumb to entrenched interests). And there would still have been no guarantee of success (we can safely say this, because that was the approach government had used in the previous four decades, during which government was spending its own funds [through Nitel], trying to do it by itself! In fact, Nitel was given a free license, to start its own GSM network; but it soon died away, unable to cope with the competition!

The point to note here is that governance efforts in the DCs, will be far more successful once policymakers develop the culture of structuring internal, institution-driven incentives to propel their programs – rather than relying solely on the coercive power of government!

Helps To Achieve Reforms Even Within Existing Political Constraints

As we saw in Slice B, dysfunctional institutions in our DCs are often sustained by powerful political forces that are benefiting from them to the detriment of the larger society. However, observe that the "self-propelling" tool reviewed in this Chapter will often allow us to improve institutional performance even within the existing political arrangements (by allowing us to improve institutional processes and programs, without necessarily having to attack the DC's balance of political powers). Nigeria's telecoms reform was a good example; it was achieved within the constraints of the nation's so-called dysfunctional federation.

How to Create Institution-Driven Incentives

Below is a possible four-step technique for creating institution-driven incentives:

1. *Open-mindedness*: The first step is to free the mind from the usual coercive inclination of government in its policies, especially in the DCs.

2. *Inventory taking*: Always start by understanding what is on the ground, including the nature of the prevailing incentives!

3. *Basic systems principles*: Ensure that the system does not violate any of the "profound" principles discussed Chapter-by-Chapter in this Slice.

4. *The strategic reform questions*: Now, ask the kind of strategic reform questions that we shall meet in Slice F (on "Regulation").

Don't Create Negative Incentives

Finally, let us note that we can sometimes inadvertently structure a system in a way that altogether creates negative incentives – the kind that incentivizes behaviors in a direction that is opposite to what government wants! We shall use Nigeria's electricity Discos (presented in the next Chapter) to illustrate this.

Chapter 11

11. Making Governance Systems Self-Enforcing

"There are obvious incentives (apart from avoiding legal sanctions) to stop at red traffic lights and to drive on the same side of the road as others … Even if I prefer to drive on the left, when I find myself in a country where driving on the right is the convention, then I will drive on the right, and others will prefer that I do this"

(Geoffrey Hodgson on "Coordination" Equilibrium, 2006)

Topics Covered in This Chapter:

- Introduction: How Systems Can Be Self-Enforcing
- Various Examples
- Reform within the existing political constraints
- Self-policing donor funding
- Turning donor help into a curse
- A Nigerian "missed opportunity" for self-enforcement

Introduction: How Systems Can Be Self-Enforcing

As we saw in the previous Chapter, sustainable institutional change often requires that thousands of public agents alter their behaviors. And, institutions work better when they (the institutions) on their own, generate inbuilt incentives that propel these public agents to act in accordance with what government wants, rather than government relying solely on its coercive power.

Another useful technique for strengthening institutional processes is to structure them (whenever possible) to become self-enforcing. When a governance system becomes self-enforcing, it does not require government agents to enforce it; instead the stakeholders themselves work to ensure compliance. Geoffrey Hodgson's example of *"coordination equilibrium"* cited above can bring self-enforcement (and stability) even though the equilibrium may not be ideal for everyone involved. As Geoffrey put it:

> "There are obvious incentives (apart from avoiding legal sanctions) to stop at red traffic lights and to drive on the same side of the road as others. … Even if I prefer to drive on the left, when I find myself in a country where driving on the right is the convention, then I will drive on the right, and others will prefer that I do this"

Notice that even though infringements will occur now and then, this category of laws will tend to be enforced by motorists themselves, because everybody wants everybody else to avoid infringements, so as to forestall perceived personal risks." In self-enforcing systems (which we can also call "self-policing" systems), the parties involved comply with the required outcome – this time, not necessarily because they are enthusiastic about doing so (as in the case of self-propelling systems) but because the arrangement constrains them to comply. This "induced" compliance is useful because at least, it is enforced by the parties concerned, which saves government from having to chase them about with whips.

Various Examples

There are many diverse ways to structure systems so that the parties concerned would have a basic tendency to police (or rail-road) themselves in the direction of government's desired outcomes.

1. *Managing micro-credit facilities*: In the DCs, many funding initiatives to support small and medium scale enterprises (SMEs) suffer from very high levels of loan defaults. Of course, government can always send its law-enforcement and special agents after the defaulters to teach them a proper lesson! However, this will fall into the coercive approach, with all the limitations (as we have been seeing in this Slice).
    We can get some effective help from the technique that the Nobel Prize winner and renowned economics professor, Muhammad Yunus (of the Grameen Bank of Bangladesh) popularized, which is now widely used by microfinance banks in Nigeria.

    ### Case 41:   A Self-Enforcing Microcredit Technique

    The technique worked approximately as follows:

    - Intending applicants would first arrange themselves in groups (of say 5 persons), which are then trained;

    - Loan would begin with only one or two members of each group;

    - Other members of the group would become eligible, only after the initial members had established successful repayment records!

    Notice that in this way, people waiting for their own loans help to ensure that existing beneficiaries are servicing their loans!
    From the point of view of a microfinance bank, this technique is somewhat self-enforcing, because the bank does not have to run after the loan beneficiaries, by itself. Instead, it has cleverly co-opted some members of the target customers (those still waiting for their loans) to ensure that those that have already received theirs, are in track. In other words, the bank has cleverly aligned the interests of those still waiting for their loans, to its own interests!

2. *Using the insurance industry for regulation*: A regulatory agency can become too cosy with the parties it regulates, either because of the so-called "regulatory capture" or due to the corruption, laxity or even incompetence of regulatory officials. According to William Sanjour, a retired U.S. Environmental Protection Agency regulator, the insurance industry can be helpful in regulating some other industries:

<u>**Case 42:**</u>   <u>**Using The Insurance Industry To Enhance Regulation**</u>

According to William Sanjour, insurance policies can be used in critical regulatory situations, to help keep regulatory agencies on their toes. As he put it (in respect of the BP's Deep-water Horizon oil rig that blew up):

- "BP has admitted, between 2005 and 2010, to breaking U.S. environmental and safety laws and committing outright fraud and paid $373 million in fines. Between June 2007 and February 2010, BP refineries in Texas and Ohio accounted for 97% of the "egregious, willful" violations handed out by the U.S. Occupational Safety and Health Administration. Yet none of this resulted in any oversight of the Deepwater Horizon oil rig that blew up … If BP had been required to carry a $10 billion insurance policy for an oil spill, I'm sure the insurance company would not have allowed the penny-pinching short cuts that the paid regulators allowed."

From the point of view of government, this arrangement can be considered self-enforcing, because government has galvanized one industry to help to keep another industry in track. In this way, government has cleverly aligned the insurance industry's interests to public interest!

3. *Corruption in the educational institutions*: Many higher education systems in the DCs are under-performing mostly because of corruption and similar vices, which manifest, not only in the administrative processes, but also in the provision of amenities, admission of students, and even students' progression.

   For example, "sorting" is a term used in Nigerian universities to describe the phenomenon by which some students rather than working hard to pass their exams, prefer to rely on "sorting" themselves out with their lecturers, to pass their courses. It can involve cash payment; or when it is a male lecturer, a female student can decide to sort herself out "in kind"! In this way, any student can pass such a lecturer's course, provided they understand what to do. The corruption can also come from the side of the lecturers – as corrupt lecturers can insist on being sorted out, before students (even good ones) can pass their courses.

   Our immediate instincts would be to inflict severe punishment on any lecturer found to be involved in such vices. However, as we saw in the last Chapter, institutions work better when we can structure some internal incentives to propel actors in the direction government wants, rather than relying exclusively on the coercive power of government. For example, the observation of Simon Kolawole of *Thisday* newspapers, in a university in England, can represent some form of self-policing mechanism:

<u>**Case 43:**</u>   <u>**The Problem of Sorting in Some Tertiary Institutions**</u>

Simon once recounted why he abandoned his MBA program in one of the local universities to go to England: Among other things, he was disgusted by how a lecturer could come into a class of 80 MBA students, and announce that his car had been stolen, and demand that every student should contribute N10,000 for its replacement. Of course, this would be with utter indifference to the very high tuition fees already paid by the students. Another lecturer could also come into the class, and announce that they had lost their mobile phone, and ask the class to contribute money for its replacement. Of course, both good and bad students would comply, to avoid being victimized. However, Simon found a different system, when he switched to a university in England. According to him:

- Two examiners would mark every academic work independently. The department would then compare. If the marks were wide apart, an external examiner would be called in to give their verdict.

From the point of view of the university, this is a self-enforcing system, because it helps to keep the lecturers in the track of the desired outcome. Each lecturer is forced to be careful with their marking, as no lecturer would like to be put on the spot with marks wide apart from what they should be – whether because of carelessness, or corruption! Sorting also becomes more complex for the students! For example, how many lecturers will a female student sleep with? It also becomes more difficult to victimize anybody for refusing to "sort"!

4. _Engaging unemployed workers in voluntary services_: As a final example, some nations pay monthly unemployment stipends to their workers that lose their jobs – to sustain them until they secure new jobs. This is a very common practice in the developed economies. This kind of program can easily be abused in the DC environment, where corruption and other vices tend to be widespread. Gary Shapiro, President and CEO of CEA, a U.S. trade association representing more than 2,000 consumer electronics companies, has a remedy with elements of self-enforcement.

<u>**Case 44:**</u>   <u>**Gary Shapiro's Self-Enforcing Proposal For Unemployed Recipients Of Welfare**</u>

According to Gary Shapiro:

"We encourage unemployment by rewarding the unemployed. All research shows the longer the unemployment payments the longer the jobless stay jobless. By shortening the duration of unemployment insurance and requiring those receiving checks to volunteer at a non-profit, both parties can benefit. By contributing to society, they can gain skills, contacts and references that will help them be successful in the next job they attain and in turn, we would see fewer people claiming unemployment [benefits]"

Notice indeed that by shortening the duration of unemployment insurance, and requiring those benefitting from it to volunteer at non-profit establishments, the system may create in-built incentives that can cause beneficiaries to want to make sincere efforts to exit the program

---

(For more, please see Gary Shapiro, _Forbes_, Jan 23, 2013)

Notice that in each of these examples, the parties concerned are complying with the desired outcome, not because government agencies are chasing them with whips (and also not necessarily because they would have wanted to) but simply because the arrangement itself railroads them into compliance!

Self-Policing Donor Funding

As an answer to the misuse of their funds, some major donor agencies, such as the Asian Development Bank (ADB) and the World Bank, now use a technique called "results based lending" (RBL). It is a self-policing tool, to ensure that the funds that donor agencies disburse to the DCs, do not end up in the private pockets of government officials, but strictly go into the projects they are meant for.

> **Case 45:** **How A Typical RBL Program Can Inspire A Prudent Use of Donor Funds**
>
> It can achieve this approximately as follows:
>
> - The project agreement will specify various phases and completion benchmarks, as well as the amount to be released for each phase.
>
> - The host government (through its implementing agency) will then commence with its own resources. Once it attains the first benchmark, it will notify the donor, and a pre-agreed independent inspection/audit team will visit for verification. The donor will release the amount attached to that phase only if the agreed benchmark is confirmed. If the project does not attain the benchmark, there will be no release of funds!
>
> - The beneficiary will then use the reimbursement to embark on the next phase. The process will continue until the execution attains the 100%, at which point the funding agency will release the final tranche.
>
> --

Notice the internal self-policing attribute of this arrangement, which ensures that donor funds go only to the projects the funds are meant for. If the leaders even spend more money on any phase of the project than they should (perhaps due to corruption), it will not affect the donor agency, which will only release the pre-agreed reimbursement for that phase.

In general, there are some important benefits of this kind of RBL arrangement:

1. *It fights corruption*: It prevents the donor funds from developing wings;

2. *It frees the donor from operational details*: It saves the donor the hassles of having to micro-manage the project in question. Once the DC understands a project's specifications, benchmarks and the amounts to be disbursed correspondingly, the DC should be free to go about the project in any way it considers most efficient, for delivering the targets.

3. *It reduces transaction costs*: Once the DC is going about the project in its own way, the donor's transaction costs attached to loans (particularly those associated with the donor's foreign consultants and experts) which the DC will usually bear, will crash – meaning that more of the funds will go into the project, rather than to transaction costs.

4. *It inspires a higher sense of project ownership*: This entire arrangement will tend to give the DC a stronger sense of ownership of the donor-financed project; while also strengthening institutions.

5. *It enhances local capacity building*: As pointed out by the OECD, many countries receiving donor funding often call on their development partners to help them strengthen their own capacities by allowing them to use local systems to manage donor projects and funds. In this way, rather than donors setting up their own (parallel) donor system, the DC will use its own public financial management system (accounting, auditing, procurement, and monitoring systems) which can be very institutions-strengthening.

Turning Donor Help Into A Curse!

It is important for a donor agency that sets out to help the poor citizens of a DC, not end up aggravating their plight. Consider the following:

1. Donor funds in the DCs have one important similarity with the revenues from crude oil exports (or the export of other natural resources): corrupt politicians and civil servants find them attractive for looting. Such funds are unlike government revenues raised by taxing citizens, to which citizens will usually be sensitive. That is why many resource-rich poor nations have remained under-developed (the so-called "resource curse") because the corruption created through such natural resources usually overwhelms good governance.

2. Therefore, donors must never take it for granted that the politicians they are dealing with are truly interested in development! As we saw before in Slice A, the DC's dysfunctional institutions are often what they are because some powerful political forces have an interest in keeping them that way.

3. When donors allow corrupt leaders to loot donor funds, it not only denies the citizens the services those funds were earmarked for, it also exacerbates the scale of corruption in the DC, and sometimes (in the case of loans) even piles up debt burdens for the nation's future generations – burdens from loans that went into private pockets.

   Therefore, donor agencies that fail to take special care to ensure that their funds are not looted, may actually be inadvertently aggravating the plight of the citizens they have set out to help! This means that donor agencies owe the citizens of the DCs, a vital moral obligation to ensure that the funds they extend to the DC achieve the purposes for which they have been set apart, rather than ending up in the private pockets of corrupt politicians, civil servants, and sometimes, the donor's own officials.

   That is also why the new generation of non-traditional donors led by China, which provide highly welcome funds to the DCs (sometimes at concessional, less prescriptive terms) owe the citizens of the DCs a moral obligation to ensure that their "easier" funds achieve the purposes they have been set out for!

A Missed Nigerian Tool For Self-Enforcement

The following Case from Nigeria's electricity sector, can serve to illustrate a missed opportunity for a good dose of self-enforcement.

Case 46:   Discos & Estimated Billing

In 2014, the Nigerian government of President Goodluck Jonathan privatized the nation's electric power system, in a major policy initiative to tackle the nation's decades of dismal electricity services. Before then, government's own Power Holding Company of Nigeria (PHCN) was the monopolistic supplier of electricity nationwide. In the privatization arrangement, government "unbundled" PHCN into several distribution companies (Discos) and generating companies (Gencos), as well as the Transmission Company of Nigeria (Tracon).

Each Disco now in private hands, remained a monopoly in its area of power distribution – it would receive power from the transmission system, distribute it to its consumers, and then bill them accordingly. A key hallmark of a well-managed Disco should be its energy distribution efficiency – relating the total energy distributed successfully to consumers, to the energy received from the transmission system. A high efficiency was very important, especially because the overall quantity of electricity generated in the country was abysmally low; so there was no room for wastes. Government expected each Disco to promptly modernize its distribution and billing infrastructure, for high operating efficiency. This should include modern devices for metering each consumer, as most consumers were not metered at the time of privatization.

Unfortunately, the Discos were allowed to retain a provision of the PHCN era, called "estimated billing", which allowed PHCN to estimate bills for customers that had no meters. PHCN usually exploited this provision to bill customers even when its power supply was poor. Now, allowing the private-sector Discos to retain this provision (*without strict regulation*), in the weak institutional environment of the country, was a reform disaster:

- Any arrangement that could potentially allow a private service-provider to make money without working for it, was sure to be abused. This had therefore created a future regulatory flashpoint!

- Note that one powerful tool in the hands of the regulator, for keeping the Discos on their toes (especially in the absence of clear market forces) should have been a rigorous regime of metered billing! It would have made a Disco desperate to distribute whatever power it received very efficiently, in its own self-interests – thereby making the Disco's self-interests (rather than pressure from the regulator) to be propelling it towards the energy distribution efficiency desired by government! That important self-policing opportunity was lost to the low-hanging loophole that "estimated billing" presented for robbing consumers!

- The estimated billing arrangement was also bad for institution strengthening in other ways.

    - *For example, creating an opportunity for a Disco to make money without working for it, sowed the seed for bribery, and backhand dealings (as the Discos would naturally strive to prevent such a profitable loophole from being blocked).*

    - *In fact, with that kind of loophole, why should a Disco even bother anymore about distribution efficiency? Why should the Disco even be in*

> *a hurry to rectify any faults, or to attend to customers' complaints in the distribution system, since there was no financial pressure on the Disco to rectify the faults on the system (since the Disco had found a way to make its revenue non-dependent on the power it distributed)? This meant that customers might even have to start bribing the Disco's officials, before the officials would attend to their faults!*

Adedeji Badejo's lamentation is typical of institutional output one could expect from the negative incentives created by that institutional arrangement:

> *"... I bought a prepaid meter in 2008, and quite early in 2011 the meter stopped working. Consequently, I was made to pay fixed sum till a new billing system was introduced. In the first instance, the only alternative [the Disco] could provide is for me to buy a new prepaid meter, which was annoying and irritating. For a family of three (wife and a kid), it is so surprising that my monthly bill had jumped from an initial N5,000 to almost N30,000 in a two-rooms apartment ... "Many things are wrong with this system. Firstly, there is no known template or yardstick for determining the actual electricity consumption, since there is no meter to be read nor monitored. I dare say somebody somewhere arbitrarily determines the electricity consumption and cost. Just like that. What a manner of an unfair system could this be? This is unfair. This is what Nigerians are passing through virtually every month ..."*

(Source: For more on the Adedeji Badejo story, see Vanguard newspaper, 17-9- 2015)

We can compare this nightmarish experience with the institutional output one would have expected if there was no un-regulated "estimated billing":

- Every Disco would have been desperate for distribution efficiency, so as to make the best possible from whatever power it received.

- This pressure for distribution efficiency would have propelled such a Disco to look for the best technical and commercial hands available, for its operations (rather than for example, employing relations and mistresses);

- This efficiency pressure would also have propelled such a Disco to make the necessary investments in infrastructure for reliable distribution and metering.

- There could even have been a boost in economic activities, as each Disco aggressively (on its own), pumped money into the sector in these necessary investments.

As we shall emphasize repeatedly in this book, reform is most successful in the institutional environment of the DC, when there is something internal to a system that is propelling that system towards desired outcomes (rather than just the coercive threat of government). With the near absence of market forces in Nigeria's electricity market, a diligent pursuit of metered billing could have provided a measure of that propulsion.

Chapter 12

12. Structuring Governance Systems "*Along*" The Grain

"Institutions are what they are because the political actors in any given society have an interest in keeping them that way ... Many development agencies act as if leaders in developing countries want to do the right thing, if only they knew how, and that development assistance should therefore consist of sending smart people from places like Washington out to teach them, perhaps accompanied by some structural adjustment arm-twisting"

(Francis Fukuyama in his review of Acemoglu and Robinson's "Why Nations Fail", The American Interest, 2012/03/26)

Topics Covered in This Chapter:

- Introduction: Systems Flowing "Along" The Grain
- Structuring systems to flow "along" the grain
- Examples of systems flowing along the grain
- Examples of systems flowing against the grain
- Problems of Systems Flowing Against The Grain
- Conclusion

Introduction: How Systems Can Flow "Along" The Grain

We all know instinctively that it is a lot easier to push a car down a slope than up the hill. This is because when pushing it down the hill, we shall be leveraging the force of gravity (meaning that gravity will be making our work easier for us). However, when pushing the car up the hill, not only shall we lose that help from gravity, but we shall actually be working (or going) against it.

The same principle applies when we play a ball in the direction of the wind than against the wind; or swim down a surging stream, instead of going against the surge of the water.

Incidentally, this same phenomenon exists in human behavior in various ways. For example, it is easier to move in the same direction with a surging crowd, than to try to find our way in the opposite direction through that crowd. Similarly, our politicians find it safer to play to the gallery and be on the popular side of issues, in line with public sentiments, than to stand against popular opinions, and risk the brunt of public anger. Even when they want to go against popular views, they are wiser to start by empathizing with the popular views, especially when emotions are high, before then working gradually from inside, to reverse those emotions.

The foregoing are examples of a principle that work wonders in social and governance systems – the principle of structuring programs and systems to flow *"along"* the grain, rather than *"against"* the grain. We shall call it the "woodworker" technique, a term popularized by the reform godfathers, Hammer & Champy, in line with the woodworker's habit of always *repositioning* his wood, to work *along* the grain, rather than *against* the grain!

In practice, it is the technique of restructuring the prevailing incentives to align the interests of the regulated parties to the desired outcomes. It is a lot easier when government policies (and indeed, institutional procedures and programs) flow along the grain, rather than against it! Let us now use an illustration:

<u>Case 47:</u>　　　<u>Capitalism vs. Socialism</u>

Man is basically a selfish creature, who is at his best, whenever he is pursuing his self-interests – those things that will give him private rewards or give him comparative advantage. Now, here is how the world's major systems of government (socialism and capitalism) roughly appear to handle this natural tendency of man.

Socialism tends to frown at this selfishness, in favor of a one-for-all and all-for-one society. On the other hand, the American capitalism, rather than seeking to cage this selfishness, allows everybody to be selfish, and to go ahead and pursue activities that are self-rewarding. But it has structured its system in such a way that as each man is pursuing his self-rewarding ventures, he will also be creating goods and services, and jobs and income for others; as well as wealth for the society as a whole!

Without bothering about the ideologies of capitalism and socialism, let us appreciate that the American capitalism tends to leverage (rather than fight) the natural tendency of man to be selfish! It tends to flow "along" the grain!

Similarly, in reforming those situations in which people may be energetically pursuing self-interests that are harmful to the larger society, we can often successfully restructure the incentives involved, in such a way that government policies for arresting the situation, can leverage the zeal of the people concerned, rather than fighting it (that zeal) head-on. This is different from the usual coercive mind-set of our DCs – which is to attack such people head-on; and which will inevitably tend to pitch the policy against the flow of the wits, resourcefulness (and sometimes, even desperation) of the people concerned.

<u>Case 48:</u>　　　<u>How Two Catholic Dioceses Manage Tribalism</u>

Tribalism is a major challenge in many DCs. People will tend to treat a person not according to the person's personal merits, but rather, in line with their prejudices against the tribe the person belongs to. For example, in Nigeria, an Edo man can hate another man very decisively, simply because that other man is of the Igbo tribe, irrespective of whether the latter is of a gentle and noble character. And so on! This tribalism is very rampant, even among the people of God.

Now, here is how two dioceses of the Catholic Church in Nigeria are handling the challenge:

- The Lagos Archdiocese tends to be cold towards tribal societies in the church, preferring to have everybody forget their tribes and work together as one big family of God. Unfortunately, people in the Archdiocese have remained tribal, and tribal societies have remained even if unofficially. Sometimes, some tribal societies even hold their meetings outside the church, in the homes of parishioners.

- The Abuja Archdiocese of the same Catholic Church takes a different approach: It encourages people to identify with their tribes! For example, most parishes earmark specific Sundays every month for tribal associations meetings. For that Sunday, such a parish is in effect saying to the parishioners: *"Go and join your people, and plot how you can as a people contribute to the growth and development of the parish"*! In addition to this, some parishes hold cultural festivals, during which the various tribes display and entertain others with their cultural shows, dances, and dishes.

Note that the Abuja approach which tries to leverage (rather than attacking) the strong tribal emotions of parishioners, has the potential to work along the grain, rather than against it! Perhaps the Catholic Bishop of Abuja, Most Rev (Dr.) John Onaiyekan, is an experienced woodworker!

When this "woodworker" principle is used to restructure institutional incentives that are producing counter-productive outcomes, the structured system will still allow the persons concerned to continue to pursue their self-interests (as in the Abuja Diocese and American capitalist examples); but now with the difference that their activities will also be yielding the results that government wants!

As we have seen continuously in this Slice, nothing can be better than when people are internally propelled to be doing what we want them to do, not just because they are afraid of the consequences of not obeying a rule, but because they really want to do so! The woodworker principle can be a powerful tool for creating that internal propulsion.

Examples of Systems Flowing "Along" The Grain

There are often opportunities to structure systems, policies and programs to flow along the grain. These can be governance, social, political and even military systems. For example, we learn from Quora's Susanna Seltzer, of how the Parthian Calvary, in one of the most devious military strategies ever used, usually leveraged the strength of an enemy's fortified army to fight and defeat that army, instead of fighting the enemy head-on!

<u>**Case 49:**</u>   <u>**The Parthian "Shot"**</u>

As explained by Susanna Seltzer, the Parthian Empire was in modern day Iran, from about 250BC to 250AD. The Parthians were exceptionally good horsemen. Their most deadly instrument of battle was the "Cavalry Archer", a horse-mounted soldier with bow-and-arrow.

The Parthian cavalry archers would pretend to become frightened and retreat. The enemy would give chase on their horses. They usually wouldn't notice that the Parthians were retreating in a careful formation. The Parthians would wait until the enemy was entirely focused on the pursuit, at full gallop, holding tight to their horses – defenseless!

A horn would then blow; and in unison, the Parthians would turn backwards on their horses and rain arrows upon the enemy, which would by now be at full gallop! The enemy had been tricked into vulnerability by believing that it was chasing a frightened and retreating army. The pursuing solders were often not even aware of the sudden reversal until being struck!

The Parthian Shot was a trick that laid waste to many opponents!

- Source: Adapted from Quora, http://www.quora.com/ *(August 15, 2015)*

Notice in this example that instead of fighting the fortified (and perhaps stronger) enemy head-on (working *against* the grain), the Parthians in effect "repositioned" their battles in a way that enabled them to work *along* the grain – by even leveraging the enemy's own strength, to defeat it!

The policy of Nigeria's President Yar'adua, prescribing tenures (for Directors and Permanent Secretaries in the federal public service) might also have flowed along the grain, at least in reference to all the people that were to decide its fate.

<u>**Case 50:**</u>   <u>**Nigerian Policy On Tenures For Directors & PermSecs**</u>

In Nigeria's federal public service, the positions of Directors and Permanent Secretaries (PermSecs) were "permanent" in the sense that those lucky to attain such posts would remain there until they died or reached the official retirement age. In Nigeria's corrupt environment, these people naturally became very rich and powerful, amassing enormous wealth over the years – and inevitably becoming kingmakers that determined who in their states of origin would become senators, governors, and so on. In other words, they were very powerful indeed!

In January 2010, the government of President Umaru Musa Yar'Adua jolted the system by announcing a new policy (apparently crafted by his Head of Service of the Federation at the time, Mr. Steven Oronsaye), prescribing tenures for Directors and Permanent Secretaries. The policy set 4-year tenure for permanent secretaries in the Federal Civil Service, renewable only once. Directors would also have eight-year tenure. All those that had already served beyond these limits were asked to go immediately. The policy was meant to address several issues, such as:

- The grave succession crisis plaguing the Service (and its inability to renew itself) because of chronic lack of vacancies at the top directorate level, where subordinate officers were often retiring ahead of their superior "permanent" officers;

- The pervading loss of morale and growing frustration from officers who were overdue for promotion but could not be promoted, because the top was saturated by "permanent" officers;

- Long years of stagnation as the directorate level manpower dominated the service at the expense of the development of the lower cadre; and

- The inability to inject fresh blood into the service, at the senior level

President Yar'Adua's policy was very jolting because these people had up to that point, been untouchable. The policy generated very bitter and stringent opposition, even from some sections of the country, which dominated the top echelon of the service, and felt that a mass retirement of top civil servants would affect them more adversely.

However, it scaled through, because it flowed along with all the critical stakeholders in a position to obstruct it! For example:

- The new federal administration of President Yar'Adua liked it because it would address all the issues highlighted above;

- It would also provide the administration the cherished opportunity to appoint its own Directors and permanent secretaries, rather than just "living" with those it met;

- All the political officeholders liked it because it would prevent the permanent secretaries from treating them as transient "short timers" that would soon vacate the arena for them;

- The state governors most of whose elections might have been funded by the super-rich permanent secretaries, liked it (even if they didn't necessarily say so) because it would give them the opportunity to recommend new persons from their states to be appointed to fill the resulting vacancies (who would now be their own choices);

- The immediate subordinates of the Permanent Secretaries and Directors (i.e. those in line for promotion) were jubilant and eager for their bosses to go – and even started "counting days" for their bosses!

- The lower cadre also liked it because it would create a more robust opportunities for growth and development of the Service.

Examples of Systems Flowing "Against" The Grain

Just as we can structure governance systems to flow along the grain, we also have governance systems flowing against the grain! In fact, in the DC environment, government systems and programs generally tend to flow against the grain, probably because of the coercive (command and control) mindset of government. When institutions are weak and dysfunctional, they tend to be characterized by processes and programs that flow against the grain.

In general, a government policy or program can be said to be flowing against the grain, if for example, it is something people comply with only when they feel that enforcement agents may be watching; or if we are trying to force it down the throats of those concerned, who would rather do things differently; and so on. For example, in contrast with the previous example on the tenures of Directors and PermSecs, which went well with most stakeholders, the Nigerian monetization policy under President Olusegun Obasanjo, did not go down well with its critical stakeholders.

Case 51:   Nigeria's Monetization Nightmare

The goal of the monetization policy was to slash the escalating cost of governance (particularly the so-called "recurrent" expenditure) by relieving government of the burden (and corruption) associated with providing basic amenities to public officers. The high and growing "recurrent expenditure" was leaving less and less to government for capital development.

Accordingly, President Obasanjo decided to monetise the fringe benefits of public officers, such as residential accommodation, furniture, utility, domestic servants, motor vehicles, fuelling and maintenance of transport facilities, medical treatment, leave grant, meal subsidy and entertainment.

The top civil servants and political officeholders (including federal legislators and Ministers) who enjoyed all these fringe benefits (and probably, profited from the loopholes associated with their implementation), were also the very people expected to implement the monetization policy! Therefore, from the point of view of these critical stakeholders, the reform program was headed against the grain!

Incidentally, President Obasanjo's term ended before he could muzzle the policy through; and within months of his departure, the next government was already telling a Senate Committee that it was set to reverse the policy, because it *made nonsense of the normal official protocol that should be accorded to Ministers and other top-ranking officials*". No top-ranking official complained!

(For more, please see Thisday, 11 December 2007)

Another flagship policy of the Nigerian government, which can be said to be going against the grain, is the public procurement system. As noted by the OECD's *Post-2015 Reflections Paper*, the procurement sector presents multiple opportunities for corruption because of the high financial interests at stake in public procurement, the large volume of transactions, and the close interaction it provides between the public servants and the private sector.

<u>Case 52:</u>   **Nigeria's Public Procurement Problems**

Nigeria's Public Procurement Act, 2007 established the National Council on Public Procurement (NCPP) and the Bureau of Public Procurement (BPP) as the regulatory authorities responsible for monitoring and oversight of Public Procurement in Nigeria.

The challenge before this policy is daunting, considering that in a corrupt environment, the efforts to eliminate Public Procurement corruption are going against the resourcefulness and ingenuity of:

- The corrupt civil servant in the awarding agency looking for what can enter their private pockets;
- The private contractor looking for whatever it can get;
- The political appointee that needs to channel patronage to some persons and also make money;
- The elected official desperate to recoup the past campaign expenses, and set up the war chest for the next election;
- The oversight legislator that needs to do a similar thing;
- The BPP field officer who is surely not a saint; and so on!

All these stakeholders who are critical to the policy's success, are themselves inclined to cheat the system! It is therefore a process that flows hopelessly against the grain! In fact, the BPP cannot in all honesty, vouch for anybody in the entire value chain, not even its own staff! No wonder, corruption has continued unabated despite all the reform activities around the nation's public procurement process!

Today, a good way to truly have a chance of eliminating the procurement corruption, is to restructure the process in such a way as to begin to leverage (rather than constantly fighting) the zeal and resourcefulness of these major stakeholders! I am aware that, the Center For Leadership Support & Social Progress (CLSSP) has worked out a very creative strategy for doing so.

(See CLSSP's "A New Presidential Initiative Against CORRUPTION", June 2011; cflsasp@yahoo.com)

Problems of Systems Flowing Against The Grain

The reason we must avoid policies and systems going against the grain, is because they are usually full of problems!

1. *They usually don't work*: Any new government policy (or reform) that moves against the grain is certain to fail. It is just a matter of time, before it is effectively overwhelmed by the constant onslaught of the normal vices that are prevalent in the DCs – corruption, tribalism, nepotism, impunity, and so on.

2. *Expensive to implement*: Any government policy (or program) that moves against the grain is usually expensive to implement, because it must involve a strong enforcement infrastructure for pushing it against the grain. This will include strong enforcement teams for surveillance, arrest, and prosecution of culprits. Besides, the enforcement presence will need to be everywhere.

3. *Breed corruption*: Policies and programs that move against the grain are usually a big source of corruption, and a fertile ground for those other vices that are prevalent in the DCs – tribalism, nepotism, impunity, and so on. This is because violators and any apprehended culprits will strive to compromise the enforcement agents.

4. *Difficult to Regulate*: Any program or system flowing "against" the grain in the DC environment is a regulatory nightmare! The regulator will perpetually be up against the flow of the zeal, resourcefulness and even desperation of the parties it is regulating! Even when the parties appear on the surface to be cooperating, it is only a matter of time before the regulator discovers that they have all the while been wrecking some havoc underneath! We can ask Nigeria's BPP what it must have been going through, trying to make the procurement system corruption-free!

    The same thing goes for the country's main anti-corruption agency, the EFCC. We highlighted earlier how frustrating the agency must be finding its mandate of fighting corruption coercively in an environment of widespread corruption. Funke Egbemode's joke on the frustrations of Mrs. Farida Waziri (the EFCC Chairperson at the time) can be an apt illustration:

> "She starts a case. Our hope of wrestling the corruption monster to the ground is renewed. Then the suspect recruits 10 Senior Advocates of Nigeria [SANs] who procure 10 different court injunctions with 10 different confusing names. The case is stalled. When or if it eventually goes to court, the first SAN whisks out one injunction saying the court has no jurisdiction. The second SAN brings out the one that says because Mrs. Waziri covers her head all the time, she cannot prosecute men. The third lawyer throws his own on the table saying the red color of the EFCC means it is a commission of witches and wizards. Therefore, the suspect is being witch-hunted. The judge gives up and tells Waziri to take her troubles somewhere else. The lawyers guffaw and smile to the bank. Another case joins the others in the dust".

See Sunday Sun newspaper, April 19, 2009

5. *Propensity For Empire Building*: One of the reasons for the large unwieldy octopus that the Nigerian public service has grown into (causing the nation to spend over 70% of its annual budget as recurrent expenditure), is the tendency of the governance systems and programs to flow against the grain! As noted before, a policy flowing against the grain will tend to require an active infrastructure for enforcement, for pushing it "against" the natural inclination of the parties concerned – because those parties will be striving to circumvent it.

    The moment such a policy comes up, the next thing that comes to mind is "enforcement"! Inevitably, we gradually become obsessed with the logistics of enforcing compliance: we want more enforcement officers, local council offices, state offices, regional offices, and of course, a new befitting Head Office. Before realizing it, we are into "empire building"! Hardly do we ever look back to appraise the overall strategic impact of the policy, otherwise it will surprise us to see that the intervention system we set up to correct something, is now itself as much in need of reform, as what we originally set out to correct! According to Dr. Osita Ogbu, the CEO of Nigeria's National Planning Commission (NPC), and Chief Economic Adviser to President Obasanjo:

> "Sometimes what happens is not intended. You set up a small unit to manage something, and it evolves on its own, and suddenly becomes a parastatal"!

6. *Reliance on Exceptional Individuals*: Programs going against the grain can only be effective when government is able to find outstanding citizens to drive them – persons who can enforce compliance in a "no-nonsense" way, without yielding to pressures of corruption, special interests, and other vices.

Because of the national tendency of systems in the DCs to push *against* the grain, the natural mind-set of their people has become that things will only work well, when government is able to find outstanding individuals to drive them.

Case 53: Outstanding Persons Pushing Against The Grain

Many of the successes recorded by Nigeria since its democracy returned in 1999, are indeed attributable to outstanding individuals. For example:

- The successes recorded by President Obasanjo's administration in the fight against corruption were usually attributed to the no-nonsense leadership of Mallam Nuhu Ribadu, the EFCC's Chairman at the time;

- Similarly, the successes that government recorded in its fight against fake drugs at the time were also attributed to the fearless leadership of late Dr. (Mrs.) Dora Akunyili, the Director-General of NAFDAC;

- Similar things can be said of Mallam el-Rufai as the Minister of the federal capital territory (FCT), when he was fearlessly demolishing buildings and other structures he found to be in violation of the city's master-plan, not minding who they belonged to; and so on!

- In fact, at the height of Mallam el-Rufai's exploits, someone even advised government, if it thought that PHCN's problems were intractable, to simply send Mallam el-Rufai to PHCN, and then watch to see if PHCN would not change within six months. (PHCN was the name of government's monopoly agency in charge of electricity at the time).

----

7. *Never Attains Stability*: Policies and systems moving against the grain never attain stability, especially in the DC environment. Even if such a system starts out strongly (perhaps with a person of strong character as the driver), it will only be a matter of time before it loses steam.

Consider the following:

a. The outstanding individual will not always be there; besides, in a DC, somebody that starts out as "outstanding" often succumbs eventually to the overwhelming forces of corruption, tribalism, intimidation and other vices;

b.   Even if an outstanding individual is found today, there is nothing in the kind of patronage system common in DCs to guarantee the continuous supply of such individuals! Institutions in the DCs, often accused of being blind to merit, are particularly not conducive for the emergence of such outstanding individuals! Instead, it tends to scorn merit, and to even subject potential eagles (persons with good potentials) to the ordinary lives of fowls!

On the other hand, policies, systems and reforms flowing "*along*" the grain create stable systems. The US Constitution is a classic example of this stability.

Case 54:   The Stability of The American Constitution

We saw before how the US system of government seemed to be flowing along the grain. The American Constitution driving that system, is often cited as a classic embodiment of stability.

During its over 200 years, the United States has grown from 13 colonies to 50 States, and the population has increased by thousand-folds. The country has gone through economic booms and depressions. It has changed from an agricultural economy to an industrial economy, then to an information economy, and now to the globalized economy. It has fought major world wars. It has even fought a civil war, and abolished slave trade.

Yet that Constitution has been able to hold together, the enormously diverse interests of the American State, successfully handling the delicate balance of political powers, the separation of church and State, and so on. Even most spectacular, it has all this time successfully subordinated the awesome U.S. military to civil control! Equally remarkable is that since their original constitutional amendment in 1789 (the Bill of Rights) only about 15 amendments have been found necessary! A stable system hardly needs amendment

The inspiration, vision, and stability of that constitution have attracted admirers from all parts of the world! Perhaps these American founding fathers were "woodworkers"!

We can compare the stability of this system with the Nigerian seaports system, which the federal government of Nigeria ordered to commence 24-hour operations.

Case 55:   Pushing The Seaports Against The Grain

When we looked at the Nigerian government's directive to private seaport operators (to whom the seaports had been concessioned) to commence 24-hour operations at the nation's seaports, one wondered why such a directive had to come from government, considering that the more goods the port operators cleared, the higher the revenues (and profit) they would make! The round-the-clock-operations should have been an initiative of the port operators themselves!

However, if these private port operators felt cold towards the policy (if it was a policy that moved against the grain), it would only be a matter of time before the port operators devised other tricks, even if they appeared (on the surface) to be complying with the directive!

For example, importers and freight forwarders were accusing the operators of deliberately creating congestion at the ports so as to generate demurrage charges; and of deliberately creating bottlenecks and contrived delays that could only be overcome by bribery.

According to Lucky Amiwero, President, National Council of Managing Directors of Nigeria's Licensed Customs Agents, the terminal operators *"are having a field day"*!

Other stakeholders interviewed by The Sun newspaper, were even more specific:

- "You will go now to APMT terminal to pay your port charges, 5 to 10 days they will not position your container, and the demurrage will be counting; and after they position it, you must pay for the demurrage before you take delivery. The demurrage thing is a deliberate rip off game"!

(For more details on the complaints & outcries at our ports, see Thisday newspaper, 15 Jan 2012; Daily Trust, 3 January 2012; The Guardian, Thursday, October 27, 201; & The Sun newspaper, October 10, 2011)

This just goes to underscore how any policy that goes against the grain tends never to attain stability! The regulators can never sleep with both eyes closed, because they will be moving from one patchwork to another!

8. *Undue Demands on Political Will*: Systems flowing against the grain make very difficult demands on leaders – testing their so-called "political will"! For example, when law enforcement agencies in a DC bring corruption cases against an influential politician or civil servant, alarm bells will go off from all over the country (as the culprit presses all possible "buttons") mounting pressure on influential persons to intervene).

That is why much of the successes we attribute to agency heads should primarily go to the leaders that appoint them, who provide the political cover for them to work!

Case 56:   **Some Demands On The Political Will of Nigerian Presidents**

Consider the demands that the following cases must have made on the Presidents of Nigeria.

- Mallam Nuhu Ribadu's successes as EFCC chairman during the era of President Olusegun Obasanjo, could only have been possible with the strong political support he received from the President. It came at a political cost to the President (the so-called political will) to stand resolutely behind the Chairman, even when he was going after powerful persons!

  The issue of "political will" surfaced again after President Obasanjo's term ended in 2007: Despite Nuhu's boasts to jail corrupt governors once their tenures (and immunity) were similarly over in 2007, he himself was humiliated out of office by the new administration of President Yar'adua. Many people accused the new President of lacking the "political will" to prosecute the governors!

- The same thing can be said of the achievements of Professor Attahiru Jega, as the Chairman of INEC (the national electoral body)! Those achievements might very well not have been possible if President Goodluck Jonathan had not gone out of his way as follows:

  - *He appointed a known radical to head that pivotal electoral Commission (on which his re-election would depend) not minding that the Professor belonged to the Fulani-Northern part of the country, who were the President's main opponents!*

  - *He simultaneously gave the Professor a free hand to run the Commission the way he (Jega) wanted.*

The achievements of Jega therefore came at a major cost to the President – including the political will to sacrifice his re-election, which by the nation's tradition, he could conceivably have ensured!

Conclusion

By way of emphasis, let us highlight the following points before finally leaving this topic:

1. It is usually possible, to creatively structure public policies, to make them flow "along" the grain, rather than "against" the grain;

2. Any regulatory framework that continues to need strengthening (such as more directives, more prosecutors, more field offices and enforcers, and more demands on "political will") may be pushing <u>against</u> the grain, and should be reviewed;

4. There is a natural relationship between corruption and systems flowing <u>against</u> the grain:

   a. Any institutional procedures or processes "going *against* the grain" will usually be vulnerable to corruption.

   b. Conversely, any institutional arrangement in which corruption is thriving will tend to have one or more processes going "*against*" the grain!

Chapter 13

13. Measuring Something – Anything!

People always behave differently, when they know they are leaving a track!

(Osborne and Gaebler, 1992)

Topics Covered in This Chapter:

- Introduction: Creating A Track For People
- The benefits of OM
    - Always triggers improvements
    - Tool for institutional accountability
    - Prevents us from rewarding failure
    - Facilitates reform even within existing political constraints
    - Can help to make public service more results-oriented
    - Often creates a "wow" effect
    - Tool for igniting competition in the public service
    - Enriches policy decisions
- The challenges of OM
- Revisiting SERVICOM

Introduction: Creating A Track For People

In this Chapter, we shall look at operations measurement (OM), another one of the behavior-shaping tools treated in this Slice. Calling it *"operations measurement"* deliberately avoids the over-used term, performance measurement (PM), because what we want here will be simpler, less technical, but more strategic than the typical rendition of PM.

As highlighted in the opening citation by Osborne and Gaebler, people indeed tend to behave differently, when they know they are leaving a track! Consider the following example:

Case 57: **A Principal's Attendance Register**

The principal of a public school in Lagos (Nigeria) once told me what an ordinary attendance register had done for her. Her teachers (many of whom were "well-connected" and drove expensive cars to school) were in the habit of reporting late to work. It did not matter to them that she, their principal, usually reported as early as 7.00am. Some of her teachers complained of traffic hold-up on the way; some said they lived too far away from the school, and one explained that it was not safe in her neighborhood for a woman to be outside before it was fully daybreak!

Then she introduced an attendance register (for teachers to record their arrival at work each day) on which she ruled a line once it was 8.00am, to mark out the latecomers. The impact amazed her! Within one week of the register, the problem of teachers' lateness disappeared! Suddenly her teachers – all of them, including the one that lived in an unsafe neighborhood – started coming early!

From Paul M. Romer, World Bank's Chief Economist and Senior Vice President, we also get the case of Hernando de Soto of Lima, Peru:

<u>**Case 58:**</u>   **<u>Hernando de Soto's Observation In Peru</u>**

"In the summer of 1983, a group of researchers working with Hernando de Soto got all the permits required to open a small garment business on the outskirts of Lima, Peru. Their goal was to measure how long this took. I read de Soto's book, 'The Other Path', decades ago, but I was so astonished by the answer it reported that I remember it today: 289 days. De Soto's conjecture, which turned out to be right, was that measuring and reporting would create pressure for improvements in the efficiency of government. In the foreword to the revised edition of his book that he wrote in 2002, de Soto reports that because of changes to regulations and procedures, the same business could get all the required permits in a single day!"

(Paul M. Romer, Chief Economist and Senior Vice President, The World Bank, in his foreword to the World Bank's <u>Doing Business report</u>, 2017)

These examples illustrate this powerful behavior-changing principle pointed out by Osborne and Gaebler, which can be turned into a powerful institution-strengthening tool:

- People always behave differently, when they know they are leaving a track!

It is sometimes not too important that what we are measuring may not be "perfect". In fact, the title of this Chapter that says *"Measuring Something – Anything"*, is just to emphasize that even non-perfect measures can often trigger changes, and are therefore usually better than not measuring at all!

The Benefits Of Operations Measurement (OM)

Let us now highlight several institutional benefits of operations measurement (OM) in the context we are applying it here.

Benefit# 1: It Triggers Institutional Improvements

This is actually the star benefit of OM. As we saw in the two examples above, everybody tends to behave differently when they know they are leaving a track! As pointed out by Osborne and Gaebler, the simple act of beginning to measure performance, tends to have a dramatic effect on the behavior of public servants and their organizations! That is what makes OM such a powerful behavior-changing tool. An old management adage says that _what gets measured gets done_!

It is amazing what operations measurement (as advocated here), can do for institutions. It can be a tool for channeling the priorities of public servants to the things that really matter to the publics that they serve.

Case 59: Potential Role Of OM In The Judiciary

In January, 2016, Nigeria's President, Muhammadu Buhari in a town hall meeting in faraway Ethiopia, reportedly complained that the Judiciary of his country was his main headache in his fight against corruption. Incidentally, one veritable tool for strengthening that institution (the judiciary) in our DCs can be OM. And this is not just in relation to corruption, but in various other respects.

Consider the following:
- Tanzania now measures the percentage of court cases outstanding for 2 years or longer. According to an International Development Association (IDA) report, this had the effect of crashing such cases in Tanzania from 70% in 2005, to 14% in 2011!

Now, the question is "Why can't other DCs replicate the Tanzanian initiative?" Imagine even stretching the Tanzanian measure slightly to include for each court, statistics such as:

- Number of new cases received during the year;
- Percentage successfully completed;
- Percentage carried forward;
- Total case load being carried
- Percentage of judgments appealed;
- Percentage of judgments overturned
- Percentage of judgments sustained; and so on

(For more on President Buhari's visit to Ethiopia, please see Vanguard, 31-1-2016)

The reengineering godfathers, Osborne and Gaebler, related the effect of OM on the Madison Police Department (Wisconsin, USA).

Case 60: The Madison Police Department Example

According to Osborne and Gaebler, the Madison Police Department had just started seeking out feedbacks from the persons they encountered, and sending the responses to the officers concerned, as a kind of personal feedback system. One officer got a feedback that was quite critical. He read it aloud to his colleagues, quite sarcastically, expecting them to agree that it was ridiculous. And there was dead silence! It was clear to him that the group did not necessarily agree with him.

> That officer was very surprised! That kind of change in peer relations can have a big impact on people.
>
> --

In this example, the focus of OM was on the interactions of the police with the public. Note that we can similarly focus it on any other aspects of police services, and try to begin to create a track in that area – bearing in mind that people tend to behave differently when they know they are leaving a track!

These examples also show how OM can be a tool for channeling the activities of government officials towards the issues that really matter to their publics – by beginning to track their performances on those issues. Otherwise, in many DCs, public officials tend to be on their own, concerned more about themselves than about the public they are supposed to be serving. For example, some DCs spend as much as 70% of their annual budgets as "recurrent" expenditure (mostly salaries and allowances of officials, and some other overheads), as if government's only business is to take care of its officials!

It should be emphasized continuously that in many cases, all we need to do is to start measuring something related to an issue of interest to us. The experience all over the world is that even non-perfect measures on such issues can often be better than no measures at all! Let us not fall into the trap of *"paralysis by analysis"* – when we do nothing month after month, year after year, because we are trying to develop a comprehensive performance measurement system! We should just begin with something that reasonably tracks the issue of interest; and then progressively improve on it, going forward.

> - Also, as we saw before, institutional quality is best assured, when something internal to the institution propels behavior towards that quality, rather than when we merely proclaim it as a directive. OM can play that "propeller" role in many governance systems!
>
> --

Benefit# 2: Tool for instituting accountability

This is a vital issue, and we have dedicated a whole Chapter in Slice D to it. However, we can note here that often, a simple OM can trigger 3rd-party analysts, focus groups, or researchers to begin to evolve independent accountability parameters! And their reports will usually provide further guidance on how to strengthen the OM system.

Benefit #3: Prevents us from rewarding failure

Operations measurement can form a basis for rewarding excellence! As pointed out by Osborne and Gaebler, a major incentive to the laxity in government operations, is that no one can say if the public servants do anything worthwhile, because in many cases, nobody actually measures anything! This is even more pronounced in the DCs.

Osborne and Gaebler have also noted that when you expect *nothing* from people, you usually get it – nothing! We cannot say we are rewarding success if we are not taking steps to identify it; and if we are not rewarding success, how are we sure we are not rewarding failure?

<u>**Case 61:**</u>   <u>**Are They Rewarding Failure?**</u>

If we are not taking steps to reward success, how are we sure we are not rewarding failure? Consider the following:

- PHCN was Nigeria's electric power supply monopoly agency, before the power sector privatization. One would have expected that when it did not supply power, consumers would not have to pay. But PHCN cleverly devised the concept of "estimated" billing, which allowed it be sending bills to consumers on "estimate" basis, without bothering to read their meters. Of course, PHCN soon capitalized on that and abandoned meter reading altogether! Even in a month of particularly lousy services, PHCN would still send its estimated bills to customers! What then was the "estimated bill" arrangement rewarding? Failure?

- There is also this tendency across many DCs, that when the police fails in its work, and the crime rate goes up – that's when the police force typically gets more attention – more budgets, more personnel, more allowances! What then are we rewarding?

- And the "mother of all rewards" for failure could be from Nigeria's political campaigns for 2003 general elections. One of the governors, who was seeking re-election, was contending with a hostile electorate, on account of his very poor performance during his first term in office. The Governor's father was said to have very wittingly disarmed his audience with a poser that went like this:

"If you send your child to school, and he fails, what is the proper thing to do? Is it not to ask him to repeat?"

Benefit #4: Aids reform within existing political constraints

Notice that OM, as we have seen from these examples, will often allow us to improve overall institutional performance, by helping us to create behavioral changes in the targeted institutional processes – something we can often achieve within the constraints of the prevailing political arrangements of a DC, without having to bother too much about the DC's balance of political forces.

Benefit #5: Makes the public service more results-oriented

As we saw before, one very serious problem in the typical DC is a public service that is not only corrupt and full of nepotism, but also very self-centered – a bureaucracy that is anything but results-oriented. In its day-to-day operations, the public service bureaucracy in a typical DC, simply keeps on "keeping on", with "activities" (that usually have to do with spending money) without really bothering about whether those activities are making any impacts.

Because of the importance of this particular benefit, we have dedicated a whole Chapter in the next Slice, to it – which looks at the concept of becoming "outcome-focused".

Benefit #6: Often creates a "wow" effect

The "wow" effect is the dream of service providers in the private sector! When a customer experiences a "wow", it means we have given them a pleasant surprise and exceeded their expectations! It means that we have addressed their needs in unexpected ways! The simple act of beginning to measure institutional performance can often reveal something no one might have thought of!

> **Case 62:**   **Operations Measurement In Oregon's DEQ**
>
> Oregon is a state in the United States. Traditionally, pollution complaints at the state's Department of Environmental Quality (DEQ) had been handled by whoever happened to receive them in the office.
>
> As pointed out by John M. Bernard, the department then decided to establish a measure to gauge the agency's responsiveness to complaints. Even just implementing a formal complaints intake process, had a profound impact! They suddenly became aware of where geographically most of the complaints were coming from, as well as the sources of the pollution – which the DEQ never thought about before, but now found extremely useful!
>
> ---
>
> *(For more details, see "Governing The States & Localities", June 1, 2012)*

Benefit #7: Tool for igniting competition in public service

In Slice G, we shall see how competition creates institutional innovation and better cost-effectiveness in government operations. That is what we see every day in the private sector. Because competition is generally absent in government operations, public services tend to be stale, inefficient and over-priced to government.

OM is a powerful tool for igniting competition in government operations. For example, it can help to identify those individuals (or teams) at the top and bottom of the performance ladder; and no one wants to be seen at the bottom, because it can be very threatening! Many people do not know that we can simulate competition even in the public sector, and make public servants (either directly, or indirectly through their agencies) compete with each other, or with the private sector in the services that they deliver. OM can be the tool!

Remember also, as we saw before, that in the institutional environment of the DCs, service improvement is best assured, when something internal to the institution (institutionally driven) propels it, rather than when we merely issue directives or make laws. We can use OM to play that "propeller" role by deploying it very deftly.

Let's again use the education sector to illustrate this point, starting with the *Beacon Schools* program in England, highlighted by Parrado & Loeffler:

<u>**Case 63:**</u>   <u>**UK's Beacon Schools Program**</u>

The Beacon Schools program identified high performing schools across England. It was designed to build partnerships between these schools. It identified examples of successful practices, with a view to sharing and spreading those practices to other schools, to raise standards in pupil attainment.

Each Beacon School (whether nursery, primary, secondary or special school) received around £38,000 of extra funding a year, usually for a minimum of three years, in exchange for a program of activities enabling the school to collaborate with others to disseminate good practice and raise school standards. The Beacon Schools program was phased out in 2005, replaced by the Leading Edge Partnership program for secondary schools.

- Please see Parrado & Loeffler's Draft Report of 31 January 2013

There are many possible ways that a DC can adapt this technique in its own school system. Let us use Nigeria's "unity" schools to illustrate it.

<u>**Case 64:**</u>   <u>**Accountability Systems For Secondary Schools**</u>

Nigeria has many federal government colleges (called the "unity" schools) which are owned, funded and managed by the federal government, through the federal ministry of education.

Now consider the following OM posers:

- How do these unity schools compare academically? Which unity schools are at the top of the performance ladder, for example, in English, mathematic and sciences, respectively; and which ones are at the bottom?

- How do the unity schools that are demographically similar (for example, those located in the state capitals) compare across the country?

- How do specific unity schools compare with demographically similar State government and private schools?

As simplistic as these measures may appear, they will begin to leave a track, and every system behaves differently when it knows it is leaving a track!

In fact, the mere act of beginning to measure them and to disseminate the results will trigger various institution-strengthening phenomena. For example:

1. It will be very threatening to the principals and teachers of the schools at the bottom of the ladder, which will trigger them to improve! Think of the pressure that will be on the Principal of the school at the bottom, for example, during the school's parents-teachers-association (PTA) meeting!

2. This will set the stage for a healthy academic competition between the schools, which will make the teachers (and other workers) in these schools better focused. Notice how we

would have thus used OM to ignite competition among public sector workers! Notice also that playing up "academics" in the school system will tend to prevent other vices (such as drugs and cultism) from filling the void!

3. This competition may even motivate some schools to start providing value-added services (such as special lessons, and counselling) to beef up performance.

4. The statistics will also begin to make available to the public some hard facts on the schools – something they do not currently have – and a solid basis for choosing between the schools.

5. The statistics will also ultimately provide a clear basis for beginning to reward institutional excellence (for example, for promoting one principal or teacher over another, especially since their promotions are handled centrally by the federal education ministry). This will thus help to curb the influence of nepotism in the system, and generally ensure that it is not rewarding "failure"!

The quality and depth of these benefits suggest that Nigeria's national intervention agencies – such as the Tertiary Education Tax Fund (TETF) which mostly carry out physical projects in the schools – can sometimes make important impact by intervening in ways that trigger competition.

OM can also provide a yardstick that an intervention agency can leverage for spending more money in one school over another.

Benefit #8: Enriches policy decisions

In a typical Nigerian bank today, the CEO will by Monday morning, be looking at the operating results for the period that ended on Sunday night (because online banking is 24 hours a day, seven days a week)! Compare this with a typical public agency in a DC, where the Chief Executive (CEO) may not see the agency's operating results until several months after. The quality of decisions of the two CEOs cannot be the same!

Strong institutions treasure up-to-date operations data that can drive fact-based decisions. OM can generate the data!

Case 65:　　The Real Cost To The Public Of Nigeria's Universities

Let us use the numerous federal government universities owned and funded by Nigeria's central government, as an illustration.

Consider the following posers:

- How much is government spending per year to fund each public university? What is this cost on a per-student basis?
- How has this per-student cost varied in each institution, over the years; and why?
- How does the per-student cost vary from one public university to another, and why?

- How does the per-student cost compare with the school fees charged by the private universities? And so on!

To press this point further, let us assume that government, and all its education intervention agencies (such as the TETF) spend N2 billion per year on a given public university, whose student population is 5,000. The annual expenditure on this university will work out as N400,000/student.

Suppose also that a certain private university is charging $350,000 per student, each year. Notice that this will be lower than the average cost of N400,000 for the public university.

This hypothetical scenario would suggest that with the same level of expenditure of N2 billion per year, government can assist more students by budgeting N350,000 on each student, and allowing the money to follow the student to whatever university (public or private) he or she chooses to attend? In other words, instead of one university gulping N2 billion per year from government for the sake of just 5,000 students, government can use the same level of expenditure to help 6,250 students (25% more students) while perhaps, also creating a better quality of institutional performance (by putting the money in the hands of the students)!

In particular, the fact that government funding now follows each student to whatever institutions they select, will create some kind of competition between the universities, for the students and the funds that follow them – which will drive up institutional quality.

Notice how different policy ideas are already coming to mind! Even this hypothetical scenario shows the kind of qualities that OM can bring to the policymaking table!

The Challenges of OM

Despite all the foregoing benefits, there are some challenges of OM that we should particularly bear in mind:

1. _Resistance_: People usually do not want their performances to be measured. Some officials can see OM as very threatening; and will often work (even if subtly) to frustrate an OM program.

2. _Gaming_: Those that an OM program is likely to put in a negative light, may try to "game" their results.
   Gaming can take several forms, including:

   a. Making results appear more favorable than they really are, which would be misleading, and perhaps even help to achieve one of the goals of the opponents of OM – to undermine the integrity of its results. Officials can also look for ways to improve their measured scores without improving underlying performance!

   b. Focusing efforts on the specific parameters being measured, at the detriment of other areas. For example, a school can focus all its efforts on Maths and English, at the expense of all other subjects, if Maths and English are the criteria that OM uses in ranking schools. As to the World Bank put it:

> "… We can see this problem arise in other domains, such as when teachers' salaries are indexed by student evaluation scores; there is a risk that this will dampen the incentive for creativity, which is harder to measure. Ranking universities often leads them to try to game the system and move resources and effort away from some important but unmeasured dimensions to the narrower tasks that are tracked and measured"

(For more details, see the World Bank's Doing Business 2016 report)

One imperative for handling "gaming" is to keep OM very "dynamic", improving continuously, and always taking context and trends into account.

3. *OM Can Become Too Technocratic*: The focus of the OM program should be on the key stakeholders (especially the public and private clients of the government unit in question), so that it can lead to outcomes that will really matter to them and (very importantly) which they will understand. This means putting these stakeholders at the forefront, right from the design stage, to ensure that the program reflects what really matter to them; otherwise, the outputs may be too technocratic.

4. **The issue of Comparability**: When we use OM to foster competition, or to identify those at the top and bottom of a performance table, we must try to make the performance measures truly comparable.

As an example:

a. Even a relatively simple measure like "unit costs of outputs" may not be truly comparable between organizations if their accounting methods are different;

b. The performances of two state governors may not be truly comparable, if the revenue bases of their states are not comparable;

c. The differences in outcomes as captured by OM may depend on factors that are outside the control of the parties being measured. For example, the performances of two federal government schools may not be truly comparable, if one is in a depressed area (that can only attract disadvantaged pupils) while the location of the other allows it to select only the brightest pupils, perhaps through a highly competitive national admission tests. And so on!

All the same, there are techniques for improving comparability. For example, when the OM program is an initiative of a higher authority, it can impose some formats and standardization of measures.

5. *Paralysis by analysis*: We can sometimes bug down an OM program with unending analysis, including the quest to make the OM all-encompassing. Unfocused analytical exercises and data overload create "paralysis by analysis" – a transformational poison that slows down reform programs, and ultimately makes them unrealistic.
    As has been emphasized in this Chapter, it is sometimes not too important that our parameters may not be "perfect". Even imperfect measures are often better than not

measuring at all! We should just begin with something that reasonably captures the issue in question; and then progressively improve the parameters, going forward.

Revisiting SERVICOM

We can now revisit Nigeria's SERVICOM program, whose mission is to make government workers and their agencies more service-oriented. When we looked at it earlier, we noted that it would be difficult to realize the noble objectives of a program such as SERVICOM through mere policy directives from the top, in the institutional environment of the DCs, where vices such as corruption, tribalism, nepotism, and impunity are prevalent.

OM can come to the rescue. For example, SERVICOM can focus on instituting localized OM programs for government units that would reflect the needs of the public that each unit serves. It can even sensitize other central and regulatory agencies (as the case may be) to begin to institute similar programs across the service. SERVICOM's role would be to provide guidance that would help to ensure that each OM program reflects the most urgent needs of the public that each agency serves.

For example, to help check the abuse by university lecturers, an OM program for each university can focus on something as basic as "course evaluation". SERVICOM can incentivize the National Universities Commission (NUC), which regulates university education in Nigeria, to institute such an evaluation as a core policy.

Case 66:   **Course Evaluation in Higher Institutions**

Remember the story of how frontline columnist, Simon Kolawole of Thisday newspapers, abandoned his executive MBA program in one of Nigeria's universities. Among other things, he was disgusted by how a lecturer could walk into a class of 80 MBA students, and announce that his car had been stolen, and demand that every student should contribute N10,000 to replace his car, with utter indifference to the very high tuition fees already paid by the students. Another lecturer could also announce that he had lost his mobile phone, and ask the class to replace it; and so on.

If the university begins to actively collate students' end-of-course feedbacks, and eventually communicate such feedbacks to the lecturers (or use other "sunshine" techniques, as we shall discuss in the next Chapter) the feedbacks will start to create a track; and everybody tends to behave differently, when they know they are leaving a track!

(For Kolawole's story, see Thisday Newspaper, October 31, 2005)

Notice that we can easily have several such OM programs, with each focusing on a different area of operations of the university. This will help in restructuring the incentives that the university lecturers (and other workers) face.

Now, if OM programs such as these help to improve the standard of public education, the private education segment will have no choice but to improve even more; otherwise, nobody will want it! Therefore, the overall effect is a strategic improvement in institutional quality!

Chapter 14

14. Using "Sunlight" To Trigger Institutions Reform

"Information is the first step to formulate choice. Greater information exposes the sources of economic rents in the economy, increasing the pressure to dismantle them. It helps to identify institutional weaknesses and provide alternatives to the status quo, and thus creates demand for change"

(World Bank Chief Economist, Mustapha Nabli, at the IMF-AMF High-Level Seminar on Institutions and Economic Growth in the Arab Countries, Abu Dhabi, UAE, December, 2006)

Topics Covered in This Chapter:

- Introduction: Sunlight As A Disinfectant
- A "sunlight" example
- Benefits of "sunlight"
- Various other sunlight examples
- Some examples of areas requiring more sunlight
- Sunlight & FOI laws

Introduction: Sunlight As A Disinfectant

In the last chapter, we saw the benefits of OM. Now, the natural next step, once OM has generated the relevant data, is to shine light on it – the "sunlight"!

By "sunlight", we mean putting relevant institutional information in the public space, with the sincere intention to inform the public. This is a fundamental ingredient for institutional reform, because it illuminates that darkness in which inefficiencies, corruption, economic rents, and other institutional vices take place, thereby creating public awareness on these vices. This awareness in turn plants the seed for the emergence of the coalitions that can begin to press to dismantle them.

Unfortunately, the kind of openness that citizens in the advanced economies take for granted, is often unheard of in many DCs! Mustapha Nabli makes this point in respect of some Arab countries:

> *"The Arab world has much to do to create openness in terms of information. Little government information is accessible by the public (a few countries have recently begun to publish some government statistics). Freedom of the press is carefully monitored and circumscribed in most countries. Use of the internet is often controlled. There are, of course, a multitude of restrictions on citizens from mobilizing for change, in terms of restrictions on civil society and the like. These are symptomatic of the institutional challenges facing the region."*

Any leader that wants to drive change needs to have the liver continue with the usual clampdown on information, does not yet have enough liver to drive change!

Some Sunlight Examples

One commendable application of sunlight as a regulatory tool is in Nigeria's banking industry.

> ### Case 67:   Sunlight in Nigeria's Banking Industry
>
> Nigeria's central bank (the CBN) has been using this sunlight technic as a very powerful tool in steering the banking industry. For example, banks in Nigeria, under the regulatory guidelines must release their independently audited results to the public, after the regulatory authorities have approved the accounts. A very commendable aspect of this sunlight technique (which other regulatory agencies can learn from) is that it has been highly dynamic and context-sensitive!   For example, the CBN insists on minimum disclosures, forcing the banks to disclose certain sensitive information that some of them might not have wanted to volunteer to the public!
>
> That is why, for example, each bank's annual report today will contain the details of:
>
> - The bank's insider transactions, such as how much of the outstanding loans went to insiders;
> - The bank's contraventions of rules and guidelines during the period being reported; and so on
>
> Similarly, in response to some sharp practices (for example, a bank taking money from another bank to shore up its position on its year-end date) the CBN has mandated all banks to close their financial years on the same day, 31st December.

Let us try to note some of the important benefits of CBN's effective use of this sunlight technique as a regulatory tool:

1. It makes the industry's stakeholders (including customers, shareholders and the investing public) better informed on the performances and quality of management of the banks;

2. The published information serves as a feedstock data for third-party analysts, who now become empowered to carry out rigorous independent assessment of the banks (for the benefit of the wider stakeholders) thereby complementing the regulator's work!

3. Stakeholders are confident that even if the regulators miss some things, the third-party analysts may not. These analysts have in effect, complemented the efforts of the regulator, by becoming another layer of oversight.

<u>**Case 68:**</u>　　　**<u>Sunlight – Tajikistan's Civil Service Register</u>**

According to the International Development Association (IDA), Tajikistan had by 2011, developed a civil service register, listing:
- All the approved posts;
- Their grades; and
- Their specific occupants

This had also become automated and accessible by the country's 47 government bodies.

(Source: For more details, please see IDA's report, "IDA at Work: Building Strong Institutions for Sustained Results")

This "sunlight" innovation has the potential to create efficiency within the civil service, discourage nepotism and tribalism in the staffing of the service, and even help the public in navigating through the establishment

<u>**Case 69:**</u>　　　**<u>Sunlight – Kenya's The Prime Minister's Office</u>**

According to the IDA, the Office of Kenya's Prime Minister has a Performance Contract Department, which evaluates and issues public reports on the performances of the nation's public agencies; and this has already crashed the waiting times for various services:
- Passports:　　　　　　　　from 60 to 10 days
- National ID cards:　　　　　from 90 to 18 days
- business licenses:　　　　　from 30 to 1 day

(Source: For more details, please see IDA's report, "IDA at Work: Building Strong Institutions for Sustained Results")

Benefits of Sunlight In The DCs

From the foregoing, we can in general, expect sunlight to create the following important institution-strengthening benefits for a DC:

1. *Bridging unequal access to information*: Sunlight will help to bridge the unequal access to information, of all the institutional stakeholders;

2. *Unveiling of institutional vices*: Sunlight will tend to unveil the dark secrecy within which institutional vices (such as corruption, nepotism and economic rents) thrive. This will in turn create the awareness that will gradually mobilize the coalitions for institutional improvement.

3. *Deepening of oversight*: Sunlight will also begin to empower third-parties (including the press) to start carrying out independent analysis of the statistics, for the benefit of the public or all stakeholders. This deepens the oversight quality on institutions as these third-parties effectively become institutional watchdogs. This will tend to strengthen regulation, because wherever corruption is widespread (and regulatory officials can easily be complicit), it is far more reassuring if the regulator is not regulating in darkness (or secrecy)!

4. *<u>Making public institutions sensitive to public needs</u>*: As pointed out by the World Bank in its World Development report (WDR97), elements of "Voice and partnership" (such as service delivery surveys to solicit client feedback) are important in promoting public sector effectiveness and good governance. Once such surveys create data on client feedback, the sunlight technique becomes a great way to make public officials sensitive to such feedback – for example, by publishing the survey results! Otherwise, government officials can very well get the feedback, but do nothing with it!

5. *<u>Creating competition among public service</u>*: Sunlight can also be used to trigger competition among public organizations, as we have already discussed under OM. It complements the outcome of OM.

Examples of Institutional Programs Requiring More Sunlight

In general, the more open a government institution becomes with its operations, the more open to potential criticisms it will also become; and that is why sunlight is so institution-strengthening – and also why we can expect that most public programs in the DCs can use more sunlight. Let us use a few examples to illustrate this.

<u>Example #1</u>: Nigeria's new pension system can be strengthened with more sunlight.

<u>Case 70:</u>   **<u>More Sunlight For Nigeria's Pension System</u>**

We have already looked at Nigeria's Pension Reform Act (PRA) 2004 that revolutionized pension administration in the country.

This new pension system is an example of the many governance institutions in Nigeria that can creatively leverage this sunlight technique. For example, the pension fund regulator, PENCOM can mandate the private-sector pension fund administrators (PFAs) and pension fund custodians (PFCs) which are managing the fund, to always disclose their detailed audited accounts and annual reports in their websites, for the benefit of all stakeholders – or at least publish annual reports just like the banks! PENCOM can also learn from Nigeria's CBN, and set out the minimum parameters that each report must contain.

What are the likely impacts?
- Nigerian workers and even independent analysts can begin to assess them meaningfully, and to determine how one PFA compares with another, just like they can assess the banks.

- This will not only put these PFAs and PFCs on their toes, but will also provide Nigerian workers a more informed basis for choosing one PFA over another.

- The PFAs and PFCs can argue that they are limited liability companies and therefore should not be mandated to publish their annual accounts! But PENCOM can remind them that they are not just ordinary private companies doing ordinary private businesses – they are managing the retirement future of millions of Nigerian workers on trust!

Example #2: Nigeria's Federal Character Commission (FCC), another agency of the federal government, can similarly leverage the "sunlight" technique very creatively:

Case 71: More Sunlight For Nigeria's FCC

The 1999 Constitution of the Federal Republic of Nigeria is very emphatic on what it describes as "federal character", which is the equitable distribution of government offices among Nigeria's federating units.

To underscore the seriousness of this issue, the Constitution set up a special body, the Federal Character Commission (FCC), to:

- Work out an equitable formula subject to the approval of the National Assembly for the distribution of all cadres of posts in the public service of the Federation and of the States, the armed forces of the Federation, the Nigeria Police Force and other government security agencies, government owned companies and parastatals of the states;

- Promote, monitor and enforce compliance with the principles of proportional sharing of all bureaucratic, economic, media and political posts at all levels of government;

  - Take such legal measures, including the prosecution of the head or staff of any Ministry or government body or agency, which fails to comply with any federal character principle or formula, prescribed or adopted by the Commission.

Many Nigerians have been complaining about the apparent impotence of FCC in the face of flagrant violations of the federal character principle by government ministries, departments, and agencies (MDAs).

The sunlight from Tajikistan can trigger some ideas in FCC: For example, what if the FCC begins to publish regularly the staff distribution statistics (and the federal character compliance status) of the various MDAs, which will reveal the MDAs at the bottom and top of the compliance table. This will likely tame the impunity of the MDAs, because it will start to leave a track; and as we have seen, everybody behaves differently, when they know they are leaving a track!

Example #3: The sunlight of Nigeria's Federal Tenders Journal can use some enhancement.

Case 72: Better Sunlight For Nigeria's FTJ

Nigeria's Federal Tenders Journal (FTJ) is a commendable initiative of the federal government, designed to put information on government's procurements in the public domain. The MDAs advertise their procurement notices in the journal.

The first few editions of the journal raised hopes of taming the monster of the nation's public procurement corruption. However, the journal has remained the same over the years, almost in its original form, even while the corruption it is trying to discourage has since graduated and even acquired many postgraduate degrees!

This author is aware that a non-governmental organization, the Center for Leadership Support and Social Progress (CLSSP) has been advocating some interesting reviews for the FTJ, to make it more dynamic and context-sensitive, in line with the mobility of the corruption it is seeking to discourage.

In general, the information we are putting out in every sunlight program must continuously be context-sensitive so as to remain meaningful. Corruption is very mobile and dynamic. Those perpetrating it and other societal vices are usually very resourceful, and continuously devise means of circumventing the latest control measures. Therefore, any measures a DC is putting out to checkmate corruption cannot afford to remain static!

Sunlight & Freedom of Information (FOI) Laws

Let us make the following points on the FOI laws, which are becoming widely enshrined by many DCs, but which are not always effective. FOI laws, as noted by the OECD, are a fundamental pillar of transparency, which enshrine in legislation, citizens' "right to know", thus enhancing government accountability and promoting informed participation in policymaking. However, merely having an FOI law in place is not enough!

There should also be institutionalized mechanisms for disclosure! For example, the law can provide for budget transparency in terms of:

1. Public availability of the budget document, once presented by the Executive arm of government; and what is finally approved after the legislative input; and

2. Each agency's previous budget and implementation statistics.

Finally, it is important to note that technology has made it very simple (almost costless) to make information available: An agency can simply post the information on its website.

Slice D: Strengthening Institutions By Strengthening Organizations

The initiatives presented under this Slice concern individual organizations and how they can perform optimally. It is important to note that unlike what we saw in the case of institutional processes and programs, making organizations perform optimally in the DC environment, can sometimes be a dicey business. In the DCs, the performance expectations of political leaders from the agencies of government are often influenced by personal, tribal and parochial interests – sometimes even more than public interests. Therefore, such agencies are not likely to be preoccupied with optimizing performances, especially when doing so will impair their abilities to serve those other interests.

Nevertheless, the initiatives presented here (including structural efficiency, accountability, and benchmarking) are handy tools for those situations that the leadership of an organization may be truly interested in enhancing institutional performance.

Chapter 15

15. Streamlining Organizational & Functional Overlaps

> " ... Added to this was the amputation of police powers by the proliferation of law enforcement agencies like the FRSC, the NDLEA, EFCC, ICPC, NCDSC and the like, all sharing from the same begging bowl and not improving the state of security and law enforcement in any substantial manner. And this is typical of us. First responders to any situation all over the country is the police and even if they were indicating problems, why did we not confront those problems and strengthen them rather than creating new agencies with new problems? The fact that we are debating the issue of state police today indicates that we are still confronted with a major problem"
>
> --
>
> *- Fola Arthur-Worrey, former Director of Public Prosecutions for Lagos State, and Head of the Lagos State (Nigeria) Security Trust Fund, complaining about the proliferation of law-enforcement agencies in the country (Dec 2012)*

Topics Covered in This Chapter:

- Duplications, Overlaps & Fragmentation In Government Operations
- Other causes of DOF
- Some obvious drawbacks of DOF
- How to detect DOF

Duplications, Overlaps & Fragmentation In Government Operations

Considering the numerous programs and agencies that government usually operates, often running into hundreds (and thousands in some cases) we should not be surprised to find some duplications and overlaps in government operations.

The United States Government Accountability Office (GAO) has identified three main forms of this challenge – duplications, overlaps, and fragmentations (which we shall simply call DOF here):

1. *Duplication*: When two or more agencies or programs of government are engaged in the same activities, or provide the same services to the same beneficiaries

2. *Overlap*: When multiple agencies or programs of government have similar goals, engage in similar activities or strategies to achieve them; or target similar beneficiaries

3. *Fragmentation*: Those circumstances in which more than one government agency (or more than one organization within an agency) is involved in the same broad area of national need, and opportunities exist to improve service delivery

In the DCs, duplications, overlaps, and fragmentations (which we shall simply call DOF here) are almost a way of life, and one of the hallmarks of their weak institutions. They can occur even at the level of a single government office – where for example, many persons can be in an office bumping into each other and carrying out duties that one person alone should be able to handle!

Various Causes of Duplications, Overlaps & Fragmentation

Some duplications, overlaps and fragmentation should not be surprising in typical government operations because of the sheer size and complexity of those operations.

But there can be other causes, including the following:

1. *Inadequate homework*: If government introduces new programs without thoroughly taking into account what is already on ground, some DOF can arise. As an example, I once worked with a Permanent Secretary on a project that reviewed the various intervention programs of a central government to tackle the problems of poverty and unemployment. We discovered an incredibly large and unwieldy number of individual programs that was sure to make duplications and overlaps a definite certainty!

Case 73:	Duplications Of Intervention Programs Against Poverty & Unemployment

   We discovered numerous intervention programs including the following:

   - YouWin (Youth Enterprise with Innovation in …) a collaboration of the Ministries of Finance, Communication Technology, and Youth Development, and the private sector
   - UNDP's micro credit scheme (under the fourth Country Program for the nation)
   - Fadama programs, including Fadama I, II, & III)
   - Family Economic Advancement Program (FEAP),
   - Financial Inclusion (FI) strategy for the nation, developed in collaboration with 48 other stakeholders, to reduce the level of financial exclusion to 20% (from about 46.3%) by 2020.
   - Industrial estates, set up to encourage business incubation and reduce overhead costs;
   - Industrial Revolution policy of the Ministry of Trade and Investment
   - Various programs under BDS (Business Development Service)
   - Special Public Works Program
   - Various other MSME financing policies (in the pipeline) to address such issues as movable collateral, Group Loan guarantees
   - Commercial Agriculture Credit Scheme (CACS), a 200 billion fund set up by the Central Bank in 2009, in collaboration with the Federal Ministry of Agriculture and Water Resources
   - DFIs (various government DFIs pooled under Bank of Industry to provide developmental, non-commercial loans)

- Entrepreneurship Development Centers (EDCs), Central Bank's effort to supplement the efforts of SMEDAN and others in skill acquisition and business management
- Facilities by the World Bank, African Development Bank, and other international financial institutions (including SME 1 and SME 2) facilitated & guaranteed by the federal government
- Micro credit scheme (the 50 billion micro credit scheme, launched by Mr. President in February, 2008)
- Micro Finance Banks policy, which gave rise to hundreds Microfinance Banks, to take finances to the poor, more effectively
- MSME Bank (as practiced in Thailand, Malaysia, Pakistan and elsewhere) which is already in the pipeline;
- A 200 billion MSME Development Fund (MSMEDF), to be established by the Bank before the end of 2012, to promote the development of the Microfinance sub-sector, to support Micro, Small and Medium Enterprises, and target 60% intervention at women entrepreneurs;
- A 200 billion Refinancing and Restructuring Facility (RRF) was therefore, introduced by the Central Bank in March, 2010. It was enhanced by 35.0 billion in 2011;
- National Job Creation Scheme (NJCS) for which the Federal Government earmarked 50 billion in the 2011 budget;
- National Poverty Eradication Program (NAPEP),
- National Youth Employment and Vocational Skills Development Program;
- The national MSME Project (a pilot initiative of the Federal Government and the World Bank presently already on-going in some States), with the investment promotion agency as the executing agency;
- Nigerian Agricultural Credit Guarantee Scheme Fund (NACGSF);
- The national incentive-based risk sharing system for agricultural lending;
- People's Bank lending (Government's social lending)
- Poverty Alleviation Programs (various)
- Public Works, Youth and Women Employment (Component of the Subsidy Reinvestment and Empowerment Program) being implemented by the Federal Ministry of Finance
- Rural Banking Scheme, designed to help break the circle of poverty by integrating the rural, low-income segment into the production process.
- Rural Banking Scheme, instituted in 1977
- Small and Medium Enterprise Credit Guarantee Scheme (SMECGS)
- Small and Medium Enterprises Equity Investment scheme (SMEEIS) was a voluntary initiative of the Bankers' Committee approved at its 246th Meeting held on 21st December, 1999. The Scheme was discontinued in 2009.
- Small-scale Industries and Graduate Employment Program
- SME 11 loan project (negotiated with the World Bank) to expand credit delivery to SMEs;
- SME 200 billion Credit Guarantee Scheme (CGS) was also established in March 2010 to provide partial (80%) guarantee to banks to lend to SMEs

----

Another important feature of these programs was that they were independently introduced (and were being managed) by different agencies of government. We identified nearly 20 of such agencies:

<u>**Case 74:**</u>　　　<u>**Some Of The Multiple Agencies Managing The Intervention Programs**</u>

- The Bank of Industry;
- Central Bank;
- Industrial Development Centers; and
- National agency for technology incubation;
- National Directorate of Employment;
- National Economic Reconstruction Fund;
- National Fadama Coordination Office;
- The Agricultural Cooperative & Rural Development Bank;
- The Export-Import bank;
- The Agricultural Insurance agency;
- The Bank for Commerce and Industry;
- The Industrial Development Bank;
- The national Investment Promotion agency;
- People's Bank (for government's social lending)
- The SME development agency;
- The National Microfinance Policy Consultative Committee;
- Presidential Standing Committee on Inventions and Innovations (PSCII)
- Industrial Revolution committee, involving the private sector and other stakeholders; and
- The National Committee on Job Creation (NCJC)

With disparate government bodies introducing and managing individual programs for poverty alleviation and employment generation, it was very unlikely that government was doing a thorough inventory taking on the programs (and monitoring how they were faring, and how they could be improved!

2. *Turf enlargement*: In the private sector, there is no room for duplications and overlaps, because nobody wants anything that will eat into profit! The focus is usually to operate every unit as efficiently and cost-effectively as possible. If a unit fails to live up to expectations, the solution is straightforward – "heads" will "roll"!

But the situation we find in the public sector in the DCs is very different: If a public program is not delivering the required output, government can just go ahead to introduce a new program (perhaps, according to a new vision) rather than taking the trouble of reforming the existing program into that vision. That was certainly what was happening in the foregoing case of government efforts to tackle the problems of poverty and unemployment.

It must also have been responsible for the proliferation of law-enforcement agencies in some DCs – the kind that Fola Arthur-Worrey, former Director of Public Prosecutions for Lagos State, and Head of the Lagos State Security Trust Fund, talked about (at this Chapter's opening citation).

Finally, let us note that this problem is not necessarily limited to the DCs, because it is still an on-going challenge for even some of the advanced economies of the world, as captured by the United States Senator, Tom Coburn (of the Republican party), from Oklahoma State:

3. <u>*Social welfare mindset*</u>: In some DCs, government employment is often seen as a way of alleviating poverty – by putting a large number of people on government payroll. In that case, efficiency and cost-effectiveness may be less important than the perceived social and political value of directly offering jobs to many people. This mindset might have featured in the proliferation of law enforcement agencies in Nigeria.

4. <u>*Lack of political will*</u>: Even when government realizes that it needs to trim its administrative bureaucracy, to free funds for developmental programs, the political will to sack workers may be lacking, because streamlining (which will involve retrenching government workers) can be politically unpopular! Consequently, successive government administrations can turn a blind eye to obvious DOF cases!

5. <u>*Nepotism*</u>: A new political administration will usually want to put its own people into the system, not caring whether the system is already saturated – not just because of nepotism, but also as a way of distributing political dividends. Even when the workforce is already bloated, such an administration may jump at the slightest opportunity to create a new program or agency, as a means of creating space for its own people. This mindset might again have featured in the proliferation of law enforcement agencies in Nigeria.

Some Obvious Drawbacks of DOF

Between them, duplications, overlaps, or fragmentations (DOF) can result in any combinations of the following problems:

1. <u>*Cost/wastes*</u>: If one agency can handle the needs of a given service or program, and other agencies are also created to start carrying out those same functions, we are creating extra sets of offices (including building and office spaces, executive management and staff, administrative and logistics systems; all of which are avoidable.

2. <u>*Bloated cost of governance*</u>: Some poor DCs, facing severe challenges of poverty, illiteracy and infrastructure (and are therefore in dire need of development projects), are still spending the bulk of their annual budgets (sometimes up to 70%) as "recurrent" expenditure – mostly for the salaries and allowances of government officials, as well as for other overheads. What then is left for capital development? An important factor in high governance costs is often the DOFs of the over-bloated bureaucracies.

3. <u>*Unjust appropriation of national budget*</u>: Note that when government spends the chunk of the national budget on just the needs of its officials (as discussed above), who may comprise less than 1% of the population, it amounts to a very unjust distribution of the nation's resources, and a very obvious pointer to weak institutions! In a DC, people are looking up to government to fund education, healthcare, and basic infrastructure such as housing, roads, electricity, and portable water. If the DC is spending the bulk of its budget on just its officials, the public service is certainly self-Centered.

4. _Excessive burden on citizens_: Duplications, overlaps and fragmentations often mean that citizens have to deal with multiple government agencies instead of just one. This tends to bounce citizens from one government office to another, rather than making things simpler for them. Let us use Nigeria's JAMB as an illustration.

<u>Case 75:</u>   **JAMB, Post-JAMB & DOF**

The Joint Admissions and Matriculations Board of the Federal government of Nigeria (JAMB) conducts the national admissions examinations for candidates seeking to get into the nation's limited tertiary schools. As at 2006, about 1.5 million kids passed out of Nigeria's secondary schools each year (according to Funmi Ogundare), but the tertiary schools had spaces for less than 500,000 of them. The situation is most likely worse today; so these kids face very competitive JAMB-administered examinations.

JAMB is required to conduct a single exam for all candidates during each admission year, and then to assign successful candidates to schools of their choices (if they outperform other candidates seeking those same schools). JAMB should also ideally reassign a high-performing candidate that fails to meet their school's cut-off mark, to other available schools (if they performed better than the other candidates seeking those schools); and this should continue until all the available spaces are filled. Before the JAMB era, individual schools had their separate admissions exams, which required each candidate to continue to apply (and often travel) to different tertiary institutions, until they secured a place.

Therefore, the JAMB initiative represented a very useful social service in the sense of:

- Saving candidates the inconveniences and costs associated with having to take multiple admissions examinations from multiple tertiary schools (each such exam would have involved examination fees, as well as travel and accommodation costs).

- Providing a common benchmark with which universities assessed all candidates for admission.

- Enabling Nigerians residing outside the country to come home and take a single JAMB examination, rather than making multiple trips to take the independently scheduled examinations of different institutions.

- Also by pooling all candidates together, JAMB has the potential to minimize the chances of any topmost performing kids missing out. For example, assume that candidate John applies to school "A" but is unable to meet the cut-off mark for that school. JAMB should be in a position to offer him admission into any other school whose cut-off mark he meets, so that John is not left out, while candidates with lower scores secure admissions into those other schools.

Due to the nation's severe educational capacity constraints, the desperation of the applicants often meant that they employed all kinds of tricks to cheat in the JAMB exams. The tertiary schools then started to argue that JAMB exams were no longer reliable. However, instead of working with JAMB to strengthen the process, each tertiary school eagerly went back to conducting its own duplicate admission exams, which now came to be known as the "post-JAMB" exams.

So Nigerians kids and their families are now having to contend with both the JAMB exams, as well as the very school-specific exams that JAMB was originally created to stop!

----

5. _Putting the hapless citizens under siege_: Another form of this excessive burden on citizens occurs where corruption is widespread, and where government officials tend to prey on businesses and citizens alike. In that environment, DOF means that members of the public will have to deal with multiple agencies and their predatory officials – and will now find themselves having to "settle" multiple sets of predatory hands!

6. _Putting businesses under siege_: This is still another form that excessive burden! At a time of vocal calls for the reduction of government's burden on the economy (particularly, the regulatory burden on businesses) any duplicated or overlapping functions of government's (particularly those that interface with businesses) can be very adversarial to the economy! We can use the complaints of the Lagos Chamber of Commerce and Industry (LCCI) in Nigeria as an example.

Case 76:   Remi Bello on the Siege From Overlapping Agencies

In July 2014, Mr. Remi Bello, the LCCI President, cried out against the excessive regulatory burden on Nigerian businesses due to the overlapping roles of multiple government agencies. He singled out the roles of the Standards Organization of Nigeria (SON), the National Agency for Food Drugs Administration and Control (NAFDAC) and the Consumer Protection Council (CPC), especially in the industrial sectors "like cosmetics, beverages, food, drinks, health and confectionary". According to Remi:

> "Each of the agencies prefers to carry out an independent analysis of the same product with the attendant cost and loss of man hours … SON normally does the calibration of equipment through their meteorology department. Weight and Measures does the verification to ascertain if the equipment is calibrated. After the verification exercise and it is established that the equipment is calibrated, the Weights and Measures department still imposes prohibitive charges on industries
> _(See BusinessNews, July 19, 2014)_

----

7. _Information duplication_: One consequence of the duplications and fragmentations of government functions is often the proliferation of data, as different agencies and programs set up and maintain independent databases on the same subjects – with each of them often attracting its own charges.

<u>**Case 77:**</u> **Proliferations of Citizens' Biometrics Systems!**

The Nigerian Identity Management Commission (NIMC) is a government agency mandated to establish, own, operate, maintain and manage the identity database of Nigerian citizens. If the NIMC had got its job done, it would have enabled Nigeria to have something as useful as the United States' social security number, or Estonia's e-ID.

However, the NIMC has not been able to do so; and because of that, different Nigerian government agencies are happily setting up independent databases of citizens, for their own uses, instead of helping to fix NIMC's problems.

Some examples:

- Nigeria's electoral body, INEC, maintains its own biometric database of all registered voters, which it uses to conduct elections in the country. INEC carries out a continuous registration of voters;

- The National Population Commission is working on its own biometrics-based census to help eliminate ghost and multiple respondents, and make census outcomes easier to audit;

- The Federal Road Safety Corps (FRSC) sets up an independent database of citizens to whom it has issued driving licenses;

- There is also a separate set of biometric data captured on citizens when they apply for vehicle number plates;

- The Central Bank of Nigeria has set up a Bank Verification Number (BVN) system as central identity system for all bank customers in Nigeria. This is perhaps the country's most successful national biometric database;

- There are similar biometric data systems for other government agencies, such as JAMB, NECO, NYSC, and so on!

Each of these parallel data systems implies additional cost to the nation, and also to the citizens, who have to pay to the individual agencies to get captured in their databases. This would not have been necessary if government had simply insisted on getting its central (NIMC's) biometric database functional.

----

8. *Poor service delivery*: Ultimately, civil servants achieve more, when they are busy, than when they have nothing to do. For example, if in an office, ten poorly remunerated persons are carrying out a function that one person alone could handle, they will tend to be lazy and unmotivated (spending all their time gossiping), and negatively reinforcing each other. Dr. Osita Ogbu, the CEO of Nigeria's National Planning Commission (NPC), and Chief Economic Adviser to President Obasanjo talks about what the NPC once did, when it had to disengage some of its workers, even before their severance benefits were ready:

The same thing happens at the level of agencies and programs. For example, remember we earlier saw the bewildering number of government agencies and programs, targeted at poverty reduction. As the case below shows, the figures from Nigeria's National Bureau of Statistics (NBS), suggest that despite all those agencies and programs, the nation's population in poverty has actually been rising, instead of going down!

Case 78:   **Trend of Nigeria's Population In Poverty, 1980-2010**

Year	Population in millions)	%In Poverty
1980	65.0	26.3
1985	75.0	46.3
1992	91.5	42.8
1996	102.3	65.6
2004	126.3	54.4
2010	163.0	69%

(Source: Adapted From Nigeria's National Bureau of Statistics (NBS), HNLSS 2010)

Notice in particular, the dramatic rise of the nation's population in poverty from 68.7 million in 2004, to 112.47 million in 2010 – not minding all these programs and expenditure!

9. *The challenge of coordination*: When different agencies are implementing parallel services or running parallel programs, coordination becomes difficult, especially if different ministries or organs of government are overseeing the implementation. For example, look again at all the intervention programs of the Nigerian federal government on poverty alleviation and employment generation, as well as the various agencies that are independently managing these programs. They can only pose a coordination nightmare.

10. *Interagency "turf" wars*: Even in individual organizations, officials whose job functions overlap, tend to struggle for turfs and to undercut (rather than complement) each other. It usually gets worse if the overlap is between independent agencies or programs of government!

11. *Poor job satisfaction*: When government has too many people on its payroll and spends an excessive proportion of the annual budget as workers' salaries and wages, chances are that it will not have the capacity to pay the workers competitive wages to the workers, leading to a disgruntled public-sector workforce. Poor remuneration also means that such a Service will not be able to attract quality manpower.
    Dr. Osita Ogbu, former NPC's CEO and Chief Economic Adviser to the President, put it this way, in respect of Nigeria's National Planning Commission (NPC):

Detecting Duplications, Overlaps & Fragmentation

In view of the adverse effects of duplications, overlaps and fragmentation (DOF) on institutional performance, each DC must endeavor to streamline them. Wherever any case of DOF is detected, the proper thing is to assign a "reason code" to it, to justify its continued retention, and why it should not be streamlined to possibly improve institutional performance.

The following techniques can help the DC's CRT to detect where cases of DOF may exist:

1. *Inventory taking*: Detecting duplications, overlaps and fragmentation (DOF) is usually an important by-product of inventory taking, which we looked at in details earlier.

2. *Periodic review*: As a way of increasing efficiency, and reducing wastes, the CRT or a Committee (or study team) of government, can occasionally review the structure of government operations and make recommendations.

> **Case 79:**   Steve Oronsaye's Presidential Committee Report
>
> In August 2011, Nigeria's President Goodluck Jonathan set up a "Presidential Committee on Restructuring and Rationalization of Federal Agencies, Commissions and Parastatals", headed by Mr. Steve Oronsaye. The Committee in its report presented to the President in April 2012, established that the federal government had a total of 541 parastatals, commissions and agencies, out of which 263 were statutory. The Committee recommended shrinking the 263 statutory agencies to only 161, because of what it found to be "duplications and overlaps in their mandates".

3. *The independent "watchdog" approach*: The United States has its Government Accountability Office (GAO) as an independent body that works as a watchdog, continuously studying government operations for ways of increasing efficiency, and reducing wastes. Part of the mandate of the GAO is to detect any opportunities that may exist for making government operations more cost-effective – including opportunities for streamlining government.

> **Case 80:**   The United States GAO
>
> The U.S. Government Accountability Office (GAO) is an independent, nonpartisan agency that works for Congress. Often called the "congressional watchdog," GAO investigates how the federal government spends taxpayer dollars. The head of GAO, the Comptroller General of the United States, is appointed to a 15-year term by the President from a slate of candidates Congress proposes
>
> The GAO is mandated by public laws to review government operations and produce annual reports. It can also work at the request of congressional committees or subcommittees, and undertakes research under the authority of the Comptroller General.

It generally supports congressional oversight by:

- Auditing agency operations to determine whether federal funds are being spent efficiently and effectively;
- Investigating allegations of illegal and improper activities;
- Reporting on how well government programs and policies are meeting their objectives;
- Performing policy analyses and outlining options for congressional consideration; and
- Issuing legal decisions and opinions, such as bid protest rulings and reports on agency rules
- Advising Congress and the heads of executive agencies on ways to make government more efficient, effective, ethical, equitable and responsive

The GAO's work leads to laws and acts that improve government operations, saving the government and taxpayers billions of dollars.

Chapter 16

16. Instilling A Culture Of Organizational Accountability

I wish we would have had a better relationship with Mayor Nutter, but I don't know how we could have done that. He used to call me at 11 at night to yell at me. The option would have been to do what he wanted, which would have been sacrificing our independence. Part of that is the nature of the relationship. You're criticizing people and giving demerits in their career advancement

(Philadelphia Controller Alan Butkovitz, explaining why the relationship between the Executive (a Mayor) and the auditor (Controller) cannot be too good)

Topics Covered in This Chapter:

- Introduction
- Auditing
- Benefits of auditing government operations
- Challenges of auditing government operations
- Strengthening the Audit Institution
- Being a good Audit Institution

Introduction: Government & Accountability

In this Chapter, we shall look at "accountability", a very important attribute of strong governance institutions.

We are all used to the high accountability standards that government sets for businesses under its control. For example, the Nigerian government not only wants them to prepare accurate annual accounts, but also to get the accounts certified by independent external auditors, publish the results (for some classes of businesses) and pay taxes as appropriate. Various agencies of government follow up on all these rules to ensure compliance.

Yet, government does not always attach the same level of importance to accountability in its own operations! Every year in a typical DC, many government ministries, departments and agencies (MDAs) go through the routine of preparing and defending their budgets, without being required to account rigorously for the funds they collected in the past. Some MDAs can continue this way for years, without anybody thinking that anything is wrong!

In the DCs therefore, government's position on accountability seems to be *"Do as I say, and not as I do!"*

<u>**Case 81:**</u>   <u>Pentascope & Nitel</u>

When Nigeria deregulated its telecoms sector in 2001, which allowed private telecoms providers to enter the market, the nation's former monopolistic telecoms services provider, Nitel (and its subsidiary, M-Tel) could not cope with the competition from the new entrants. In 2003, government contracted a Dutch telecoms firm, Pentascope, to manage Nitel and M-Tel, hoping it would turn them around.

In 2004, after one year of the contract, Pentascope outraged many Nigerians, when it declared a loss for Nitel running into billions of Naira – something Nigerians had never heard from Nitel! But the highly respected columnist, Ijeoma Nwogwugwu, saw even the declaration of a loss as a credit to Pentascope!

Quoting her:

- "… Today we are told that Nitel after one year of Pentascope, declared a loss of N19 billion … The truth of the matter is that Nitel and its managers had no way of knowing if it was operating profitably or not. Prior to 2003, the company's accounts had not been audited for over a decade, nor had it paid an iota of dividend to its owner, the federal government of Nigeria, for ages".

In other words, as bad as the news from Pentascope might have been, the company had at least updated the accounts of Nitel after so many years!

(For more details, see Business Times, March 14-16, 2005)

Government organizations can be considered accountable, when they are subject to thorough oversight processes that are open to the public. In such an environment, these organizations will be less susceptible to the various vices that tend to be prevalent in the DCs, such as corruption, fraud, nepotism and impunity.

Accountability is a key attribute of effective public institutions. In fact, there is no way a DC can have strong governance institutions if there is no accountability in its operations. It is the starting point for good governance. If a DC's political leadership is not willing to commit to accountability, it is not yet ready for effective institutions – because they go together!

Auditing

Auditing is a special attribute of accountability, which we have singled out for more detailed discussion, because of the pivotal role it plays in enhancing institutional effectiveness. It is a form of performance measurement (PM) during which we examine the performance of an organization (mostly financial performance), verify its records-keeping and the appropriateness of its operating controls and security. If it is sincere, auditing has the potential to enhance institutional accountability in government operations.

Every year, government rakes in money in billions and trillions, which it spends on behalf of the citizens, on a variety of programs and projects. Auditing helps to keep track of how all that money is being spent, and to watch out for any weaknesses in operating controls and security. That precisely is why we cannot expect bureaucrats in the DCs (where corruption and other vices are widespread) to be enthusiastic about auditing. Nobody usually is, because the auditor, by the nature of their work, will always be highlighting people's shortcomings.

Benefits of Auditing Government Operations

The following are some of the obvious benefits of auditing in a DC environment:

1. ***Tool for parliamentary oversight***: If Parliament votes public funds for an MDA, it is only natural that Parliament should seek to know how that MDA has used the money! Independent audit findings provide guidance to Parliament in its oversight and appropriation functions.

2. *Promoting transparency*: Even if an MDA is prudent with funds, nobody can be sure, until it gets audited. When an MDA puts its audited accounts in the public domain, it projects transparency, which assures citizens and other stakeholders that the officials in the MDA are not misusing public funds. The OECD has more insights on this:

> "Government organizations which uphold principles of integrity and disclosure, and are subject to objective and thorough oversight processes, are more accountable to the public and less susceptible to corruption and the mismanagement of funds which can divert precious resources away from governments' goals."
>
> --
>
> *(See OECD's Post-2015 Reflections)*

3. *Credibility of financial statements*: It is not enough for an MDA to prepare its own financial statements – there is far more credibility after an independent body (the auditor) has certified them. Government even requires this of the private businesses it regulates!

4. *Identifying any control weaknesses*: An external auditor is not only tasked with verifying the correctness of an MDA's financial information, but also with confirming that the MDA's operations have adequate internal controls that safeguard public assets. Auditing helps to identify internal control weaknesses, including financial risks and vulnerabilities; and to suggest mitigation steps.

5. *Fraud detection*: Auditing can sometimes uncover fraudulent or illegal activities that might have taken place, although auditors like to point out that fraud detection is usually not the main goal of auditing;

6. *Performance auditing*: As explained by Dave Yost, the special case of performance auditing, which examines an MDA's economy, efficiency and effectiveness, creates the additional benefits of bringing to the table, ways of enhancing economy (keeping costs low), efficiency (getting the most out of available resources), and effectiveness (meeting the objectives set for the MDA).

7. *Data for sunlight*: Finally, note that the "sunlight" we looked at earlier is only meaningful if there is some performance information that it can disclose! Auditing will usually create such information!

From all these, we can see that a robust and independent auditing of government operations, will help in strengthening governance institutions.

Challenges of Auditing Government Operations

Even in the developed nations, the relationship between government officials and government auditors is usually at best "polite". The auditor by the nature of their work will often be criticizing people or highlighting their shortcomings, which is neither good for the career advancement of the civil servant, nor the re-election scheming of elected officials! In a typical DC, where governance institutions are weak, the challenges of auditing government operations are even greater!

For example, when corruption is widespread in a DC:

1. Nobody in government is really interested in a proper audit – not the executive arm, not the legislative arm, and not even the judiciary! The reason is not "rocket science" – only a foolish rat will like to invite a snake into its hole!

2. The audit reports tend to be irrelevant, and of little or no influence on government's decisions. This can be very disillusioning to the public-sector auditors. All too often, the audit reports end up in remote file cabinets, where they gather dust – especially when their conclusions are politically unpopular.

3. The operations of government auditors are usually not well-funded, to enable the auditors do their jobs independently. The executive and legislative arms of government easily use "budget power" to tame whatever exuberance these auditors may develop!

4. A good example of a weakened audit institution can be found in Nigeria's Auditor-General of the Federation.

> **Case 82:**   **Constitutional Constraints On Nigeria's AuGF**
>
> In 2014, a prominent civil rights activist, Femi Falana, wrote to Nigeria's Auditor-General of the federation (AuGF) requesting it to audit the accounts of the state-owned oil giant, NNPC, because of some controversies at the time about some missing funds.
>
> In its highly publicized response, the office of the AuGF reminded the activist that:
>
> - Section 85(3) of the nation's constitution did not empower the office to audit the accounts of (or appoint auditors for) government statutory corporations, commissions, authorities, agencies, including all persons and bodies established by the Act of the National Assembly.

- The constitution only empowered the AuGF to provide the NNPC and other similar bodies with a list of auditors qualified to be appointed as external auditors and from which they could then appoint their own external auditors.

(For Femi Falana, see Thisday & The Citizen, March 3, 2014)

5. Now, what really does Section 85(3) of the Nigerian Constitution say about the powers of the AuGF?

Case 83:   What Section 85(3) Of The Nigerian Constitution Says

Here is what Section 85(3) of the Nigerian Constitution says about the powers of the AuGF:

- Nothing in subsection (2) of this section shall be construed as authorizing the Auditor-General to audit the accounts of (or appoint auditors) for government statutory corporations, commissions, authorities, agencies, including all persons and bodies established by an Act of the National Assembly,

- "But the Auditor-General shall
    - *Provide such bodies with a list of auditors qualified to be appointed by them as external auditors and from which the bodies shall appoint their external auditors,*
    - *Provide guidelines on the level of fees to be paid to external auditors; and*
    - *Comment on their annual accounts and auditor's reports thereon".*

Source: The 1999 Constitution of the Federal Republic of Nigeria

Public commentators in Nigeria have been lamenting this seeming absurdity of giving Ministers and heads of agencies the powers to self-appoint auditors to investigate their own activities. As Robert Ekule put it:

> "It is a pity that section 85 of the 1999 constitution ... created to shield corrupt leaders because they all know where to steal from. The lack of transparency we see in government sphere today is aided by the section ... As it stands now, there is no agency clearly given the mandate to audit and publish findings of corporations like the NNPC. It should be the office of the AGF to detect missing money if empowered ... I find it hard to believe that Nigeria is one of the very few countries in the world without a functioning Auditing Act"

(For more details, please see Business Day, March 22, 2015)

Instead of this Nigerian case, a DC that is interested in strengthening its audit institution can look at the powers of the Auditor General of South Africa.

<u>**Case 84:**</u>   <u>**The Robust Powers Of The Auditor General Of South Africa**</u>

The South African Constitution guarantees the independence of the Auditor General of South Africa (AGSA) and stipulates that the AGSA is subject only to the constitution and the law.

The constitution also unequivocally empowers the AGSA to audit and report on the accounts, financial statements and financial management of:

- All national and provincial state departments and administrations;
- The administration of Parliament and of each provincial legislation;
- All municipalities and municipal entities;
- All constitutional institutions; and
- Any other institution or accounting entity required by national or provincial legislation to be audited by the AGSA.

(Source: Auditor General of South Africa, AGSA)

It is interesting that since 1999 when democracy returned to Nigeria, the nation's Parliament has passed many anti-corruption laws, such as creating the Independence Corrupt Practices and other related offences Commission (ICPC) and the Economic and Financial Crimes Commission (EFCC) as anti-corruption agencies. Yet it has not adequately empowered the nation's most basic institution for fighting corruption – which is the office of the AuGF! Ironically, instead of untying the hands of the AuGF, government found it more convenient to keep it shackled, while creating interventionist agencies.

Strengthening The Audit Institution

In general, here are some of the main tools for strengthening the audit institution, for the benefits of any DC that is interested in doing so:

1. *Auditor independence*: This will empower the institution to function without being inhibited by the other arms of government that it will be checking. Some key elements of this independence include:

2. *Financial autonomy*, such as the kind that Parliament enjoys, including financial capacity to take the kind of steps necessary to draw attention to its audit reports. For example, the auditor general's budget should not be at the pleasure of the executive arm of government, but rather a direct charge on public funds.

3. *Administrative autonomy* for recruiting, promoting and disciplining its staff: Government auditors, for example, should not belong to the mainstream civil service that is managed centrally.

4. *Reporting line*: The auditor general should report directly to the legislature, rather than to the executive. Equally important, no other MDA controlled by any arm of government, should in any way control the operations and administration of the office of the AuGF.

5. *Full control of the audit*: The auditor general should have the right to decide the nature of its audits, the timing, and the reporting.

6. *Mode of appointment of the auditor-general*: Section 86 of the Nigerian Constitution prescribes that the AuGF "shall be appointed by the President on the recommendation of the Federal Civil Service Commission (FCSC) subject to confirmation by the Senate". This kind of arrangement may not create enough auditor independence, especially in DCs, where governance institutions are very weak! For example, a meddlesome Nigerian President easily controls the FCSC!

   Some alternative arrangements for appointing the auditor-general include by citizens' election. An auditor that emerges that way will report directly to the citizens of the state, with neither the state governor nor state legislature having any direct oversight over its work.

   Case 85:   **Auditor Emerging Through Elections**

   In the United States, some state auditors emerge through state-wide elections. For example, the Auditor General for the State of Michigan is appointed by a majority vote of the legislative members. That of the State of Illinois is nominated by the Legislative Audit Commission, and appointed by majorities of both Houses of the Legislature; and so on

   ----

   When an auditor-general's position is by appointment, one can expect it to be based on cognate qualifications, such as a solid background in accounting and auditing. But when the position is filled by election, anybody can get elected, including someone with little financial experience. Voters can use other criteria, such as uprightness, or reputation for cutting waste and corruption, or even the size of a candidate's campaign purse.

7. *Removal from office*: It is important that threat of removal from office does not become a tool for compromising the auditor-general's independence. Different techniques are used to mitigate this danger.

   - For example, Section 87 of the Nigerian Constitution prescribes that a person holding the office of the Auditor-General of the Federation shall be removed from office by the President acting on an address supported by two-thirds majority of the Senate praying that he be so removed for inability to discharge the functions of his-office (whether arising from infirmity of mind or body, or from any other cause) or for misconduct.

8. *Tenure Renewal*: The auditor-general is expected to be independent from the other arms of government; however, if the tenure is subject to renewal, the likely interest of the auditor in tenure extension can compromise the independence!
   Various techniques are used to mitigate this threat:

   a. An auditor-general can hold office until retirement: For example, Nigeria's 1999 Constitution allows the AuGF to remain in office until retiring age, except when removed as discussed before;

   b. There can also be long tenures – For example, the United States' Comptroller General is appointed for a 15-year term, while the Auditor General for the State of Illinois serves a ten-year term.

9. *Right to audit all government operations*: the auditor general should have the right to audit every unit of government that spends public funds. This effectively means all government operations! This will enable a DC's auditor general to play an effective role in strengthening institutions.

10. *Right of Access*: the auditor general should have the right of access to all physical and nonphysical data, which they believe will facilitate their audit work, from any organization it is empowered to audit. This includes the right to obtain any explanations they may demand.

11. *Right to do performance auditing*: The auditor-general should have the right to undertake performance auditing, which examines government's <u>economy</u> (ways of keeping the cost low), <u>efficiency</u> (ways of getting the most out of available resources), and <u>effectiveness</u> (ways of meeting set objectives).

12. *Right to do proactive auditing*: This refers to the kind of "interventionist" auditing that the Government Accounting Office (GAO) does in the United States. The GAO can audit projects at a much earlier stage, which can help to detect problems, when they are still in the making.

13. *Auditing the auditor*: In Slice G, we have devoted a Chapter to "monitoring the monitors" – which looks at this and other institutional procedures that can help to ensure that the empowered government auditor (and other public officials handling sensitive duties) remain faithful to their mandates.

Being a Good Audit Institution

In addition to the foregoing steps that government needs to take to strengthen the audit institution, the institution itself needs to take firm steps to instill confidence in its work, recognizing that it can never enjoy automatic deference on issues, unless it earns the deference. Here are some tools that the institution can use to instill credibility and respect for its works:

1. *Technical competence*: It is not enough to statutorily empower the audit institution to audit all government operations; the institution itself must take steps to ensure that it acquires the in-house expertise to discharge that duty! This calls for recruiting, training and retaining qualified staff, who will not only understand what they need to do, but can also stand their ground and defend their audit positions effectively.

Technical competence particularly includes:

    a. *Financial expertise*: This is a prerequisite for proper auditing;

    b. *Digital literacy*: The auditor-general's office cannot go very far in its work in this era of globalization, if it is not overflowing with digital literacy, especially considering how technology is now transforming governance (which we shall see in the next Slice).

c. _Benchmarking_: The auditor-general's office must continue to study (and learn from) what other audit institutions around the world are doing. We shall look at "benchmarking" in details in the next Chapter

2. _Giving firepower to audit reports_: Government auditors must take steps to make their reports very influential, because the other arms of government will certainly not do it for them!

<u>Case 86:</u>   **Alan Butkovitz's Suggestions For Giving Firepower To Auditors' Reports**

From Alan Butkovitz, Philadelphia Controller, (in the US), we can get some hints that government auditors will find very helpful in drawing attention to their works:

- Becoming the expert on the subject you are involved with, so that it gradually becomes hard to argue with you;

- Developing a good relationship with the media, and perhaps even becoming a useful resource to them; and

- Backing up reports with multimedia effects:

> "We developed video audits. We have found they have devastating impact. For example, we did our third review of the condition of school buildings. The video that showed the bathrooms clogged with human waste that isn't cleaned up -- that had the school district surrender. Traditionally it has been able to deny the situation".

(Source: Please see Governance, January 7, 2016)

3. _Keeping tab on field staff_: Government auditors must also take steps to shield the field staff from becoming compromised. Various tools for doing this are discussed in the next Chapter on "monitoring the monitors", including limiting the ex-audit staff from accepting appointments from any other government unit within a specified number of years of leaving the audit work;

In conclusion, empowering the audit institution is fundamental to creating strong national institutions; and this empowerment demands very hard work from the audit institution itself! Luckily, there are many global resources today that a DC's audit institution can leverage to enhance its technical competence. Constant benchmarking will also keep it abreast of what similar institutions across the world are doing.

Chapter 17

17. Benchmarking Institutional Performance

"In the private sector, benchmarking has become standard practice for helping businesses identify processes that need improvement and has enabled many of the world's most well-known and successful businesses to drive down administrative costs. However, although benchmarking studies target administrative areas (e.g., finance, HR/payroll, procurement, and IT) and government is largely administrative in nature, benchmarking has rarely been applied to the public sector. The conventional wisdom has been that state governments are organized and funded so idiosyncratically that benchmarking lacked application."

(Better Government Competition, 2006)

Topics Covered in This Chapter:

- Introduction To Benchmarking
- Types of benchmarking
- Benefits of benchmarking
- Challenges of Benchmarking Government Operations
- How To Create The Appetite For Benchmarking

Introduction To Benchmarking

Harold Wilson (1916-1995), the two-term English Prime Minister and Statesman, once described the cemetery as the only human institution that rejected progress. However, even the cemetery is today changing; it cannot help noticing how the world around it is changing!

Similarly, we are in the "click" age; no one should be stuck with a bureaucracy of red tape and long waits, or a bureaucracy, which still bounces citizens from one office to the other.

Benchmarking is the technique of striving to improve how we are doing things, by looking at how others are doing theirs. It is one of the governance practices that can help in strengthening governance institutions, once there is a basic desire to improve things. Applied to an organization, benchmarking in the words of Joseph Blakeman of the Center for Urban Transportation Studies (CUTS), University of Wisconsin-Milwaukee,

"is a process to determine who else does a particular activity the best and emulating what they do to improve performance".

In the private sector, where the pressures of market forces are always pushing organizations towards improvements (so they can remain in business) benchmarking is an indispensable and highly treasured management tool. Let us use some examples to illustrate it, starting with a story by Hammer & Champy:

<u>**Case 87:**</u>　　　　<u>**Ford, Mazda & Benchmarking**</u>

As recounted by Hammer & Champy, Ford Motor Company, America's auto giant, was in the early 1980s, like many other American multinationals, searching for how it could cut its administrative overheads. One area that Ford targeted was the Accounts Payable department for its North American operations, which employed over 500 persons. Ford figured that through several reform measures, it could achieve as much as a 20% reduction in that unit – bringing the number down to about 400. Ford managers beat themselves on the chest, believing that this was pretty good – until they visited Mazda in Japan, where Ford had earlier acquired a 25% stake!

During the visit, the Ford team was surprised that Mazda used only 5 persons for its Accounts Payable unit! Although Mazda was a smaller company than Ford, the difference (500 vs. 5) was too big to attribute to just the size differential. In the end, this discovery was to change Ford's concept of Accounts Payable! It was to lead to a transformational change in the way Ford did business with its suppliers, which was its source of the accounts payable. By the time Ford finished, it only needed 125 persons for an entirely new process it now called "vendor payment"!

(Source: adapted from Hammer & Champy, 1994)

From Zairi and Leonard (1994) and also Blakeman (2005), we can recall the following story about an American company, Xerox, once the world's largest manufacturer of copiers:

<u>**Case 88:**</u>　　　　<u>**Xerox, The Japanese & Benchmarking**</u>

As recounted by Zairi & Leonard (1994), Xerox was the largest manufacturer of copiers in the world in the 1970s. However, Japanese manufacturers were making better copiers, selling them for less, and making good profit. This prompted the company to benchmark itself with its direct competitors to determine what it could do better.
The results were astonishing:

- Xerox's ratio of indirect to direct staff was twice that of direct competition;
- It had nine times the number of production suppliers;
- Assembly line rejects were in the order of ten times worse;
- Product time to market was twice as long;
- Defects per 100 machines were seven times worse.
- Xerox's Japanese joint venture, Fuji Xerox, was performing well.

The findings forced some changes. Over the next five years, Xerox would have to increase productivity 18% to keep up with its competitors. It did this through a strategy known as leadership through quality, which became the foundation of the revival of the company. For example, Xerox benchmarked L.L. Bean, a Maine outdoor sporting goods retailer, because of their excellent warehouse procedures that are now the standard at most companies.

And by the time it won the Malcolm Baldridge National Quality award in 1989, it had benchmarked almost 230 performance areas!

Source: adapted from Zair & Leonard (1994), and Blakeman, J. (2005)

Benchmarking is also growing very rapidly in the public sector, where it stands to bring a lot of benefits to any organization striving for progress.

Types of Benchmarking

Benchmarking has evolved over the years (and across various economic sectors), and today, takes many diverse forms that include the following:

1. *Reverse engineering*: This was actually how modern benchmarking started. Reverse engineering involves tearing apart (or opening up) the product of another firm, examining and improving the components, and then putting them back together to form a superior product. Many Asian manufacturers used this technique to catch up and compete with hitherto superior American and European companies.

2. *Results benchmarking*: In this case, what is of interest is the output from our processes. Here, we measure our results and compare them with the results that others are getting; and then look for what we can improve. What does a kilometer of road construction cost in country A compared to country B? This form of benchmarking can help a DC to see its deficiencies relative to other nations.

3. *Process benchmarking*: In this case, what is of interest can be any of the organization's processes of converting inputs into outputs. The ultimate goal here is to improve overall results, by identifying any weak processes and improving them. The Ford's "accounts payable" case above had to do with "process" benchmarking.

   Except when there is a genuine thirst for improvement within an organization (perhaps because jobs and careers are at stake) many public agencies in the DCs are not likely to have successful process improvement – because some kinds of inefficiency may be deliberate, to facilitate vices such as corruption. In that case, a process benchmarking program may end up as a lot of grammar and reports, but without real substance.

   On the other hand, if we initially focus on "results" benchmarking, the outcome can even begin to create the pressure for improvement – which if it catches on, can then trigger genuine interest in process benchmarking!

4. *Competitive benchmarking*: This is where we use a competitor (or an organization providing similar services) as the benchmark. For example, a federal government school can use another demographically similar (and well performing) school as its benchmark.

5. *Internal benchmarking*: They say "charity begins from home"! In internal benchmarking, we use another cost center within our organization, as a benchmark. For example, what can the north-western operations of the Nigerian Customs Services learn from the Eastern Zone? What can the Western Zone of the Peoples Bank (a publicly-owned microfinance bank that gives peasant loans) learn from the relatively high loan repayment rate of the Northern Zone? And so on. Internal benchmarking, whenever it is applicable, can often be

a cheap and an economical way to start the benchmarking journey, to gain experience inexpensively, before venturing outside.

6. *External benchmarking*: This is the normal kind of benchmarking, where an organization uses another organization as its benchmark. Both Ford and Xerox in the cases above did "external" benchmarking. Similarly, a public sector logistics department can use one of the private-sector courier companies as a benchmark; and so on! External benchmarking can also involve out-of-category organizations as benchmarks – i.e. an organization that may be engaged in very different primary activities, and perhaps, even have different objectives. From Joseph Blakeman of the Urban Transportation Studies of the University of Wisconsin-Milwaukee (USA), we learn of how Remington, a shotgun shell manufacturer in the United States, got ideas on how to make shinier shells, from Maybelline's lip stick containers.

7. *Functional benchmarking*: In functional benchmarking, what matters is how somebody else carries out a particular function (for example, payroll, budgeting, procurement, etc.) regardless of whether that organization belongs to a different sector of the economy.

    Functional benchmarking is particularly useful for monopolistic organizations that carry out unique services, which may not readily find similar organizations to benchmark. Even if an organization's primary activities (and even goals) are unique, its payroll function, inventory management, procurement and other functional activities may have many things to learn from how somebody else handles those activities.

8. *International benchmarking*: This is a special kind of external benchmarking, where the benchmark is outside the national boundaries. Both Ford and Xerox in the cases above did "international" benchmarking, since these American firms used companies in another country, Japan, as benchmarks.

    The need for international benchmarking will usually be strong in our DCs. For example, Nigeria can use the Brazilian electronic voting system as a benchmark for improving its own electoral system. Peru can seek to improve its governance system by using the e-gov system of Estonia as a benchmark. Mexico's education ministry can try to find what propels the high literacy rate of Vietnam; and so on.

<u>**Case 89:**</u>   <u>**Interesting Initiatives From Tajikistan**</u>

Many DCs may want to take a look at how Tajikistan manages it civil service. According to the IDA, Tajikistan in 2010 filled 2,514 vacancies in its civil service (below the political level positions) through a competitive recruitment process. This represented 82% of the 3,065 vacancies filled. Prior to 2006, there was no competition-based recruitment system in the country. Equally interesting was the country's new civil service register, listing all approved posts, grades and their occupants, which had become automated and now accessible to 47 government bodies.

(Source: For more details, please see IDA's report, "IDA at Work: Building Strong Institutions for Sustained Results")

In the private sector, international benchmarking is taken for granted, because with globalization, businesses face pressures not just from local competitors, but increasingly from global competitors.

9. *Peer Review*: Sometimes, governments or their institutions can peer-review themselves on a voluntary basis. For example, in the United States, the National State Auditors Association (NSAA) carries out external peer reviews on its members every three years to ensure that their audits satisfy the auditing standards. Another example involving some DCs is the African Peer Review Mechanism (APRM).

Case 90: **African Peer Review Mechanism (APRM)**

The APRM is a mutually agreed instrument founded in 2003, which member states of the African Union (AU) voluntarily acceded to, as a self-monitoring mechanism. Membership of the APRM is voluntary and open to all member countries of the AU. APRM's primary purpose is to foster the adoption of policies, standards and practices that lead to political stability, economic growth, sustainable development and accelerated sub-regional and continental economic integration through sharing of experiences and reinforcement of successful practices. A typical Review Mission may last for two to three weeks, excluding the preparatory team meetings and the writing of the Country Review Report.

Benefits of Benchmarking in the Public Sector

Some of the benefits that benchmarking can bring to institutional performance include the following:

1. *Governance improvement*: Any government leader in the DCs truly interested in national progress, will be very pleased with what it can learn from how similar leaders are strengthening their institutions.

    Benchmarking will usually open government eyes to where it needs to reform itself. For example, if benchmarking shows that state government "A" spends 70% of its annual budget as staff salaries, while it is an average of 30% for the other states in the country, then state "A" will need to ask why!

Case 91: **Several Benchmarking Prospects From IDA**

From the International Development Association (IDA), the World Bank's Fund for the Poorest, we get the following examples of what the DCs can gain from collaborative benchmarking:

- In Nepal: Electronic bidding in the Department of Roads first introduced in 2007 has been extended to other line ministries in 2012 - any procurement over Rs2 million (approximately $23,000) must come under e-bidding.

- TSA in Nepal: Over 12,000 (of 14,000) separate government bank accounts have been closed and consolidated into the Single Treasury Account (TSA). The TSA coverage in real time, of the revenues and expenditures of government in 2012 was 95% for expenditure and 98% for revenue

- Performance Evaluation in Kenya: The Performance Contract Department in the Office of the Prime Minister evaluates the performance of public agencies and issues public reports.

  Waiting times for various services dropped sharply as follows:

  - *Passports:*   *from 60 to 10 days*
  - *National ID cards*   *from 90 to 18 days*
  - *business licenses*   *from 30 to 1 day*

- In Armenia: An Electronic Document Management System (EDMS), which was piloted in 2008, had been rolled-out to the entire civil service of Armenia, including all ministries and 10 regional governors' offices. As at the time of IDA report, the system had:

  - *Cut processing time for incoming correspondence within the entities by about 12 times;*

  - *Cut the communication within the government (which once would last a full business day in Yerevan and about three business days with the regions) to only a few seconds;*

  - *Dramatically reduced government expenditure on courier and postal services; and so on*

  (Source: IDA, the International Development Association)

2. <u>*A tool for creating pressure on public agencies*</u>: In the private sector, the pressure for improvement comes from market forces, which ordinarily are absent in the public sector. This absence explains why the public sector tends to be inefficient, wasteful and corrupt.

   Government can use benchmarking (as we saw under OM) to create a similar pressure for improvement in the public sector – for example, among schools, hospitals, police units, courts of law, licensing offices, tax offices, and local authorities. Benchmarking of similar services will reveal the relative performances of the service providers. This inevitably will start leaving a track, which is a powerful incentive for improvement – because everybody behaves differently, when they know they are leaving a track.

3. <u>*Leapfrogging*</u>: By seeking to launch into where the benchmarks are, a DC can save itself the trials, mistakes, frustrations, costs and pains that characterized the evolutions of those other nations to their present positions! In this way, benchmarking will enable a progress-minded DC to leapfrog.

4. <u>*Making government citizens-sensitive*</u>: As we saw in Slice B, when we looked at the political nature of institutions, public servants, in many DCs, are often in their own world, driven sometimes, almost completely by self-interests that are in conflict with public interests. We saw several examples of this in Slice B, for example, from the open declaration of the Nigerian President, Olusegun Obasanjo, of how the interests of his nation's civil service were in conflict with national interests. Benchmarking can be a powerful tool for focusing the activities of public servants on things that matter to citizens, by generating the data that can build up the momentum and pressure coalition for reform.

It can generally improve awareness of citizens and stakeholders on how an organization stands relative to others – for example, in terms of products, services, processes, results and outcomes. This insight will tend to foster better management, by putting citizens and other stakeholders in a better position to begin to hold their leaders accountable.

5. *Tool for improving user choice*: Notice also that by creating citizens awareness on how an organization stands relative to others, benchmarking will put citizens in a better position to make informed choices (for example, on which federal school to choose over another).

6. *It is not always about copying*: Benchmarking is not just about copying what others are doing. Sometimes we are even able to improve what we observe from others – because even if an organization is the best in its class, it can never mean that what it is doing cannot be improved further! In fact, the technique of reverse engineering (we saw earlier) proves that even the wonderful product of today can be further improved!

   More importantly, what we learn from benchmarking can trigger other ideas and game-changers, even in unrelated areas.

Challenges of Benchmarking Government Operations

There are many possible challenges that can face benchmarking in a typical DC:

1. *Lack of incentive to improve*: In the private sector, organizations are usually under the constant pressure of market forces; and they must continue to innovate in whatever they are doing, so as to remain in business. Therefore, productivity tools such as benchmarking are taken for granted.

   In the public sector on the other hand, especially in the DCs, there is usually no such pressure for improvement. Often nobody bothers about efficiency or productivity, as long as procedures are followed. There are therefore little incentives to improve things! Also, people often get appointed into government positions in the DCs, not on the basis of merit, but more likely because of their tribes, or connections to powerful persons. So, why should the officials so appointed bother about benchmarking – to highlight how relatively unsuitable they are for the positions they occupy? Instead, their interests are more likely to be on things that will facilitate any "returns" (payback) they are obliged to make to the godfathers that influenced their appointments! It is these godfathers that will also intervene on their behalf, if they need protection! What makes a big difference is when external factors (such as revenue plunge or looming privatization) put pressure for improvement.

2. *Political concerns*: Many governments and their agencies will be cold towards benchmarking for fear that the results can be falsified, or that the opposition can make political capital out of anything unfavorable.

3. *Cultural & administrative differences*: There can be strong variations in the ways countries, states and localities organize their administrative functions and processes, and measure results. For example, the administrative structures may vary; the education structures may be different; so can the judicial system; and so on. If we have to benchmark across such institutional environments, the first step will be the important task of creating standard definitions, protocols, and measures from their dissimilar environments.

   It means that if we are using benchmarking to foster competition, or to identify those at the top and bottom of a performance table, it is vital to ensure that the performance measures are truly comparable, so that we neither cause the stakeholders to misinterpret the results, nor unfairly put unrealistic pressure on those disadvantaged by the results. For example, two schools may not be truly comparable (even if they are both federal government schools), if one is in a depressed area (that can only attract disadvantaged pupils) while the location of the other allows it to select only the brightest pupils, perhaps through competitive national admission tests.

If we recognize that our benchmarking parameters can unfairly put some organizations at a disadvantage, we must design the study to take the differences into account; and/or limit the distribution of the results to knowledgeable stakeholders, who can take the factors at play into account, in interpreting the differences.

4. *Constraints of confidentiality*: In the private sector, some organizations can refuse to participate in benchmarking for fear of giving away their trade secrets. This can also happen in the public sector, where some governments may be reluctant to open up their operations and data for benchmarking, for "security" and other reasons.

5. *Gaming*: When benchmarking is likely to put some of the parties in a negative light, those not favored may try to "game" their scores, to make them appear more favorable than they really are. We looked at "gaming" earlier, under OM.

How To Create The Appetite For Benchmarking

Like all other reform measures, benchmarking is most successful and beneficial when there is a hunger for it. In the private sector, this hunger comes from the market forces, which tend to put every organization on their toes.

Here are some possible situations that can create the thirst for benchmarking (and even other reforms) in government operations.

1. *Competition between agencies*: When there is competition between government agencies, such as schools, licensing offices, courts of law, and so on; the agencies that find themselves at the bottom of the performance table will be under pressure to know why others are doing better, while the agencies at the top will strive to remain there. The thirst for benchmarking will shoot up!

2. *Competition from private service providers*: Sometimes (often due to budgetary pressures) public-sector workers are forced to compete with private-sector service providers, to prevent the public services in question from being outsourced. The units under threat will likely begin to benchmark. We shall look at this kind of competition in details in Slice G.

3. *Awards*: In other to improve services generally, government through the CRT can institute some awards for agencies that are performing well – while reprimanding those agencies at the bottom. Those at the bottom will be eager to understudy those doing well (benchmark) to improve.

   For example, there are several awards by various governments in the United States, which inspire agencies and other organizations to improve their performances (and of course to benchmark), for example in areas such as:

   a. *Academic*: Best students performances in national tests; Students assessments results; and so on;
   b. *ICT*: Extent of migration of services online; quality/functionality of official website, and so on;

Chapter 18

18. Striving To Be Outcome-Focused

"If a service provider is to be responsible for achieving the outcomes, it must have control over the process and the method of delivering those outcomes."

(James North in "Outcome-Based Contracting Is On The Up: Who's Doing It, Why, And What You Need To Know About It", 13 May 2014)

Topics Covered in This Chapter:

- Introduction: Outcome-Focused Governance
- The public sector is obsessed with procedures
- The private sector is obsessed with results
- What About Results-Focused Governance
- And Even Outcome-Focused Governance
- Flavors of outcome-based contracting
- The benefits of outcome-focused policymaking
- The challenges of outcome-focused policymaking
- Going forward

Introduction: Outcome-Focused Governance

According to a report by James North, the Washington State Lottery (WSL) in the United States, for many years, paid its advertising agency a fixed percentage of the contract value (for example, 15%) as fees – covering specified tasks, such as advertising services, production activities, printing and media buys. That was until WSL overhauled the contract structure to link the fees directly to the number of lottery tickets sold!

What the WSL did by the new contract structure was effectively "outcome-focused contracting"! We can expect the new arrangement to force the advertising agency to become more innovative to make its adverts more "effective", rather than merely carrying out agreed activities.

This Chapter looks at "outcome-focused" policymaking; which is one of the new behavior-shaping practices that are helping to strengthen governance institutions.

The Public Sector Is Obsessed With Procedures

The public sector tends to be obsessed with rules, procedures and due process, perhaps in a bid to guard against the misuse of public funds. In particular, in an environment where corruption is widespread – as in many DCs – the preoccupation is with ensuring that bureaucrats follow due process. Hardly does any bureaucrat get blamed for poor results, as long as the rules and procedures have been followed!

In fact, even good results can be spurned, if the processes leading to them violated approved guidelines or procedures. Kanu Agabi, Nigeria's former Attorney-General and Presidential adviser on ethics & good governance, put it this way:

> "… And then there is the due process rule. This means that it is not enough to achieve the results desired by law. We must achieve those results using the procedure laid down by law. Only when that procedure has been followed can the law accept the results"

Typically, the bureaucracy becomes very comfortable in its day-to-day operations, with just following its rules and due process, without bothering that it may not be solving any problems, nor making any useful impacts!

The Private Sector Is Obsessed With Results

Unlike the public sector, the private sector tends to be focused on results – with the operators always looking at how to improve the bottom line (the profit, return to shareholders, return on investment, and so on). James North uses Rolls Royce as an example:

Case 92:   **Rolls Royce Engine Pricing Model**

> Over 20 years ago, Rolls Royce transformed its support and maintenance contracting model for engines used in commercial jets. Instead of charging customers for repairs, maintenance and the provision of spare parts, customers paid a fee per hour based on the number of hours of flying time for an engine.
>
> The company apparently recognized that directing the contractual arrangement to the real underlying need of the customer – keeping a jet in the air – could deliver greater satisfaction to the customer whilst at the same time reducing inefficiencies and increase its own revenue. This contractual structure has since become the industry standard in commercial aviation.
>
> --
>
> *(Source: James North, 2014)*

In the private sector, people pay for results, not necessarily for activities or even "efforts" – except of course, to the extent that the results people see embody the efforts that went into those results. As an example:

1. You will always hear of the "bottom line" – i.e. such things as <u>profits</u>, <u>dividend declared</u>, <u>return on investment</u>, <u>return on assets</u>, and so on! Nobody really worries about the procedures used, the number of meetings held, or hours of hard work, except to the extent that all those become reflected in the bottom-line.

2. Manufacturers of goods are increasingly required to specify the performance standards for which they guarantee their goods. Many manufactured equipment come with minimum

performance specifications – such as power output ratings for electricity generators, fuel consumption ratings for cars, and so on.

3. Even at the level of the private individual, the man, who wants to buy a ram in the market, buys the ram on its own merit – i.e. according to what he sees (the result)! He is not bothered about the efforts that might have gone into rearing the ram, except of course to the extent that those efforts are reflected in the fowl he sees!

What About Results-Focused Governance

Being *results*-focused in government operations means that the bureaucracy will constantly be checking to see how far the results from its individual programs are meeting set targets. Some examples of this would include:

1. The number of new communities that have benefited from portable water for a given budget – and an explanation for any deviation from the set targets;

2. The number of patients treated in a primary healthcare program for a given budget, and an explanation for any deviation from the set targets;

3. The number of unemployed youths that have been trained on entrepreneurship skills, under a given budget, and an explanation for any deviation from the set targets; and so on

In the same way, being results-focused in our budgeting will require that we regularly define measurable targets for our budgets, and subsequently demand of the MDAs, what they have achieved with those budgets. It will require that they support whatever reports they present, with independently audited accounts.

For example, in the healthcare industry, there are now various arrangements that allow governments in varying degrees, not only to increasingly pay only for results, but also to even pass some of their risks to the contracted providers.

From William D. Savedoff, we get the following examples:

1. *Fee-for-Service* by which healthcare providers are paid an agreed fee for each service they render to a patient

2. *Case-Based Payments* by which healthcare providers are paid an agreed fee for each case that is treated, not minding the variations in type or intensity.

3. *Capitation* by which healthcare providers are paid a fixed amount for each person enrolled in their care and are expected to render all services required by that individual during the period of enrolment

And Even Outcome-Focused Governance

While becoming results-focused would be a big achievements for many DCs, some governments across the world are already going beyond that and becoming increasingly *outcome*-focused. Being *outcome*-focused means defining the desired outcomes (not just results) and then hinging contracts obligations on their attainment. It means, for example, means that we are no longer merely interested in the "number of *youths that have been trained to become employable*". Rather we should now be evaluating the training on the basis of the number that has started working after the training, and the number still on their jobs after six months of the training – or after one year, two years, and so on. As an illustration, let us see from the Beeck Center, how Australia paid its workforce development consultants.

<u>Case 93:</u>　　　　**<u>Australia's Employment Funding Model</u>**

Funding to providers in the Australian Employment Funding Model is spread across three types of payment tied to individual job seekers:

- Upfront service payments to fund the minimum services required by Australia's Department of Employment for each job seeker;

- Placement payments for each job seeker successfully placed in a job; and

- "Employment outcomes" payments after 13 and 26 weeks of successful employment.

Each of these payments is weighted based on a set of criteria. For example:

- Job seekers are separated into different "streams" based on their assessed level of disadvantage and work-readiness, with payments more heavily weighted to the more disadvantaged streams;

- The length of unemployment is measured, with payments more heavily weighted toward job seekers with longer periods of unemployment; and

- After a job placement, the length of employment is measured, with payments more heavily weighted as length of employment increases.

(Adapted from: Georgetown University (The Beeck Center for Social Impact & Innovation): Funding For Results: A Review of Government Outcomes-Based Agreements, November 2014)

Being <u>*outcome*</u>-focused forces the bureaucracy to become sensitive to the ultimate social impacts that government programs are making. It involves a fundamental evaluation of whether the outcomes of policies meet the original policy objectives. Consider the case of the Tennessee Department of Children's Services, reported by the Beeck Center for Social Impact and Innovation:

<u>Case 94:</u>　　　　**<u>Tennessee's Children in State Custody</u>**

According to the Beeck Center, the Tennessee Department of Children's Services (TDCS) in the State of Tennessee (in the United States) faced a crisis in May 2000, of meeting the needs of the State's most vulnerable children: those in state custody. At the time, the TDCS contracted with nearly 100 different service providers to care for these children. The state paid the providers on a "per diem", "per child" basis. This meant that the longer the child stayed in a facility or received a service, the more funding the provider received from the state – implying that there were really no incentives for providers to act swiftly to move children out of the system and into permanent homes.

No wonder then (as reported by the Beeck Center) many of the children were languishing in emergency shelters for periods of six months or more. Others were constantly shuffled between multiple facilities and family placements. More than one in three children in the state system had been living within the system without a permanent home for over two years. These children had little hope for reunification with family, adoption, or even finding appropriate foster care. The TDCS then considered an outcome-based system for managing the problem, which would align child welfare funding with each provider's ability to quickly place the foster-care children into permanent homes.

In the end, it came up with three relevant measures:

- The number of days children spent in providers' care in the fiscal year;
- The number of children that left providers' care to permanent placements, including adoption; and
- The number of children that returned to providers' care after previously exiting to permanent placements

When a provider met a pre-agreed baseline performance goal, it received a share of the state's savings, and if it performed below the baseline, it would reimburse the state for cost overages. This created an incentive for the providers to focus on each child's long-term placement. They also now had flexibility in the methods they used in attaining the goals, because they needed freedom to innovate and be creative in making the required outcomes.

With this new system, the TDCS by 2010, had cut in half the average time a child spent in state care – from over 22 to 14 months.

Adapted from: Georgetown University, The Beeck Center for Social Impact & Innovation: Funding For Results: A Review of Government Outcomes-Based Agreements, Nov 2014

The Advance National Open Apprenticeship Training Scheme (ANOATS) of Nigeria's National Directorate of Employment (NDE) can be similarly made more outcome-focused.

Case 95: **Efforts of Nigeria's NDE**

The NDE is the federal government agency with the responsibility for creating employment for Nigerian youths. According to Mr. Edem Duke, one of NDE's State Coordinators, the NDE had a program (the ANOATS) designed to enhance proficiency, add more value to the skills already acquired by the participants, and help them start their own businesses after the three months training period. The training covered areas such as computer maintenance and repair, electrical installation, website design, auto-mechanics and others.

Now, to make this program more outcome-focused in line with the principles of this Chapter, the NDE can further link the consultants' payments to parameters such as:

- The number of trainees that successfully start their own businesses after the training,
- The number that remain in business for specified time benchmarks, and
- The number that successfully service their loans

The consultant should also be given the flexibility to design the program for optimum achievement of these targets, including even allowing each consultant to determine the skills their participants should be trained on – based on the skills the consultants believe the economy needs.

(Information on Mr Edem Duke downloaded from the NDE website, May 2016)

Flavors Of Outcome-Based Contracting

For a DC that may be interested, there are presently many flavors of outcome-focused contracting initiatives, such as:

1. Pay for Success (PFS) contracting;
2. Social Impact Bonds (SIB);
3. Pay for performance (PFP or P4P) contracting;
4. Results-Based Financing (RBF);
5. Performance-Based Financing (PBF);
6. Performance-Based Contracting (PBC);
7. Payment by results (PBR); and so on

The underlying principles are almost the same, and practitioners sometimes even use some of their names interchangeably!

Here are some highlights on PFS and SIB:

1. *Pay for Success (PFS) contracting*: This approach will enable a government to pay only for programs that successfully deliver the desired outcomes. As explained by the Beeck Center, government typically sets a specific and measurable outcome that it wants achieved (such as a specific reduction in asthma-based hospitalizations, teen pregnancies, or homeless populations). It then contracts to pay an external organization—sometimes called an intermediary—if, and only if, the organization accomplishes the desired outcome, by an agreed future date. A third-party evaluator determines whether the outcome has been achieved.

    Often, the intermediary designs the services necessary for achieving the agreed outcome, and turns to investors to bear the upfront cost by contributing the working capital needed to implement those services. The investors are incentivized by charitable reasons or by the prospects of a big return on investment. If the outcome is achieved, government releases the pre-agreed amount. Payments can rise for performance that exceeds the minimum target, up to an agreed maximum payment level.

However, if the outcome is not achieved, government is not bound to pay, and the investors do not get repaid with public funds.

2. *Social Impact Bonds (SIB)*: This is similar to the PFS, and is mostly used for financing social innovation. As explained by Hanna Azemati et al, government under the most common SIB model, contracts with a private intermediary to obtain social services. Then government pays the intermediary if the performance targets are achieved. Payment is funded at least partially, from the cost savings that government achieves through successful outcomes.

Performance is measured by comparing the outcomes of individuals referred to the intermediary, against the outcomes of a control group. If the intermediary fails to achieve the minimum performance target, government does not pay. Payments typically rise for performance that exceeds the minimum target, up to an agreed maximum payment level.

The intermediary obtains operating funds by raising capital from independent, commercial or philanthropic investors who provide up-front capital in exchange for a share of the government payments that become available if the performance targets are met. The intermediary uses these operating funds to contract with service providers to deliver the interventions necessary to meet the performance targets.

The New York City's Rikers Island prison project, as highlighted by the Hanna Azemati team, can serve as a good illustration:

Case 96:   <u>New York City's SIB For Rikers Island Prison</u>

According to the Hanna Azemati and team, New York City established the first SIB in the United States. The initiative provided services to 16- to 18-year-olds who were jailed at Rikers Island, with the aim of reducing recidivism and its related budgetary and social costs. Services were delivered to approximately 3,000 adolescent men per year from September 2012 to August 2015. MDRC, a prominent non-profit research organization, served as the intermediary, overseeing day-to-day implementation of the project and managing the two non-profit service providers who were delivering the intervention. Goldman Sachs funded the project's operations through a $9.6 million loan to MDRC. The city was supposed to make payments ranging from $4.8 million (if recidivism was reduced by 8.5%) to $11.7 million (if recidivism was reduced by 20%). Bloomberg Philanthropies guaranteed the first $7.2 million of loan repayment.

(Adapted from: Hanna Azemati, Michael Belinsky, Ryan Gillette, Jeffrey Liebman, Alina Sellman, & Angela Wyse: Social Impact Bonds: Lessons Learned So Far, John F. Kennedy School of Government, Harvard University)

The Benefits of Outcome-Focused Policymaking

In general, we can expect the benefits of outcome-focused policy-making to include the following:

1. *Responsible public stewardship*: Outcome-based contracts fund outcomes, not the activities of bureaucrats. They can thus be a powerful tool for focusing the activities of public servants on the things that matter to citizens – things that can make real impact on their lives and communities. If the needs and views of stakeholders are taken into account

while designing an outcome-focused policy, the end-results will tend to address the outcomes that really matter to them.

2. *Increased transparency and accountability for results*: Outcome-based contracts help to ensure that public funds are spent for agreed outcomes, which may prevent budgets from being looted. Most outcome-based contracts require little or no government payment unless the projects have achieved their required outcomes.

3. *Increased potential for innovation*: Once government defines outcomes for a service provider, and tie payment to the achievement of those outcomes, the service provider must in turn be given the freedom to pursue the targets innovatively. This means that the service provider must be allowed room to innovate and become creative. Therefore, one important benefit of outcome-based contracts is that they generate innovations in public service provision – including innovations for which there would otherwise not have been any incentives.

4. *Innovation in Tight Fiscal Times*: Indeed, as pointed out by Hanna Azemati and team, outcome-focused contracting offers government an answer to a question all policymakers face in difficult fiscal times – how they can keep innovating and investing in promising new solutions, when they cannot even afford to pay for everything they are already doing! Outcome-focused contracting provides such an opportunity – because it transfers the burden and risks of innovating to the private service providers, who must strive to innovate to be able to achieve the agreed outcomes, and optimize their profits. Meanwhile, government while carefully noting the innovations, will only pay if the outcome is achieved.

5. *Institutional strengthening*: All these translate to stronger governance institutions, compared to the conventional approaches, which fund activities that can be endless but with negligible social impacts.

6. *Potential for longer-term benefits*: While the focus of an outcome-focused contract is on the achievement of the specified outcomes, these outcomes can themselves be predictive of longer-term benefits:

    c. If outcome-focused policymaking leads to stronger governance institutions (as we saw above) all the other benefits of strong institutions will follow!

    d. As a specific example pointed out by Hanna Azemati and team, if outcome-focused investments in prenatal healthcare create the immediate outcomes of improved infant healthcare, improved maternal healthcare, and lower healthcare costs, these may in turn create longer-term benefits, such as reduced future spending on special education, reduced crime during teenage years, and increased adult earnings!

7. *Lower administrative burdens and costs*: In an outcome-focused contract, the contractor usually has the freedom to innovate to achieve the required outcomes. This also means that government no longer needs to micromanage the project (worry about the day-to-day project administration), as well as the resources that micromanaging the project would have required.

8. *Private-public convergence*: Outcome-based contracts create a meeting point for the private sector (which is driven by profit) and the public sector (driven by social good). In an outcome-based contract, government (after defining the required outcomes) does not

impose prescriptive process specifications. This frees the private service provider to pursue innovative and cost-effective solutions.

This can be a 'win-win' situation for both parties:

a. First, in a typical outcome-based project (such as an SIB contract), the better the outcome delivered by the contractor (over and above an agreed threshold), the more profit the contractor makes. So the private contractor, driven by the quest for profits, is incentivized to deliver the greatest outcome possible (which will also be a "win" for government)!

b. Government is also able to leverage the private-sector's expertise, resources, creativity and vibrancy (all of which it usually lacks) in delivering social services – and (sometimes) only uses a part of what it saves from the improved outcome, to compensate the private contractor.

e. Notice also how this kind of arrangement makes the private contractor implicitly more responsive to social needs!

The Challenges of Outcome-Focused Policymaking

The common challenges of outcome-focused policymaking include the following:

1. Outcome-focused contracts are complex and novel. Structuring them requires rigorous data analysis and other preparatory works – and (as noted by the DFID) good capabilities in design, management and negotiation, not just on the side of government, but also on the side of funders and intermediaries.

2. It is often difficult to find a project with a convincing probability of success.

3. It may not always be easy to find contractors willing to accept the risks of contracts, where payments are tied to outcomes!

4. The pool of available charitable (or philanthropic) funds is limited.

5. The outcomes may take a while to manifest, and (as pointed out by Hanna Azemati et al) contractors may be concerned about future governments reneging on success-based commitments made today. This can be a major issue in the DCs, where political successions tend to be very adversarial.

6. Confusions can sometimes arise as to whether an outcome has resulted from an intervention (the contract) or by other socioeconomic factors, or even by chance.

7. Contrary to the excitement about government using its savings from outcome-focused interventions to pay for those contracts, it is often difficult to find interventions that truly pay for themselves!

Going Forward

Notwithstanding these challenges, governments across the world are finding outcome-focused contracts very attractive, which is why such contracts are gaining popularity. Here are some guides for a DC that wants to become outcome-focused:

1. The starting point is a basic shift in mind-set from the traditional transactional pricing model.

2. Hanna Azemati et al have identified several types of interventions that appear to be getting the most attention across multiple jurisdictions:

   a. Projects that aim to reduce recidivism among those released from prison or jail;
   b. Services for at-risk youth such as those aging out of the foster care and juvenile justice systems;
   c. Homelessness prevention services;
   d. Prenatal, early childhood, and preschool services;
   e. Preventive health care interventions such as those for asthma or diabetes;
   f. Home-based services designed to keep elders out of nursing homes;
   g. Employment/workforce development services;

3. It is good to be guided by an experienced consultant, even when a government MDA has officials experienced in outcome-focused contracting.

4. In identifying what projects to undertake, a very good idea could be to solicit suggestions from the public. According to Hanna Azemati et al, Massachusetts and New York (both States in the United States) in this regard, issued requests for information (RFIs) in an effort to collect suggestions from the public, for outcome-focused projects.

5. From Hanna Azemati et al, we learn of how the same State of Massachusetts managed the concerns about future governments reneging on success-based commitments made today: The State set up a sinking fund to steadily fund the payments over the life of a contract, rather than requiring a future legislature to appropriate payments.

6. If a DC finds it difficult to get contractors or other third party philanthropic investors willing to take up a project's risks, government may consider sharing some of the risks, at least initially, to help institute a culture of outcome-focused projects in the country.

Slice E: Leveraging Technology To Create Strong Governance Institutions

Technology presents an exciting window of opportunity to the DCs for leapfrogging their institutional weaknesses, and cutting off the institutional learning curves that the developed economies had to pass through. This Slice looks at this, and also attempts to show why every DC must strive to become a part of the surging global digital economy. In general:

1. Technology has been the greatest economic change agent of this century, which has powered many national economic transformations, including stunning third-world economic development miracles.

2. Technological advancements can be highly disruptive of institutions. As we shall see shortly from Geoff Colvin (Fortune's senior editor-at-large), every major technological turning point in the last 200 years created major social and economic disruptions. And the world is on the verge of another technological turning point, which may be the most disruptive ever, and which is expected to stretch governance institutions (even in the developed nations) to their limits.

3. This latest technological revolution will be catching many DCs in a pitiable state of unpreparedness – with poor infrastructure, weak institutions, poverty, illiteracy, and crippling social tensions, wars and conflicts. What becomes of each DC in the unfolding dispensation will significantly depend on the strategy it adopts today towards technology – which can lead to important opportunities for leapfrogging poverty and underdevelopment, as well as severe consequences for failing to become proactive right away.

4. The political leadership in the typical DC still sees globalization as something that concerns only the advanced nations, unaware that it is already everywhere, and perhaps, even quietly eating up their poor economies into further poverty!

We shall loot at all these issues in this Slice.

19. Leapfrogging Poor Institutions Through E-Governance

The most striking thing about Estonia's e-government system isn't the way it allows anyone to file taxes, vote, or receive a medical prescription, all in a matter of minutes and from a single website. The technology behind it is smart, but not magical. The real surprise is that more countries have yet to build similar systems of their own.

(Leonid Bershidsky in the article, Envying Estonia's Digital Government, Bloomberg View, Mar 4, 2015)

Topics Covered in This Chapter:

- Introduction
- What is e-government?
- Examples of e-gov applications
- The concerns about e-gov
- A Lucky Opportunity For Leapfrogging

Introduction: What Is e-Government?

In the early 1990s, Estonia was just one of the poor Baltic States that gained independence from the old Soviet Union, perhaps even the most "backward" technologically. It was struggling with all kinds of problems, including high inflation, food and fuel shortages, and an unfriendly "big" neighbor.

However, for many years now, Estonians have not been required to physically visit their banks, because they are conducting 98% of banking transactions via the internet! They are unconcerned with what time their banks open or close, or where they are located, since the internet bank is open 24 hours a day. The expression "going to the bank" has all but disappeared from their diction, because an Estonian would rather just "log in" to the bank!

The widespread use of internet banking (e-banking) in Estonia is just one aspect of the stunning transformation of Estonia into the digital economy! The most striking thing about this phenomenal breakthrough is not that the people are today doing almost everything online! The real surprise as Leonid Bershidsky points out, is that more DCs are yet to build similar systems of their own!

Case 97: The Estonian e-gov Model

When Estonia started planning its online governance system, it had to adopt a simple, scalable architecture, because it lacked the resources for a huge centralised system. Many nations are today coming to study that model – which Estonia now calls the X-Road!

(See Vahtra-Hellat, Anu (2015) & Estonia public website, Estonia.eu)

The good news for our DCs is that technology (for example, e-governance) can allow them to leapfrog weak institutions, and cut off the institutional learning curves that the developed economies (including even Estonia) had to pass through. That is why every DC should today pay very close attention to it.

E-government (or simply, e-gov) stands for <u>electronic</u> government, and refers to the extensive use of information and communications technology (ICT) in governance. Some people like to call it <u>online</u> government, e-<u>state</u>, <u>Internet</u> government, or even <u>digital</u> government. The Research Foundation of the State University of New York defines it as follows:

> "The use of information technology to support government operations, engage citizens, and provide government services"

Here is something that may surprise many DCs: e-gov is one area in which small nations are recording surprising upsets against the "big" developed nations of Europe and America. For example,

1. Brazil is a leading nation in electronic voting system (EVS). Lin and Espinoza (2014) point out that since 2000, EVS has been the only voting method in Brazil's general elections. Neither the United States, nor Japan, nor any of the advanced European countries, has matched Brazil's experience in this area.

2. The United Nations (UN) conducts an e-government survey every two years that assesses the levels of use of the technology among its 193 member States. The report helps to guide member nations on how to take advantage of this new, powerful governance tool.

    For the 2014 survey, two Asian "Tigers" topped the world – South Korea (1st) and Singapore (3rd) as shown in the Case that follows! These countries have overtaken the United States, Canada, Europe and Japan in e-governance! In fact, since the inception of this survey in 2003, South Korea has consistently led the world as the topmost e-gov nation.

<u>Case 98:</u>　　　<u>UN's Top 10 E-Government Nations, 2014</u>

Below are the world's top nations in e-governance, based on the United Nations E-Government Survey for 2014:

- 1st　Republic of Korea
- 2nd　Australia
- 3rd　Singapore
- 4th　France
- 5th　Netherlands
- 6th　Japan
- 7th　United States of America
- 8th　United Kingdom of Great Britain and Northern Ireland

- 9th   New Zealand
- 10th   Finland

(Source: the United Nations E-Government Survey, 2014)

Later in this Slice, we shall peep deeper into how the forward-thinking government of South Korea is positioning the country as the emerging global technological powerhouse of the future.

As another example, more than 700 persons from 36 different nations have visited Estonia to study its phenomenal expertise and rise in e-government! According to Estonia's e-Governance Academy (eGA) a non-governmental, non-profit organization that shares Estonia's experience in the areas of e-government, e-democracy, and ICT education, these visitors come even from developed economies, such as Canada and Japan!

In general, e-gov is today powering the following key functions of government:

1. <u>Services</u>: It enables government to deliver its usual services "online" to those governed, so that they do not first have to come to its offices. For example, it allows us to do business with our government from anywhere we may be – at home, anywhere else in the country, and even outside the country!

2. <u>Democracy</u>: It has ushered in a new era of active citizens engagement, where government's relationship with those governed, is shifting from a "government-to-us" approach, to a "government-with-us" approach! For example, technology is creating opportunities for greater citizen participation in governance (citizens engagement), which is where the future of public service delivery is headed!

3. <u>Administration</u>: It has allowed nations to create integrated administrative governance systems (with streamlined processes, including electronic records) that work seamlessly behind the scene to provide superior service to citizens, while minimizing human errors and corruption.

Examples of e-Gov Applications

A good way to explain e-gov is to highlight some of the growing number of e-applications that nations are rolling out. Note the numerous references made to Estonia: This is because Estonia's e-gov achievements can serve as an inspiration to our DCs. The data on Estonia has been based on information from both Estonia's government website [estonia.eu, accessed November 2015] and the Estonia's eGA.

- According to estonia.eu, as at the beginning of 2012, almost 90% of Estonians already had such identification cards. The Estonian ID card serves as an identity document and, within the European Union, also as a travel document. In addition to its physical use, the card is also used as proof of ID when utilizing online services. In other words, the ID card is the key to almost every innovative e-service in Estonia.

   This is an important lesson for many DCs that tend to proliferate parallel identity systems. For example, the Nigerian nation has various citizens' ID systems, one for elections, another for driving licenses, another for the banking system, another for immigration offices, and so on!

Some of the most common e-gov applications that nations are rolling out include.

1. *e-ID*: This serves as a basic identity tool, for utilizing online services, including e-banking, e-voting, e-tickets, e-health, and so on. For every transaction of a citizen, it verifies that the identity information presented is not fake; for example, that it belongs to the that particular citizen; not a non-citizen, and not a deceased person. The system uses reliable biometrics information to identify citizens, including facial recognition techniques.

2. *e-voting*: This is an area in which institutions in our DCs can potentially reap huge benefits from technology. It takes the traditional ballot paper process online, in a way that brings answers to many of the problems bedeviling the electoral institution in the DCs. It can validate voters biometrically, guide them audio-visually through the voting process, transmit and collate all the votes instantly, keep flawless records, and easily make those records available wherever they may be needed.

- Brazil is setting the pace in EVS, which was used as the only voting method for Brazil's 2000, 2002, 2004, and 2006 elections. Since 2005, everyone in Estonia has had the opportunity to vote in this way, according to estonia.eu. The number of e-votes and voter turnout in recent elections indicate the positive effect of the e-voting system on general voter turnout.

E-voting limits the role of electoral violence, including voter intimidation, and the snatching of electoral materials.

<u>Case 99:</u>   <u>Voter Intimidation In Nigeria</u>

Voter intimidation and electoral violence have become such a big challenge to Nigeria's democracy. For example,

- During the nation's 2015 elections that brought President Muhammadu Buhari to power, many Nigerian voters living in the northern part of the country (and who had naturally registered there as voters), had to flee to other states, to escape the violence that was being threatened. Most of those voters would ultimately have been unable to vote, because the country's cumbersome electoral system required people to vote only from the voting places that registered them – unless they had been able to go to designated offices to transfer their names to new voting locations (something that needed to be done way before the election day).

- When those elections finally arrived, violence was not in short supply! For example, even Mikaila Abdulahi, the electoral commissioner for Kano state (a state in the north-western part of the country), was burnt alive together with his entire family, by a mysterious fire!

- Other electoral officials have apparently taken note of Mikaila's fate! For example, the nation's electoral body has since admitted that its officials were knowingly registering underage voters, to avoid being attacked by the communities that presented them for registration; and that its officials were even becoming reluctant to be posted to those violence-prone parts of the country.

(See Punch & Daily Post newspapers, February 15, 2018; & Ahmad (2018) for more on the death of Mikaila Abdulahi)

By empowering citizens to vote from their homes, or from wherever they may be (without having to go to queue up in any designated polling centers to be able to vote), and by allowing votes to be transmitted and collated electronically (without the need to handle ballot papers) e-voting practically vaporizes the opportunities for electoral violence and voter intimidation.

Other advantages of e-voting include the following:

a. It boosts voter turnout (citizens participation in elections), because of its convenience. For example, it enables a voter to e-vote from anywhere they may be, even while on the road, travelling!

b. E-voting records can instantly be accessed, in any order required, unlike the ordeal of rummaging through physical records;

c. E-voting records can instantly be transmitted (made available) anywhere they may be needed, without requiring the logistics of transporting physical ballot papers;

d. They will not have any problems of being defaced or torn; nor become otherwise unrecognizable, unlike physical ballots papers;

e. E-voting records will not deteriorate over time

3. *E-democracy*: Here, the focus will be on citizens' engagement platforms (CEPs): The CEP is an online and interactive platform that government can create for engaging citizens. It enables citizens to anonymously ask questions, share their views (including consent and opposition) in policy-making.

In this way, it empowers citizens to influence the way they are governed.

a. CEPs enable government to leverage the knowledge and experiences of citizens for policymaking, especially in implementing difficult decisions;

b. CEPs enhance transparency and accountability in governance, by helping to make data available, which enables citizens to engage government in an informed manner.

c. CEPs boost citizens participation. For example, if a city was holding a mere town-hall meeting, not everybody with a suggestion will be able to attend, because of geography, time, and cost. But an online platform will allow citizens to participate from even their bedrooms, and at their own times, even at midnight!

d. CEPs eliminate the barriers that social status, timidity, disability, prejudice, and poor finances might have imposed on some citizens.

4. *e-Procurement*: Governments are now using the internet to support their public procurement processes.

This can involve:

a. *e-tendering*, including the online publication of procurement notice, download of tender documents, online clarifications and bid opening; online submission of bids (so that individuals will not have to travel to state and federal capitals to drop tender documents in boxes); and more.

b. *e-purchasing* including online catalogues, e-reverse auctioning, or e-RTD ("Requests to Tender); and

c. *e-invoicing* and *e-payment*.

E-procurement has popularized the so-called "reverse" auction, in which multiple firms compete with bids for a government project. As the auction progresses, each firm tries to offer lower bids than its competitors (for the same project specs), in order to win the project. That is why it is called "reverse" auction, because in a normal auction, people who are competing to buy an item will rather be raising their bid prices, so as to win. Reverse auction therefore pushes down prices, typically shaving off about 20% from what projects' cost would have been.

- Mexico was one of the first emerging countries to migrate its public procurement to the internet, with the system it called "Compranet".

- In 2014, the Kenya became the first country in East Africa to launch an e-procurement system, which it called IFMIS. Quoting Kenya's President, Uhuru Kenyatta, during the launch of the system in Nairobi:

  > "Over the years, we have heard complaints from Kenyans that the government is being overcharged for goods and services that it purchases. By introducing transparency and accountability through e-Procurement, we expect to eliminate the abuse of our procurement system."

5. *Electronic document management system (EDMS)* helps government to manage its documents, including keeping track of what it has done with them, and by whom. It crashes communications time between government units, and cuts communication costs.

- Armenia has since 2008 rolled out an EDMS covering the entire civil service system, including all ministries and regional governors' offices. The system has reduced internal communication within government, which once lasted a full business day in Yerevan and about three business days with the regions, to only a few seconds! No courier or postal services are needed for communication anymore.

6. *e-Taxes*: This allows citizens to declare and pay their taxes through the internet. Among other benefits, its convenience can boost citizens' compliance in tax payments.

- According to estonia.eu, this service has become so popular among Estonian residents that way back in 2012, over 94% of income tax declarations were presented through the e-tax system.

7. _e-Business Registration_: This allows the people to register their businesses online, without having to go to any government office. It therefore bypasses the corruption and bureaucratic frustrations of manual business registration.

   - According to the estonia.eu, an entrepreneur can create a company in Estonia through this e-process, even directly from home. Company registration takes only about 18 minutes! Currently, the system requires an Estonian ID card, but recognizes ID cards from Belgium, Portugal, Lithuania, and Finland. Work is on-going to enable many other nations' citizens use the e-register system in Estonia.

8. _e-school_: This allows schools to interact more actively with parents, using the internet, in the study process.

   - Since 2003, Estonian schools have been using a web-based school-home communication system, to engage parents more actively in the study process, make information on subjects more available to children as well as to parents, and facilitate the work of teachers and the school management. According to estonia.eu, the system allows parents for example, to follow the marks given to students, their absence from classes, and the content of lessons, homework and assessments given to students.

9. _e-Admissions_: This system unites the higher-education databases with the students' admission test results, thus greatly simplifying the exchange of information between the user and the university in the higher-education application and admission process.

   - According to estonia.eu, all Estonian students are required to take state exams at the end of high school. The results are entered directly into the information system and every high school graduate may retrieve them through a special state portal. Upon completing high school, students may submit applications to universities via the state's internet-based application system

10. _e-Health_: This includes e-data, which enables different healthcare professionals to share a patient's data online; e-prescription, which enables electronic transmission of prescriptions from doctors to pharmacies, e-records (keeping details of treatment histories, prescriptions, hospitals, doctors, test results); and so on.

    - Estonia's e-prescription system sends all prescriptions to a central database, which the pharmacist can access – reducing the risk of mistakes. Prior to launching the system in January, 2010, patients, according to estonia.eu, had to carry paper prescriptions with them to pharmacies. This had several weaknesses: it was easy to lose the paper, the handwriting of the doctor could be illegible, and pharmacists could misinterpret prescriptions and issue wrong medications, and so on.

11. _Various others (m-parking, -ticket, etc)_: Governments are rolling out various other e-services. For example, Estonians can use mobile phones to pay for parking (m-parking), or to purchase tickets on public transport or theatre without cash (m-ticket); and so on.

    - Only tourists to Estonia buy paper tickets on the capital city's public transportation system. Locals buy their bus tickets via the internet and their virtual ticket is registered in their personal ID card, which can be checked by a card reader carried by conductors. Paper tickets have been almost completely consigned to the dustbin of history!

Let us conclude with the following spotlight on Estonia, again because that nation's e-gov achievements should serve as an inspiration to all our DCs.

Case 100:   Concluding Spotlight on Estonia

Estonia ranked 15th in the 2014 United Nations E-Government Survey report. This final spotlight on Estonia is appropriate, because from the viewpoint of our DCs, Estonia is an inspiring e-gov success story. Almost any activity can take place over the internet in just a few clicks. In fact, most Estonians would not even consider doing things the old-fashioned way, like physically visiting an office, when the process can easily be completed online.

Consider the following statistics on Estonia's e-gov exploits, as at 2015:

- 80% of the population aged 16-74 years use the internet;
- 83% of households have internet capabilities;
- 98% of households with children have Internet capabilities;
- All Estonian schools are connected to the internet;

- Rapid Wi-Fi internet connections are available in more than 1007 public places, in many places, free of charge (the area of Wi-Fi internet is steadily growing, encompassing all of Estonia);

- 98% of banking transactions in Estonia are conducted through the internet;

- In 2013, over 95% of income tax declarations were presented through the e-Tax Board;

- Cabinet meetings have been changed to paperless sessions using a web-based document system;

(Source: adapted from Estonia's public website)

The Concerns About e-Gov

Some of the concerns that people have expressed about e-governance tend to center on the following issues:

1. <u>Vulnerability of e-gov systems to cyber-attacks</u>: This vulnerability is real, but other countries are managing it successfully;

2. <u>Technological displacement of workers</u>: This is likely to weigh heavily in the minds of policy makers in the DCs, where public service employment tends to be highly political, and where government tends to be the greatest employer of labor. We shall therefore use the whole of the next Chapter to look at it!

3. Lack of equality in public access to the internet;

4. Possibility that the information on the web may not be reliable;

5. <u>Potential of abuse by government</u>: There is some chance that a DC's government can eventually abuse its access to huge citizens' data, which may even foster dictatorships. There is also the possibility that government groups (especially in the DCs) could use government's privileged position on the e-platform to influence and bias public opinion.

While these concerns point to areas that a DC must watch in any e-gov initiative, other nations have managed them successfully. Beside, as we shall see clearly in this Slice, technology adoption is not an option for our DCs; it is imperative!

A Lucky Opportunity For Leapfrogging

The good news for the DCs is that technology offers them a dramatic opportunity to leapfrog both their weak institutions and under-development. As we shall see shortly, it is no longer valid for a DC to say it is hampered by lack of infrastructure! Mobile telephony has made that untenable!

During the past four decades, the developed economies crunched technologically from mainframe computers to mini computers, then to desktop computers, then to laptops and now to mobile smartphones. The early users of e-gov crunched through these earlier generations of computers (mostly the desktops)! However, what is happening today all over the world is that even in the DCs, people, who never had computer experience, are now happy users of mobile phones, which are far easier to use than computers. In fact, governments and businesses are under pressure to migrate whatever ICT services they have for citizens to the mobile platform, which is where the citizens are presently located!

<u>**Case 101:**</u> **<u>Pressure To Migrate To The Mobile Platform</u>**

As noted by Goh Shufen (Principal at Marketing Consultancy R3 Worldwide), companies are under pressure all over the world, to offer customers a platform that provides full functionality on a smartphone. Mobile is so important because in many markets, a smartphone is the first and only channel that people have to get online – people have leapfrogged desktop PCs and gone straight to mobile. In Asia's developing markets there is a willingness to adopt new payment technologies. The success of mobile platforms in China for example, demonstrates that people are comfortable using their phones to manage financial transactions.

(See HSBC Bank Plc. Navigating The Digitised Landscape, 20 December 2016)

Without doubt, the mobile revolution creates an important leapfrogging opportunity for our DCs:

1. Since mobile phones are equally widely used in the DCs, a DC does not have to worry about the resources for making computers available, and training citizens to use them – which would have been the case for computer-based e-gov solutions! The citizens are already connected to their mobile phones, and are already reasonably mobile-literate! In fact, the leapfrogging that Goh Shufen talks about is even more dramatic in the DCs, where "mobile" is becoming the choice means of communication between individuals – meaning that a mobile-based e-gov solution can promptly become available to a sizable proportion of the DC's population.

2. An e-gov solution developed for the advanced economies on the mobile platform, can conceivably be adapted to the DC environment. But remember that rather than adopting such a solution blindly, it will be wise to align its technical specifications to the key institutional principles we discussed in Slice C for restructuring incentives

In view of all these, any DC that says it is waiting for infrastructure to improve, before launching into (at least) a basic e-gov program, is not yet ready! In any case, the waiting will never end, considering that the infrastructure has been "trying to improve" for decades – thanks to weak institutions, and to the corruption and other vices that thrive in the weak institutions.

Instead, launching into e-gov quickly will now itself create the pressure for further improvement in national infrastructure, which may even benefit from the savings that e-gov can begin to spawn (by for example, reducing the losses to corruption). As noted earlier, a country like Estonia is a good starting point, because of the simplicity of its e-gov model. It is a scalable model, which can allow a DC to start small, with minimal investment, and then expand.

Chapter 20

20. Appreciating The Impact Of Technology On Jobs

For as long as computers have existed they've been scaring people, eliminating jobs, creating jobs, devaluing some skills, and exalting others. Yet it would not be correct to say of today's situation that it was ever thus. It wasn't. ... As computers begin to acquire some of the most advanced cognitive and physical human skills, we confront a new reality. In a way that has not been true before, the central issue for the economy and for all of us who work in it will be the answer to the question: What will people do better than computers?

(Fortune's senior editor-at-large, Geoff Colvin (June 16, 2014)

Topics Covered in This Chapter:

- Introduction
- The 1st technological turning point
- The 2nd turning point
- The 3rd turning point
- Technology & displacement of workers
- Who harvested these benefits?

Introduction: Technology Evolution & Jobs

In the DCs, leaders tend to have the mindset that anything to do with computers will take away people's jobs. That is why we have this Chapter – to review the past major technological trends, their institutional disruptions, and impacts on national employment!

Indeed, in the last 200 years, the world has witnessed some major technological turning points. Each turning point represented a major advance in technology, and a disruption of the way the economy worked, with all the consequences of such disruption. The following highlights on the first three turning points have been adapted from the great work of Geoff Colvin, *Fortune*'s Senior editor-at-large:

The First Technological Turning Point

The world's 1st major technological turning point was the arrival of the "factory" and industrial technology, causing 19th century production to shift from small artisanal shops, to bigger and more efficient factories. Geoff used the old artisanal gun maker to illustrate how the nature of jobs changed: The highly skilled gun maker would typically carve the gun's stock, cast the barrel, engrave the lock, file the trigger, and painstakingly fit the pieces together.

However, the arrival of the gun factory created a novel division of labor – where separate workers were required to do each of those jobs, or even portions of them, using new machinery, to produce components that were identical. As the number of factories increased, the economy now wanted low-skilled factory workers, rather than highly skilled artisans!

This had the effect of devaluing the highly skilled artisans, which created major upheavals and angry protests in different sectors of the economy by those it was disintermediating!

Case 102: Remembering The Luddites

In England for example, textile artisans protested violently against a new textile technology that was disintermediating them with less-skilled, low-wage laborers. Some rampaged about destroying the known installations of the "evil" technology. This crystallized into a region-wide rebellion in north-western England that required a heavy military deployment to suppress! The members of this movement came to be known as the "Luddites".

(Story on the Luddites adapted from Wikipedia, the free encyclopaedia)

The "Luddites" became the face of the movement against the advancing technology, because of the "evil" they believed it portended, particularly in the area of massive displacement of workers.

The Second Technological Turning Point

The 2nd technological turning point occurred in in the 20th century, as technology advanced more quickly, and electricity became widely available. This gave birth to a wide range of new household and industrial goods and services that were based on electricity supply. In particular, it gave rise to greater sophistication of factories, creating the need for more skilled workers. Companies also started getting larger and more complex, and started to require better-educated managers. As Geoff put it:

"Now the unskilled were out of luck, and educated workers were in demand. Through most of the 20th century, Americans responded by becoming better educated as technology continued to advance, producing an economic miracle of fast-rising living standards."

The Third Technological Turning Point

The 3rd technological turning point has been on since the 1980s, when ICT developed to a point where it started to take over many blue-collar and white-collar (routine and medium-skilled) tasks:

1. *For the blue-collar workers*, robots were taking over all kinds of factory jobs, including welding tasks.

<u>**Case 103:**</u>　　　<u>**Proportion Of Americans Employed In Manufacturing &**</u>
<u>**Agriculture**</u>

From David Rotman (2013), we can get the following insight on the impact of this displacement:

- The proportion of Americans employed in manufacturing dropped from 30% in the post–World War II years to around 10% today; and

- By 2000, only 2% of Americans worked in agriculture, compared to 41% in 1900; and so on.

(Source: David Rotman, 2013)

2. *For the white-collar workers*, a new flotilla of technology-driven tools were bringing new efficiencies to the workplace, and eliminating the need for many categories of jobs. For example, instead of the separate workers that a typical accounts department would usually have for maintaining its various ledgers (such as purchase ledger, sales ledger, nominal ledger, and others) integrated accounting systems were emerging, which could do these ledgers automatically – with far more accuracy, and in seconds, rather than the days and weeks that humans used to require!

Similarly, office secretaries, who hitherto received messages for their bosses, started seeing the emergence of new mobile devices that allowed clients to reach these bosses directly, wherever they might be! Poor secretaries: The devices continued to grow in sophistication, to the point where these bosses were becoming able not only to receive messages directly, but even to treat and respond to them by themselves, from wherever they might be, without reference to their secretaries!

The growing spread of the internet was particularly eating into some categories of white-collar jobs. Online shops started to emerge to decrease the need for physical shops. Instead of going to a "travel agency" to book a flight, we started seeing how we could do that ourselves online. Martin Ford's Silicon-Valley-based software firm was a good illustration of this phenomenon:

<u>**Case 104:**</u>　　　<u>**Martin Ford's Silicon Valley Software Firm**</u>

According to Martin, his Silicon Valley software firm used to put its programs on disks and ship them to customers. The disks were made, packaged and delivered by workers. But it gradually became possible for Ford's customers to just download the software through the web, directly into their computers — meaning no more disks, no more packaging, and of course, no more workers for packaging and delivery!

(Source: Martin Ford, Christian Science Monitor, January 24, 2013)

Technology & Displacement Of Workers

Now that we have appreciated the world's major technological turning points, we are now in a position to look at the very important issue (which is highly sensitive in the DCs) of what the impact of their adoption of technology can be on national employment.

Clearly, as we have outlined, advances in technology have been displacing certain types of human jobs. However, they have also tended to create even many more jobs of new categories – often with second and third-order effects. For example, the factories of the *1ˢᵗ turning point* above definitely devalued the previously prized skills of the artisans; but they created work for many others, such as low-skilled factory workers, their managers and administrative staff!

In addition, they created other high-quality second and third-order jobs for the economy, such as:

1. Engineers constructing the factories;
2. Utility industries supplying gas, power and water to them;
3. The construction industry putting up roads and rail links;
4. Auto industry building vehicles for wheeling all the products.
5. Robust media system;
6. Marketing and brand specialists that were now needed for presenting all these services to potential users;
   And so on.

With all these people generating values and incomes, prosperity soared, leading to new demands for other goods and services – for schools, hospitals, restaurants, shops, sports and recreation; and so on – which in turn started to create their own categories of second and third-order high-quality jobs in the economy; and this further blossomed prosperity.

Steve Lohr has used the technology giant, Google, to illustrate the second and third-order effects:

> *"Take the Internet and Google: The search giant employs thousands of people — programmers, mathematicians, statisticians, marketing and sales people, administrators and managers. But its success ripples to create other jobs as well: service workers and suppliers of everything from computers to food. Real estate brokers and car dealers have benefited from Google's wealth. "More broadly, the spread of Internet technology has meant that most companies have their own Web sites. The companies hire software programmers, computer technicians, graphics designers and online advertising salespeople. And the job-creating ripples continue. "Smarter computing technology, experts say, ought to make the most skilled workers — in science, the arts and business — even more productive and prosperous by freeing them from routine tasks. Their prosperity translates to spending that creates jobs in stores, schools, gyms, construction and elsewhere."*

> *(Steve Lohr (June 24, 2010))*

Of course, another source of new jobs was the existing businesses, which became more efficient and more competitive by virtue of the efficiencies that technological improvements had heralded. Since businesses became more competitive, their volumes of operation increased, creating the capacity to afford more hands.

Deloitte researchers (Ian Stewart, Debapratim De and Alex Cole) studied the employment records in England and Wales for every decade since 1871, as well as labor data from 1992. They found that during that period of about a century and a half, computers, machines and robots did indeed eat up many jobs; but they ended up creating more jobs than they destroyed. Routine jobs declined the most because they could easily be substituted by technology, while cognitive, non-routine jobs exploded during the period! Let us join Hope King on the details:

<u>Case 105:</u>   <u>**The Findings Of Deloitte Researchers, Ian Stewart, Debapratim De & Alex Cole**</u>

- Decline   Job Type
- -82%   Footwear and leather working jobs (since 1992)
- -79%   Weavers and knitters
- -70%   Metal making and treating process operators
- -57%   Typists and related keyboard occupations
- -52%   Secretaries
- -51%   Energy plant workers
- -50%   Farm workers
- -44%   Metal machine setters and setter-operators

(Source: See Hope King, August 19, 2015)

Compare these with the cognitive, non-routine jobs that seemed to have exploded during the period! Not only was this category of jobs outside the immediate displacement reach of ICT, new technologies actually boosted the productivity of those handling such jobs!

<u>Case 106:</u>   <u>**More Findings Of Deloitte Researchers, Ian Stewart, Debapratim De & Alex Cole**</u>

- Increase   Job Type
- +909%.   Nursing jobs (since 1992)
- +580%.   Teaching jobs
- +365%   Management consultants and business analysts
- +195%   I.T. managers
- +183%   Welfare, housing, youth & community workers
- +168%   Care workers and home carers
- +156%   Actors, dancers, producers, show hosts, etc
- +132%   financial managers

(Source: See Hope King, August 19, 2015)

Another feature of these technological advances is that the new high-tech jobs arising from technology have tended to be not only high-paying, but also increasingly very fast, and more resilient to economic downturns.

These have been confirmed by a recent study by California's Bay Area Council Economic Institute (BACEI) in the United States that compared technological (high-tech) jobs to other kinds of jobs for the 10-year period, 2001 to 2011:

<u>Case 107:</u>   <u>**From The California's Bay Area Council Economic Institute (BACEI) Report**</u>

The report shows that high-tech jobs have been more resilient over the past 10 years to economic downturns than other private sector industries, pay more, create more indirect jobs by far than any other industry, and hold the most promise for continued growth.

Among the key findings:

- Employment growth in tech jobs — defined as those most closely related to science, technology, engineering and math (STEM) — outpaced gains in all other occupations by a ratio of 27 to 1 from 2001 to 2011.

- For each job created in the high-tech sector, approximately 4.3 jobs are created (multiplier effect) in other local goods and services sectors across all income groups, including lawyers, dentists, schoolteachers, cooks and retail clerks, among many others.

- By comparison, traditional manufacturing has a multiplier effect of 1.4 jobs. Therefore, the jobs multiplier effect in the high-tech sector is significantly higher than for almost any other sector.

- Demand for high tech occupations will be considerably stronger than demand for other workers at least through 2020.

(See BACEI's report "Technology Works: High-Tech Employment and Wages in the United States", 2015)

It seems therefore that mankind has always adapted whenever technology crushed some jobs – by inventing entirely new categories of work! And the improved technology has tended to make the new jobs more productive and higher paying! That is why the fear of technological unemployment, which Geoff Colvin describes as *"the 200-year-old terror that has never arrived"*, has so far, remained unfounded!

- "Practically every advance in technology has sparked worries that it would destroy jobs, and it did destroy them — but it also created even more new jobs, and the improved technology made those jobs more productive and higher paying. The fears of Luddites past and present have always been unfounded. Technology has lifted living standards spectacularly ...
- "Fear of technological unemployment is as old as technology, and it has always been unfounded. Over time and across economies, technology has multiplied jobs and raised living standards more spectacularly than any other force in history"

(See Fortune, June 16, 2014; July 23, 2015)

Who Harvested These Benefits?

It is important to emphasize that all the foregoing benefits (the creation of new categories of jobs and economic prosperity) have gone basically to the nations, which through proactive policies, have strived to become a part of the global digital economy. Even within such nations, the states, localities and cities that most embraced technology (for example, by articulating the most proactive technology-friendly policies) usually reaped the greatest benefits.

Of particular interest to our DCs should be that these benefits have by no means, been limited to the advanced economies. Several countries that used to be low-income (such as Estonia, India, Brazil, Costa Rica, Dubai, and others) have also benefited heavily from digital economy, and launched themselves into the "knowledge economy"!

On the other hand, those countries that failed to board this surging "technology train", have not only found themselves thoroughly left behind by others, but often as we shall shortly see in the coming Chapters, have even found themselves "on the menu" of those in the train!

Chapter 21

21. Bracing Up For Another Tech-Driven Disruption (The Real Tsunami)

"At the hardware store, the guy who used to cut keys has been replaced by a robot. In the law office, the clerks who used to prepare discovery have been replaced by software. IBM Watson is replacing researchers by reading every report ever written anywhere. This begs the question: What can the human contribute? The short answer is that if the job is one where that question cannot be answered positively, that job is not likely to exist."

(Robert Cannon, Internet law and policy expert, predicting the unfolding impact of the rampaging of technology on jobs, 2014)

Topics Covered in This Chapter:

- Introduction: The Tsunami on the way
- The assault from robotics, artificial intelligence & big data
- Some important attributes of the imminent TTP
- So what are humanity's best options?

Introduction: The Tsunami On The Way

If the DCs are worried about their present technological gap relative to the advanced economies, there is still some more bad news on the way! Economists, analysts and technology futurists such as Mark Mills, now believe that with the rampaging robots (both the automation of physical things, and virtual robots in the form of artificial intelligence and machine-learning), another major technological turning point is imminent – the fourth technological turning point, and is expected to herald a potentially unprecedented disruptive effect on national economies and institutions.

The purpose of this Chapter is to highlight these raging capabilities of technology, and their unprecedented assault on the work areas that had been the exclusive domain of humans.

The Assault From Robotics, Artificial Intelligence & Big Data

A major source of this looming TTP is the dramatic developments in the fields of robotics (both the automation of physical things, and virtual robots in the form of artificial intelligence and machine-learning), and similar disruptive technologies. As we saw before, practically every previous major technological advance did spark worries that it would destroy jobs; and as Geoff Colvin noted, it did indeed destroy them —

many of them! However, contrary to the fears of the Luddites, it has also always created even more new jobs than it destroyed – because each new technology usually heralded new opportunities and jobs; and workers also adjusted their skills over time! The improved technology also made those new jobs more productive and higher paying. This has remained the pattern for nearly 200 years!

Recall also that since the 1980s, ICT has been displacing workers involved in repetitive, routine and medium-skill jobs, under what we classified as the 3rd technological turning point. All this time, two important classes of jobs remained safe:

1. <u>The jobs of the "knowledge" workers</u>: ICT could not handle the problem-solving, discretionary, coordinating and cognitive tasks involved in high-skill jobs. Rather, it actually made those jobs more productive by ushering in new tools for doing them more efficiently. In this way, managers, engineers, architects, physicians, lawyers, pilots, and other high-skill workers felt not only safe, but also became more productive.

2. <u>The jobs of the low-skill workers</u>: Similarly, ICT could not handle the physical tasks involved in the bottom, low-skill jobs. Robots for example, were only good at closely prescribed, repetitive tasks, such as we see on assembly lines; but could not unpack a carton, clean a room, prepare a meal, or help an elderly person. So cooks, home-helps, security guards, gardeners, and such low-skill workers also felt safe.

In this way, only the middle-skill workers bore the disruptive effects of the 3rd technological turning point. All that has now changed; and very rapidly too! Dramatic technological advances in recent years are now suddenly threatening both the low-skill and the cognitive (high-skill) ends of the job spectrum!

<u>**Case 108:**</u>   <u>**Geoff Colvin explains The Assault Of ICT On Low & Cognitive Skill Jobs**</u>

Technology is advancing steadily into both ends of the spectrum, threatening workers who thought they didn't have to worry.

- At the top end, what's happening to lawyers is a model for any occupation involving analysis, subtle interpretation, strategizing, and persuasion. The computer incursion into the legal-discovery process is well known. In cases around the country, computers are reading millions of documents and sorting them for relevance without getting tired or distracted. But that's just the beginning. Computers are also becoming highly skilled at searching the legal literature for appropriate precedents in a given case, far more widely and thoroughly than people can do. Humans still have to identify the legal issues involved, but as North-western University law professor John O. McGinnis points out in a recent article,

  > "Search engines will eventually do this by themselves, and then go on to suggest the case law that is likely to prove relevant to the matter."

- Advancing even deeper into the territory of lawyerly skill, computers can already predict Supreme Court decisions better than lawyers can. As such analytical power expands in scope, computers will move nearer to the heart of what lawyers do by advising better than lawyers can on whether to sue or settle or go to trial before any court and in any type of case. Companies such as Lex Machina and Huron Legal already offer such analytical services, which are improving by the day…

- Developments at the opposite end of the skill spectrum are at least as surprising. In the physical realm, robots have been good mainly at closely prescribed, repetitive tasks — welding on an auto assembly line, as an example. That's all changing radically. Google's autonomous cars are an obvious example, but many more are appearing. You can train a Baxter robot from Rethink Robotics to do all kinds of things — pack or unpack boxes, take items to or from a conveyor belt, carry things around, count them, inspect them — just by moving its arms and hands ("end effectors") in the desired way…

- Still more advanced is a robotic hand developed by a team from Harvard, Yale, maker of the Roomba vacuum cleaner and many other mobile robots. So fine are its motor skills that it can pick up a credit card from a table-top, put a drill bit in a drill, and turn a key. As one of the researchers, Harvard professor Robert Howe, recently told Harvard Magazine.

> "A disabled person could say to a robot with hands, 'Go to the kitchen and put my dinner in the microwave,'"

The overwhelming message seems to be that no one is safe.

(Source: see Fortune, June 2, 2014)

In June 2014, the Associated Press (AP) <u>announced</u> that it would use a robot to produce up to 4,440 robot-written corporate-earnings reports per quarter. That amounted to more than ten times what AP's human reporters were then producing!

<u>**Case 109:**</u>   <u>**Kevin Roose On the Shock Waves Created By AP's Announcement**</u>

From Kevin Roose, we can feel the shock waves created by that announcement!

- "By this point, we're no longer surprised when machines replace human workers in auto factories or electronics-manufacturing plants. That's the norm. But we hoity-toity journalists had long assumed that our jobs were safe from automation. (We're knowledge workers, after all.) So when the AP announced its new automated workforce, you could hear the panic spread to old-line news desks across the nation. "Unplug the printers, Bob! The robots are coming!"

(See NY Magazine, July 11, 2014)

Similar incursions are taking place in other white-collar areas – such as post office work, online marketing, customer service works, anesthesiology, surgery, diagnostics, X-ray jobs, and so on!

In particular, this disruption is hitting even those skill groups that have been at the pinnacles of skilled labor – lawyers, doctors, pilots, and investment bankers – taking over tasks, which (by most experts) only a few years ago, computers were supposed to be no good at! Erik Sherman provides more insight on the medical professionals:

<u>Case 110:</u>   <u>Erik Sherman On Robots' Assault On The Medical Profession</u>

- "IBM's Watson, well known for its stellar performance in the TV game show "Jeopardy!", has already demonstrated a far more accurate diagnosis rate for lung cancers than humans – 90% versus 50% in some tests. The reason is data. Keeping pace with the release of medical data could take doctors 160 hours a week, so doctors can't possibly review the amount of new insights or even bodies of clinical evidence that can give an edge in making a diagnosis … There have already been demonstrations … of how a robotic system could potentially remove tumors from tissue. There is also at least one hair transplant robot on the market, allowing one surgeon to oversee multiple procedures at the same time.

(Source: see Fortune, February 25, 2015)

Frank Tobe, publisher of The Robot Report (a publication that tracks and analyses the robot industry) has used Fedex, a global, US-based courier company, to provide insight on the assault on airline pilots:

"Look at FedEx. They hope that by 2020 they will have a pilot center with three or four pilots that fly the FedEx fleet (of hundreds of planes) around the country"!

From Stefan Kip Astheimer, Vice President for strategy at wealth management firm Howe & Rusling, we learn about a similar attack on investment advisors:

"One trend in the investment industry over the last few years has been the advent of 'robo-advisers. These are automated services that are replacing personal financial advisers, financial planners and stockbrokers for younger individuals and individuals who don't have complex investment needs."

W. Brian Arthur, a visiting researcher at the Xerox Palo Alto Research Center's lab in the United States and a former economics professor at Stanford University, sees an "autonomous economy", far more subtle than the idea of robots and automation doing human jobs!

<u>Case 111:</u>   <u>W. Brian Arthur On The Autonomous Economy</u>

Here is what W. Brian Arthur says about the "autonomous economy", going beyond the idea of robots and automation doing human jobs:

- It involves digital processes talking to other digital processes and creating new processes, enabling us to do many things with fewer people and making yet other human jobs obsolete: It is this onslaught of digital processes that primarily explains how productivity has grown without a significant increase in human labor. And digital versions of human intelligence are increasingly replacing even those jobs once thought to require people. It will change every profession in ways we have barely seen yet

----

(Source: MIT Technology Review, June 12, 2013)

As Brynjolfsson and McAfee have noted, ICT can already drive cars in traffic, understand and produce natural human speech, write clean prose, and beat the best human "Jeopardy" players in the game! In all these, Geoff Colvin asks a profound question:

Case 112:   A Poser From Geoff Colvin

In 2014, the Associated Press began publishing thousands of articles about US corporate earnings. Most were not written by humans. Similar software is taking on Wall Street, synthesizing and analyzing data at a pace people can't match. If you're going to the doctor for a screening, you'll probably be sedated by an anesthesiologist, unless you happen to be at one of the hospitals using Johnson & Johnson's Sedasys anesthesiology machine, in which case you might be sedated by a plastic box.

There is no doubt the robots are coming. In many cases, the robots are already here. The question now is what that means for the rest of us.

(Source: See Business Insider, August 19, 2015)

The answer to this poser, according to Geoff Colvin, is that the 4th technological turning point may have arrived; and this time, the overwhelming message seems to be that no one is safe! Unlike the previous turning points, the speed of change has been very sudden; so sudden that nobody is prepared for the readjustments that humanity and governance institutions need to make – not the education institution, and not the other governance institutions, even in the advanced economies.

It appears that the old technological unemployment, the 200-year-old terror that never arrived, may finally be here! As Geoff Colvin put it:

"The luddites may be smiling in their graves!"

What The DCs Must Know About This Technology Tsunami

Clearly, another technological revolution is imminent; and analysts, economists and technology futurists believe it will have implications far more dramatic than anything the world had ever witnessed before! Experts' opinions also seem to converge on some issues:

1. *It is already here*: If anybody needed any proof that the disruption is already here, they should listen to MIT economist, David Rotman, drawing attention to the "great" decoupling in recent years, of employment, wages and salaries on one hand, from the impressive productivity and growth of the US economy.

"Productivity is the amount of economic value created for a given unit of input, such as an hour of labor. It is a crucial indicator of growth, wealth creation and national progress; and usually rises with total employment in an economy, because as businesses generate more value from their workers, the country as a whole becomes richer, which in turn fuels more economic activity that creates even more jobs."

(David Rotman, MIT economist & expert on the connections between jobs and technology (June 12, 2013))

Indeed, Erik Brynjolfsson, a professor at the MIT Sloan School of Management, and his co-author, Andrew McAfee, have shown how the productivity line in the United States economy diverged from the employment line, as from 2000 – with productivity continuing to rise robustly, while employment started sagging. By 2011, a significant gap had appeared between the two lines, implying economic growth without a parallel increase in job creation – which they called the "great decoupling", and have attributed to technological displacement:

- "A wonderful ride has come to an end. For several decades after World War II, the economic statistics we care most about all rose together as if they were tightly coupled. The US gross domestic product – the economy – grew and so did productivity – our ability to get more output from each worker. At the same time, we created millions of jobs, and many of these were the kinds of jobs that allowed the average American worker, who didn't have a college degree, to enjoy a high and rising standard of living. …

- But productivity growth and employment growth started to become decoupled from each other at the end of that decade [1990s] … and they show no signs of closing. We're creating jobs these days, but not enough of them … There are several explanations for this, including tax and policy changes and the effects of globalization and offshoring. We agree that these matter, but we want to stress another driver of the Great Decoupling: the changing nature of technological progress".

(Source: See The Christian Science Monitor, December 12, 2012)

2. ***We humans are a hopeless mismatch:*** It is useless trying to ignore or compete with technology in whatever jobs it invades! The odds seem decisively stacked in its favor! As an illustration, Jomati Consultants, a leading British-based strategic consultancy to the legal profession, studied the comparative economics of robot lawyers vs. human lawyers. Let us join Julius Melnitze on the conclusions:

Case 113:　　Robot Lawyers vs. Human Lawyers

- "Salaries for lawyers [junior lawyers, associates and paralegals] doing these types of tasks [low-level knowledge economy work, like due diligence] which also include file and data checking, collation, data linking, and document improvement, is in the range of $100,000… Licensing fees for bots smart enough to work independently in a leading law firm will initially cost about $500,000 with the cost going down over time.

- "Even at this price, the bots would be worth the cost as they can work 24 hours a day, 7 days a week with no downtime, thereby eclipsing the chargeable hours of the most workaholic lawyers," the authors conclude. As well, a handful of bots could work on many matters at the same time and would be instantly accessible at any moment to anyone in the firm no matter where they were. They would learn as they work and become more efficient over time … They would not get tired. They would not seek advancement. They would not ask for pay rises."

(Source: Law Times, 08 December 2014)

As another example of how hopelessly better technology can be, consider the story that a "business-beat colleague" of journalist Kevin Roose, did for the Associated Press (AP), on Alcoa Inc; the giant American metals company. The most impressive part, though, was how long the story took to produce: less than a second! Hear Kevin Roose:

- *"That impossible-sounding deadline was possible because the AP's story wasn't written by a person at all. It was the product of a piece of software — a robot, really — created by a Durham, North Carolina-based company called Automated Insights. The AP announced last month that it would use Automated Insights' software, called Wordsmith, to produce up to 4,440 robot-written corporate-earnings reports per quarter, more than ten times the number its human reporters currently produce ... What a robot can do ... is churn out stories at a superhuman pace. Last year, Wordsmith, the company's software, produced 300 million stories — more than every other media outlet in the world combined. This year, Wordsmith is expected to work even harder — producing more than a billion stories"*

(Source: NY Magazine, July 11, 2014)

3. *It keeps getting better:* It is not just that we are a hopeless mismatch, as bad as it is! Even more bad news is that technology as awesomely powerful as it has already become, is still improving at an alarming speed! While humans actually start to slow down with age, the machines are getting better and better with time!

Case 114:   Technology Is Not Slowing Down With Age

The following insight from <u>Geoff Colvin</u> explains how technology is not slowing down with age.

- "I'm surrounded by technology that's better than I am at sophisticated tasks. Google's autonomous car is a better driver than I am. The company has a whole fleet of the vehicles, which have driven hundreds of thousands of miles with only one accident while in autonomous mode, when one of the cars was rear-ended by a human driver at a stoplight. Computers are better than humans at screening documents for relevance in the discovery phase of litigation, an activity for which young lawyers used to bill at an impressive hourly rate. Computers are better at detecting some kinds of human emotion, despite our million years of evolution that was supposed to make us razor sharp at that skill. One more thing. I competed against Watson [IBM's intelligent robot] two years ago. Today's Watson is 240% faster. I am not. And I'll guess that you aren't either. Most things in our world slow down as they get bigger and older: A small start-up can easily grow 100% a year, but a major Fortune 500 firm may struggle to grow 5%. Technology isn't constrained that way. Today's systems, as awesomely powerful as they are, will be 100% more awesomely powerful in two years. In a decade they'll be 32 times more powerful".

(Source: Geoff Colvin, Fortune, June 16, 2014)

Clearly, the mismatch is all round! While today we describe the educated workforce as "white-collar", and use "blue-collar" for the junior, less educated workers, Amy Webb, the CEO of the strategy firm, Webbmedia, has made a prediction:

"The collar of the future is a hoodie!"

So What Are humanity's Best Options?

Geoff Colvin thinks that we humans **should stop being "Machine-Like"**: It is wise to begin to envisage the areas in which the advancing machine will be better, and start keeping away from there! For example, the jobs we do in the workplace have over the years, tended to be predefined, hierarchical, routine and regimented, with clear divisions of labor. These are precisely the ways of the computer! In other words, our factories, shops, warehouses and construction sites presently tend to be structured in the way of the machine!

Similarly, the analysis, research, strategic thinking and many cognitive tasks of the white-collar workplace flourish on intellect and memory power – the very capabilities that computers have amassed at a horrifying pace in recent years. We can get some very useful insight from David Brooks and Geoff Colvin:

Case 115:   Time For Man To Become Less Machine-Like

According to David Brooks:

> In the 1950s, the bureaucracy was the computer. People were organized into technocratic systems in order to perform routinized information processing. But now the computer is the computer. The role of the human is not to be dispassionate, depersonalized or neutral. It is precisely the emotive traits that are rewarded: the voracious lust for understanding, the enthusiasm for work, the ability to grasp the gist, the empathetic sensitivity to what will attract attention and linger in the mind. Unable to compete when it comes to calculation, the best workers will come with heart in hand.

Geoff Colvin makes the same point even more elaborately:

> Since the dawn of the Industrial Revolution—the machine age—much human success has derived from our being machine-like. For decades, most of the physical work in factories and the mental work in offices were repetitive and routine. They were designed to be that way; that's why Henry Ford complained, "Why is it every time I ask for a pair of hands, they come with a brain attached?"

It was the kind of work for machines to do, only the machines of the era couldn't do it. The machines improved, slowly at first, then rapidly, driven by the ever-quickening advance of infotech. Now they can actually do most of the machine work of our world.

(See New York Times, Feb 3, 2014)

In the dramatically escalating race against the machine, the experts are saying that it is now time for man to return to being human, and stop trying to be machine-like! We shall look at this some more in the next Chapter.

Chapter 22

22. Why Every DC Must Strive To Play In The Global Digital Economy

The digital divide between … high and low or middle income countries is substantial … As an example in 2013, a vast majority of the population used the Internet in Sweden (94%), Estonia (79%) and Singapore (74%). This is in contrast to Costa Rica, Georgia or Egypt where less than half of the population had access to the Internet. This disparity becomes particularly acute with low-income countries such as Guinea-Bissau (3%), Madagascar (2%) or Somalia (1%)

- The United Nations E-Government Survey, 2014

Topics Covered in This Chapter:

- Globalization, Digital Economy, Knowledge Economy
    - Globalization Explained
    - What About The Knowledge/Information Economy
    - And Also The Digital Economy
- The Dreadful Consequences Of Being Left Behind
    - Intensifying poverty
    - The quiet economic poaching already going on
    - Growing Global Competition Even For Local Jobs
- Why Making The Efforts Is Worthwhile
    - The Digital Economy Is Achievable
    - The Medal Of Success Will Be (More Than) Worth It

Globalization, Knowledge, Information & Digital Economies

The goal of this Chapter is to demystify the big-sounding global digital economy, and encourage every DC to strive to play in it. Let us start by providing some insight on some of the favorite buzzwords of the on-going information and communications technologies (ICT) revolution.

Globalization Explained

We can think of globalization as the worldwide integration of national economies through technology, trade, investment, and labor. Because of trade liberalization and advances in technology and transportation systems, firms in the global economy can now split their operations across multiple nations. Such a firm can afford to break up a production process into small, specific slices; and perform each slice in any nation where it can be done optimally – for example, where the firm can find the best combination of business friendliness, political stability, workforce quality and cost.

This is especially possible because it costs practically nothing today to process information in one country, and transmit it to another country (or even continent) in a split second. People in different countries and continents can now work together as if they are in adjacent rooms of the same building! For example, the staff of a multinational company (MNC) in India and their counterparts in the United States can now work as if they are in the same building! All these represent globalization in action! Melina Kolb describes globalization as

- the growing interdependence of the world's economies, cultures, and populations, brought about by cross-border trade in goods and services, technology, and flows of investment, people, and information

As explained by the United Nations Conference on Trade and Development (UNCTAD), goods and services increasingly cross international borders multiple times as they become processed into finished products. It has become a relentless international zigzagging of goods and services as they progress from raw to intermediate products, and then to finished goods. Even the finished goods may additionally be exported to other countries.

Globalization is truly blurring national boundaries, and integrating the nations of the world more economically than many DCs may realize, shattering geographical boundaries of nations, and turning the world into the so-called "global village"!

What About The Knowledge (or Information) Economy

The knowledge economy and globalization are intertwined! The basis of the knowledge economy (or fully, knowledge-based economy) is essentially the creation, distribution, and application of knowledge. Timothy Hogan (2011) defines it as:

- The characterization of an entire economy in which the production, distribution, and use of knowledge plays a key role throughout the economy

As explained by Hogan, there will usually be two sectors in a knowledge-based economy (KBE):

1. The knowledge-intensive sector made up of those industries whose firms employ advanced technologies and have highly educated and skilled workforces, and

2. The sector that is not knowledge-intensive, composed of industries with less educated/skilled workforces that use "traditional" production processes.

If a nation's knowledge-intensive sector makes a significant contribution to its overall economic growth, it will usually indicate that the nation is into the information economy.

- For example, Timothy Hogan (2011) estimated that on average, nearly 70% of recent economic growth in the United States and other advanced economies was attributable to technological change.

- Similarly, in his analysis of the United States' economy, Jorgenson (2014) in an apparent agreement with Hogan, found that in the period, 1995 to 2002, about 70% of the economic growth could be attributable to the knowledge-intensive sector.

The information economy started with the 3rd technological turning point of the 1970s and 80s, which we looked at earlier.

And Also The Digital Economy

What we call the digital and knowledge economies are intertwined! We can think of the digital economy as a worldwide network of economic activities that are driven by ICT. The Asian Development Bank Institute (ADBI) defines it as:

"A broad range of economic activities that use digitized information and knowledge as key factors of production"

(ADB's February 2018 event tagged "Understanding the Digital Economy: What Is It and How Can It Transform Asia?")

While it may appear too far-fetched, asking every DC to strive to be a part of the global digital economy (since the typical DC is still grappling with the basic problems of poverty, illiteracy, and poor infrastructure), the truth is that:

1. The DC today really has no choice, because, as we shall see shortly, the consequences of being left behind by that economy, are simply dreadful!

2. A DC can successfully get into that economy, and many hitherto poor nations have indeed made it. In fact, it is easier to play in that economy today, than it is to "industrialise" in the traditional sense.

3. Successful transition will launch the DC into the new, unprecedented opportunities that the global digital economy is creating for nations across the world – the kind of opportunities that are transforming many hitherto poor nations, such as India, China, Vietnam, Argentina, Brazil, Costa Rica, Chile, Indonesia, Estonia, Korea, Mexico, and Puerto Rico.

Although some people tend to differentiate between the "digital economy", "information" economy and "knowledge" economy, such differentiation is not necessary for our purposes in this book; so we shall often use the terms interchangeably.

The Dreadful Consequences Of Being Left Behind

Digital economy is expected to become "the economy" in the immediate future! Economic activities, jobs, and prosperity are all shifting to the digital realm; and at a very rapid rate too! For example, the proportion of workers in the USA that are still involved in manufacturing, as pointed out by John Mauldin, is already less than 9%!

Therefore, the consequences of being left behind in the emerging technological revolution will be dreadful. Let us look at some of the consequences that are already manifesting.

Intensifying poverty

As we have seen, the digital economy has been the obvious driver of prosperity and economic development across the world in recent years. Therefore, any DC that fails to strive for the digital economy is likely to remain in poverty! It will even be more so, going forward, as the surging technological advancements continue to place escalating premium on the digital literacy. As JP Rangaswami (the chief scientist for Salesforce.com) put it:

> *"The effects (of emerging technology) will be different in different economies (which themselves may look different from today's political boundaries). Driven by revolutions in education and in technology, the very nature of work will have changed radically—but only in economies that have chosen to invest in education, technology, and related infrastructure."*

Interestingly, the DCs that think they can remain outside the digital economy, may not even have the luxury of remaining poor in peace! Various phenomena, such as those described below, will additionally be intensifying the poverty in such DCs, in a way that will viciously make the poor even poorer!

The Quiet Economic Poaching Already Taking Place

Many policymakers in the DCs see globalization as something that concerns only the advanced nations, without realizing how hard it is already hitting their own nations! One dreadful consequence of ignoring the digital economy comes from the quiet economic poaching already taking place!

We can use a typical online purchase to illustrate this. Each time somebody makes an online purchase in a DC, the implication is that somebody else in Asia, Europe, America (or wherever else the clever guy may be) has made a quiet non-physical export to the DC! In many cases, the people through whom we are making the purchase may not even be the owners of what we are buying! They may only have just created a website that simply links buyers to sellers! In fact, in many cases, people selling items on the internet, may be selling what they themselves have not seen physically! Somebody in India could be selling something to us that is located in faraway America, Israel, Europe, or Africa! In fact, the guy in India could be selling something located in Nigeria, to another person who is in Nigeria! That shows how technology, has collapsed national borders.

Even an online transaction as simple as downloading an anti-virus software, has a similar implication! That downloading implies that somebody in Asia, Europe, America (or wherever else the developers of the software may be) has made a quiet non-physical export to the DC! Thousands of this can take place all over the DC during a given period, without much notice; meanwhile, the DC's customs officials will be at the entry boarders, focused intently on physical imports for collecting their import duties!

That internet purchase also means that the foreign developers have denied work to the local software engineers in the DC, who would have provided the solutions locally, or at least come to do the installation! The clever foreigners have not only made a quiet export to the DC, they have even remotely done the installation, from the comfort of their own country – further reducing the DC's need for its own local software engineers! This is a serious poaching!

There is a more serious aspect of this kind of economic poaching that many DCs may not fully be aware of. Consider the following:

1. Because the staff of a multinational company (MNC) in one country and their counterparts in other countries can now work as if they are in adjacent rooms of the same building, an MNC with operations in a DC already has the technology to domicile some of the works associated with its operations in the DC (for example, the administrative, financial and logistics aspects of the work) in any other country or countries. This means for example, that a multinational oil company operating in Nigeria now has the means to domicile all the administrative and logistics work for its Nigerian operations, in another country (or continent), where it finds a better combination of business friendliness, workforce efficiency, political stability, and of course, cost. It can then choose to use only skeletal field staff in Nigeria!

2. This is bad news for those DCs that are only counting on their natural resources (such as oil and solid minerals) to attract MNCs. In the past, such an MNC would domicile everything needed for its DC's operations, inside that DC – which usually boosted employment and economic activities in the DC. Today however, the MNC can just as easily carry out those administrative and support operations from any other country or continent of the world, where it gets the best value!

3. Remember that even the portion of the operations it chooses to domicile in the DC, may now be largely technology (robot) driven, as we saw in the last Chapter!

4. Therefore, even when a DC attracts international extraction of its natural resources, the associated employment and economic activities can very well be taking place in other, more conducive countries!

5. Note that when an MNC chooses to do most of its work for a DC from other countries, it means that money generated in that DC is being used to create employment and other economic activities in those other countries – in other words, to enrich those other countries, while perhaps leaving any associated environmental degradation for the DC. That is how merciless the global economy has become to nations that are outside the digital economy.

6. It also means that those local administrative policies (such as "expatriate quota") which some DCs have been using to compel foreign companies to employ and train the locals, are becoming largely hollow!

7. In other words, the host DC will increasingly not be able to enjoy even the benefits of the mineral resources being extracted from its territory, if a large chunk of those benefits is following the jobs to the other nations that make better business sense to the investors.

8. In particular, this kind of economic poaching makes it an illusion for a DC to think that it can successfully be outside the influence of globalization, or that the digital economy is only the business of the advanced nations! Not any more – It is either a DC gets on board the technology train, or risk becoming a meal to those nations that do.

In view of all these, we can see that the consequences of failing to strive for the digital economy are no longer limited to being left behind by other nations – any DC that fails to board the technology train, may simply find itself <u>in the menu</u> of those nations that do!

The Growing Global Competition For Local Jobs

It is not just that technology has affected where workers can now work from, it is also transforming who their competitors can be even in local job markets! This is another dreadful consequence of staying outside the digital economy! For example, workers in a DC historically competed for local jobs in the DC mostly with other locals. But now that technology can allow other people to do the jobs of the DC from their own countries and continents, it means for example, that workers in Nigeria are now competing for local jobs with workers in other countries, who can as well do those local Nigerian jobs from their own countries! This is another havoc that globalization is quietly visiting on the DCs!
And the implications for the local job market are equally scary:

1. Local professionals seeking jobs from an MNC operating in their DC, will not only have to square up among themselves, but now increasingly against other professionals in other countries around the world, who can equally do the MNC's jobs in the DC from their countries.
   This means that the DC's local professionals will increasingly have to become globally competitive, even to qualify for the local jobs of MNCs operating in their country! If an MNC finds that its interests are better served by workers elsewhere, it can easily use such workers to do most of its local jobs in the DC!

2. With the education institution in near ruins in most DCs, how many DCs can produce workers that are globally competitive?

What all these show is that globalization is already quietly eating into the local economies of the DCs. Unfortunately, many leaders in the DCs do not seem to appreciate this; and still view globalization as something remote and taking place among only the advanced nations! The only option available to the DC is to strive to become a part of the digital economy. How they can achieve this is the subject of the next Chapter.

Why Making The Efforts Is Worthwhile

Let us again in this Section reiterate the important benefits of striving to become a part of the global digital economy.

The Digital Economy Is Achievable

The first reason to strive is that a typical DC that makes sincere efforts (as opposed to the empty political mantras) can indeed begin to play in the digital economy! This is mainly because the economics of knowledge in our globalizing world, and the economics of traditional goods and services, are not the same, as explained by Professor Timothy Hogan of the Arizona State University:

> **Case 116:** **Some Insights On The Knowledge Economy (From Timothy Hogan)**
>
> From the explanations of Emeritus Professor Timothy Hogan of the Arizona State University, we can get the following insights on the economics of knowledge:
>
> - The economics of knowledge in our globalizing world differ from the economics of traditional goods and services.
>
> - The world's stock of knowledge in our globalizing world, is much more accessible all over the world than in the past, making it much easier to undertake knowledge-based activities all over the world, even in previously poor nations.
>
> - In fact, the process of creating new knowledge and making investments in human capital and technology, is now taking place in many nations across the world, including many otherwise poor nations.
>
> - Knowledge in our globalizing world can produce economic value not only to the party that created the knowledge, but also (through diffusion) to many other users, cities, regions and nations.
>
> --
>
> *(Source: The Productivity and Prosperity Project (P3) of the Arizona State University)*

While the digital economy has provided enormous growth and prosperity to many nations, the phenomenon driving it (which as explained by Hogan, is the process of creating new knowledge and investing in human capital and advanced technologies), is now taking place in many multiple nations across the world. In fact, the advanced economies of the world, which had thrived on technological edge, are somewhat uncomfortable about what is becoming a relative leveling off of the field. Hogan provides some insight on this in respect of the United States:

216

<u>**Case 117:**</u>   <u>**US Concerns About The leveling of Opportunities**</u>

According to the Emeritus Professor Timothy Hogan of the Arizona State University, the processes that the United States has relied upon to produce economic growth and prosperity— the creation of new knowledge and investment in human capital and advanced technology — will surely continue, but similar processes are occurring around the globe.

Concerns have been increasing about how the United States can successfully compete and prosper in the global community of the 21st century. The business community, government officials, and other policymakers are working to develop policies aimed at strengthening and stimulating the U.S. knowledge economy (exemplified for example by the Task Force on the Future of American Innovation).

(Source: The Productivity and Prosperity Project (P3) of the Arizona State University)

The Medal Of Success Will Be (More Than) Worth It

The ultimate incentive for striving to play in the global digital economy, is that any DC that succeeds can harvest benefits that include the following:

1. *Avoiding the foregoing dreadful consequences*: Any DC that wants to avoid the dreadful consequences highlighted above, must strive to become a part of the digital economy!

2. *Institution strengthening*: The digital economy, including technologies such as e-gov and the internet of everything (IoE), will help to strengthen institutions in the DC, and enable it to leapfrog its institutional weaknesses.

3. *Economic boom*: This should be the greatest attraction of the KBE to the DCs. The creation, distribution, and application of knowledge — which are the basis of the knowledge economy — have been the most important factor responsible for the dramatic rise in living standards in the countries that have keyed into it. For example, as we saw earlier, Jorgenson (2014) found that about 70% of the economic growth of the United States, in the period, 1995 to 2002, came from the knowledge-intensive sector.

   That is also what we have seen in the economic boom of nations such as <u>India</u>, <u>China</u>, <u>Vietnam</u>, <u>Argentina</u>, <u>Brazil</u>, <u>Costa Rica</u>, <u>Chile</u>, <u>Indonesia</u>, <u>Estonia</u>, <u>Korea</u>, <u>Mexico</u>, and <u>Puerto Rico</u> that have succeeded in beginning to play in the digital economy.

   This ability to play in the digital economy is also expected to be the decisive driver of economic growth and prosperity in the unfolding 4th technological turning point.

Chapter 23

23. How A DC Can Make The Transition

"The jobs that the robots will leave for humans will be those that require thought and knowledge. In other words, only the best-educated humans will compete with machines; and education systems in the US and much of the rest of the world are still sitting students in rows and columns, teaching them to keep quiet and memorize what is told to them, preparing them for life in a 20th century factory."

(Howard Rheingold, an internet sociologist, 2014)

Topics Covered in This Chapter:

- Getting ready for the transition
- Other technical steps towards the transition
- It is not dreadfully capital intensive
- You must get your FIPA right

Getting Ready For The Transition

As we argued in the last Chapter, striving for the digital economy is a worthwhile venture for every DC – not just because of the huge rewards of success, but also because of the dreadful consequences of remaining outside that economy! Yet, despite the successes that many nations have recorded from making the transition, the odds against it, for a typical DC, are significant! The purpose of this Chapter is to suggest how a DC can successfully make the transition. Let us also bear in mind that making this transition is a very serious business, not the kind of empty mantras that political leaders often dish out.

Here are some of the initial considerations:

1. *Patriotism & vision*: The DC must have a leader with vision and real passion for the nation's future – a leader with the liver to break away from parochialism and obsession to:

   a. Amass wealth (for self, family, or loyalists);
   b. Cling to power at all costs;
   c. Ensure that power remains within the family, tribe or religious group;
   d. Use state institutions principally for clinging to power;
   And so on.

2. *An effective FIPA*: As we have seen, foreign direct investments (FDIs) including outsourcing opportunities, are a favorite path to this transition. But they are not easy to secure, as many nations are competing for them – very fiercely. That is why every DC striving for this transition needs to have an aggressive and highly focused foreign

investment promotion agency (FIPA) to help in driving its national efforts. We have set out a separate subheading in the Chapter to discuss this agency in more details, because of its importance.

3. *Awareness creation*: One of the early tasks for the FIPA will be to conduct an elaborate series of workshops for policymakers and top officials of all the tiers of government, on globalization and the digital economy, so that they can become aware of what is at stake, and the very high sense of urgency required.

4. *Assess the comparative strengths*: Another early task of the FIPA will be to do an assessment of the DC's comparative strengths. The DC will be wiser to start by identifying the sector(s) where it can have relative competitive advantages, including high-growth potentials. It can then focus its outsourcing (and other FDI) efforts on those sector(s), confident that all initiatives to develop the sector(s) – such as educational programs and special sectorial incentives – will be consistent with the DC's overall long-term economic development interests.

Some of the factors that can confer competitive advantage on a DC include the following:

a. *Local input prices*: This is one of the most important reasons why firms in the advanced economies outsource – i.e. to reduce production costs, so that their goods and services can remain competitive. For example, if labor costs are 90% less in Vietnam than in the US, a product manufactured in the US will be significantly more costly in the international market than one made in Vietnam, using identical processes. So in order not to be at a disadvantage with other competitors in the international market, the US firm will seek to build its production facility in Vietnam.

However, as noted by Erran Carmel, while low wages will initially attract foreign outsourcing jobs, competing simply on low wages will ultimately not be a sustainable strategy. For example, national software industries that do not add value beyond simply being the "low-cost producer" will soon see their projects shift to newer lower-cost destinations, in a "race to the bottom" (of the wage scale).

b. *Rule of law*: One of the most important considerations of the foreign investor is the protection of their investment in a DC. Any DC that is serious about attracting FDI, must appreciate this, and facilitate the rule of law, rather than viewing this legal recourse as confrontational.

Case 118:   **When MTN Went To Court**

Earlier, we looked at the huge fine of $5.2 billion (N1.04 trillion) that the Nigeria's telecoms regulator, the NCC, slammed on the Nigerian operations of MTN in October 2015. One of the initial reactions of MTN was to go to court, to challenge the fine.

Segun's Adeniyi of Thisday newspapers, who clearly understood how the nation's institutions worked, seemed to remind MTN of the implications:

- "Now that the company has decided to go to court after admitting its guilt in writing to the Presidency … so many other things have come up about MTN operations in Nigeria and the manner in which the company might actually have been breaking our laws, especially on remittances and taxation. These are issues that the relevant authorities are now looking into since the company wants to fight."

----

c.   *Reliable labor force*: No firm will want its work to be bogged down in another country by labor bottlenecks, either because of lack of requisite skills, or labor turnover, or because enough workers are not available, or even due to union-related activities. A DC with business-friendly labor policies, which also has an effective pool of educated and skilled workforce, will be at an advantageous position. National labor practices (union activities) can be a big issue. A potent workforce is the outcome of deliberate government policies.

Case 119:   **Vietnam's Proactive Education System**

For example, from TMA Solutions, we can get some insight on Vietnam's proactive policy of developing a technological labor force.

- As highlighted by TMA Solutions, mathematics instruction has long been the strong suit of Vietnam's educational system. In addition, government has since been trying to train people across the country in computer skills, such that today, the country has thousands of university and college graduates who are keeping up with the demand for professionals in the Vietnam software outsourcing industry.

- The net outcome, as highlighted by the Vietnam Economic Times, is that the country's overall literacy rate is as high as 96% with 80% of the country's college graduates holding degrees in the sciences.

----

d.   *Language:* It is very helpful when both international parties in an outsourcing program are at ease with a common language, so that communications can flow, not only between the top management teams, but also at the level of the schedule officers that will be interacting on a daily basis. Since English has always been the dominant language of business (especially computing), English skills tend to be critical. This has been one of the factors behind India's success in outsourcing – the abundance of skilled, English-speaking manpower. A DC unfamiliar with English may therefore find it useful to popularize the study of English in its educational curriculum.

Case 120:   **Teaching Of Maths & Science Subjects In Indigenous Languages In Nigeria**

In May, 2017, there were media reports about the move by the federal government of Nigeria to start teaching Mathematics and Science subjects in indigenous languages. In line with this, government had set up an inter-ministerial committee (involving the Ministry of Science and Technology and the Ministry of Education), to develop the capacity of the local languages to serve as effective tools for teaching mathematics and science subjects.

Government considered that this policy would:

- Help Nigerian students to understand mathematics and science subjects better;

- Promote the application of science and technology for national development; and

- Speak to the concern of the government over the low interest in mathematics and the science subjects by students

It is important that this policy does not in any way weaken Nigeria's native competitive advantage in English-speaking manpower (being a former English colony), at a time that many non-English-speaking nations are striving to popularize the language in their own education curricula.

(For more details, see Premium Times, May 31, 2017)

e. *Intellectual property protection:* The outsourcing project will usually involve proprietary information; and so the prospective foreign firm will be very interested in the kind of policies a DC has in place for protecting trade secrets and intellectual property-rights.

f. *Socio-political stability:* No foreign firm will want to outsource to a country with a history of upheavals and uprisings – for example, where ethnic or religious tensions are high, such that projects can be disrupted by political crisis; or where its employees visiting the country can easily be targeted or even kidnapped.

g. *Economic Stability:* This is also very important. No foreign firm would want to outsource to a country where economic policies are turbulent (for example, where exchange policies can change rather dramatically). Are there any preferred sectors? What are the tax rates? And so on!

Similarly, general incentives that apply to all companies that meet prescribed conditions, are more credible and stable than those offered to a specific investor on a somewhat discretionary basis. In this sense, rather than offering special concessions to a prospective investor, it is better to carry out reforms (even if inspired by that investor) that improve the DC's overall competitiveness. From experience, special concessions can also arouse future opposition, unlike reforms that improve a DC's overall competitiveness.

Finally, a DC that is a part of some international trade treaties and pacts will ordinarily be more attractive than one that is not.

Other Technical Steps Towards The Transition

The following are other specific steps that each DC striving to become a part of this all-important digital economy, can consider. The DC's FIPA will usually find itself pushing for these.

1. *Telecoms deregulation*: A vital step for launching into the technology arena, is high national mobile penetration – which in many cases, telecoms multinationals will provide at

no cost to a DC! In fact, these multinationals have been paying license fees to nations for the privilege to provide them with mobile services! For example, MTN and other telecoms companies each paid a whopping $285 million to the Nigerian government (as license fee), for the right to come into the country and provide telecoms services. Therefore, a DC that has not deregulated its telecoms sector, should consider doing so!

2. *Serious attention to education*: For a nation to be relevant in the emerging technology-intensive era, it needs to start aggressively to develop a workforce that will be educated, highly skilled, and digitally literate! According to JP Rangaswami, the chief scientist for Salesforce.com:

> "The effects (of emerging technology) will be different in different economies (which themselves may look different from today's political boundaries). Driven by revolutions in education and in technology, the very nature of work will have changed radically—but only in economies that have chosen to invest in education, technology, and related infrastructure."

Education will hold the key to future prosperity of not just the DCs but all nations. Because of its importance, we shall devote the whole of the next Chapter to it.

3. *Encouraging firms to use the internet*: The Chinese government has been promoting local digital economy, through its *"Internet-Plus"* policy, which encourages firms to begin to use the internet in their operations. The hope is that this will facilitate healthy development of e-commerce, ultimately increase their international presence. Our DCs can take a cue from that!

4. *Strive for outsourcing opportunities*: The DCs that are able to create the enabling environment for a thriving outsourcing industry will immediately gain extra job opportunities, economic prosperity, and technology transfer, which will come with outsourcing. The technology transfer will become a foothold into the digital economy!

Technology has greatly simplified the logistics of coordinating project activities across nations and continents. Today, a firm in the global economy can afford to break up the production process into small, specific slices; and perform each slice in whatever nation it can be done optimally – for example, where the firm can find the optimum combination of political stability, labor quality, workforce efficiency, and cost savings.

Consequently, businesses (including the technological companies in the advanced nations, under intense global competitive pressure, are constantly shopping for prospective outsourcing partners across the DCs; and this has been transforming the economies of many hitherto poor countries.

Today, international outsourcing spans a wide variety of business functions, such as:

a. Software development;
b. Customer care;
c. Production, testing and assembly plants;
d. Medical transcription;
e. Medical billing services;
f. Database marketing to Web sales/ marketing;
g. Accounting;
h. Tax processing;
i. Transaction document management;
j. Telesales/ telemarketing;
k. HR hiring and biotech research

We should also expect that the production of most of the hardware and software systems that will drive the imminent 4th technological revolution, will be outsourced to many low-cost DCs. Imagine the knowledge, skills and future productive capacity that this will generate in the benefiting DCs! It will give such DCs a leap into the information economy!

5. *Leveraging Diaspora linkages*: Some DCs have thousands of citizens in the advanced nations, who originally travelled there for education, as refugees and asylum seekers; or otherwise in search of greener pastures. A DC's FIPA can facilitate liaison programs with these people (especially those that have risen to responsible positions in their foreign lands). If properly incentivized, these Diasporans can help in channeling investments projects to their home nations. They can even help in packaging their home nations to become more attractive for FDIs.

> **Case 121:**   **Erran Carmel's Examples of Diaspora Linkages**
>
> Here is some insight from Erran Carmel on the role that Indian professionals in the Diaspora have been playing in this regard:
>
> - According to Erran Carmel, the success of the Indian software industry is due in part to the successful and well-placed diaspora of Indians in US high-tech firms. This generation of Indians came to the US for education, stayed on and rose to influential positions in these firms. We see these diaspora linkages in other countries that have succeeded in high technology - Israel, Taiwan, Korea, China, and Ireland. The "brain drain" has become a "brain gain" in the ties and know-how that have been forged between firms in the home countries and the countries of the diaspora.
>
> - These scientists and engineers left their home countries and, many years later, returned, or invested in, or encouraged acquisitions in their home countries. In the case of Israel, many of the US technology firms' R&D centers (e.g., Intel, Microsoft) were established as a result of Israeli expatriates working for the US technology companies who wanted to repatriate to the home country

6. *Importing the "seed" human capital*: A DC, guided by its FIPA, which does not immediately have the right calibre of domestic human capital, but can otherwise secure outsourcing businesses, can leapfrog the home-grown human-capital deficiency, by importing and using foreign professionals. Here is an example from Barbados, as reported by Erran Carmel:

> **Case 122:**   **Leapfrogging The Home-Grown Human-Capital Deficiency In Barbados**
>
> As noted by Erran Carmel, Barbados in the Caribbean was the base of a (briefly) successful IT services firm that imported software professionals (mostly from India) to work on projects for large US customers.
>
> Panama subsequently created a new technology park in former US Army bases, with plans to emulate this model by importing hundreds of software professional from outside Panama.

(For more details, Please see Erran Carmel, 2003)

7. *Creating contract linkages*: Sometimes, an advanced country wants to provide aid to a DC, or a multinational company (MNC) is seeking to sell a product to the DC. In either case, the DC, most likely guided by its FIPA, can specifically ask that a given chunk of the project be outsourced to local firms, as a way of helping the DC in local capacity building.

India today is not only a foremost emerging technological nation, but also an outsourcing capital of the world. Manu Joseph, editor of an Indian newsweekly, shares some insights on how this seed was sown in India:

Case 123:   How India Won GE's Software Outsourcing

According to Manu Joseph, editor of an Indian newsweekly, Jack Welch, the chief executive of General Electric (a United States multinational company) was once in India to persuade the country to place an order for G.E. aircraft engines. Present at the meeting was Sam Pitroda, a technology adviser to the Indian Prime Minister, Rajiv Gandhi. After Mr. Welch said what he wanted from India, Mr. Pitroda said,

"Fine, but first we want you to outsource $10 million of I.T. software work to India."

Jack Welch, G.E.'s famous boss, was somewhat surprised (startled), but he finally said,

"Fine. Done."

And G.E. became the first U.S. company to outsource software work to India!

(For more details, see "The Coalition of Competitors", by Kiran Karnik, the former president of India's National Association of Software and Services Companies, NASSCOM).

8. *Technology clusters*: A DC under the well-packaged guidance of its FIPA, can consider creating a pilot technology cluster (a technology park, much like the industrial or free-trade zones that many DCs already have) where it can provide a relatively higher level of infrastructure (power supply, connectivity, security, and so on) than in the rest of the country. The people in the DC, who will play in the global software outsourcing market, require such infrastructure.

If well implemented, the park will serve as a vital local technology incubation engine, which in due course (especially with other encouragements) can begin to attract outsourced jobs from the developed economies.

All things considered, it is wise to locate the cluster near a major university or other research institution, so that:

a.   The cluster can take advantage of the university system, which creates knowledge (through research), and produces the scientists, engineers, and other skilled individuals it will need; and

b.   The university (being itself a vital node for the creation and diffusion of knowledge in the knowledge economy) can benefit from the enhanced level of infrastructure of the cluster.

<u>**Case 124:**</u>   <u>**Symbiotic Relationship Between Universities & Technology Parks**</u>

From Hulsink etal (2008), we see that the Silicon Valley (SV) area of California, and the Boston/Route 128 area of Massachusetts (both in the United States) can be good illustrations of this symbiotic relationship between technology parks on one hand, and universities and research institutions on the other.

The SV area, which is now a renowned high-tech region, featuring extensive cutting-edge technologies, office blocks, large-scale shopping centers, and a close-knit network of highways, was originally a very rural community, known for growing fruits and vegetables. As pointed out by Wim Hulsink et al, the nearness of Stanford University played a key role in SV's transformation: the university was continuously seeking to commercialize new knowledge and innovations through contract research, and by promoting start-up and spin-off companies (all of which the SV area was fertile for).

Similarly, the high concentration of universities, research institutes and hospitals in Boston/Route 128 area, helped to transform the area into a beehive of ICT firms, which have made Massachusetts one of the most technologically advanced states in the United States.

(For more details, see Hulsink, Wim; Manuel, Dick & Bouwman, Harry (2008))

9. *<u>Demo site arrangement</u>*: A DC, propelled by its FIPA, can seek some form of collaborative arrangement that will lure technology multinationals to come and set up pilot "demo" systems within the country – much like Brazil did with its Águas de São Pedro project.

<u>**Case 125:**</u>   <u>**Brazil's Pilot Smart City of Águas de São Pedro**</u>

As noted by Roberta Prescott, Brazil is transforming its city of Águas de São Pedro, located about 187 kilometers from São Paulo, into a pilot smart city, in partnership with technological giants, Telefónica Vivo, Huawei and other partners. Already they have deployed smart solutions in the areas of health, education, security and tourism.

According to Roberta Prescott, the city did not have to spend its own money on the project, which had effectually turned it digital. Instead, technology multinational, Telefónica Vivo, made the main investment of about $576,000 on the project. Other multinational partners, such as Huawei, also made investments. The common goal of the companies was to make Águas de São Pedro a demo city (or showroom) for their technologies, for the benefit of other cities and nearby nations – knowing (as they say) that "seeing is believing"!

(For more details, Please see RCR Wireless News, August 18, 2015)

An important point to note from the Águas de São Pedro project is that this kind of project does not always have to be an initiative of the central government; a state government, local council, city (as in Águas de São Pedro) can also initiate it! It depends on the arm of government striving most aggressively for the information economy!

It Is Not Dreadfully Capital Intensive:

An interesting paradox of the digital economy, is that despite being all about technology, it is not as capital intensive as a DC would ordinarily fear! It is more about knowledge and ideas, than capital.

For example, some of the biggest names in global ICT today, started out as unserious jokes – sometimes in the innovators' bedrooms, or garages! We can also even consider the phenomenon of the so-called virtual companies: These are companies that exist on the internet (usually, doing energetic business through the internet), but without physical offices anywhere. A creative person with only a laptop (of late, even smart phones), can take time to design a beautiful and effective website on the internet, and use it to trade. In the internet, it can afford to compete with the biggest multinationals, even without having much of physical assets! This is possible because the company provides its customers all the information they need about whatever it is selling, so the customers have no need for its premises! What the company is selling may even be located in other countries and continents!

We can use the well-known garments company, Li & Fung (as presented by wikibooks), as an illustration.

Case 126: Li & Fung, The Garments Company

As Li & Fung, which operates in the global garments industry, receives an order, it uses personalized Web sites and e-mail to fine-tune specifications with the customer. It then feeds those customers' instructions into its intranet to find the right supplier of raw materials and the right factory for assembling the clothes.

For example, Ada Liu, Li & Fung's Division Manager, explains how she once juggled an order for pants from a major American clothing brand: She had the fabric woven in China because the factories there could dye it the dark green indigo she needed, and she chose fastenings from factories in Hong Kong and Korea, because they were the most durable. Then she sent the raw materials to Guatemala for sewing. Why did she choose Guatemala for the sewing?

- "For simple things like pants with four seams, Guatemala is great! They can do things quickly, and it's close to the U.S. Delivery takes only a few days."

As the order moved through production, the client could make last-minute changes through the Web site, which tracked the entire production process. For example, until the material was woven, the client could cancel the order online. Until the fabric was dyed, the client could change the color. Until it was cut, the client could change the design or size; and so on!

What if production problems arose in Guatemala? Li & Fung would simply tap into its worldwide network and send the order to another country to avoid delays.

In the past, when the company was run by phone and fax – for example, when Li & Fung would get an order for 50,000 khaki cargo pants, and deliver the goods five months later – such adjustments were difficult and were a source of disputes. But with improved technology, adjustments had become easier to accommodate and effect, reducing disputes and making customers happier.

Now, here is the most interesting thing about Li & Fung: it owned no factories, no machines and no fabrics. Instead, it dealt only in information, on a far-flung network of more than 7,500 suppliers in 37 countries, from Madagascar to China to Guatemala. According to William Fung, the Managing Director,

> "There are no secrets in the actual manufacturing. I mean, a shirt is a shirt, we would rather build on something proprietary, like what information it takes to make that shirt faster or more efficiently"!

- Source: wikibooks.org (as at 28 August 2002)

The explanation by William Fung, the Managing Director, also illustrates an important and growing feature of the global economy: The world has become a global village! We can see how Li & Fung is able to break up the production process into small, specific slices; and to perform each slice wherever it can be done optimally! The world has indeed become a global village!

You Must Get Your FIPA Right!

Every DC striving for transition to the information economy needs to have an aggressive and knowledgeable foreign investment promotion agency (FIPA) to help in driving its national efforts. Such a FIPA can be pivotal in attracting foreign direct investment (FDI) and in the DC's successful transition.

In many DCs, governments in good faith set up FIPAs as a part of the public service. The problem is that in the prevailing weak institutional environments of the DCs, such FIPAs tend to acquire the same corrupt, ossifying and docile features of the DC's civil service system. As pointed out by Andrés Rodríguez-Clare, the DC's organized private sector is in a better position than government, to launch an effective FIPA, as a non-governmental agency.

The first job of the FIPA would be to push for institutional reforms to facilitate FDIs, including the kind of 1st-generation reforms discussed in Slice B. These initial steps will help to create the right climate, as well as build up the "pressure coalition" and momentum for institutional reform. This pressure coalition is vital in weakening the resistance to reform, which is always very strong. We can use Costa Rica's CINDE to illustrate how aggressive and knowledgeable a FIPA needs to be in the fiercely competitive global FDI market!

Case 127:   How Costa Rica Won A Major FDI From Intel

As reported by Andrés Rodríguez-Clare, many analysts believe that Costa Rica's ground-breaking success in attracting Intel (the United States-based global technological giant) in 1996 to build the plant for one of its newest chips in Costa Rica, would have been unthinkable without CINDE!

Thanks to its increased understanding of the electronics industry, CINDE learned that Intel was starting the site selection process for an assembly and testing plant for one of their newest chips. Given that Costa Rica was not on Intel's "long list" of possible sites and not without some skepticism from Costa Rica's highest authorities, CINDE's specialists on FDI attraction started a campaign to make sure that it was at least included in the list. Thanks to the knowhow that CINDE had accumulated through a few years of focusing on the electronics industry, they were able to put together an effective presentation of the country and finally enter the list in November of 1995.

The next step was a visit from Intel to Costa Rica in April of 1996. Intel used the visit to talk to representatives of several high tech multinationals already in the country; and the glowing reports and optimism of the executives at those multinationals were a decisive factor for Intel in favor of Costa Rica. After this visit, Costa Rica became one of the top contenders in the list, which at that stage included Argentina, Brazil, Chile, China, India, Indonesia, Korea, Mexico, Puerto Rico, Singapore, Taiwan, and Thailand. Having already 3 plants in Asia (Malaysia, China and Philippines), Intel decided it was necessary to diversify, so it dropped the Asian countries from the list. Additional research involving many visits by Intel representatives to the different locations narrowed down the list to just four countries: Brazil, Costa Rica, Chile and Mexico.

Chile's lack of emphasis on the electronics sector and air transportation logistics, made it an awkward strategic fit for Intel. Brazil, on the other hand, had a lot to offer but Intel felt the business environment, at that time, would not exactly suit the type of operation they were considering. Finally, Intel rejected Mexico because of its mandatory union rules and the fact that the incentives it offered were specific to Intel and somewhat discretionary, making them less credible and inferior to Costa Rica's more general and stable conditions.

- Intel finally announced its choice of Costa Rica in November 1996!

(Adapted from Andrés Rodríguez-Clare (2001))

That singular project would later become a watershed, which made a major contribution to Costa Rica's efforts towards the digital economy.

It is doubtful if a FIPA patterned like a typical government agency, could have mustered the kind of inspiration, agility and capabilities that propelled CINDE to success in that epoch national assignment. Not only was CINDE pivotal in convincing Intel to even put Costa Rica in its list of possible locations, CINDE was also credible and consistent in conducting research and promptly supplying the information that Intel demanded.

As noted by Andrés Rodríguez-Clare, CINDE itself was a private, non-political, non-profit organization, founded in 1983 by prominent business people, and financed by grants from the US-AID. In a similar way, NASSCOM, India's best-known pressure group, has played a pivotal role in creating the myth of Indian software genius.

In general, the organized private sector (OPS) in a DC should not be indifferent to public policies regarding foreign direct investments (FDIs). Good policies to encourage FDI create collateral improvements in business climate, as well as pressures for institutional reforms – all of which are ultimately beneficial to both incoming investors and existing businesses. A DC's OPS can inspire a non-governmental agency in the pattern of CINDE or NASSCOM.

Chapter 24

24. Repositioning The Education Institution

"We're not just going to wake up in 2031 and be a developed country, we have to work at this, and the people who will be contributing to the economy by then are in school today."

(Nivi Mukherjee, co-founder of Kenya's educational eLimu, referring to Kenya's National Vision 2030 (for the economic sustainability of the country), July 2013)

Topics Covered in This Chapter:

- Why Education Deserves Special Attention
- Why the education institution deserves special attention
- The proposed areas of focus for each DC's education institution
- Challenges facing these educational goals
- Interesting opportunities for Leapfrogging

Why Education Deserves Special Attention

The education institution can play a very vital driving role in the unfolding technology revolution, which is why every DC needs to pay a very special and urgent attention to it. The purpose of this Chapter is to highlight the profound role that this institution can play in the DCs in the surging technological revolution. The advanced nations are presently trying frantically to reposition their education institutions; and if they are doing so, our DCs should even be more desperate about it!

Here are some of the roles the education institution can play:

1. *Preparing the workforce for the emerging economy*: As Barack Obama, President of the United States of America, put it:

> "…History shows that the nations that do best are the ones that invest in the education of their people. You see, in this information age, jobs can flow anywhere, and they typically will flow to where workers are literate and highly skilled and online."

Similarly relating education to the unfolding technology revolution, JP Rangaswami (the chief scientist for Salesforce.com) put it this way:

> "The effects (of emerging technology) will be different in different economies (which themselves may look different from today's political boundaries). Driven by revolutions in education and in technology, the very

nature of work will have changed radically—but only in economies that have chosen to invest in education, technology, and related infrastructure."

2. *Human capital quality is becoming preeminent*: As technology surges at a stunning pace, a central factor for national prosperity is expected to be human capital. Even today, the most successful companies in the global economy are already those built on *human capital*, rather than on the traditional *financial capital*, as had been the case! As Geoff Colvin put it:

> "…Microsoft and Google understand perfectly well that their success is built on human capital. Both companies are famous for the scorching intelligence of the people they hire and for the brutally rigorous tests they impose on job applicants. Bill Gates has said that if you took the twenty smartest people out of Microsoft it would be an insignificant company, and if you ask around the company what its core competency is, they don't say anything about software. They say it's hiring. They know what the scarce resource is."

(Source: See Talent Is Overrated)

3. *Each DC needs to start producing globally competitive workforce*: This is a key role for the education institution, as we saw earlier. Professionals in every DC will now increasingly need to be globally competitive, to be able to secure even what would have ordinarily been the local jobs in their country – because other nationals can now as increasingly perform those "local" jobs remotely from their own countries!

4. *As a matter of human rights for citizens*: Historically, even in the advanced countries, low literacy levels, as aptly pointed out by UNICEF (1999), always go side-by-side with menial jobs, poor job prospects, low salaries, poverty and crime. Education is the single most vital element in combating poverty and exploitation – and a human right.

    Education is also a force for social change. In a DC, the people, who are educated, are always an important building block in the crystallisation of the coalition for good governance; they will begin to assert their rights, and resist being ruled like a herd of cattle!

Possible Focus Areas For A DC's Education Institution

There is a kind of convergence of expert opinions on what the focus areas should be for the education institution, as nations scramble to adjust to the surging technology:

1. *Digital literacy*: According to Stewart Riddle of the University of Southern Queensland (Australia), digital literacy includes skills such as

> "Coding, data synthesis and manipulation, as well as the design, use and management of computerized, digital and automated systems".

Success and prosperity in the emerging dispensation will require these skills, which experts believe will remain in short supply globally in the next few years, as the world economies struggle to fill the new jobs that technological is creating.

An abundance of digital skills in a DC will:

a. Enable the DC's workforce understand, operate and be at home with the emerging economy that will be driven by robots, artificial intelligence, internet of everything, big data, and others;

b. Put the DC's workforce in a position to be able maintain and even add value to the systems;

c. Foster ICT-driven creativity, innovation and entrepreneurship in the DC, which will in turn foster prosperity and job creation;

d. Enable the DC benefit from the digital revolution, rather than being turned into a meal for other more proactive nations.

2. _Some other complementary skills_: Some analysts and futurists have made predictions on some other skills that will become increasingly valuable as technology gallops ahead. As an example:

a. Stewart Riddle has argued that success in the new work order will require not just digital literacy, but also skills of lateral thinking, innovation, problem-solving, collaboration and entrepreneurship;

b. Aaron Smith and Janna Anderson have argued that demand for creative and curating activities will grow exponentially; and

c. Geoff Colvin has argued that the skills of empathizing, collaborating, creating, leading, and building relationships will become more valuable.

Looking at these predictions, we can see that technology appears to be making our _"deeply human capacity for feeling and empathy"_ suddenly valuable in the emerging workplace. Not only that the robot does not have these interpersonal skills ("yet", as Geoff Colvin would add), employers worldwide are saying that cognitive skills are no longer enough. They need people who can understand what the patient, client, or customer is really feeling. The men and women with such hybrid skills are set to win in a world that increasingly favors what Geoff Colvin calls a combination of high technological literacy and deep social sensitivity.

The DC's education institution needs to be cognisant of this! The good news is that culturally speaking, _"social sensitivity"_ may be "native" to many communities in the DCs! Consider the following real life experience:

Case 128: **Natural Potential For Empathy In Many DCs**

Many years ago, while in a village in Eastern Nigeria, it never seized to amaze me how everybody my host and I met, seemed to stop to greet us with repeated "welcome ... welcome ... welcome ... how are you? Your people? Welcome ... welcome ..." in their language. Practically every person we met, including those with heavily-laden baskets on their heads, and those that didn't necessarily know my host, would spend what looked like eternity greeting us with sincere interest. If my merely smiling and nodding, without speaking, gave me away as a visitor, a new round of greetings would start, welcoming me, wishing me well, and trying to find out if I would stay long enough for so and so event!

When I think about that experience today, I can't help wondering whether it wasn't an indication of an interesting cultural potential for social sensitivity and empathy, which could be honed! Ironically, once any of these natives migrated from their villages to the cities in search of better life, they would likely hurry to do away with their "village" habits, in their haste to become city-like!

3. *Time to revisit the conventional career advice*: Developing nations used to be advised to focus their educational efforts on the STEM subjects (science, technology, engineering and Maths) for producing scientists, technologists and engineers. Well, that is still fine for the DCs, because they have a huge digital gap to bridge. However, the foregoing picture of the future suggests that the most valuable human STEM products of the future will be those that can additionally empathise. According to Geoff Colvin:

> • The emerging picture of the future casts conventional career advice in a new light, especially the nonstop urging that students study coding and STEM subjects—science, technology, engineering, math. It has been excellent advice for quite a while; eight of the 10 highest-paying college majors are in engineering, and those skills will remain critically important. But important isn't the same as high-value or well-paid. As infotech continues its advance into higher skills, value will continue to move elsewhere. Engineers will stay in demand, it's safe to say, but tomorrow's most valuable engineers will not be geniuses in cubicles; rather they'll be those who can build relationships, brainstorm, collaborate, and lead.

> *(See Fortune, July 23, 2015)*

Challenges Facing These Educational Goals

From all that we have seen in this Slice, the work for the education institution of the future is already set out – nurturing digital literacy in the DCs, nurturing the other skills that the jobs of the future will demand, producing globally competitive workforce, and shaping and reshaping citizens for the race against machines.

In repositioning this institution for these tasks, the challenges that policymakers can anticipate, including the following:

1. *Weak institutions, including Corruption*: The project of getting the education institution in a DC to perform this flagship role, must contend with the corruption, self-centeredness and generally weak governance institutions. Even getting the education institution to recognize and acclimatise to the new and urgent role it must play, will in itself be a massive project! To illustrate this, let us remember our earlier example, where we used Nigeria's education sector to illustrate the apparent insensitivity of the nation's public service to the people it was serving.

<u>**Case 129:**</u>   <u>**The Challenge Of Getting The Education Institution Up To Speed**</u>

Earlier, in Slice B, we used Funmi Ogundare's submission on the enormity of the challenges facing the Nigerian education institution, to illustrate what appeared to be the insensitivity of the public service in the DCs, to the peoples' needs. For example, according to Nigeria's Appropriation Act 2006, the Ministry planned to spend 78% of its total budget as recurrent expenditure (roughly for staff welfare and some other overheads) leaving only a paltry 22% for all the capital projects begging for attention in the sector!

Remember also that even when years later, the size of its overall budget had increased by a whopping 155% (an increase one would have expected to go entirely into capital projects), we observed that it was rather the Ministry's recurrent expenditure that exploded in size, by a whopping 189.0% which represented 88.0% of the total education budget! That left an even more miserable 12% for capital projects in the sector!

Will it not be a challenge to get institutions in this form, to rise promptly to the urgent task of striving for the digital economy?

2. *Massive illiteracy*: Many DCs will be starting from very poor literacy levels! In some parts of Nigeria for example, one can find many generations of citizens that are stack illiterates, absolutely unable to read or write in the conventional sense! These people are also for the global economy, where jobs are being created for only the highly educated, highly skilled, and digitally literate! This means that the education institution has far more work to do in a typical DC, than in the developed nations!

3. *Out-of-tune curricula*: There is also the challenge of old-century education models that are continuing to prepare young people for jobs that no longer exist! As Smith & Anderson) put it:

> "[we are] still sitting students in rows and columns, teaching them to keep quiet and memorize what is told to them"!

There will also be the challenge of faculty members that may not be in a position to impart the required education experience on their students. Tenure and promotional criteria may need to be re-weighted to reflect digital criteria.

4. *Budgetary constraints*: This is of course a major factor. Many DCs will be hard-pressed to muster the budget needed to revamp their education institutions, including upgrading the teaching staff, and equipment.

Interesting opportunities for Leapfrogging

Even with these challenges, technology is also creating some new and interesting opportunities for reengineering the education institution in the DCs.

Some of these opportunities include prospects for leapfrogging the present educational impediments:

1. *Distance learning*: A DC can leverage the growing popularity of "distance learning" to put education within reach of many more citizens, who might otherwise have been shut out by limited physical capacity! Many nations are making a departure from the historic perception of the tertiary school as being one-dimensional (physical) – because "distance learning" and other technologies are increasingly making the tertiary school multi-dimensional (both physical and virtual)!

2. *Global campuses*: The DCs can also strive for local sites from the big universities in the advanced countries that are increasingly establishing tech-driven overseas campuses.

3. *Corporate-academic partnerships*: Tertiary education should be relevant to the skill needs of the economy. The business community, which will be in dire need of the right skills and workforce, will be eager to partner with the education institution. This is therefore a time to make corporate-academic partnerships an important and decisive part of the tertiary education experience in the DCs – so that the education institution can be producing what the economy needs, rather than what it can!

4. *Digital flexibilities*: This includes using technology in new creative ways that leverage the new opportunities it has opened up – for example, to boost collaboration, enhance revenue, and create new markets.
   In particular, technology can now help an educational institution to:

   a. *Crash operating costs* – including deploying automated self-service programs, streamlining activities, such as course registration and career services; and more; *also boost revenue* – for example, by using e-marketing and social-networking tools for fundraising, and for redefining connections with alumni; and

   b. *Collaborate better and enrich content* – for example, with research partners across the globe;

5. *Forward-looking curricula*: Technology can now assist an education institution in the DC to leapfrog and join the efforts towards forward-looking curricula, including those curricula seeking to leverage the unique attributes of learners.
   For example:

   a. *Curricula that release learning from the constraints of traditional institutions and methods*: In particular, "online competency-based learning", is breaking down learning not by courses or even subject matter, but by competencies; it then blends competency-based training with online learning. This can potentially revolutionize education in the DCs, by releasing learning from the constraints of traditional methods. As noted by Weise & Christensen, it has a potentially disruptive power, by helping students through targeted learning outcomes, customized support, and portable skill sets that employers care about – all potentially explosive as employers create value networks that help students connect directly with potential job opportunities.

   b. *Curricula that seek to leverage the special attributes of students*: Technology can now allow education to hone on the important attributes that students may have, for best education experience. For example, Americans use "Generation Y" (or "millennials") to describe individuals born between 1982 and 2001. Amy Lynch, who has studied the millennials and the American culture shaping it, has found that they tend to have special capacity for multi-tasking and short learning curve; and to be at ease with technology; and that they tend to be impatient with long, boring lectures. Such millennials abound in other countries, including the DCs. As _Smith_ & _Anderson_ put it, these are not the people we should put in rows and columns, and teach to keep quiet and memorize what is told to them!

All these are opportunities that a DCs stands to reap by quickly and proactively repositioning its governance institutions (including the education institution) for the surging "technology and ideas" economy.

Slice F: Strengthening Institutions By Strengthening Regulation

While the education institution (treated in the last Chapter) can play a driver's role in repositioning a DC's population for the emerging digital economy, the regulatory institution can play a similarly central role in the overall reform and strengthening of governance institutions.

We also saw in Slice B, how the Crack Reform Team (CRT) could drive the institutional reform both directly and indirectly through other channels. Perhaps, the most important indirect channel through which the CRT can drive its reforms, is the regulatory institution.

The purpose of this Slice is to spotlight this institution, including the central role it can play in our DCs, not just in institutions reform, but also in generally reinventing governance.

Chapter 25

25. Leveraging Regulation To Strengthen Institution

"Removing administrative barriers…can set an economy on a path to greater prosperity and development."

(Kaushik Basu, Senior Vice President and Chief Economist, World Bank's Doing Business for 2015)

Topics Covered in This Chapter:

- Defining regulation
- A Very Sensitive Governance Institution
- What It Can Do To The Economy
- What Of Weak Regulatory Institution
- When do we need regulation?

Defining Regulation

Regulation is basically, a tool that government uses to put its laws and policies into action, facilitate economic interactions, and protect citizens and national interests, without unnecessarily hindering the development of the private sector. According to Baroness Deech of Cumnor, Chairperson of the UK Standards Board (and for a time the Gresham Professor of law), regulation is

> "the supervision of professional activity in the interest of the public as a whole, their welfare, their rights and their future, where those elements would be at risk were there no regulations"

Similarly, the World Bank's Public-Private-Partnership in Infrastructure Resource Center (PPPIRC) defines regulation as

> "The monitoring and control of a sector or business by Government or an entity appointed by Government"

Usually, this "entity" that government appoints to "monitor and control", is the regulatory agency.

A Very Sensitive Governance Institution

There are many reasons why a DC should pay very close attention to its regulatory institution. For example:

1. *It can have awesome powers*: By the nature of its mandate, a regulatory agency typically interprets the laws for its sector, creates guidelines to implement them, and enforces those guidelines.

    This means that the agency can effectively exercise all three of legislative, executive and judicial powers in its sector! It particularly exercises judicial powers when it adjudicates in the many matters that arise in its sector. Note that if this institution effectively exercises all three of legislative, executive and judicial powers – the exact thing that a sovereign state does – it means that the sovereign state has effectively outsourced a section of governance to the regulator!

2. *It is the government people see*: The interface that the citizens and economic agents (business organizations) have with government (the governance institutions they see) will mostly be whatever their regulators become to them. In other words, the governance that the regulated parties "feel" is largely the governance they experience from their regulators!

3. *Can exercise far-reaching discretionary powers*: The legislations that create regulatory agencies usually empower them to exercise significant discretion in their day-to-day operations. This power of discretion can have far-reaching implications, especially in the institutional environment of the DC, where the regulator can often get away with impunity. As Loucks and Gorman (2012) put it:

    > "... In the real world, disparate treatments occur. The regulator may have improperly construed Congressional intent and adopted more stringent rules than intended. Or, in reviewing one citizen's application, the regulator may misapply its own rules and hold that citizen to a higher standard than required. Or, an individual may choose to avoid the barrier and act in defiance of the regulation. Whether the rule is ever applied to that person will depend on the vagaries of enforcement: whether the offensive behavior is observed, recognized ... and thereafter punished by those charged with enforcement ... How a regulator uses such powers, and as to whom it chooses to enforce them, will have a disparate impact among similarly situated individuals. Not all regulators are created equal; a citizen may have the misfortune of engaging in regulated activity in a jurisdiction with an aggressive regulator. Because all human endeavors, including regulation, involve mistakes (or worse), those residing in an aggressively regulated environment will from time to time suffer from regulatory mistakes that their competitors situated elsewhere will be lucky to avoid. In American society, these vagaries of regulatory behavior constitute the legal norm ... it is no defense to assert "everyone else was doing it, how come I am the only one getting punished"

    (For full details, please see Forbes, May 2, 2012)

Another factor that helps the regulator get away with impunity is that regulation can sometimes be too technical for political leaders, who therefore often lack the capacity to provide effective oversight on the regulators. For example, few political leaders in the DCs can be expected to have the background needed to understand the regulatory issues in the areas of industrial standards, finance, securities, health, technology, and so on. Bryce C. Tingle, an expert on finance and securities regulation, put it this way (in reference to Canada's securities market):

- "Securities regulation is an obscure subject and very few politicians enter politics with the background needed to have informed opinions about it. As well, almost no member of the public votes on the basis of the quality of securities law; it would be a foolish politician that invested a lot of his or her time on it. Thus, of all the implausible assumptions behind the national scheme, the notion that the Council of Ministers will be an effective check on the regulators is surely the most noteworthy"

(For more details, please see Financial Post, December 22, 2014)

4. *A potential driver of reforms*: If there is a problem in a sector, we should look upon the regulator to navigate and structure the sector to address the problem and optimize institutional performance.

    For example, some of the most transformational reforms in Nigeria were carried out by regulators:

- It was a regulatory agency (the Nigerian Communications Commission, NCC) that midwifed the nation's telecoms sector reform of 2001, which revolutionized the nation's telecoms industry, and made it one of the fastest growing telecoms market in the world!

- It was also a regulatory agency, the Central Bank of Nigeria (CBN) that midwifed the nation's 2004 bank capitalization program, which revolutionized Nigeria's financial sector.

    This also means that wherever institutional performance is weak, it is probably because the relevant regulator is not on top of its mandate. If a central anti-corruption agency (such as Nigeria's EFCC) seems to be galloping from one sector to another, pursuing corruption culprits, it must be that the respective regulators are not on top of their sectors – they are not able to navigate their sectors to arrest the problems and optimize institutional performance! For example, if the EFCC is spending a lot of its time chasing corrupt and fraudulent operators in the capital market), it can suggest that the market regulator is NOT on top of its mandate (not able to optimize the sector's institutional performance). And so on.

5. *A potential extension of the CRT*: The potential capacity of the regulatory institution to drive reform, makes it a ready tool for the CRT. Indeed, the CRT can optimize its performance by leveraging the potentials of the regulatory agencies, and using them as an extension of its own operations. For example, if the CRT develops a template for reform, it should be able to count on each regulator to replicate it in the sector the regulator is overseeing. That way, each regulator will become the driver of the CRT's reform in its sector.

    This relationship is in the interest of the CRT because:

a. It will enable the CRT to record greater achievement;

b. The CRT has a limited lifetime: In a typical DC, the CRT is not likely to outlive the administration that set it up! In the special situation that the tenure of the administration ends before a particular reform is completed, chances are very good that the reform will be disrupted, if it is driven directly by the CRT. But the reform has a better chance of surviving if it is driven by a regulatory agency, which is a corporate body with the advantages of perpetual succession, continuity and institutional memory!

c. Reform is not always a "one-off" business – something that a Committee or taskforce (such as the CRT) can get into, execute, and then forget! It is often a continuous process, because even when a system has been put into the desired track, it must continue to be "steered", to ensure that it remains on track.

d. Reforms carried out by regulatory agencies, are more likely to be "internalised" by the civil servants who do not see the regulators as "short-timers" – unlike the CRT, who they know will soon be gone.

What It Can Do To The Economy

When the regulatory institution is working well – which means, facilitating economic interactions, and protecting citizens and national interests, without unnecessarily hindering the development of the private sector – it will tend to set the economy on a path to greater prosperity and development (using the words of Kaushik Basu, World Bank's Senior Vice President and Chief Economist). Many advanced nations, unlike the DCs, have long recognized this critical role of the regulatory institution, and are paying close attention to it.
Consider the following:

1. The government of the United Kingdom (UK) has a special body, the "Better Regulation Task Force, which advises it on regulatory issues. Indeed the UK government has done extensive work on regulation, from which DCs across the world can gain a lot of insight.

2. The United States has very vocal political constituencies campaigning against excessive regulation, which they regard as excessive government interference.

3. The advanced economies consistently score better than the DCs on the World Bank's _Ease Of Doing Business_ rankings! What an irony! The poor countries that should be most desperate to develop and grow out of poverty, are the ones putting the most obstacles in the way! As the World Bank put it

> "… The countries that most need entrepreneurs to create jobs and boost growth—poor countries—put the most obstacles in their way … Latin American countries have very high regulatory obstacles to doing business. But African countries are even worse…"
>
> ---
>
> *(Source: World Bank's Doing Business report for 2016)*

Good regulation does not just fall from Heaven; it is something that government and the regulator must have to work hard to achieve.

What Of Weak Regulatory Institution

Regulation is bad when the regulator is not regulating well. Baroness Deech defines bad regulation as the regulation that

> does not achieve its ends, is overly expensive, intrusive, resented and rigid, and lacking in understanding of the objectives of the overseen.

Weak regulatory institution frustrates and stifles business development! As the World Bank put it:

> *"Indeed, regulation can overburden businesses, making it virtually impossible for them to operate. Consider business registration. If the process is too complex— as in Equatorial Guinea, where completing the formalities to start a business takes 18 procedures and 135 days – it can deter entrepreneurs from even starting a new business. And if resolving a commercial dispute takes too much time—such as the 1,402 days in Guatemala—it can reduce the number of potential clients and suppliers for a company. Where courts are inefficient, firms are more likely to do business only with people they know. How regulations and regulatory processes are designed makes all the difference"*
>
> --
> *(Source: World Bank's Doing Business report for 2016)*

All the notorious vices that stifle development – *corruption, poor corporate governance, red tapes, frustrating paperwork, long waits for permits, the predatory public officials, and so on* – thrive in weak regulatory environment. Naturally, such economies, as noted by Richard W. Rahn (the Director-General of the Center for Global Economic Growth) produce *fewer jobs, less international competitiveness, less freedom, and a lower standard of living for most people.*

Weak regulatory institutions are a favorite of the DC's elites – in fact, the regulatory institution in general, is usually the most elite-dominated governance institution in the DCs. Regulation is often the tool the elites use in their predatory sorties on citizens and businesses.

When Do We Need Regulation?

The emerging wisdom is that government should no longer introduce regulation recklessly. Regulation can be very expensive, not just to government that will have to set up the machinery to administer it, but also to the citizens and businesses that will have to live (and comply) with it, and ultimately, to the economy, which can be retarded by a stunted private sector. Indeed, in the advanced economies, governments are now very careful about intervening in the affairs of citizens and businesses.

As a general guide, government intervention will tend to be necessary in the following situations:

1. *To structure the marketplace*: A DC needs to create the basic structures, which will facilitate business operations (the enabling environment). According to the World Bank:

> "Countless transactions are required to set up and operate a business. When starting a new business, entrepreneurs need to establish a legal entity separate from themselves to limit their liability and to allow the business to live beyond the life of its owners—a process requiring commercial registration. To operate their business, entrepreneurs may need a simple way to export and import; they may need to obtain a building permit or acquire property to expand their business; they may need to resolve a commercial dispute through the courts; and they are very likely to need an inflow of funds through credit or new equity. Regulation is at the heart of all these transactions. If well designed, regulation can facilitate these transactions and allow businesses to operate effectively; if badly designed, it can make completing these transactions difficult".

(Source: The World Bank's Doing Business Report, 2016)

2. *When there are no better alternatives to regulation*: According to UK's DBIS, government should always assess the potential impact of every new regulation, and only go ahead with it when:

   a. Government cannot achieve those goals through other methods, such as by simplifying, modifying or improving the enforcement of existing regulation; or by encouraging self-regulation; or by providing clearer information to the public; and so on;

   b. An analysis of the costs and benefits of the new regulation shows that it is preferable to all the other options.

3. *To mitigate risks*: Think of the aviation industry and the gravity of the dangers involved: Can we trust the industry not to cut corners in its pursuit of "profit" at the grave expense of public safety? Similarly, think of the drugs that we take: Can we truly trust the producers to test them thoroughly on their own, if nobody is independently ensuring they that do? Another example is the threat that industrial and toxic wastes pose to the environment: Can we trust companies on their own, to ensure utmost safety standards in the disposal of these wastes – without cutting corners?
The risks posed by some industries are too serious to be left to the mere expectation that all businesses will behave responsibly!

4. *To manage monopolistic markets*: Monopolistic markets arise because it is sometimes better for the society when a single supplier provides services (such as electricity, municipal water, and gas supply) in a geographical area, instead of multiple firms wastefully deploying crisscrossing assets. Since the restraining force of competition will not be present in a monopolistic market, regulation can help to protect consumers from possible irresponsible behaviors of the firms that have been allowed to function as monopolies.

5. *To protect the public in other ways*: In general, the goal of business is to make profit – as much profit as it can. The pressure to make this profit sometimes causes businesses to overlook necessary precautions, or even make shortcuts that may be harmful to the society in the long-run. James O'Toole, Director of the Neely Center for Ethical Leadership at the University of Southern California, gives some other examples:

"In the 1970s the growing problem of air pollution in the U.S. would not have been addressed if the nation had waited for the auto industry to voluntarily introduce catalytic convertors. If virtuous manufacturers had taken the lead and adopted those costly devices, they would have found themselves at a significant price disadvantage against converter-less competitors … Similarly, society can't depend on the benevolence of convenience-shop owners not to sell cigarettes and booze to minors. Indeed, the laws prohibiting such sales benefit virtuous shop owners because they prevent their less scrupulous competitors from gaining the advantages of increased market share."

6. *To reduce market information asymmetry*: Information asymmetry tends to make the marketplace dubious and fraudulent. Unscrupulous businesses exploit this asymmetry to dupe consumers, or to make good profit without adding positive value – which can prevent the market from developing in an economically helpful direction. Regulation can reduce this asymmetry, for example, by creating disclosure standards that can put most of the stakeholders in a position to begin to make informed decisions.

7. *To acquire policy expertise*: One of the core goals of a regulatory agency should be to blossom the sector it is regulating. For example, the agency regulating the aviation sector should seek to create a vibrant aviation sector; the regulator for the telecoms sector should target a vibrant telecoms sector; and so on. The competent regulator usually acquires expertise on its sector, and guides government policies in that sector, including guiding government objectively on any incentives that may be appropriate for the sector.

8. *Where the powers of the parties are not well balanced*: Sometimes, government's intervention is necessary to set equitable rules, when the powers of the parties in the marketplace are not well-balanced.
Consider the following:

   a. An entrenched firm can try to run smaller insurgent firms out of the market, so as to allow the bigger firm to be in a position to begin to dictate the market conditions. That kind of situation would call for government's intervention, to protect such smaller firms and engender innovation.

   b. Sometimes a small consumer suffers some grave damage but cannot take legal action because they are a mismatch to the strong financial muscles of the defendant firm. Similarly, an individual consumer can sometimes absorb a damage from a business organization because the damage is not worth the efforts that seeking redress would require from the consumer. However, when such damage is being replicated across thousands or millions of consumers, the overall effect can become very huge for the firm. The experience of Segun Adeniyi, the Chairman of the Editorial Board of Nigeria's ThisDay newspapers, can serve to illustrate this point:

   Case 130: **When The Cost Of Seeking Redress Outweighs The Damage: Adeniyi's Experience**

   The following narration of Segun Adeniyi of his experience, can serve as an illustration of the kind of damages that individuals can suffer, which (from the viewpoint of any single individual) may not be worth the cost of seeking redress:

"A few days before the commencement of the 2014 FIFA World Cup tournament in Brazil two years ago, I received one of those unsolicited SMS on my Globacom line. It was from a number, 5836 and I was being asked to subscribe to it if I wanted to be receiving results of World Cup matches. I just deleted the message as I do several of those SMS that are being used to defraud people. That notwithstanding, I kept receiving messages about results of matches I had already watched and a week into the competition, I got another SMS that my "subscription" had expired and had been renewed. They did that about three more times. Of course the amount we are talking about is N50 which was being taken without my asking – thus practically stealing my money! "I know many Nigerians in my position, who are victims to this sort of impunity. People hardly complain because the amount being taken, albeit without their authorization, is usually small. In my own case, perhaps I was defrauded of about N200 by those behind number 5836. Small potato, but when you multiply that sum by about a million subscribers for instance, then we are talking big money here".

(Source: See The Verdict, Thisday July 14, 2016)

Situations like these would call for government's presence, and rules that can protect consumers from predatory firms.

9. *Where disorder would otherwise arise*: Government's regulation will also be useful in the marketplace, if the individual businesses are likely to otherwise act in ways that would be ultimately harmful to themselves.

> **Case 131:**   **Examples Of Where Regulation Can Prevent Firms From Harming Themselves**

- In a sector where businesses should best operate as natural monopolies (such as the power sector), regulation can help to carve out geographical markets for the firms, which will prevent them from wastefully deploying crisscrossing infrastructure.

- Regulation can also help firms in the telecoms sector to interconnect and pool resources, rather than each firm having to erect its own masts and other infrastructure, even in locations where existing masts are under-utilized.

- Another example is what can happen in the event of a firm becoming insolvent: As highlighted by the World Bank in its Doing Business report, each creditor will have an incentive to grab as much of the insolvent firm's assets as possible, even if it is in their collective interest to see the insolvent firm restructured! Regulation can help replace the "grab" tendency with an organized, rational approach.

Notice also that in these situations, regulation will tend to reduce the litigations that would otherwise be very rampant.

10. *To create trust*: In some sectors, government regulation is required to create trust. For example, the banking sector has an important role to play in the economy; but banks can only do banking if citizens are confident enough to take their hard-earned money to the

banks. To ensure that the sector plays its important role in the economy, government needs to step in and set (and enforce) the rules that will not only protect depositors, but also galvanize the industry's activities towards the direction that will be helpful to the economy.

11. _To incentivize a market_: Responsible regulation will usually create the catalyst that an industry needs to blossom – by creating rules in the marketplace that can facilitate positive interactions without unduly hindering business development. As the World Bank put it

- A well-designed land administration system, by providing reliable information on the ownership of property, makes it possible for the property market to exist and to operate. It is no surprise that land markets barely function in countries with no property registry, such as Libya and Timor-Leste.

(Source: The World Bank's Doing Business Report, 2016)

Chapter 26

26. How Regulators Can Do Quality Regulation

"These differences persist across the world: the countries that most need entrepreneurs to create jobs and boost growth—poor countries—put the most obstacles in their way … Latin American countries have very high regulatory obstacles to doing business. But African countries are even worse!"

(The World Bank: Doing Business Report, 2005)

Topics Covered in This Chapter:

- Introduction
- Understanding effective regulation
- Regulator's internal housekeeping
- Regulator's internal structure
- How to regulate along the grain
- Examples Of Situations Demanding "Along-The-Grain" Regulation
- Today's DC regulator must leverage digital technology

Introduction

The regulatory institution stands to play a commanding role in strengthening institutions; but that is only if the regulators are themselves up to speed. Because of the importance of this institution, this Chapter and the next will particularly dwell on the proper structuring of regulatory agencies.

Understanding Effective Regulation

Effective regulation is when a competent regulator, working in good faith, will be helping its sector to function in an orderly manner, discouraging frauds and sharp practices, and enhancing the integrity of the system and confidence in it. Effective regulation involves striving constantly to strike a balance between flexing the regulator's enormous powers and "responsible" regulation.

We can look at it in terms of the famous *principles of good regulation* developed by UK's Better Regulation Executive (BRE), which have since been variously enhanced:

1. *Proportionate*: Regulators should only intervene when necessary, prescribing remedies that are commensurate to the risk posed. Regulatory and enforcement activities should <u>not</u> place more than the minimum necessary burden on the regulated parties. The burden must not be out of proportion to the benefits of the regulation. The impact of regulation on small businesses should continuously be taken into account.

Regulation should be guided by the fact that all those that want to do genuine business (and they are always in the majority) also prefer a sector that functions with integrity, in an orderly manner, which discourages frauds and sharp practices, and in which there is confidence.

2. *Accountable*: Regulators should not play "gods" over the regulated parties; they should justify the decisions they make, and be subject to public scrutiny. There must be effective channels for complaints and appeals. They must be open to other options for achieving policy objectives.

   Regulation should not create administrative barriers (such as long waits for permits and lots of paperwork); it should not stifle innovation, or hold down better performers. Finally, the regulator must not be guilty of what it is regulating against – enforcement activities must follow due process. The regulators must be able to justify the resources they utilize through value-for-money reviews.

3. *Consistent*: Government rules and standards should be consistent across regulators. When regulators overlap in a sector, they should work in harmony. New regulations should be predictable (rather than jolting), and should take other existing regulations into account.

4. *Transparent*: Regulators should be open, and consult widely across the stakeholders, so that final policies are the products of wide consultations. The regulated parties should be given necessary time and support to comply. Rules and policy modifications must be well publicised and accessible. Stakeholders should be able to have relevant market information to strengthen market discipline. Finally, regulators should not lure innocent regulated parties into violations to entrap them, but should rather be open and accessible to them.

5. *Targeted*: Regulators should be focused on the problem, and minimize side effects. Those regulated parties responsible for the most risky activities should get the greatest regulatory attention, and bear the greatest regulatory burden.

As Baroness Deech put it, "right touch" regulation means always asking what risk the regulator is trying to regulate, being proportionate and targeted in regulating that risk, finding ways other than regulation to promote good practice, using regulation only when necessary, and watching out for unintended consequences.

In effect, "right touch" regulation means:

1. Striving to regulate "along the grain", as we shall discuss shortly;

2. Ensuring that enforcement activities are guided by clear guidelines, so that they will not apply differently to different regulated parties, nor be too dependent on the personality of individual regulatory officials;

3. Constantly evaluating the overall impact of regulation, including its competitive effects on any economic players in the market;

4. Being very clear on the goals & objectives of every new regulation, so that the regulated parties not only understand what the regulation seeks to achieve, but are also aware of what will come next; and are therefore in a position to plan ahead. The regulatory guidelines should be easily accessible, and in plain, easy-to-understand (not just legal) language.

<u>**Case 132:**</u>   <u>**Ensuring That Regulatory Guidelines Are Easily Available**</u>

One of Nigeria's landmark privatization reforms was the 2005 deregulation of its maritime sector and concessioning of its seaports (which the Nigerian Ports Authority had hitherto managed) to the private sector, by the administration of President Olusegun Obasanjo.

However, in a very bizarre arrangement, Nigeria's clearing agents have been crying out that they could not get hold of the concessioning agreement, to be able to determine the limits of the new private-sector terminal operators, who had taken over the seaports.

According to Lucky Amiwero, the President of Nigeria's National Council of Managing Directors of Licensed Customs Agents,

> "With the high charges at the ports, there is nobody to complain to, and there is no law with which to sue the terminal operators for breaching the terms of contract … Even the terms of agreement, which the Bureau of Public Enterprises (BPE) made with the terminal operators, are being kept secret!"

(For more details on the maritime complaints, see Thisday newspaper, 15 Jan 2012; Daily Trust newspaper, 3 Jan 2012; The Guardian newspaper, Oct 27, 2011; The Sun newspaper, Oct 10, 2011)

5. Providing meaningful opportunities (including online, as pointed out by the OECD in its Post-2015 Reflections Paper) for the regulated parties and the public to contribute to the process of preparing draft regulatory proposals, and becoming guided by superior arguments and analysis;

6. Showing the regulated parties the side benefits (when applicable) that they can realize from a new regulation, so as to discourage "box ticking" compliance.

<u>**Case 133:**</u>   <u>**An Example Of The Side Benefits of Regulatory Compliance**</u>

From Treasury Today, we have the following note on the benefits that the United Kingdom's banks could realize from complying with the extra data that the banks were requested to provide to the regulator (a requirement that the banks considered burdensome):

> "… It is also creating an environment that enables banks to make better business decisions; if they have the data for regulators, they can build the information for their own benefit. With 85% of respondents believing better business decisions came from improved data models and infrastructure created as a direct result of regulatory influence, this is surely a positive observation. There is truth in the expression 'if you can measure it, you can manage it' and … better management information systems (MIS) within banks are bound to facilitate better decision-making, at least in terms of steering the organization around revenues, costs and return on capital"

(Source: see Treasury Today's Regulation: Don't Just Tick The Box, Jul 2015)

Regulator's Internal Housekeeping

Governments, especially in the DCs, are very good at setting high standards for businesses they oversee, but without applying similar standards to their own operations – a case of *"do as I say, but not as I do"*!
Here are some suggestions to help regulators avoid falling into that mold:

1. *Good regulation*: Sincerity of purpose, guided by the principles of good regulation discussed earlier

2. *Learning organization*: The regulatory agency must strive to be a knowledge-driven organization, not a docile government bureaucracy that will itself be in need of reform!

   Instead, it should target a credible, values-based culture, which inspires not just positive perceptions and confidence in the sector, but also respect for regulation. For example, there should be:

   a. Institutionalized mechanisms for complaints and resolution, rather than for example, the regulator being defensive of its performance;

   b. A strong appetite for knowledge and for performance improvement;

   c. A culture of benchmarking with the best global practices;

3. **Quality staff**: The regulatory agency must strive to attract quality staff, for example, through effective recruitment, good corporate culture and fulfilling job schedules, fair remuneration, and very high bar of entry.
   The issue of remuneration will always be a challenge, because the regulatory agency staff will usually be interacting with industry counterparts that are very well remunerated – which exposes them (especially the good ones) to poaching, and even enticement with future job prospects.

   <u>**Case 134:**</u>   <u>**The Regulatory Challenge of Retaining Good Staff**</u>

   We can use this insight from The Economist in respect of UK's banking industry regulator, the FSA, to illustrate the kind of challenges a regulator typically faces to retain good staff:

   > "Another reason for the FSA's failures could be that it struggles to keep good staff. Ian Mason, an ex-regulator who now works for Barlow, Lyde & Gilbert, a law firm, reckons that many of the people considered "experienced" bank supervisors at the FSA have worked there for just two or three years. Keeping people of even such limited experience is a challenge, he says. Many might be earning £50,000-70,000 a year, which is probably a quarter of what they could get by moving to private firms"

   (Source: see The Economist, 27-Mar-08)

   While the agency cannot compete on remuneration, it can still attract quality staff by striving to be a center of excellence, offering professional challenges, and a sense of duty.

4. *Accountability*: The regulator must be accountable, for example by firmly putting internal mechanisms in place, for seriously evaluating its own performance and failures; and for performance reporting;

5. *Monitoring The Monitors*: The regulator must also put internal mechanisms in place, as suggested later in this Slice (under "Monitoring The Monitors") to ensure that its officials are not easily compromised; and to quickly detect when a compromise occurs.

Regulator's Internal Structure

As pointed out above, a regulatory agency should ideally be a knowledge-driven organization, rather than another government bureaucracy that will itself be in need of reform. It should not be a dumping ground, for the children of the elites, or for the friends, families and mistresses of government officials. Regulation is a serious business that calls for serious-minded professionals and knowledge workers, who should ideally be organized dynamically.

It can for example, have a "flat" organization structure, where:

1. Anybody can walk up to anyone anywhere, and talk about anything;

2. Members of the private sector can easily come in on secondment, be able to fit in, and later go back to their sector;

3. Someone can become a coordinating Director for a tenure, and then step down and become an ordinary Director, while a colleague takes over as the new coordinating Director; and so on.

How To Regulate "Along" The Grain

As we saw in Slice C, one of the interesting techniques for strengthening institutions, is to begin to structure its programs and systems "*along*" the grain. Incidentally, there is no better governance institution to leverage that technique (and indeed, most of the tools profiled in Slices C and D) than the regulatory institution!

Once the regulator decides that an existing policy or program is running "against" the grain, some basic policy options should immediately come to mind for restructuring it:

1. *Inventory taking*: As discussed in Slice C, this is always the first step – to gain clarity on what is on ground, "*where we are*" relative to "*where we want to be*", and "*why we are where we are*". Once we know "*why we are where we are*", we can now target our regulatory intervention at the counter-productive incentives, in a way that will take us from "*where we are*" to "*where we want to be*".

Let us illustrate this with the challenges facing the Nigerian health institution.

Case 135:   Strategic Questions On Nigeria's Healthcare

With respect to the deterioration of healthcare in Nigeria, and the exodus of Nigerians to other countries for medical treatment, the healthcare regulator, as part of the inventory taking, can do a brainstorming session:

- Why has the private sector not effectively intercepted this huge and steady flow of healthcare money out of the country, by bringing the desired quality into the country – the way the private sector has exploited gaps in government services in the other sectors of the economy (such as in education, broadcasting, aviation, banking, and telecoms)? Why has it not happened in healthcare? After all, patients who can afford to travel abroad for treatment, can (more than) afford the cost of local treatment, even if expensive, as long as it is the quality they need!

- Why have none of the foreign hospitals (some of which even advertise their services in Nigeria's local media), not been incentivized enough to set up such world-class hospitals in Nigeria, perhaps as subsidiaries?

- What of even those outstanding Nigerians in the Diaspora, many of whom are distinguished medical professionals, in world-class facilities all over the world: why are they not incentivized enough to set up such world-class hospitals in Nigeria?

- Why has the NHIS, Nigeria's profound healthcare initiative, been unable to propel the private sector to intercept this huge and steady flow of healthcare money out of the country?

- One of the cardinal goals of the NHIS Decree 35 of 1999 was to harness private sector participation in the healthcare services. This has largely been achieved, considering that private hospitals and HMOs today dominate the NHIS. Why then are we not seeing the famed private-sector performance from them?

- Another key objective of the NHIS Decree was to provide a "high standard of healthcare" for Nigerians! Why are we not seeing the high standard of healthcare?

- Indeed, Dr. Godswill Okara of the MLSCN did also lament that Nigeria used to rank 4th in healthcare in the entire Commonwealth, in the 1960s and 70s! What is it that is frustrating "world-class" performance, even from the private-sector participants in the nation's health sector?

(Source: For Dr. Osahon Enabulele & Dr. Godswill Okara, please see Thisday, 23 Oct 2012 & Punch, February 19, 2013)

The goal of strategic posers such as these is to help us to gain clarity on "*where we are*", relative to "*where we want to be*"; and "*why we are where we are*".

2. _Restructuring the counter-productive incentives_: Of course, once we have the clarity sought above, we can target our regulatory intervention at the culpable incentives – to move us from "_where we are_" to "_where we want to be_".

Case 136:   How To Structure The Strategic Intervention

To help us structure our strategic intervention, we can start with posers such as the following (as suggested by Osborne and Gaebler, but with some additions):

- What really does the society need from the institution?
- What is the society getting?
- Are people in the sector motivated to excel?
- Are operators accountable for their results?
- Do rewards reflect performance?
- Are we leveraging the full potentials of the sector?
- How does it benchmark with similar ones?
  And so on.

To be able to target our intervention at each counterproductive answer that is thrown up, we can further seek insight (as suggested by Osborne and Gaebler) on what may be lacking:

- Information?
- Demand?
- Supply?
- Choice?
- Competition? And so on!

Note that if we are able to have clarity on what is lacking, and successfully bring it in, we will not only succeed in regulating along the grain (by restructuring the unwanted incentives), we can even find ourselves on our way to a self-propelling system!

3. _Structuring 3rd parties as monitors_: Another tool that can be helpful in regulating "_along the grain_" in the DC environment, is sometimes to cleverly structure other 3rd parties into the process.
   There are conceivably different ways of doing this:

   a. _Liability insurance_: In some special situations, we can significantly strengthen regulation, by requiring the regulated parties to carry liability insurance policies. We can borrow from the example suggested by William Sanjour (a retired US government regulator, and member of the Board of Directors of the National Whistle-blowers Center) in reference to the massive San Juan river oil spill disaster of 1972:

      "… If BP had been required to carry a $10 billion insurance policy for an oil spill, I'm sure the insurance company would not have allowed the penny-pinching short cuts that the paid regulators allowed. If the laws are written intelligently, insurance companies can be a significant instrument for regulation"

b. *<u>By encouraging whistle-blowing</u>*: This is also a tool that a regulator can use to channel activities along the grain. It is like coopting everybody in the system into additional eyes of the regulator. In some situations, it may even be advisable to make explicit provisions in the enabling legislation for protecting and rewarding whistle blowers. As President Obama puts it, workers can be the "eyes and ears of enforcement!" Again, the advice of William Sanjour is instructive:

> "Congress ought to consider not merely protecting whistle blowers, but rewarding them. When a whistle blower's charges prove correct, they should be given a cash reward in proportion to the importance of the revelation. Whistle blowers cost much less and are far more effective than salaried government enforcement officials"

c. *<u>By empowering citizens</u>*: Citizens can sometimes be empowered to help in the enforcement of a regulation designed for their benefit. Again, William Sanjour:

> "Organizations such as "Citizens for Health and Environmental Justice" and "Global Community Monitor" teach citizens how to get actively involved in the enforcement of government regulations. For example my friend, environmental activist Denny Larson, founded the Bucket Brigade movement, which helps citizens, living near air pollution sources, get their own resources to test the air quality for themselves and inform EPA enforcement officials if the air is toxic. EPA should be sponsoring this movement as well as sponsoring citizen water pollution testing. Again, if laws are written intelligently, concerned citizens can also be a significant instrument for regulation"

Citizens can also be galvanized to start taking independent actions directly against careless operators, without having to go through any government agency. Again, William Sanjour:

> "One of the best examples of this is the use of liberal citizen suit provisions, especially with treble damages. In statutes that have this provision, citizens can hire a lawyer on a contingency fee basis and bring action directly against a violator without having to go through any government agency. If they win, the polluter pays a fine equal to three times the damages that is split between the citizens and their lawyers"

In general, striving to regulate "*<u>along</u>*" the grain will provide many important benefits to the regulator, including the following:

1. *<u>It will make the regulator's job lighter</u>*, because the regulated parties will on their own, be going in the direction of the outcome that the regulator wants – allowing the regulator to concern itself with mostly the deviants. Compare this with when the regulator will have to be running after practically everybody in the system!

2. *<u>It will reduce the role of enforcement</u>*, and thus prevent regulation from being too dependent on the personality of individuals;

3. *<u>It can stabilize</u>*: In the DC environment, any regulation that relies too much on enforcement will (as we saw in Slice C) usually lose steam in the long run.

For example:

a. The enforcement officials are themselves not monks; they ultimately usually get infected by the vices of corruption, tribalism, nepotism, and so on, which are prevalent in the environment;

b. Important and powerful elites usually have vested interests in the regulated entities, to which rulers have to pander; so there is also a limit to how far a regulator can go with "being tough" and "stepping on toes".

4. *It reduces the regulator's visibility*: Sometimes, a sector works better in the background, quietly and competently steering things, without using excessive refereeing to spoil a good ball game!

Examples Of Situations Demanding "Along-The-Grain" Regulation

Below are some examples of situations that call for *"regulating along the grain"*, rather than continuing with the usual coercive posture of government.

Example#1: Consider the following regulatory challenge that the Nigerian government faced in its maritime sector:

Case 137:   Nigeria's 24-hour Seaports Operations

In December 2011, Nigeria's federal Minister of Finance and the Coordinating Minister for the Economy, Dr. (Mrs.) Ngozi Okonjo-Iweala, directed Nigeria's private-sector terminal operators (to whom government had concessioned the nation's seaports in 2005) to commence 24-hour operations at the nation's seaports. It was a time of massive congestions and delays in cargo clearance at the nation's ports, which were delaying cargo turnover and negatively affecting the nation's maritime economy. There were loud and disturbing complaints from the nation's maritime stakeholders, including clearing agents, importers, and shippers about how the terminal operators were managing the ports.

(Please see Thisday newspaper, 15 Jan 2012; Daily Trust, 3 January 2012; The Guardian, Thursday, October 27, 2011; The Sun newspaper, Monday, October 10, 2011)

Our interest here will be on the 24-hour directive – the fact that the directive came as an order of government, rather than as an initiative of the port operators themselves! If the sector was functioning properly, the revenues of the port operators should depend on the quantity of cargoes they processed – such that the more they processed, the higher their revenues (and profits). If therefore there were plenty of cargoes waiting to be processed, why was the initiative (of extending the working hours) not from these operators themselves, who should have been searching obsessively for whatever could help them process more cargo and generate more revenues? Why did government need to compel them through a directive? The port operators were either naïve, or they were (more likely) deriving more benefits from not clearing more cargoes, than they would from trying to clear more cargo.

Notice that if the port operators had opened better means of making money (than striving to clear more goods) the directive, as well intentioned and necessary as it might have been, would be pushing "against" the grain. And like all policies going against the grain, it would never provide a permanent solution to the problem, as the regulated parties would strive to circumvent the policy – even if they were showing outward compliance!

<u>**Case 138:**</u>　　　<u>**Circumventing The 24-Hour Ministerial Directive**</u>

Indeed, circumvention appeared inevitable. There were already allegations by importers and freight forwarders accusing the terminal operators of deliberately creating contrived delays, bottlenecks and congestions that could only lead to demurrage charges and bribery.

For example, quoting a stakeholder interviewed by The Sun newspaper:

"You will go now to APMT terminal [one of the terminal operators] to pay your port charges, 5 to 10 days they will not position your container, and the demurrage will be counting; and after they position it, you must pay for the demurrage before you take delivery. The demurrage thing is a deliberate rip off game"!

(Please see Thisday newspaper, 15 Jan 2012; Daily Trust, 3 January 2012; The Guardian, Thursday, October 27, 2011; The Sun newspaper, Monday, October 10, 2011)

This suggests that even if the terminal operators kept their offices open 24 hours/day, they might be using other means to sustain the gains they were deriving from delayed cargoes.

Example#2: Our next example has to do with the "riot act" that Nigeria's electricity authorities read to the nation's private-sector electricity distribution companies (Discos).

<u>**Case 139:**</u>　　　<u>**NERC's Riot Act To Discos on Energy Rejection**</u>

In 2014, Nigeria's federal government under President Goodluck Jonathan privatized the nation's electric power sector. Before then, government's Power Holding Company of Nigeria (PHCN) was the monopolistic supplier of electric power nationwide. Government "unbundled" the distribution segment of PHCN into several electricity distribution companies (Discos), and the generating segment into several generating companies (Gencos), while retaining ownership of the transmission segment.

In November 2014, at a ministerial platform in Abuja, the Minister of Power, Prof. Chinedu Nebo, threatened to severely sanction any Disco found rejecting the power allocated to it.

In August 2015 (almost a year later), the Nigerian Electricity Regulatory Commission (NERC) was still threatening to sanction Discos that continued to reject the electricity allotted to them. All this was in a nation experiencing acute electricity shortage, with government very desperate to get more power supply to the people.

(See Leadership, Nov 25, 2014 & The Nation, August 05, 2015)

A Disco was supposed to be making its money when it received power from the transmission system, and distributed it to its consumers, who it would then bill for what they consumed. If Discos were rejecting the electric energy that was supposed to be their source of livelihood, something must be amiss! Either the Discos were too naïve, or (more likely) that they had found an easier way of making money without distributing power!

Notice that if the Discos had found such means of making money (than striving to distribute more electricity) the directive, as well intentioned and necessary as it might have been, would nevertheless be pushing "against" the grain. And like all policies going against the grain, especially in the DC environment, it would never provide a permanent solution to the problem, as the regulated parties would strive to circumvent it!

Again, the ultimate solution should be to try and gain clarity on the factors at play (through "inventory taking") and seek to restructure the counter-productive incentives.

Example#3: Our final example will come from Nigeria's lingering health-sector challenge.

Case 140: Nigeria's Lingering Health Sector Challenge

At the 2012 Physicians Week in Abuja, Dr. Osahon Enabulele, the President of the Nigerian Medical Association (NMA) lamented that as many as 5,000 desperate Nigerians were travelling abroad monthly for treatment, and spending over 500 million annually! The Head of Civil Service of the Federation, Mrs. Winifred Oyo-Ita, recently updated the loss to about $2 billion yearly, due to loss of confidence in the nation's health system.

In its editorial of 1st June 2017, Nigeria's "Sun" newspaper lamented the nation's poor health indices, including ranking 140th out of 195 countries in the first global healthcare access report of 2017, and a doctor/patient ratio of 1:4250 as against the recommendation of 1:600 by the World Health Organization (WHO), and 1:170 for the Caribbean country, Cuba.

(On Winifred Oyo-Ita, see Seriki Adinoyi, Thisday, Sep 14, 2018; Also see The Sun, 1st Jun 2017; Jethro Ibileke, PM News, Sep 11, 2012; & Patrick Ugeh, Thisday, 30 Jan 2013)

Some Nigerians have advocated a total government ban on medical treatment abroad (especially of public servants), so as to create the incentives to resuscitate the national healthcare system, and also stem the outflow of the nation's scarce foreign exchange. That can be helpful; but it will still be pushing *against* the grain, because the people to enforce the policy – the public officials – are the first set of people gaining from it. And you can trust that people will strive to circumvent such a ban.

Again, in a matter such as this, it is wiser to try to gain some insight into the incentives at play, because if those incentives remain, a ban will ultimately be frustrated in other ways. Even when the regulator has to make an immediate intervention that flows against the grain, the intervention should only be an interim measure, because the only remedy that will endure will be the one that successfully restructures the counter-productive incentives.

Today's DC Regulator Must Leverage Digital Technology

An important aspect of the regulator's internal housekeeping in today's DC environment, is to enthusiastically embrace digital technology. In the previous Slice, we saw the disruptive power of technology, and the pivotal role it could play in the DCs in strengthening governance institutions, and driving future prosperity and development.

In addition to all those advantages of technology in governance, which we highlighted earlier (when we looked at e-gov), we can particularly note that technology brings the following special benefits to regulation:

1. Private businesses in the DCs are aggressively migrating their operations to digital platforms. Nigerian banks are an example. The regulator will find it difficult to regulate these businesses unless it is itself very digital.

2. Automation will help the regulator to be more effective, responsive, and leaner.
   For example,

   a. Its services can be available 24 hours a day, seven days a week;
   b. Professionals can apply for licenses online;
   c. Citizens can conveniently lodge complaints against licensees (by doing so online); and the regulator can review such complaints during the renewal of licenses;

   d. Citizens can even check the legitimacy of anybody claiming to be a licensee before engaging them (for example, check whether the licensee is duly recognized by the regulator),;

   e. Integration across government functions and agencies will become possible, ultimately offering businesses and citizens a genuine one-stop shop for government interactions.
      For example,

      i. Instead of applying separately to different arms of government for related services, one application can serve, with the work of one agency being automatically accessible to others;

      ii. If a licensee is indicted for an infraction, it can become visible to the entire sector;

      iii. The DC can begin to build real databases (of business registration, licensees, permits, and so on) the kind of data that many advanced nations are now opening up to their publics, free of charge, to promote and drive entrepreneurship and value-added ICT services;

Chapter 27

27. How The Political Leadership Can Facilitate Quality Regulation

"We need to tackle regulation with vigor to free businesses to compete and create jobs, and give people greater freedom and personal responsibility ....I want us to be the first Government in modern history to leave office having reduced the overall burden of regulation, rather than increasing it."

(U.K.'s Prime Minister, David Cameron, in his letter to all Cabinet Ministers, April, 6 2011)

Topics Covered in This Chapter:

- Introduction
- Discarding some wrong notions
- The referee should not become a combatant
- Keeping regulators off our backs
- Other tools for more responsible regulation
- Other challenges of good regulation
- Regulatory independence & its benefits
- And Some Concerns About That Independence

Introduction

The political leadership in the DC has a very important role to play in strengthening the regulatory institution; and that is what we shall look at in this Chapter.

Discarding Some Wrong Notions

The starting point is to discard some wrong notions that the practice of regulation in the DCs might tend to suggest. For example:

1. *Regulation is not a tool for raising funds*: Government should not see regulation as a tool for toll collection from citizens and businesses.

<u>**Case 141:**</u>   <u>**Some Complaints About Using Regulation To Raise Funds**</u>

Regulators in the DCs are often accused of being primarily concerned with how they can collect more and more money from those they regulate. Consider the following:

- The verdict of the CEO of a company whose application for a license had been stuck with one of the regulators in Abuja, Nigeria's capital city (as reported by BusinessDay, Nigeria's local business newspaper):

    > "Regulatory agencies and government bureaucracy now operate as toll roads and view businesses as cash cows to be milked".

- The verdict of BusinessDay, following its investigation and research, on the N100,000,000 civil penalty (including a whopping N60,000,000 as the cost of investigations) that Nigeria's Consumer Protection Council (CPC) slammed on Coca-Cola Bottling Company, for allegedly violating CPC's orders and laid-down safety standards and regulations:

    > "N50,000 was the highest penalty such an infraction should attract".

    If indeed, N50,000 was the highest penalty the law empowered the CPC to levy for that alleged infraction, was it not interesting that the N100 million included a whopping N60 million for investigations alone!

- The verdict (on this CPC's fine) of the Nigerian Employers Consultative Association (NECA), the umbrella organization of employers in the "Organized Private Sector" of Nigeria:

    > "The CPC, in its bid to survive in a dispensation of tight fiscal policy and diminishing budgetary funding, has resorted to sleazy and untoward methods that are inimical to the sustenance of the real sector of the economy"
    >
    > ---
    >
    > *(For more details, please see BusinessDay, Nigeria, December 1, 2014)*

In some DCs, government agencies regularly roll out rules, whose real goals appear to be to raise funds for the agencies concerned. Sometimes, agencies at different tiers of government (for example, at the federal, state, and council levels) roll out independent rules and regulations, as if they are unbothered about the collective yoke on businesses and citizens!

Ironically, while the advanced nations that have a lot of businesses are making efforts to nurture those businesses, so that they can "lead the economic recovery", the DCs which should be doing everything to nurture businesses, seem to be putting the few businesses they have under siege! What a way to perpetuate poverty! The outcry of Nigeria's Hotel Owners Forum Association (HOFA) is very instructive and typical:

<u>**Case 142:**</u>   <u>**HOFA On Multiple Taxes By Multiple Agencies**</u>

According to Onofiok Ekong, National President of the Hotel Owners Forum Association (HOFA) of Nigeria, hotel operators are faced with "daunting challenges", including "multiplicity of taxes", such as:

- consumption tax,
- value added tax,
- company income tax,
- withholding tax,
- health certificate,
- waste operation permit,
- vehicle emission fee,
- contravention charges,
- business premises, and
- administrative charges for environmental audit

According to Mr. Ekong, the numerous taxes were negatively affecting the industry, and causing closures and outright change of purpose.

(Source: Premium Times, June 22, 2013)

The DCs must learn from the advanced nations, where regulation is careful not to stifle economic growth. As the UK's Department for Business, Innovation and Skills (DBIS) put it:

> "We want business to lead the economic recovery. So we need to remove all unnecessary burdens on business, making sure regulators continue to provide important protections. We know that poorly thought-out regulations cost businesses time and money. So we are identifying and reducing these through the Red Tape Challenge. Sometimes the regulation is not the problem. Inconsistent or inappropriate enforcement causes problems, or could just work better"

2. *Regulation is not a tool for settling political scores*: Government should also not see regulation as a tool for settling political scores and teaching business owners (of a specific ethnic group, nationality, political affiliation, or religion) some bitter lesson! Using regulation in this way degrades the institutional quality.

3. *Regulation is not an employer for the elites*: Finally, government should not see the regulatory institution as the employment provider for the children, friends, families and mistresses of the elites. Indeed, regulation is usually one of the most elite-dominated governance institutions in the DCs!

<u>**Case 143:**</u>   <u>**Regulatory Agencies As The Choice Place For Elite Employment**</u>

In the developed economies, the private sector is the employer of choice for young people. Very few of them want to work for government. For example, in the United States, the survey by the National Association of Colleges and Employees (NACE) for the class of 2015, found that the percentage of university students planning to enter public service declined for the 5th consecutive year, with just 2% planning to enter the public service in 2015.

In contrast, a similar poll in Nigeria will likely find the reverse to be the case, because most young people will do anything for a chance to work with the federal government – especially regulatory agencies, such as the CBN, TETF, NDIC, NNPC, NCC, PENCOM, INEC, FIRS, NHIS, PPPRA, and so on. These are examples of where you will likely find the children of the elites!

(Source: For the NACE survey, please see Steve Dobberowsky: "Succession Planning in the Public Sector? Not Impossible"; Rework, March 2, 2016)

In general, when regulation is not about national interest, but politically targeted, or designed to raise money, it tends to be overly intrusive, resented, and bad for development. In such an environment, the regulated businesses are often helplessly at the mercy of predatory government officials; and spend a lot of time and money sorting themselves out with sorties of government agencies. This translates to frustrations, higher costs of doing business, lower profitability, less international competitiveness – and ultimately, fewer jobs and poor living standards for citizens.

The Referee Should Not Become a Combatant

It can be very institution-weakening, when a regulatory agency is also an active service provider in the sector it is regulating. We shall look at this as a separate Chapter in this Slice.

Keeping Regulators Off Our Backs

Policymakers in the DCs must not inadvertently make regulation an obstacle to development. They must be careful in crafting the enabling legislation for regulatory agencies, so as not to provide ladders for regulators to unnecessarily climb on the back of businesses. Such ladders can sometimes be quiet or subtle, as in Nigeria's NHIS Decree:

Case 144:   NHIS & Excessive Government Presence

Nigeria's National Health Insurance Scheme (NHIS) Decree No 35 of 1999 authorizes the NHIS governing Council to register private and public health maintenance insurance organizations for the Scheme. But according to Section 19(3) of the Decree, registration of an organization under the Scheme

- "shall be valid for such period as may be determined by the Council; and may be renewed at the expiry of every registration, so however that, no registration shall be renewed unless the organization concerned has complied with guidelines issued under this Decree"

Consider the following: This Section of the Decree has given to the Council the powers to:

- Determine on its own, the validity period for registration, after which an organization must come to renew its registration;

- Determine (using its own criteria) whether the organization has complied with guidelines;

- Decline to renew the registration if the Council determines that the organization has not complied with guidelines

These provisions although well-intended, create a definite potential for rent collection – in the institutional environment of the DCs! For example, the Council can decide to set the validity period (of registration) to just 2 years, which will compel the regulated organizations to be frequenting the Council for renewal. Notice in addition that each time the renewal is due, the Decree has empowered the Council to delay action, or even decide outright (in the case of an organization that may fail to sort itself out) that there has not been compliance; and so refuse to renew the registration!

Notice that these have the potential to unnecessarily incentivize the Council to climb on the back of the regulated businesses! In the institutional environment of the DCs, incentives such as this will facilitate corruption, arm-twisting, blackmail, score-settling, and perhaps, even outright expropriation – all of which degrade institutional quality!

Compare this with an arrangement that merely makes provision for renewal fees (even annual fees), and allows the regulated parties to go about their businesses – while the issue of suspension of registration can come up if there is a serious contravention of the laws.

Other Tools For More Responsible Regulation

Below are some factors that policymakers should take into account in matters that have to do with regulation:

1. *Impact assessment for every new regulation*: Regulation is expensive, both to government, the regulated parties, and potentially to the economy. That is why our DCs need to halt their reckless creation of regulatory agencies.
   Every proposal for new regulation should come with an impact assessment, and only progress if:

   a. Government cannot achieve the goals in question through other methods (such as by simplifying or modifying existing regulations; improving the enforcement of existing regulations; encouraging self-regulation, and/or providing clearer information to the public); and

b. An analysis of the costs and benefits of the new regulation shows that it is preferable to all the other options.

The impact assessment should be made available to the trade associations of the sector concerned, for their review, comments and inputs.

2. *Mitigating the adverse impacts of new regulations*: To ensure discipline in the reckless creation of regulatory agencies, policymakers in the DCs should pay attention to what is happening in the advanced economies. For example, the **UK Department for Business, Innovation and Skills (DBIS) has found that** one of the biggest problems of businesses in the UK is the number of new regulations they have to comply with, which costs them both time and money – prompting the UK government to start some new initiatives that the DCs can learn from!

<u>Case 145:</u>   <u>**Some Initiatives In The UK To Mitigate The Impact of New Regulations**</u>

According to the DBIS, the programs of the UK government that help to mitigate the impact of new regulations, include the following:

- *One-in, two-out program*: This prevents policymakers from creating new regulations that increase business costs, unless they will simultaneously take out two existing regulations! In introducing a new regulation with cost implications for business, policymakers must remove or modify an existing regulation with double the cost to business

   According to the DBIS, this program builds on an earlier 'one-in, one-out' rule that applied from January 2011 to December 2012, during which period government departments not only met the target but exceeded it.

- *Common commencement dates (CCD) initiative*: This prevents policymakers from introducing new regulations haphazardly, or anytime they please. Instead, new business regulation can only come into force on 6 April or 1st October. Ahead of this, government will publish the list of the upcoming regulations, giving businesses and the public advance notice, to help them plan ahead.

(Source: the DBIS' Policy paper 2010 to 2015, Updated 8 May 2015)

If regulation can be such a burden to businesses in the relatively business-friendly environment of the advanced economies, one can only imagine what it is doing to businesses in the DCs!

3. *Regulations review*: This implies a periodic review of existing regulations, with the aim of improving (or altogether, getting rid of) those that have become unnecessary, redundant or duplicated. The review should not be an all-civil-servants affair! The **DBIS** "*Focus on Enforcement (FoE) scheme*" provides a very good guide on this to our DCs.

<u>**Case 146:**</u>   **UK's Innovative Regulation Review Initiative**

Below is how the DBIS has explained its "Focus on Enforcement (FoE) scheme":

> "This pilot scheme gives trade associations and representative business groups the dominant role in identifying enforcement issues, rather than civil servants. This will encourage reform to benefit their industries. The initiative also provides the opportunity to present findings directly to ministers and regulators. We invited applications from trade associations and other representative business groups to lead reviews. They looked at how regulation enforcement, by national regulators and local authorities, affected their area or sector. We received 14 applications. The winning bids were from the Fresh Produce Consortium (FPC) the National Farmers' Union (NFU) and techUK. These organizations made the best case for why a particular area needs review how they would carry out the review in an effective, inclusive and impartial way. They also made a successful case for government part-funding to support the work"

(Source: Please see UK Department for Business, Innovation and Skills (DBIS) "Focus on Enforcement (FoE) scheme")

As advocated by the DBIS, this review should seek the opinions of businesses and the public on:

a.   The regulations that are burdensome;
b.   The regulations that are ineffective or unnecessary;
c.   The regulations that are beneficial and should be strengthened (and how);
d.   The regulations that have created unexpected fallouts;
e.   The regulations that should be revisited or abolished

For every new regulation in a DC, policymakers can explicitly spell out a clause for this review in the enabling legislation.

4. *Structuring "sunset" clauses into new regulations*: One of the exciting regulatory innovations is the sunset clause, which puts a lifespan on a new legislation, and causes the regulation to expire automatically after a specified number of years – unless of course, government renews it. If built into the enabling legislation, it can be a very helpful tool in the DCs, for forcing government to (as a minimum) review the regulation – because the renewal process by the time the regulation expires, will inevitably call for stock-taking including public hearings and impact assessment. It will make regulators far more accountable than they presently tend to be!

    The renewal process will also be an opportunity to review any kind of independence (from direct political control) that the enabling legislation might have granted (or failed to grant) the regulator.

5. *Recognizing the peculiar compliance challenges facing SMEs* : Due to their limited resources, start-ups and small businesses tend to face far more challenges than well-established businesses, in complying with regulations – especially in coping with the onslaught of predatory government officials. Special provisions can be built into the enabling legislation of a new regulation, to tie the regulator's hands towards special programs for small businesses.

As explained by the DBIS, the "micro-business moratorium" of the UK's government can be a good example of this emerging trend:

> "On 1 April 2011, we introduced a 3-year freeze on new UK regulation for businesses with fewer than 10 employees, including start-up businesses. Known as the micro-business moratorium, the freeze applies to business regulations that came into force before 31 March 2014"

6. *Closing "revolving" doors*: A potential conflict of interest can arise if a regulatory official is free to take up employment with a firm that they regulate, after leaving their agency. The DBIS calls it the "revolving door"; and advocates a moratorium of a specified number of years before ex-regulators can take up such jobs. In the institutional environment of the DCs, this "revolving door" restriction should not even be limited to job offers, but extended to cover other forms of business relationships.

7. *Accountability*: While some form of autonomy will be useful for effective regulation, it should not be a threat to accountability. The laws setting up an independent regulator should strive to balance autonomy with accountability; otherwise, the "unelected" regulator, who is not be subject to democratic scrutiny, may be inadvertently encouraged to go out of control.
For example:

   a. How can the regulated parties challenge the decisions of the regulator?

   b. Are there vibrant trade associations for the industry that will continuously raise alarm without fear of being targeted (which would be the case should the alarm come from any of the regulated parties)?

   c. Will there be regular and vibrant independent impact assessments of regulation? From William Sanjour, we get the following example of such independent reports:

   > "A recent study of corporate fraud among U.S. companies looked at different groups responsible for fraud detection and found that corporate employees (i.e. whistle blowers) were the leading group with 19% of the fraud cases revealed, while the SEC [Securities & Exchange Commission] was the least effective group with only 7%. This in spite of the fact that SEC employees are paid comfortable salaries to uncover corporate fraud while, corporate whistle blowers risk losing their jobs.
   > "In the health care industry, the problem is the same. Some 41% of the fraud cases are brought by employees because the Federal Civil False Claims Act entitles whistle blowers to between 15 and 30% of the money recovered. Monetary rewards for whistle blowers pay benefits far in excess of the cost when compared with hired regulatory bureaucrats"

   (Source: See William Sanjour, 2012)

The key advantage of this kind of independent study is that it brings out what is working and what is not working. For example, if whistleblowing (rather than the highly paid auditors and regulatory officials) becomes the most effective tool for fraud detection, it can call for increased attention and budget for the program.

8. *Common template*: Given the profound role that regulation can play for development (as we have seen in this Slice), and the fact that the core principles of regulation are the same, the setting up of a new regulatory agency should not be treated as the customized business of a minister, which they can design as they please. The CRT should develop a common national template for regulatory agencies, which should serve as a guide. The template will provide a checklist and guidance on the various structural issues, such as impact assessment, regulatory review, revolving doors, agency accountability, sunset provisions, autonomy (or independence) considerations, and so on. It will also help to prevent the character of a regulatory agency from being too dependent on individual ministers.

9. *Monitoring the monitors*: What if a regulator goes bad? In particular, in the DC environment, where corruption and other vices tend to be rampant, what if the regulator begins to pursue other interests? In other to discuss this important issue very robustly, we have devoted a separate Chapter in this Slice to "monitoring the monitors".

10. *Configuring the horizontal structure*: By "horizontal structure" we are referring to the breadth of functions that a regulator has been mandated to carry out. If the agency carries out multiple functions (especially functions with competing or conflicting goals), it can give rise to what Carrigan & Poole (2015) have described as "priority goal ambiguity", which can impede the agency's performance. This is particularly so when an agency delivering services, is simultaneously carrying out policy and regulatory functions.

   In other to discuss this more robustly, a separate Chapter in this Slice has been devoted to it.

Other Challenges of Good Regulation

1. *The allure of discretionary powers*: As pointed out by William Sanjour, the power to enforce, is the power to control! The allure of enforcement authority can be very strong challenge to the political will to grant regulators the independence they need to get the job done.

2. *Regulatory capture*: This is the situation where the regulated parties influence the regulator and its policies. While the views of the regulated parties should always be taken into account, it is unhealthy when the regulated parties begin to control the regulator.

   Many factors lead to regulatory capture. For example, the regulatory officials may technically not be knowledgeable enough to cope with the pace of a regulated industry; or the officials can lose their voices because of the influence of corruption; and so on. But even in the best of circumstances, regulatory capture can still evolve gradually over time, as a natural fallout of the daily interactions between the agency officials and the regulated parties.

   From William Sanjour, we get more on this in the context of the United States:

   > "The regulated community constantly deals with regulatory agencies through congressional committees, the courts, and meetings with top government officials. This is what the public sees, but it does not stop there. Industry also constantly interacts with individual agency employees at every level, working directly with the field inspectors and permit writers responsible for making regulatory decisions. For example, the inspector general of the Minerals Management Service concluded that officials in the agency had frequently consumed alcohol at industry functions, had used cocaine and marijuana, and had sexual relationships with oil and gas

company representatives. When I was in charge of writing regulations I too was the object of this courtship, showered with flattery, meals, trips, and hints of future employment".

(Source: see William Sanjour, Independent Science News, May 1, 2012)

3. *The industry lobby*: As we have seen, regulated parties can be very powerful in a DC, when the private interests of the political leaders and top government officials are involved. But even on its own, an industry can develop an effective lobby, including a powerful public relations machinery, with which it can arm-twist the regulator and even the government. From William Sanjour, we can again get some insight on this lobbying power of big business in the context of even the United States:

    "As I said, we are dealing with powerful forces. The Food and Drug Administration [FDA], the Nuclear Regulatory Commission [NRC], the National Highway Traffic Safety Administration [NHTSA], and EPA [Environmental Protection Agency] among many others regulate giant corporations. As you know, big corporations have big power, money, and influence …The EPA, for instance, cannot write regulations governing the petroleum industry without the oil companies going to the White House screaming 'energy crisis!' As a result of energetic lobbying by the automobile industry, the NHTSA cannot release the millions of automobile safety complaints in its files. When the FDA wants to thoroughly evaluate a new drug, the pharmaceutical company lets loose a public relations barrage about how the bureaucratic delays are costing lives".

One critical factor in managing this industry onslaught is the level of expertise available within the regulatory agency, which can be a factor in its capacity to stand up to the industry, fact-for-fact!

Notice also that the conscientious regulator faces the same challenge that the social activist faces while confronting vested interests: The vested interests are always well informed, well organized and desperate in protecting their privileges, while the citizens whose interests the activist is protecting are largely un-bothered, uninformed and dispersed. Again, from William Sanjour:

    "After some catastrophe or new technology, Congress creates a new regulatory agency in a wave of enthusiasm, giving it money and following the same pattern of broad, vague discretionary authority to control the richest and most politically savvy forces on Earth. But the interest of Congress, the press and the public can only be maintained for a few months or years. There are a lot of other things going on. But there is one group whose interest never wanes or wavers. The life, the existence, the future of the regulated industry depends on the pressure it can exert on the regulatory agency!"

4. *The loneliness of integrity*: **All these show that t**he conscientious regulator can be very lonely indeed, in an environment that may not be interested in competence and moral integrity! Being competent, efficient and principled is usually not what the regulated industry wants – because, the regulatory agency, by its very nature, can do little that doesn't adversely affect business. In other words, no matter how gentle we make regulation, it will tend to gag!

Unfortunately, nobody – not even the most socially responsible business – wants to be gagged! From William Sanjour, we can see that even when big business appears to be in favor of regulation, it does not really want the kind of competent regulator it cannot control:

> "Regulatory agency employees soon learn that drafting and implementing rules for big corporations means making enemies of powerful and influential people ... People who like to get things done, who need to see concrete results for their efforts, don't last long. They don't necessarily get fired, but they don't advance either; their responsibilities are transferred to others, and they often leave the agency in disgust. The people who get ahead are those clever ones with a talent for procrastination, obfuscation, and coming up with superficially plausible reasons for accomplishing nothing ... People who cooperate with industry also find that its lobbyists will work for their advancement with upper management. Those who don't cooperate find the lobbyists lobbying for their heads"

Regulatory Independence & Its Benefits

One of the most important issues for the political leadership, is the political will to grant autonomy or independence to the regulator. Regulatory independence refers to the extent that the regulator can regulate without interference from the political leadership. It is very difficult in the DCs, because the leaders will not like to give away that power of discretion, especially in the minefield of toes that the regulator can step on.

All the same, regulatory independence, even if limited, can bring some important benefits to regulation:

1. <u>Fidelity to mandate</u>: Independence can allow the regulator to remain faithful to its mandate, irrespective of the changes in political leadership (and their ideologies) as one political party replaces another in government. It will help to assure businesses (which treasure policy stability) that current policies will not suffer jolting reversals if there is a change of government.

2. <u>Legacy preservation</u>: Regulatory independence gives the government in power a way to ensure that the next administration will not easily discard its current policies. It is therefore a tool that the current administration can sometimes use to insulate its important policies from future adversarial reversals.

3. <u>Professionalization</u>: Independence helps the regulator to build the capability and processes commensurate with its mandate. This includes having its own special policy on staffing, different from that of the general civil service, which can shield it from the propensity of politicians (Ministers, senators, and so on) to saturate government offices with their relations, friends and mistresses. In this way, independence can encourage professionalism in an agency.

And Some Concerns About That Independence

Despite the foregoing benefits of regulatory autonomy, there are some possible concerns about empowering a regulator to operate independently of the government in power:

1. *Frustration of electoral mandate*: A new government can come into power with its own special ideology, obviously reflecting what the electorate wants at that particular time. It is conceivable that the regulator may not to share that ideology or the new government's sense of urgency. The question then becomes whether the unelected leadership of an agency should stand in the way of the voters' mandate, as reflected in the ideology of the new government!

2. *Agency officials may not be saints*: Independence can be a double-edged sword! How can we be sure that the agency officials will not become guilty of the same vices (such as vested interests and corruption) for which we are shielding the agency from the politicians! Even when an agency has a multi-member Board, the vested interests of the Board members can possibly replace those of the politicians – and the agency's independence may make it difficult to tame such errant officials.

3. *Poor accountability*: Regulatory independence gives rise to regulators that are unelected, whose decisions may also not be subject to democratic scrutiny. As pointed out by Carrigan & Poole (2015), independence reduces an agency's political accountability, as the agency will not have obvious political overseers; and if an agency is not accountable to any overseers, it may become less accountable to the broader public that elected those political representatives.

Chapter 28

28. Strengthen Institutions By Keeping The Referee Out Of Combat

"Truth, like the cork, cannot sink. It cannot be sunk. It always floats."

(Professor Tam David-West, in his book, Philosophical Essays, 1980)

Topics Covered in This Chapter:

- Introduction
- When referees become combatants
- How combatant refereeing can weaken institution
- Some notes of caution

When Referees Become Combatants

One unhealthy phenomenon in the DC environment is the widespread practice of allowing government agencies delivering services to double as regulators – i.e. as both referees and combatants!

Jonathan Boston describes a multi-purpose agency, which is doing both policy and service delivery, as a *"single-roof"* agency, and an agency focusing on only one (either policy or service delivery) as a *"single-purpose"* agency:

1. Single-roof agency (doing both policy and service delivery)
2. Single-purpose" agency (focusing either on policy or service delivery)

The *Single-roof* institutional structure (in which an agency is doing both policy/regulation as well as service delivery) is the focus of this Chapter. It can take different forms. Here are the two common types:

1. *Type #1 arrangement*: This occurs when the regulatory agency wets its fingers in in the sector it regulates (for example by carrying out tasks for those that it regulates, which would have been better handled by the regulated parties). We can use Nigeria's PENCOM to illustrate this:

   #### Case 147:   When The Regulator Is Assigned Some Tasks In The Service Provision

   Nigeria's Pension Reform Act 2014 established the National Pension Commission (PENCOM) to (among other functions) regulate, supervise, and ensure effective administration of pension matters in the country. In particular, PENCOM supervises the private-sector Pension Fund

Administrators (PFAs) who now manage the monthly pension contributions of Nigerian workers, as well as the Pension Fund Custodians (PFCs).

However, Section 7(2) of the Act makes the following provision for when an employee leaves the service:

- Where an employee voluntarily retires, disengages, or is disengaged from employment as provided for under Section 16(2) and (5) of this Act, <u>the employee may with the approval of the Commission</u>, withdraw an amount of money not exceeding 25% of the total amount credited to his retirement savings account …

Our concern here is with the Act of requiring retirees (as underlined above) to apply to PENCOM for approval before they can withdraw from the retirement savings they maintain with their PFAs! This arrangement presumably prevents the PFAs from stealing the workers' savings, in the name of paying the retirees.

However, in the institutional environment of the DCs, this can be institution-weakening for several reasons:

- It is unnecessary! It is just like requiring bank customers to apply first to the Central Bank, before accessing their bank deposits, so that the banks will not steal the deposits; or life-insurance customers applying first to the insurance regulator, before accessing their life insurance benefits; and so on! PENCOM can never be as efficient as the private-sector PFAs in processing the applications; so as a regulator, it should see that the PFAs do their job, rather than turning itself into a bottleneck!

- PENCOM will also be doing the job for all the PFAs combined – a job that would have been thinly distributed among the PFAs, if each PFA handled its own customers! Think of the bottleneck that PENCOM will become if for example, 1,000 public servants retire in one week! What of even the case of mass retrenchment of workers!

- The arrangement creates a gaping opportunity for "rent" for the bureaucrats in PENCOM – for vices such as corruption, induced delays, arm-twisting and so on – all of which will be degrading to the institutional quality.

- Interestingly, the arrangement denies the public a true arbiter! What if a retiring staff is unhappy with how PENCOM processes their application? Who can they now complain to, since PENCOM that should have been the referee, is now the player and culprit?

Instead of this kind of provision, the regulator PENCOM should use a variety of regulatory tools to monitor and keep track of how the PFAs disburse the funds (including getting regular reports from the PFAs, and independent feedback from the retirees).

Unfortunately the public service in the DCs is dotted with similar arrangements, where regulatory agencies carry out tasks that would have been better handled by the regulated parties.

<u>**Case 148:**</u> <u>**NCC & SIM Card Registration**</u>

As another example, consider the decision of Nigeria's telecoms-sector regulator, the Nigerian Communications Commission (NCC) in 2010, to embark by itself, on a major biometrics registration of all the telephone subscribers on each of Nigeria's private operator's network, including the new subscribers that each operator was adding daily to its network.

As reported by <u>Afolabi Ogunde</u>, the NCC in 2010 announced a N6.1 billion plan to handle by itself the biometrics registration of the subscribers on each of Nigeria's private operator's network. Of course, there were many such private operators, each of which had millions of subscribers, and was continuing to issue out additional SIM cards on a daily basis.

Many analysts warned that it would end up in failure, and advised the NCC to pass the responsibility to the network operators, who were the party issuing out the SIM cards in the first place, and therefore better positioned to do the registration!

NCC defiantly went ahead with the project, but had to eventually abandon it, when it flopped as had been predicted. However, this was apparently not before it had spent the budget, because as reported by Afolabi Ogunde, Nigeria's House of Representatives did announce in April 2012, that it would probe the N6.1 billion SIM card registration project, as it could not see any recognizable value for the money spent.

(Please see Afolabi Ogunde, BusinessNews, April 27, 2012)

2. *Type #2 arrangement*: This occurs, when the regulatory agency competes with those it is regulating. We can use Nigeria's NIPOST to illustrate this:

<u>**Case 149:**</u> **Nigeria's NIPOST As A Regulator**

In December, 2015, there were media reports on how the Nigerian Postal Service (NIPOST), the government agency regulating the Nigerian courier industry, had revoked the licenses of 8 courier firms. Incidentally, NIPOST was also in the courier business itself, because it was providing its own courier services, in competition with the private courier companies.

In other words, NIPOST, in the courier business, was also the regulator of the private courier companies, which were competing with it!

(Source: see Thisday, December 14, 2015)

How Combatant-Refereeing Can Weaken Institutions

Combatant-refereeing arrangements can for example, be institution-weakening in the following ways:

1. *Conflicts of interest*: Government officials will naturally not want to be subjected to the fierce competitive rigours that can optimize service delivery. This puts a regulator-

combatant agency in an inevitable conflict-of-interest position, if it is in a position to control the tempo of competition, by being the regulator!

<u>**Case 150:**</u>　　　　<u>**A Private "Conflict of Interest" Example**</u>

Some years ago, a man, who was building a private house, retained his nephew known as John at the site, to keep an eye on the masons and laborers working there. John's real assignment was to safeguard the materials at site, ensure that the workers were busy even in the absence of the owner, and to protect the interests of his uncle in every other way. For this, the man was paying John an agreed amount, despite their being related. One day, when the man visited the site, he noticed that John had dropped one of the laborers, and taken his place. He had himself joined in serving the masons, apparently to make some extra bucks. And of course, while he was busy carrying blocks, he was likely to lose sight of the overall picture. Worse still, instead of questioning the many rest-points of the workers (since they were daily-paid workers, rather than a contract-job arrangement), John himself, now laboring to serve masons, cherished the rest – perhaps because that kind of work was not easy for him, since he was not accustomed to it.

Note that if we regard John's original assignment as somewhat regulatory, he clearly compromised his effectiveness, when he adopted a "service delivery" role that conflicted with his regulatory mandate.

This example shows how combatant-refereeing will tend to perpetuate mediocrity in a sector, because the regulator-combatant agency may not be able to move the sector beyond the horizon of its own service-delivery limitations! The private firms can only innovate within whatever framework their competitor-regulator tolerates.

2.　*Priority goal ambiguity*: When a regulatory agency focuses on either regulation or service delivery, it can build its competencies there, and gain additional dexterity by that specialisation. On the other hand, if the agency is divided between regulation and service delivery, it could face what scholars such as Carrigan and Poole, call *"priority goal ambiguity"*, in how it prioritises its goals.

For example, regulation requires competences and skills that are different from those of service delivery – the kind of skills associated with consultants, researchers, analysts, strategists, catalysts, brokers, and persons with rich private-sector backgrounds in the industries in question. These are not the everyday attributes of service delivery!

Regulation also calls for a different mind-set (and even work orientation) from service delivery. Carrigan and Poole's observation on the United States Social Security Administration (though made in a different context), can serve to illustrate this point:

<u>**Case 151:**</u>　　　　<u>**Carrigan & Poole's Mindset Ambiguity**</u>

As explained by Carrigan and Poole, the initial focus of the US Social Security Administration, when it was set up, was on paying social security recipients. The US Congress subsequently tasked the agency with evaluating disability claims. The impact was interesting: The employees became noticeably more adversarial towards the program's potential recipients than they had been. The work culture for evaluating disability claims, had apparently conflicted with their previous gentle orientation towards the recipients!

(Source: Carrigan & Poole, 2015)

According to Carrigan and Poole, empirical evidence demonstrates that priority goal ambiguity impedes agency performance, both by diminishing employee focus, motivation, and efforts; as well as by making management's role in deciding upon and communicating agency priorities more difficult. Further, agencies beset with priority goal ambiguity struggle to ensure their employees respond in a consistent manner to the issues they face in their work environments

3. *External competition*: Separation makes it easier to force improvements in the service delivery cycle. For example, it makes it easier to open up a given service to competition. A regulator that is also delivering services will certainly not be inclined to opening up the services to external competition!

4. *Economies of scale*: Separation may also allow government to consolidate related services in one agency to achieve economies of scale from shared overheads (or in other ways).

Finally, the preferred form of separation should be "*organizational*" – in which the two entities are autonomous – legally, financially and perhaps, even geographically. This is different from "*functional*" separation, which can still keep both functions within the same government entity.

Some Notes of Caution

The foregoing suggest that *single-roof*" agency arrangements (which combine both policy and service delivery) should as much as possible be avoided. However, this should be reviewed on a case-by-case basis, because the following are also true:

1. Sometimes, the line between policy and service delivery may not be so clear. Some agencies may even be involved in activities that cannot be easily classified as policy development or service delivery.

2. Policy-making and service delivery can also be symbiotic in any given area of government business. In fact, policy-making should be informed (or at least enriched) by service-delivery (implementation) experience – which suggests that policy-making cannot meaningfully take place in complete isolation of the field experiences of service-delivery; otherwise, a gulf may develop between the world that the regulator imagines, and the reality of the service delivery. This gulf can lead to what is often dubbed "ivory-tower" policy-making!

Chapter 29

29. Monitoring The Monitors

"In the 1970's, ABC News [in the United States] conducted an integrity test in Miami, where 31 wallets containing money and identification were turned over by role players to 31 police officers. Nine of the officers kept the money and were subsequently fired and/or prosecuted. Thirty years later, ABC News replicated the integrity test in Los Angeles and in New York. Twenty wallets containing money and identification were turned in to officers of the LAPD and another twenty were turned in to officers of the NYPD. All forty wallets were recovered by the officers without a single penny missing. It is unclear if the officers have become more ethical over the past three decades, or if they suspected the wallets were simply baits being offered in some type of sting operation".

(Source: Steve Rothlein, Conducting Integrity Tests on Law Enforcement Officers, Issues and Recommendations; Legal & Liability Risk Management Institute, April 2010)

Topics Covered in This Chapter:

- Introduction
- Why monitor the monitors
- How to monitor the monitors
- The challenges in monitoring the monitors

Introduction

By "monitoring the monitors" (which we can also describe as *"monitoring the regulators"*, *"policing the policemen"*, and so on) we are referring to the policy of keeping an eye on how competently and dispassionately regulators (and those other government workers whose jobs require the use of various levels of discretion) are doing their job. Indeed, the quality of state institutions depends significantly on how these officials carry out their jobs.

In the DCs, many public officials work unsupervised, and on jobs requiring them to exercise various levels of discretion; and this is in the midst of all the corruption, nepotism, tribalism and the other vices that tend to be widespread.

Case 152:   Examples Of Monitors Requiring Monitoring

Sometimes, some job functions can be very sensitive with heavy societal implications. Consider the following cases:

- The society relies on some public sector workers in the aviation sector to ensure that only airworthy aircraft are flying in our airspace. Anytime we board a plane in the airport, we are actually hoping that these workers are handling their sensitive duty with competence and integrity; and that they have not collected bribe and allowed an unfit aircraft to carry us.

- Nigeria's bank regulators have some bank examiners, who visit the banks to examine their operations and records. The regulators rely on these public-sector examiners for accurate information on the true positions of the banks. It is what these examiners report as their findings that the regulators (and the entire banking system) largely depend on!

- Similarly, Nigeria's National Pension Commission (PENCOM) supervises the private-sector Pension Fund Administrators (PFAs) and Pension Fund Custodians (PFCs) who now manage the monthly pension contributions of Nigerian workers. The retirement future of millions of Nigerian workers is depending on these public-sector workers in PENCOM, to supervise the PFCs and PFAs competently and with integrity.

- Nigeria's Federal Inland Revenue Services (FIRS) is the federal government agency responsible for corporate income tax. The FIRS has tax auditors that go from company to company, examining their records and assessing their tax liabilities. The FIRS depends on what these tax examiners report back. What if they become compromised?

These are examples of the numerous government officials whose duties involve monitoring, investigations, and various other levels of discretion. Of course they include regulators, who as we have seen, can wield enormous powers, and can sometimes be "bad". What happens for example, when the regulator is bad?

Basic Reasons For Monitoring The Monitors

Let us highlight here for clarity, some basic reasons why government should ensure that all its officials involved in sensitive duties (including duties that requires some degrees of discretion) are being faithful to their mandates:

1. *Vices are prevalent*: In the DC environment, vices such as corruption, nepotism and tribalism tend to be widespread. It is useful to have a means of shielding officials in sensitive duties from becoming infected with these vices. Equally important, we should also have some means of detecting very quickly whenever any such officials become compromised.

2. *To help regulation live up to its potentials*: As we have seen, regulation is a vital institution that can play a vital role in the development of every DC. One important way of strengthening this institution, and shielding it from the vices that are pervasive in the DCs, can be a quiet monitoring of the monitors.

3. *A lot of powers for unelected officials*: As we have seen, the regulator can wield enormous discretionary powers. It can be dangerous to pack such powers into an unelected official, without any means of holding them accountable!

4. *The buck will ultimately stop with government*: Citizens will ultimately hold government accountable for the governance carried out through the regulator and all others who exercise significant discretion in their jobs. If the regulator should get it wrong,

government will still be expected to come in and salvage the situation, because government is the ultimate custodian of every nation's wellbeing.

5. *Monitors of low-probability events*: People engaged in a low-probability event can over time become absent-minded; and then the low-probability event can just occur (at a time nobody expects)!
Therefore some mechanisms need to be in place for keeping them alert. For example,

   a. An officer monitoring transactions can become absent-minded after reviewing hundreds of transactions, without any events. If the officer begins to do the job perfunctorily (like box-ticking), the significant event can just pass unnoticed!

   b. There are some Americans, whose duty it is to look out to know when the Russians are coming, and vice versa; and this has been going on for many decades, without any events. The governments concerned must obviously be interested in sustaining their alertness, so that they are not caught unprepared.

Techniques For Monitoring The Monitors

The following are examples of institutional procedures that can help a DC in monitoring its monitors:

1. *Creating an independent investigative agency (IIA)*: Parliament can set up an independent agency for investigating any aspects of the operations of government – including the operations of the regulators. An investigation can be at the instance of Parliament (based perhaps, on reports it has received) or initiated by the IIA itself. The IIA will publish its findings, which can create public uproar and/or trigger legislative hearings.
A DC can model its IIA after the US Government Accountability Office (GAO), an independent, nonpartisan agency that works for the US Congress. Often called the "congressional watchdog," GAO carries out special investigations, sometimes requested by Congress, or initiated by the GAO itself.

2. *Using undercover stings*: In a sting operation, an official may think they are dealing with their normal clients, not knowing that what they have are law-enforcement agents disguised as clients. This makes it possible to capture graphically an officer's pattern of conduct while unsupervised.
Undercover stings can apply to any aspect of government operations, and as explained by Steve Rothlein, can produce some benefits, if well executed:

   - The mere realization that there can be a sting operation, can powerfully strengthen state institutions, by creating an aura of uncertainty in the minds of any officials intending to engage in illegal activities. Because these officials do not exactly know who they may be dealing with, they will find it wise to work according to guidelines.

Let us remember Steve Rothlein's example cited earlier as Chapter opener:

"In the 1970's, ABC News [in the United States] conducted an integrity test in Miami, where 31 wallets containing money and identification were turned over by role players to 31 police officers. Nine of the officers kept the money and were subsequently fired and/or prosecuted. Thirty years later, ABC News replicated the integrity test in Los Angeles and in New York. Twenty wallets containing money and identification were turned in to officers of the LAPD and another twenty were turned in to officers of the NYPD. All forty wallets were recovered by the officers without a single penny missing.

"It is unclear if the officers have become more ethical over the past three decades, or if they suspected the wallets were simply baits being offered in some type of sting operation".

(Source: Steve Rothlein, 2010)

In fact, the mere institution of a policy of sting operations will send a message throughout government agencies, and cage any tendencies that officials may have for illegal activities.

a. Stings can lead to an in-progress arrest of officials involved in criminal misconduct, and even produce enough evidence for successful prosecution.

b. When a sting operation leads to an in-progress arrest of an official involved in criminal misconduct, and produces evidence that can be used for successful prosecution, it helps bypass one problem identified by Steve Rothlein with reactive investigation of complaints against law-enforcement officers – it prevents allegations from turning into credibility contests between the accuser and the accused!

"The majority of these reactive complaint investigations become swearing contests between the complainants and the accused officers, including the witnesses for each side. Rarely can investigators locate physical evidence or objective witnesses to prove or disprove the allegations. Generally, less than 20% of these cases are sustained, despite comprehensive investigations that are sometimes comparable to homicide cases, exhausting every lead and documenting every aspect of the case. The vast majority of these investigations result in a finding of "not sustained", meaning failure to prove or disprove the allegation".

(Source: Steve Rothlein, 2010)

c. According to Steve, proactive targeting of officers, notwithstanding its limitations, may often be the most effective method of building a strong case against corrupt officers.

d. Even if sting operations are not used for the entrapment and possible prosecution of fraudulent officials, they can be used routinely in-house, as a tool for randomly gauging the integrity of officers in the course of their duties.

They can also be used to keep officers involved in critical but low-probability events, alert to their duties. For example, a sting operation can see the IIA regularly trying to smuggle a bomb through an airport security system, to test its reliability and keep the responsible officers alert.

A sting operation can be "random", when it is arbitrary in nature, and not focused on any specific individual; but it can also be "targeted" at specific officers – probably because those officers are suspected of misconduct, or to have "sticky fingers" (using Steve's words), or because of complaints against them.

3. _Using Monitoring technology_: Technology is also offering nations new means of keeping an eye on how people on sensitive duties are carrying on. The continuing advances in surveillance technology have led to electronic surveillance equipment that now allow for computer-based off-site tracking of targets.

<u>Case 153:</u>   <u>Private Sector Examples Of Monitoring Technology</u>

In the private sector, which is already leveraging monitoring technology extensively, management can now remotely see what workers are doing, and how they are doing it.
From Charley Richardson, we get some examples:

- "UPS drivers, for example, are watched by a "telematics" system that continuously gathers more than 200 data points. From how fast they are going and how often they drive in reverse to whether they have their seat belts fastened and their doors locked, management has access to a detailed electronic map of a driver's day.

- "On the docks, monitoring technology allows management to know exactly what crane operators, truck drivers, and maintenance workers are doing. By tracking containers, monitoring allows the boss to limit the number of "extra" moves and feed that information into scheduling programs that ensure the minimum number of workers, with the right skill levels, are on the clock.

- "In healthcare, nurses and others are outfitted with badges that track their location, sending information to a central computer when they pass near sensors ... anyone who works at a computer or operates a computer-controlled machine can be, and probably is, monitored".

(For more details, see Labor Notes, May 18, 2011)

The use of drones to hunt down human targets that may be miles and even continents away, is also an application of monitoring technology.

4. _Vulnerability analysis & forensic audits_: Vulnerability analysis (VA) looks at the structure, policies and procedures of an organization, to determine if they leave opportunities for corruption and other problems. It is a proactive measure because it helps to reveal potential vices before they occur, rather than the usual process of commencing investigation after the vices would have taken place. The CRT, or any independent party (such as the IIA), or a regulator, can carry out the VA – and on any aspects of government operations.

Forensic audits are similar, though more involving. The GAO defines forensic audit as the systematic evaluation of the effectiveness of internal controls over a program, process, and/or set of policies and procedures. It identifies ineffective controls and vulnerabilities, and uses data mining and investigations to expose areas of fraud, waste, abuse, and the effect of inadequate controls.

Both programs can target any aspects of the operations of government, particularly those that carry out sensitive duties or duties that involve a lot of discretion, to identify any vulnerabilities that may exist.

5. _Whistle-blowing program_: This is an arrangement that enables third parties to secretly report any case of fraud, waste, abuse or misuse of government resources, to an

independent arm of government, such as the IIA. It can even be internal alert by staff about a colleague's behavior.

The presence of an effective whistle-blowing program can be very uncomfortable for officials that may want to get involved in corruption and other vices – because nobody knows who may just be watching!

The program will be most effective when it is designed with reliable mechanisms for:

a.   Protecting the identity of the whistle-blower; and
b.   Rewarding the whistle-blower under pre-agreed terms, to encourage whistle blowing.

Whatever channels that are provided for whistle-blowing (such as a toll-free number or email address) would need to be well publicised (so that citizens can become aware of it). The channels should also reliably protect the identities of those making the reports.

6.   *Independent audit function*: Following the Enron scandal in the United States, and the global financial crisis of 2008, regulators in different parts of the world started requiring their corporate organizations to reengineer their corporate governance practices. This has transformed financial governance in the private sector. For example, public companies in many jurisdictions, are now required to establish independent audit committees, which can bypass the executive management and report any problems they spot, directly to the boards of directors.

These reforms in the private sector are beginning to find their ways into the public sector. In some jurisdictions, cities and states are beginning to establish independent audit functions, and even to have publicly elected (rather than appointed) auditors. An elected auditor will be far more inclined to act independently, than the one appointed.

7.   *Legislative committees*: Some parliamentary committees will usually have oversight jurisdiction over regulatory and other executive agencies. Such committees can always call for public hearing, based on the complaints (including confidential complaints) that they get.

Case 154:   **The Powers of Parliamentary Committees**

From Georgina Lawrence, we can get some insights on the inherent clouts of such committees:

- "The power of the committees rests in their ability to investigate, report and make recommendations which are laid before parliament. The committees have the power to send for persons, papers and records to appear before them … They cannot change regulatory policy, nor can they direct the regulator, or the relevant minister to take a certain course of action. The committees work primarily through the use of publicity and recommendations, and they can publish the text of their inquiries, and any recommendations made as a result of these inquiries. The committees can be quite adversarial when questioning a regulator, and although the only sanction which can be imposed is adverse publicity for the regulator, many regulators admit to being nervous of appearing before a committee. The committees, even though they cannot force change, do play an important role by facing the regulators with areas of public concern, and getting them to answer these concerns on the record.

- "Besides being a forum for the venting of public concerns, and presenting the opportunity for some potentially embarrassing comments to be made on the

All the same, parliamentary committees must exercise their powers with caution, so as not to use excessive parliamentary interference to undercut an agency's functional autonomy.

8. *Multiple regulators*: As pointed out by Bryce C. Tingle of the University of Calgary (an experienced Canadian regulator), the quality of regulation, including responsiveness and innovation, tends to be higher, when there are independent regulatory agencies at the state and provincial levels, as opposed to a single national regulator:

> "We know from research in the United States that where there are many regulators (as is the case in corporate law, where each state has its own regime) the quality, responsiveness and innovation in regulation, as well as the time needed to fix regulatory mistakes, is significantly better than where there is only one regulator (as in the case of U.S. securities law)"

9. *Vibrant trade associations*: This should be encouraged in regulated industries, because it is easier for a strong trade association to challenge a regulator on behalf of its members, than for any individual member to do so. While individual businesses may be afraid to speak out, for fear of being targeted by the regulator, their trade association will have less of such constraint.

10. *Judicial review*: A regulated business can usually challenge a regulatory decision in the courts.

But in the DC environment, only a business that has been pushed to the wall will do this, for many reasons:

    a. There is the fear of being targeted. This is because, even if the regulated party wins, it can thereafter be singled out, and be used to teach others a bitter lesson – either directly by the regulator, or more likely, in concert with other government agencies.

    b. The judicial process can be unduly long, with an uncertain result.

    c. A smart regulator might have anticipated this resort to the judiciary, and made its decisions in a way that would minimize the prospects of successful litigation. However, with the level of impunity that abounds in the DCs, few regulators will even bother!

11. *An independent ombudsman*: In some jurisdictions, there can also be an office of an independent ombudsman, empowered to hear and investigate cases concerning the operations of government, including regulatory issues.

This somehow qualifies the ombudsman as a higher authority to regulatory agencies. An independent ombudsman can typically:

    a. Investigate complaints about possible injustices it receives concerning any arm of government, including regulatory agencies;

    b. Offer its services free of charge, so as to be accessible to all citizens;

    c.   Produce reports (usually to parliament) which makes recommendations to resolve the issue in question and forestall future occurrence;

    d.   Try in all these to act as responsible neutral arbiters, rather than a mere consumer advocate

Challenges of Monitoring The Monitors

We can expect many challenges in monitoring the monitors in the DC environment, especially in implementing the different institutional procedures discussed above:

1. *Executive impunity*: It is difficult in the DC environment, for any other organ of government (including Parliament, the judiciary, ombudsman) to be truly independent of the executive arm of government; and this is true at the national level, state and council levels.

2. *The monitor can also be vulnerable*: It is often the case in the DCs that intervention agencies set up to stop some vices often end up becoming active participants in those vices. For example, this has become the lot of many anti-corruption agencies in the DCs, and can also possibly become the lot of any organ set up to monitor the monitors!

3. *Sting operations*: Covert sting operations can pose some challenges:

    a.   Conducting a successful investigations requires professionalism, meaning that there can be capacity challenges in the DC environment;

    b.   Because vices can be very rampant, the officers trained in sting operations can themselves easily go bad. When that happens, it can be extremely hard to entrap them through stings, because as rightly pointed out by Steve Rothlein, when they themselves are under surveillance, they often easily use counter-surveillance techniques to frustrate entrapment.

    c.   The sting program may be resented by officials that are the potential targets. In that sense, it can lower morale in an agency – especially if it is not carried out in an ethical manner.

Slice G: Leveraging The Private Sector To Strengthen Institutions

Chapter 30

30. Knowing How To Integrate The Private Sector

"The best tool we currently know of for producing rapid innovation, product development and jobs, is a competitive market."

(Grist Energy Series writer David Roberts, on the importance of competitive electricity market, so that utility companies can have the incentive to cut costs and innovate, May 2013)

Topics Covered in This Chapter:

- Introduction
- Appreciating the strengths of the private sector
- Appreciating the strengths of the public sector
- The all-important market forces
- Private sector workers vs. government workers
- Using "Managed Competition" To Boost Institutional Performance
- Various ways of integrating the private sector
- Knowing When Public Service Needs This Integration
- Is Privatization Always The Best Option?

Introduction

In its WDR97 report, the World Bank highlighted "competition" (for example, competitive social service delivery, private participation in infrastructure, and privatization of certain market-driven activities) as an important mechanism for promoting public sector effectiveness and good governance.

And indeed, governments all over the world, sometimes under severe funding constraints, including pressure to reduce wastes and improve service delivery, have been integrating the private sector into governance – in what is variously called private sector integration (PSI), private-sector participation (PSP), public-private partnership (PPP, 3P or P3), and so on. This Chapter looks at the various ways that PSI can be leveraged to strengthen institutions.

Appreciating The Strengths of The Private Sector

In general, the private sector performs better than government (the public sector) in the following areas:

1. *Responding rapidly to changing conditions*: While government is always slow and bureaucratic, "speed" means everything in the private sector, where profit often depends on

how quickly a firm can adapt to changing market conditions, including changing customer needs;

2. _Meeting customer's needs_: The private firm makes its income (and stays in business) by satisfying its customers (We shall see why shortly, when we look at market forces)

3. _Innovating_: We can see a lot of this in the unprecedented technological developments of recent years, driven exclusively by the private sector;

4. _Exploiting opportunities_: We can see a lot of this in in the Nigerian banking industry, which for example, was steadily exploiting the advances in technology to extend its services – compared with the relative indifference to technology, of the nation's public service.

Case 155:   PHCN Vs. The Private Sector

The Power Holding Company of Nigeria (PHCN) was for many years the government agency responsible for electricity generation, transmission, and distribution in the country. Up to when it was privatized in 2014, if you walked into any PHCN office and paid your electricity bill, you would be required to photocopy the payment receipt and paste on your house gate. That way, whenever PHCN officials from that same office came to disconnect their debtors, the photocopy would let them know that you had made payment to them!

Even when the private sector started leveraging technology to improve services, PHCN remained the same. For example, PHCN officials in the same Nigeria, were seeing how the money they paid into their bank accounts would promptly become visible in all the branches of the banks nationwide, and in all the ATMs; yet PHCN remained un-moved; and continued to rely on the customers' copies of the receipts that they themselves had issued to the customers – for evidence of payment!

----

5. _Performing complex tasks_ – Those familiar with the United States Department of Defense (DOD) will have observed that despite the security implications of allowing private organizations into such a sensitive industry, the DOD relies largely on private-sector companies as its defense contractors, to develop its complex weapons systems!

The growing realization that the private sector can outperform government in virtually all service areas, explains why the role of government all over the world, has been shifting from that of a _direct provider_ of services, to a _facilitator_ of services, who incentivizes others (by providing the enabling environment) to deliver the services. Osborne & Gaebler have used the word "steering" to describe this facilitative role of government; explaining that the term _"government"_ actually came from a Greek word meaning, "to steer".

This growing realization has also spurred the push into "privatization" across the world in the past three decades, which first swept through the developed economies of Europe and America, and more recently through the DCs.

<u>**Case 156:**</u>   <u>**The FAIR Act of the US Government**</u>

The United States Federal Activities Inventory Reform (FAIR) Act, passed in 1998, requires U.S. government agencies to conduct annual inventories to identify their commercial activities. Within this category, each activity is assigned a "reason code" to determine whether it is actually appropriate for competition—and, if not, why not. The President's Office of Management and Budget (OMB) is principally responsible for managing this process.

Appreciating The Strengths of The Public Sector

The foregoing prowess of the private sector notwithstanding, there are still some tasks on which government can justifiably claim supremacy, particularly in the DC environment. They include:

1. *Steering*: As discussed earlier, government is more at home with "steering" (i.e. policy and regulation);

2. *Services that need to be provided by a monopoly*: In the weak institutional environments of the DCs, where vices such as corruption and impunity are widespread, the only thing that can be worse than a government monopoly, is a private monopoly! Nigerians learnt this lesson in a bitter way after the privatization of the nation's monopoly electricity company, the PHCN, when the private-sector "Discos" that took over PHCN's power distribution, continued with the PHCN monopolistic arrangement. Monthly electricity charges suddenly shot up by more than 1,000% in some cases, without any noticeable improvements in power supply; and consumers were helpless, having no alternatives!

3. *Services that require compassion and human touch* (such as humanitarian services to the elderly, and the handicapped): Whenever you see a profit-driven firm showing compassion, it may be advisable to look very well – for there just might be some profit potential lurking underneath the compassion! As far as the private sector is concerned, anything that will not ultimately add to the "bottom-line" is a useless distraction!

4. *Services that come out of compelling reasons of economic efficiency*, such as when government leases out its underutilized facilities (such as lands) to the public; and

5. *Any other essential services*, which others (such as the private or non-governmental sectors) are unable to provide

The All-Important Market Forces

For our purposes here, let us understand *"competition"*, *"choice"*, and *"market forces"* as follows:

1. *Competition*: When there are alternative sources from which we can obtain the service in question;

2. *Choice*: When those receiving the service have untethered freedom to choose who they get it from (the service providers), and to change those providers at will, without hindrances;

3. *Market forces*: When competition and choice are both present

A private-sector firm under market forces, knows that the only way it can remain in business is to be meeting its customers' needs. If it is not delivering the quality the customers want, and at a competitive price, the customers will switch to other firms that offer better deals.

That is also why the firm must strive for efficiency and continuous improvement – so that it does not for example, wake up one morning to see competitors delivering the same quality (or even better quality) at lower prices!

Note that the public sector does not ordinarily face "market forces". Even when a government agency is delivering services, it usually does so as a monopoly, without competition; or it is usually subsidized. The important difference is that its survival does not depend on its performance – at least not immediately! We can recall our earlier "public vs. private" school example:

<u>Case 157:</u> **Nigeria's Public vs. Private Schools**

A ***private*** school tends to perform better than public schools, not because it necessarily has better qualified teachers, but mostly because of the institutional environment it faces. Its funding is in the hands of the people it serves! Each private school knows that if parents are not satisfied, they can readily pull out their children to other competing private schools; and money will stop flowing in! This tends to make private schools very sensitive to the people they serve!

On the other hand, the funding of a ***public*** school in a typical DC comes from government, rather than from the people the school serves. Even when the school is not doing well, it does not stop its funding from flowing in, nor its teachers from being paid; and it may even not stop the pupils from continuing to flow in, especially in the poor, and economically disadvantaged neighborhoods that cannot afford the higher cost of private education! In this way, such a public school can get away with poor and unsatisfactory performance; and can continue to perform unsatisfactorily!

The point we should therefore note, is that it is "market forces" that create the obsession of the private sector to serve us well; the pressure on the sector for continuous innovation; and drive its vibrancy. In short, it is market forces that make the private sector what it is, and primarily differentiate it from the public sector. Take away "market forces", and the private firm will tend to behave just like the public sector – usually, even worse!

Market forces also help to tame the potential temptation on the private firm to exploit consumers to maximize profits, since an exploitative firm will soon lose its customers to competitors, once there is awareness of the exploitation.

It is important to appreciate that there is really no genetic difference between public and private sector workers. As our "school" example illustrates, the institutional environment (incentives) that government workers tends to be different from what our private sector workers face.
For example:

1. *The private sector workers* know that their jobs and welfare depend on their firm's continuing survival, which in turn depends on the continued patronage of the customers. This tends to make them sensitive to the needs of customers. In fact, the usual mantra in the private sector is that the customer is the king, which encourages the private-sector workers to treat their customers as kings!

2. *The public sector workers* are under no such pressures! Their jobs are ordinarily not subject to the insecurity of the private sector. They get paid irrespective of how their agencies perform. In any case, nobody ordinarily, even measures an agency's performance – let alone tie its workers' welfare to it! That is why government workers ordinarily tend to be lazy and inefficient; and why vices such as "tribalism", "nepotism", and "corruption" thrive freely in the public sector.

If government workers come under market forces – for example, if they see their jobs under threat from any serious competition – they will become "fired up" and innovative; and sometimes even end up outperforming their private counterparts!

Case 158:　　　**Outsourcing of Phoenix Trash Collection**

As narrated by J. A. Trujillo, the city of Phoenix in 1979, decided to outsource its trash collection (budget, $154 million), in a bidding process open to both private firms and city employees, who had been handling the trash service. The city wanted to provide residents the best service at lowest cost.

It then split the city into 10 zones for 6-year contracts, which it progressively put out for bids, one zone after the other. There were 13 bidding rounds. The city employees lost the first two bids to private operators. Apparently stung by the resulting privatization and loss of jobs, they woke up; and won 7 out of the next 11 bids, , including winning the last 3 in a row!

(Source: See J. A. Trujillo's presentation at the 2010 US Conference of Mayors)

The Phoenix story is just one of many cases across the world, of government workers matching or outperforming the private sector, under certain institutional environments. We can also highlight the case of Indianapolis.

Case 159:　　　**Igniting The Genius of Indianapolis Public Sector Workers**

Indianapolis is a city in the United States. Stephen Goldsmith was the 46th Mayor of Indianapolis. While running for the city office, he vowed he would embark on wide-scale privatization to transfer the delivery of services to private contractors.

However, once elected into office, he quickly came to realize that the real answer to improving service delivery was not a blanket privatization because monopolies, public or private, were not good. Instead, Indianapolis launched a comprehensive effort that treated city departments as businesses and gave workers a voice in ways to cut costs. If a department could put in a winning bid against private competitors, the city workers would continue to provide that particular service.

As Goldsmith put it:

- "I was increasingly impressed with the inherent ability of our own employees to perform better when the system allowed them; I underestimated what they could do if we unloaded the bureaucracy off the top of their heads."

(Source - US Department Of Labor, Working Together For Public Service: Snapshot: Indianapolis)

Similarly, from Eric Schnurer, the renowned public-private policy consultant, we learn of Edmonton (Canada) where a new voucher system forced the public schools to compete with private schools. The public schools quality improved so dramatically that, as Schnurer put it,

"Within two years, there were hardly any private or parochial schools left in the market"!

Interestingly, government workers and public servants usually know how they can unlock efficiencies in their jobs – only that they ordinarily do not have the incentives to do so! Here is Eric Schnurer's favorite example:

Case 160:   Innovation by Chicago Construction Workers

When Rahm Emanuel became the 55th Mayor of Chicago in May 2011, he was in a hurry to slash city spending, including payroll; and to privatize services. And he issued a challenge to the city's unions:

- If you don't like my plans, come up with yours that will save as much taxpayer money!

The union took up the challenge with all seriousness. And interesting productivity ideas and initiatives started to come out. As an example:

- The construction workers repairing sidewalks were working the standard 8-hour shifts, 5 days/week. That meant a total of 40 hours/week. It usually took these workers 5 hours to completely pour a load of concrete, meaning they could only do one (1) load per day, which translated to 5 loads per week.

As Eric Schnurer likes to narrate, the workers on their own realized that they could still do their 40 hours/week by changing to a 10-hour shift and working only 4 (instead of 5) days per week! This enabled them to pour 2 concrete loads per day, meaning 8 loads per week! Going from 5 to 8 loads/week represented a whopping 60% increase in productivity – at no additional cost, and with additional savings on fuel and equipment rental!

(Source: see Eric Schnurer, The Atlantic, March 11, 2015)

Using "Managed Competition" To Boost Institutional Performance

The foregoing cases can actually serve as examples of how a DC can use "managed competition" to boost the performance of its public SECTOR workers. Let us additionally use "signage" collection as a specific illustration:

Case 161:   Example Of "Managed Competition" In Signage Collection

In the DCs, State and local governments usually collect signage fees from adverts on government roads and streets. Instead of government workers alone handling the collection, a DC can decide to ask for bids from private firms to handle the collection in a specified area, and for a specified number of years. The winning bidder will usually be paid a specified percentage of what it collects.

There are some basic benefits of getting such outsider bids:

- To measure the market value of the revenue possible, which can be compared to what the public-sector workers are bring in;

- To possibly subsequently jerk up that revenue threshold for the public-sector workers.

If for example, assume that government is presently realizing N10m monthly in the area using its workers. If a private firm bids a minimum threshold of N30m monthly, out of which it will retain 20%, the bid will generate more revenue for government, because even after paying the 20% (or N6m) to the firm, the arrangement will still leave government with a net of N24m (compared to the present N10m).

Note that this outsourcing does not necessarily require the retrenchment of the government workers previously handling the job. If government was keeping them when they were bringing in only N10m monthly, government will be even in a better position to keep them, now that it is receiving N24m monthly!

Instead of laying off the workers, government will have them understudy the firm, to learn its techniques. When the contract runs out, government can decide not to renew it, and rather mandate its workers to achieve the new revenue benchmark set by the firm! In this way, it can further save the 20% going to the firm!

Various Ways Of Integrating The Private Sector

In the past four decades, governments across the world have used a variety of techniques to integrate the private sector into governance – in what is variously called private sector integration (PSI), private sector participation (PSP), or public-private partnership (PPP, 3P or P3).
The forms of integration include:

1. _Deregulation_: In this case, government removes the entry barriers in a sector of the economy that it monopolises, so that private firms can enter the sector, and provide services at their own qualities and prices.

2. _Privatization_: Government sells its asset outright to the private sector – which permanently transfers the ownership and management of the asset to private hands.

3. _Concession agreement_: Government releases its asset to a private firm (the concessionaire) for a specified period (usually above 20 years), at the end of which the asset (and all the improvements made by the concessionaire) revert to government. The concessionaire is expected to invest to develop the asset, during the period of concession, and to recoup its investment through charges to the users of the improved asset.

   - In 2005, the Nigerian government concessioned its seaports (previously managed by the Nigerian Ports Authority) to private port operators.

4. _Out-sourcing_: In the most basic form of outsourcing, a government body will contract a private firm (or another public-sector supplier) to provide services that its own workers had previously provided (or have the capacity to provide) in-house.

5. _In-sourcing_: This is the opposite of outsourcing, where the government body takes back the service it has been receiving from an outside party, so that its workers can begin to handle it in-house. The government body will sometimes have to employ persons with any new skills or expertise that are necessary for carrying out that service.

6. _Management contracting_: In this case, government hands over its facility to the private sector, to manage for a given period of time, under a contractual arrangement.

   - The Nigerian power transmission system is a recent example. As highlighted before, Nigeria's federal government, in privatizing its power sector, split the previous monopolistic government-owned national power supplier, the Power Holding Company of Nigeria (PHCN), into several distribution companies (Discos), and generation companies (Gencos), while retaining the transmission segment, which it handed over to a private foreign firm to manage, under a contractual arrangement.

7. _Contracting (or competitive tendering)_: In this case, government or its agency calls for bids from private contractors or government agencies for providing a specified service (including internal bids from any units within the agency that may want to provide that service)

Note that *management contracting*, *concessioning* or *outsourcing* as explained above, are all related. Also, "outsourcing" is being stretched in different jurisdictions, in a variety of ways, such as:

1. *Build-operate-transfer (BOT)*: In this case, a private firm enters into an arrangement with government to build a facility for public use, operate the facility for an agreed number of years (to recoup its investment) and thereafter, "transfer" the facility back to government.

2. *Rehabilitate-operate-transfer (ROT)*: This is similar to BOT, but refers to the situation where the facility already exists, and the private party is to start by rehabilitating it.

3. *Various other* adjustments in the contractual terms, such as:
   a. Build-own-operate (BOO)
   b. Rehabilitate-own-operate (ROO)
   c. Build-own-operate-transfer (BOOT)
   d. Rehabilitate-own-operate-transfer" (ROOT)

Although the developed economies of the world championed this private sector integration, the DCs have since joined them. The difference is that the public sector tends to provide many more services in the DCs, such that the DCs are mostly dealing with issues of *deregulation* and *privatization*; while the developed economies now talk mostly about *outsourcing* and *contracting* of services.

Knowing When Public Service Needs This Integration

What should a DC be aiming at, when it embarks on private sector integration? Here are some possible institutional goals:

1. *Leveraging private-sector funding*: One great attraction of PSI to governments, is the funds that the sector can inject into public programs and projects. Governments that are cash-strapped can use various forms of PSI to provide services that they would otherwise not have been able to fund. We can use Nigeria's telecoms deregulation as an example.

   Case 162:   Leveraging Private-Sector Funds For Nigeria's Telecoms

   In Nigeria's telecoms deregulation, which we looked at earlier, each successful private-sector telecoms provider paid a license fee of about $285 million to government. Notice the double-win for government!

   - If government was doing the telecoms expansion by itself (for example, through government-owned Nitel) it would have spent its own funds, and there would still not have been any guarantee of successful outcome, because that's what it had been doing for several decades before then.

   - Now the private telecoms firms were using private funds to do the job, and government was at the same time, receiving huge cash payment from them as license fees (and later, taxes)!

2. *Meritocracy*: In the institutional environment of corruption, tribalism, nepotism and other vices that tend to prevail in the DCs, politicians and the elites tend to saturate the public service with their family members, mistresses or tribes-people, rather than qualified persons. However, when the service is thrown open through deregulation, and the private-sector providers are allowed to come in and compete with a government agency (which threatens jobs and even the agency's existence), the agency will tend to become thirsty for persons, who can help it to withstand the private-sector onslaught!

   Notice what this means: It means that the agency will tend to become merit-driven, which is how strong institutions should function! It means therefore that by enhancing "meritocracy", the involvement of the private sector is helping to strengthen institutions.

3. *Enhanced economic activities*: The economic institutions in the DCs tend to be stifled by the dysfunctionalities that create rent for the elites, while bottling up the potential benefits to the larger society. Deregulation is sometimes the easiest way to open up such sectors. We can use Nigeria's telecoms sector as an example.

> **Case 163:** **How Telecoms Deregulation Enhanced Economic Activities In Nigeria**
>
> The deregulation of Nigeria's telecoms sector was globally considered a huge economic success. Before this, government had spent huge funds trying to provide telecoms services through its monopoly agency, Nitel. The result remained poor, year after year, decade after decade – even after restructuring and reorganizing Nitel several times, and appointing different kinds of persons to head it. Telecoms remained so dismal in the country that even when GSM telephony had become available in smaller neighboring countries, Nigeria still didn't have it; and by the time the government of President Olusegun Obasanjo deregulated the industry in 2001, the nation could only boast of about 250,000 active telephone lines, for a population of about 160 million persons!
>
> The impact of the deregulation was phenomenal. According to data by the Nigerian Communications Commission (NCC) as at July 2015:
>
> - Active lines had exceeded 150 million; and teledensity had almost hit 110!
>
> - Exponential growth in telecoms investment, and in associated direct & indirect employment;
>
> - Crashing of connection charges from about N100,000 per fixed line in 1999 to almost zero (free SIM cards);
>
> - Exponential growth in communications and related infrastructural facilities for the economy, and in associated direct & indirect national employment
> - Exponential growth in internet penetration, in associated direct & indirect national employment;
> - Created one of the most vibrant economic sectors in the country!
>
> - Other macroeconomic effects: Booms in associated businesses, including construction, financial services, SMEs, ICT, etc.

4. *Improved service delivery*: A hallmark of weak state institutions is poor service delivery, because the parasitic elites are more interested in their control of (and rents from) state institutions, than on the effectiveness of the services from those institutions.

    Once private firms come in and begin to provide their own services at their own qualities and prices, the standards will go up; and the scarcities, queues and rationing that are often associated with dysfunctional institutions, will disappear. Citizens will experience product diversity, innovations, and ultimately, price fall.

    - This was exactly what happened in Nigeria's telecoms sector – which under government's Nitel, was characterized by poor services, line scarcity and long queues for telephone lines. All those problems vanished with the arrival of the private providers!

5. *Productive workforce*: Deregulation forces government workers to jerk up their performance, faced as they become, with the threat of losing their jobs to the private service providers. This was what the examples of Phoenix (USA) trash collection, voucher system at Edmonton Canada, the Indianapolis (USA) competitive initiatives, Chicago (USA) construction workers, and so on; showed us!

6. *Public service valuation*: Deregulation can enable the society to know the true market price of government services (whether citizens are getting good value for their tax money). Once the private sector comes into a service, there will now be a basis to compare the private-sector prices of the service, with what government itself is spending to provide it. If the government cost is too high, this awareness can help to build up the pressure coalition for reforms on the system.

7. *Empowerment of local businesses*: As we saw before, outsourcing is a special form of PSI in which (in its most basic form) government contracts out some service that its workers have been providing in-house (or could provide in-house). Government can deliberately outsource specific services to local firms, to expand the firms' scale of activities and increase their knowledge and skill base, which can even help such firms to ultimately enter the export market. In this way, government is enhancing the growth of the private sector relative to the public sector, which can boost the economy as a whole.

    - This empowerment of the private sector can take place in very diverse ways. For example, from Auriol and Picard (2009) we learn that when some European countries outsourced postal services to grocery stores and gas stations in rural areas, it not only enabled the rural communities to enjoy postal services even at extended business hours, but the shop owners also earned additional revenues!

8. *Pooling of resources*: Government can also create outsourcing to allow multiple agencies to share the resources of a private firm, rather than each agency setting up its own independent system. For example, the private firm processing payroll for one agency can use the same resources for other agencies, thereby saving government the cost of replicating those resources in individual agencies.

9. *Accessing expensive skill sets*: Government can also outsource a given program in order to leverage the kind of skills that it may not have in-house, including specialists that a government office may not want (or be able) to retain permanently.

10. *Backdoor price increases*: Government can sometimes be financially pressed, and may wish to generate more revenue through price increases (on its services) that may be politically too unpopular to effect directly. Government may also find a particular service too unsustainable at the prices it is charging. Whatever the case, PSI can help government to get the price increases indirectly, for example by leasing out the service to a private party at a rate that incorporates the expected price increase. The private party can then increase the service fee after a while – meaning that government has in effect "outsourced" the price increase! This was obviously what the Chicago parking meter concessioning (which we shall review in more details shortly) tried to achieve.

> **Case 164:**   **How The City Of Chicago Indirectly Increased Parking Meter Fees**
>
> In December 2008, the cash-strapped city of Chicago (USA) concessioned its 36,000 parking meters for 75 years, to a private consortium led by Morgan Stanley (MS), for $1.2 billion. MS paid up-front. Soon afterwards, MS hit Chicago motorists with a doubling of the parking meter rates – rates that had never been increased in the previous 20 years! This sparked mass outrage. People held protests and threatened to boycott. But there was little they could do. The deal had not only been consummated, the cash-strapped city was in fact, already spending MS' cash!

11. **Focus on Outcomes**: In Slice D, we looked at how government could improve institutional performance by striving to be outcome-focused in its operations – rather than being just obsessed with procedures. Incidentally, outsourcing allows government to specify the desired outcomes, which the private firm is obliged to deliver. It is easier for public officials to become outcome-focused, when they are preparing specifications for others, than in their own work plans!

Is Privatization Always The Best Option?

In the DC environment, where corruption and rents by powerful elites tend to make institutional services dysfunctional, some dose of PSI will often be a great reform approach. However, as we have seen from all the cases presented in this Slice, what matters really is not so much whether those doing the work are private or public, but the institutional environment under which they are doing it – i.e. the incentives propelling them.

This calls for a note of caution in many respects. For example:

1. The blanket thinking by some policymakers that the automatic solution to public-sector inefficiency is to hand over government assets to the private sector, is not always in order! Sometimes what we need is to put the public employees on their toes. The goal, as some reform practitioners now put it, should no longer be *outsourcing* or *insourcing*, but *right-sourcing*!

2. In particular, the social problems (including labor grievances, unemployment and service disruptions) that go with policies such as automatic privatization, or "let's privatize 50% in the next two years", and so on, can be avoided by starting with "managed competition", at least, to determine which provider (public or private) will offer the best value.

Chapter 31

31. Avoiding Some Common Privatization Mistakes

"Lots of Americans were disturbed to learn from Edward Snowden that the government is keeping track of their every phone call and text message. But they might have also wondered why a 30-year-old government contractor in Honolulu, with security clearance that was approved by another private contractor, had routine access to some of the government's most sensitive secrets. Even worse, two years after Pfc. Bradley Manning did the same thing, Snowden managed to download millions of pages of documents from a computer system designed and managed by private contractors without setting off a single alarm. The whole affair was an embarrassment to Washington's government contracting sector."

(Business and economics columnist, Steven Pearlstein, on whether the US government might have been reckless with its outsourcing to private contractors, while allowing the quality of its own workforce to atrophy.(Washington Post, January, 2014)

Topics Covered in This Chapter:

- Introduction
- Some basic things that often go wrong
  - Privatizing Before Deregulating
  - Failing to bring in market forces
  - Poor sequencing of the assets to be privatized
  - Failing to give the government workers a chance
  - Failing To Have A Firm Regulator In Place
  - Failing to "prime" before privatizing
- Some Other Miscellaneous Things That Often Go Wrong
- Two Other Things To Note About PSI

Introduction

We have already seen why a DC might be interested in leveraging the private sector in governance. In this Chapter, we shall look at how and why many private sector integration (PSI) projects go wrong, in the hope that our DCs can be better guided.
We shall look at the most common causes of disappointing PSI outcomes, under the following headings:

1. Privatizing before deregulating
2. Failing to bring in market forces
3. Poor sequencing of the assets to be privatized
4. Failing to give government workers a chance
5. Failing to have a firm regulator in place

6. Failing to prime before privatizing
7. Some other miscellaneous things that often go wrong
8. Some other things to note about PSI

Mistake#1: Privatizing Before Deregulating

A common PSI goof in the DCs, is to privatize government services before deregulating the sectors concerned. If a social service in a DC is being provided by a government agency that operates as a monopoly, and there is a decision to privatize the agency, the starting point should be to deregulate the sector concerned, to remove the entry barriers in the sector, so that private firms can enter the sector, and compete with the government monopoly, with their own services, qualities and prices.

There are some important institutional benefits of regulating before privatizing:

1. It will enable government to test-run the private hands in the sector, and gain valuable insights, ahead of the privatization, if it should eventually become necessary;

2. The competition from the private firms may ignite the government workers in the sector, and challenge them to sit up – which, if they do satisfactorily, can ultimately, even make privatization unnecessary!

3. Mere deregulation will mitigate potential labor unrest from the government workers of the sector, because they will continue on their jobs, doing what they were doing before, with the private sector only complementing them to fill the demand (and quality) gaps they are unable to meet. It is natural for public-sector workers to oppose privatization, but more difficult for them to oppose a deregulation that merely allows the private sector to come in and offer consumers similar services at its own quality and price.

4. The approach will forestall possible public unrest (from initial jolting private-sector pricing), because the government services will remain available (with its quality and price) while the private sector only provides an alternative to those that are interested.

5. In the event that private firms fail to enter the sector successfully, after it has been deregulated, then something must be very wrong with the institutional arrangements in the sector, which should be looked into, because it will likely be equally detrimental to a successful privatization outcome.

Case 165: Nigeria's Deregulation of Telecoms Before Privatization

One of the remarkable features of the privatization of Nigeria's telecoms sector was that NCC (government's newly constituted regulator for the sector) started by deregulating the sector, before privatizing the government agencies in the sector. This deregulation allowed private telcos, such as MTN and ECONET, to come in, set up their GSM networks, and sell their services at their own rates – while the government's agency (Nitel) continued to do its thing. Government even encouraged Nitel to set up its own GSM network.

- There was no opposition from the public to the initial higher telecom costs of the private service providers, since their services were optional, and additional to what Nitel was offering.

- Similarly, it was difficult for the government (Nitel's) workers, to make trouble (especially at that initial stage, when they were a monopoly) because their work and services continued as before.

The new private firms flourished and soon dominated the sector, to the point that Nitel and its workers no longer even had the capacity to hold the sector hostage. Notice that the story would have been different if the reform had started with a plan to privatize Nitel! Its workers would have protested vehemently, and even paralyzed the nation's entire telecom services - something they had the capacity to do at that initial stage!

Mistake#2: Failing To Bring In Market Forces

Another common privatization goof in the DCs is to hand over government facilities to the private sector without ensuring that the private owners will operate under market forces! Merely handing over a government facility to the private sector, cannot by itself, guarantee private-sector performance! We must additionally ensure (as discussed earlier) that the private party operates under market forces – the condition that brings out private-sector performance!

If a privatized firm operates without the pressure of market forces, it will tend to behave just like the public sector – usually, even worse!

Case 166:   Inadequate Market Forces in Nigeria's Seaports

Let us again return to the outcries and complaints of port users that seem to have trailed the services of the private-sector port operators after the Nigerian government's concessioned its seaports to them. Why are the new private operators apparently not striving to satisfy the port users, the importers/ exporters? Is anything inhibiting true competition in the sector? For example:

- Did any one individual (or even group of individuals) use proxy names to take over most of the seaports, during the concessioning process? If so, this would surely inhibit true competition.

- Did the new terms of operation give an importer/exporter (or their agent) the complete freedom to select where – for example, out of the many (privately operated) seaports in Lagos – that the ship should drop the cargo? If the answer was also "no" – meaning that these major port users had no say on which port operators processed their cargoes – then "choice" was severely inhibited.

(For more insights on the complaints & outcries, see The Sun newspaper, Oct 10, 2011; The Guardian, Oct 27, 2011; Thisday newspaper, 15 Jan 2012; Daily Trust, 3 Jan 2012)

If the seaports concessioning had all these defects, it would not be able to yield true private-sector performance.

We can also use Nigeria's more recent power-sector privatization as another example of privatization without market forces.

> **Case 167:** *Nigeria's Privatized Power Sector Without Market Forces e*
>
> In 2014, Nigeria's federal government under President Goodluck Jonathan, privatized the nation's electric power sector. Before then, government's Power Holding Company of Nigeria (PHCN) was the monopolistic supplier of electric power nationwide. Government "unbundled" the distribution segment of PHCN into several electricity distribution companies (Discos), and the generating segment into several generating companies (Gencos), while retaining ownership of the transmission segment.
>
> It was interesting to note that even though the private sector had taken over the electricity sector, there were no "market forces" anywhere in the distribution segment! For example, even though the Discos had gone into private hands, and there was a number of them, each Disco still operated as a monopoly in its area, and faced absolutely no competition from any other Disco.

In the above electricity case, notice that there is nothing "internal to the system" (as discussed in Slice C) to push a Disco to improve its services – except perhaps, pressure from the regulator. Similarly, nothing will restrain the Disco from the private sector's tendency to exploit consumers, except again the regulator's whip! In the DC environment, where privatized agencies are usually acquired by powerful elites, the regulator's hands will be severely tied, such that regulating such firms competently will be an outright nightmare! That is why market forces are so important in the DCs.

Even if the nation's powerful elites do not have interests in the Discos, the first thing a smart Disco will likely do, in the very corrupt environment of the DCs, will be to establish strong links to powerful politicians. With such links, it can then fight (and even remove) any regulatory officials that prove too stubborn – starting usually with sponsored media campaigns against such officials! The Disco will find this option far more profitable, than taking the trouble to make the kind of investments that can truly improve services.

Regulation of private providers of utility services in a jurisdiction of weak institutional environment, is a completely different ball game from what would obtain in the more developed economies (of for example, Europe and the United States) where governance institutions are stronger! Market forces, whether actual or simulated, are vital in DC's privatization programs, to help counter the very overwhelming forces of corruption and elite impunity.

We can compare the foregoing institutional concerns of the power sector's privatization, with how the Nigerian government privatized its telecoms sector.

<u>**Case 168:**</u> <u>**Market forces in Nigeria's Telecoms Sector**</u>

The Nigerian government commendably structured market forces into its telecoms sector during its privatization. For example,

- There is clear competition in the sector (many telecoms companies are operating competitively);

- There is clear choice, as each consumer freely chooses the service providers they want, and can change the providers at will; and

- There is no ambiguity about the regulation of the sector – the Nigerian Communications Commission (NCC) is the undisputed regulator of the sector;

- This presence of market forces has been propelling the sector towards true private-sector performance in the economy. For example, consider the following event:

- When the telecoms companies (telcos) first started, they were billing customers on "per minute" basis, which short-changed consumers. The telcos insisted that it would take years before the industry could develop the technology for "per-second-billing". But when a new telco, "Globacom", emerged and commenced business with "per-second" billing, consumers started migrating to its network; and all the other telcos scrambled and joined the per-second billing! Market forces had clearly achieved what the telcos had argued was not feasible in the immediate future, shrinking the telcos' estimate of "years" into "days"!

Mistake#3: Poor Sequencing of The Assets to be Privatized

While in Slice B, we suggested that the following factors should be considered in sequencing government's operations for reform:

1. Quick wins (to generate early benefits, and create enthusiasm for reform, including public and political support for the reform);

2. The enthusiasms of the respective ministers for the reform (a minister that is enthusiastic about the reform is likely to work for its success; and vice versa);

3. The ultimate benefits (business, social or political) that stand to be reaped from the reform;

4. The extent of disruptions and chaos that the reform can generate;

5. The cost implications (financial, social, and political costs);

6. The institutions and processes in deepest trouble;

7. The potential of specific reforms to reinforce each other;
And so on!

Mistake#4: Failing to Give Government Workers A Chance

One key advantage of deregulation is that it will enable government to offer the public-sector workers presently handling a service, the chance to play in the new dispensation. As we have seen, the private-sector workers are not genetically different from the public-sector workers; it is just that they operate under a different institutional environment.

Instead of losing their means of livelihood once their facility is privatized, many public sector workers will be very happy to compete against the incoming private firms.

<u>**Case 169:**</u>   <u>**No Seaport Terminals For Government Workers in Nigeria**</u>

In Nigeria, the maritime industry is a critical sector of the economy, which has the potential to become the 2nd highest revenue earner after oil. It also has the potential to become the regional hub of trade for the West and Central African regions.

One of Nigeria's landmark privatization reforms was the 2005 concessioning of its seaports (which the Nigerian Ports Authority hitherto managed) to private-sector port operators, by the administration of President Olusegun Obasanjo. The reform had lofty goals – such as discouraging the diversion of Nigeria-bound cargo to neighboring ports, quadrupling of cargo handling and productivity at the ports, reducing port charges, reducing the rate of pilferage in the ports, and so on.

Since there were many ports involved, it would have been very interesting to concession at least one of the ports to the government workers, and have them run their own port terminal in competition with the private-sector port operators! And who knows, they just might have performed creditably – perhaps, even outperformed the private operators!

Mistake#5: Failing To Have A Firm Regulator In Place

When a sector of the economy is about to be deregulated (or the government agencies in the sector are about to be privatized) it is important to ensure that a firm regulator is in place for the sector. Very importantly, this regulator should be independent of the government agencies that are presently providing services in that sector. The regulator will become the driver of the deregulation process, working perhaps with government's central privatization agency (if one exists).

Because a central privatization agency will be handling privatization projects across different sectors of the economy, it will not be able to give the required structuring depth that any given sector may call for – such as priming the sector, deregulating before privatizing, bringing in market forces, and so on. That is why each sector's regulator should take over and become the primary driver of the sector's PSI process.

As obvious as this may appear, it is interesting how many DCs fail this test, as the following Nigerian example shows.

<u>**Case 170:**</u>   <u>**Nigeria's Maritime Deregulation Without A Firm Regulator**</u>

In the port reforms described above, it was bizarre that government did not structure a firm regulator for the maritime sector, now that it was going to private port operators. According to Lucky Amiwero, the President, National Council of Managing Directors of Nigerian Licensed Customs Agents,

> "There is nowhere in the world where the ports are concessioned to private companies without first having a law to back it up … Who is the commercial regulator? Who is in-charge of the port and what is the function of the Nigerian Ports Authority in the new era? … … With the high charges at the ports, there is nobody to complain to, and there is no law with which to sue the terminal operators for breaching the terms of contract … Even the terms of agreement, which the Bureau of Public Enterprises (BPE) made with the terminal operators, are being kept secret!"

Unfortunately, this omission may have jeopardized the lofty goals of the entire reform. Rev. Jonathan Nicol, the General Secretary, Shippers' Association of Lagos State, lamented the grief of shippers over several charges at the ports, which according to him had "swallowed almost half of the costs of the imported goods" making the port charges "now to stand as one of the highest in the world"! As Lucky Amiwero put it, the terminal operators are "having a field day"!

Even more bizarre was that this situation remained unaddressed for nearly 10 years, despite these outcries of port users, until the government of President Goodluck Jonathan appointed the Nigerian Shippers Council (NSC) as an interim regulator in 2014, under executive order! Interestingly, the private port operators refused to recognize the NSC as their regulator, and went to court!

(For more details on the maritime complaints, see Thisday newspaper, 15 Jan 2012; Daily Trust newspaper, 3 Jan 2012; The Guardian newspaper, , Oct 27, 2011; The Sun newspaper, Oct 10, 2011.)

Mistake#6: Failing To "Prime" Before Privatizing

When a hospital surgeon wants to cut through their patient, they sedate the patient from feeling the potentially excruciating pains of the surgery. The sedation can be through anesthesia that sometimes puts the patient into a deep sleep, such that by the time the patient wakes up, the surgery is over, and the patient has a different body.

We can think of our "priming" here as the reform-equivalent of anesthesia, which is designed to sedate the citizens from feeling the pains of a potentially jolting reform. There is one form of such anesthesia that is a favorite of the federal government of Nigeria!

Case 171: Nigeria's Anaesthesia For Fuel Price Increase

Each time that Nigeria's government under President Olusegun Obasanjo wanted to increase the nation's official fuel price (which was uniform across the country), it would usually start with a sudden fuel scarcity. Within days, the scarcity would become so acute that it would force motorists to the "black market", where they would not only be paying very exorbitant prices, but often also even buying adulterated fuel that damaged their vehicles.

Sometimes, the scarcity would bite so hard that desperate motorists would be willing to pay any price, if only they could be sure that the fuel was not adulterated. With everybody now groaning under the pains of the scarcity, government would (largely to everybody's relief), quietly effect the new official price, which would be substantially lower than the "black market" price, but higher than the previous official price! And the scarcity would thereafter, progressively ease off!

The Nigerian government under President Ibrahim Babangida also practiced a variant form of this anesthesia. It would simply announce the new official fuel price, but simultaneously create a dual price regime, which allowed commercial passenger vehicles that served the masses to continue to buy from designated fuel stations at the old price, while other stations would sell to other vehicles at the new price. The commercial vehicles would have no reason to increase transport fares immediately, since they would still be buying fuel at the old rate. This arrangement would only last for a while, because government would progressively (but quietly) thin down supply to outlets that sold at the old price.

One privatization reform that did not leverage this priming principle was the Nigerian government attempt in January 2012 to remove the fuel subsidy altogether!

Case 172: No Priming For Nigeria's Aborted 2012 Subsidy Removal

Nigerians woke up one morning in January 2012 to find that fuel had started selling at N141/liter, from the previous price of N65/liter! Government subsequently announced that fuel subsidy had been removed, and gave the new "indicative" price as N141/liter! It was government's peculiar new year gift to citizens! It did not take a jolted, angry and disappointed nation long to troop into the streets in massive protests, which eventually forced government to back down!

Another Nigerian government PSI program that did not leverage the anesthesia principle was government's power-sector-reform Roadmap of 2010.

Case 173: Power Sector Privatization Without Anesthesia

Nigeria's federal government, under President Goodluck Jonathan, in giving priority attention to the power sector, set up two key organs for driving his comprehensive reform of the sector - the Presidential Task Force on Power (PTFT) and the Presidential Action Committee on Power (PACP).

In August 2010, they unveiled a reform "roadmap", which put privatization (of the state-owned distribution and generating agencies) upfront in the reform program for the sector.

This immediately created a very avoidable transformation trap: It ignited a stiff and bitter opposition from the powerful workers of the public power supply company (PHCN), who had the capacity to hold the nation to a ransom, because government was the monopolistic supplier of electricity nationwide.

Government could conceivably have minimized the force of the opposition that greeted the program (and the very huge terminal "buy off" payments it eventually made to the workers), if it had followed the anaesthesia principles of this Chapter.

One area in which the Nigerian government can still apply the anesthesia principle is in the deregulation of its downstream petroleum sector, which has been variously described as the engine-room of corruption.

<u>Case 174:</u> <u>Anesthesia For Downstream Oil Sector Deregulation</u>

Nigeria has been a major producer of crude oil for many decades; but even by 2019, it still imports most of the petrol used in the country, in a process that government restricts to a few privileged elites. Government has implemented a subsidy program ostensibly to prevent Nigerians from paying what it calls the market value of the imported fuel, and also to make the fuel available at a uniform price all over the country.

The subsidy has become both very costly to government, and (as many people have long argued) a source of massive fraud perpetrated by the government in power together with the so-called "oil cabal" – a rip-off by the elites. The subsidy opponents, who usually include opposition politicians (until they take over government, and find themselves in a position to control the subsidy), have argued that there is nothing like subsidy; and that a vicious "cabal" is just using the so-called subsidy to feed the pockets of a few vicious Nigerian elites. They argue that at the price citizens are paying for the fuel, there cannot be any subsidy at all!

Unfortunately, subsidy removal is a sensitive political issue, because:

- The masses support it in the belief that subsidy saves them from paying higher price for the fuel.

- The subsidy also prevents price differentials across the country, which would be disadvantageous to those states that are far away from the coastal (seaport) areas, particularly the highly influential north-western and north-eastern states.

- Very importantly, the "oil cabal", which controls the oil supply nationwide, has the capacity to create immediate jolting prices, if the subsidy should be removed against its will.

- If a new government becomes convinced that the subsidy should go, here is a possible way that it can apply the anesthesia principle of this Chapter:
- Government can start by creating a new regulator for the sector. The regulator should be independent of the multiple government agencies that presently exist in the sector, to ensure that the program will not be driven by any of the agencies that may presently be benefiting from the subsidy scam – as such an agency could conceivably be inclined to frustrating it!

- The regulator can then start by opening up the fuel importation business to all those interested, so that all members of the private sector (both local and international) will be free to begin to bring fuel (of defined specifications) on their own into the country, and sell at their own prices.

- Government can then apply the anesthesia principle by sustaining its subsidized fuel regime through some selected retail outlets. If indeed there is a subsidy (and many people believe there is none) the subsidized outlets will initially be cheaper, and motorists who can afford the time can queue up there, while those who are in a hurry can drive into the de-regulated outlets and buy, without queuing!

- Government will thereafter progressively thin down supply to the subsidized outlets, as the deregulated market matures.

Some Other Miscellaneous Things That Often Go Wrong

Below are some other miscellaneous things that governments often get wrong in their PSI programs:

1. *Poor contracting*: Government agencies often fail to draw up very competent contracts that will not short-change public interests. This can be out of ignorance, incompetence, or corruption. Poor contracting is one of the main causes of disappointing privatization outcomes. It can be in terms of "quiet" clauses, which are easy to miss, but whose implications (when they manifest later) can sour an entire PSI program. This is by no means limited to the DCs, as the Chicago parking meter PSI illustrates.

Case 175:   Chicago's Parking Meter PSI Debacle

The outcome of the concessioning arrangement that the cash-strapped city of Chicago (USA) entered with a private-sector consortium led by Morgan Stanley (MS) was disappointing in many ways. The concessioning empowered MS to take over the city's 36,000 parking meters, for 75 years, for $1.2 billion. MS soon afterwards, hit Chicago motorists with a doubling of the parking meter rates (something that had never been increased in the previous 20 years). This sparked mass outrage.

But, as if this was not enough, more bad news followed:

- MS notified motorists that the parking Meters must now run 24 hours a day, 7 days a week - no more grace times, for example, evenings and Sundays!

- A report then by the New York Times suggested that compared to the $23.79 million the city had made from the meters in 2008, MS was expecting a revenue haul of $46.92 million for 2009, and $79.54 million in 2010!

- Careful analysis found that the agreement, running for 75 years, would cost motorists as much as $11.6 billion – for a deal that cost MS only $1.2 billion!

- The agreement committed the city to compensate MS for any actions the city might take that impaired the revenue inflow from any of the meters, during the 75 years.

- That meant the city could not for example, block any of the roads for street festivals, nor remove any parking meter from the system for road expansion, street redesign, etc!

- The contract did not make any exit provision for Chicago! The city was stuck!

- Within a few years, the city had spent all but $125 million of the $1.2 billion, and now faced 72 years of restrictive contract that gave it no control and no exit option!

- MS would not even allow the city to grumble in peace: It was additionally billing the city for compensation penalties. Such penalties had reached $61 million in just the first few years! The city refused to pay and took the case to arbitration, and lost the lawsuit filed by Morgan Stanley for $61 million.

- When interest rates fell significantly, the city was unable to take advantage of the low rates to borrow against parking-meter revenue.

- On the other hand, MS quickly took advantage of the low rates, and recovered $600 million of its $1.2 billion upfront payment, by selling 10-year notes!

- Some city council officials who voted for the deal, naturally regretted doing so, saying they wished they had known more of the details – a bad case of "medicine after death"!

(Source: Adapted from Mihalopoulos (2009), Kaehny (2009), Cohen & Farmer, 2014)

Notice in particular that the concessioning agreement gave the city of Chicago no exit option, and also committed the city to compensate MS for any actions the city might take that impaired the revenue inflow from any of the meters – for 75 years! This is an example of the "quiet" clauses, which can easily be missed, but whose implications can be very serious.

2. _Security lapses_: Outsourcing any sensitive government services to the private sector increases significantly the risk of security breaches, which if not managed carefully can lead to disappointing PSI outcomes.

- For example, Edward Snowden (as pointed out by Steven Pearlstein) was a 30-year-old American working for a private contractor engaged by the US government. Snowden embarrassed the government by downloading and publishing millions of pages of highly classified documents from government computer systems. After the Snowden affair, it was shocking to realize that the man was working for a private contractor to the US government, with security clearance that was approved by another private contractor to the government! Worse still was that a 30-year-old government contractor [Snowden] with security clearance that was approved by another private contractor, had routine access to some of government's most sensitive secrets?

3. _Poor contract monitoring_: Another frequent cause of PSI failures is the underestimation of the importance of contract monitoring in the management of PSI programs. It is very critical, when collaborating with the private sector, for government to remain very alert, because government's goal of "common good" is often in conflict with the private sector's goal of "maximizing profit".

- For example, in the Chicago parking meter debacle discussed above, the city's policy goal for setting up the parking meters might have been to provide residents with a low-cost amenity; but as Chicago motorists quickly found out, the goal of the private firm was simply to maximize its profit!

Policymakers should always bear in mind that if a private firm can boost profit by cutting corners, it will often try to do so. This is by no means limited to the DCs, but happens everywhere!

- According to Steven Pearlstein, the US Investigations Services (USIS) was a private contractor, which was doing investigations for the US government for top security clearances (something normally done by the FBI). After the Snowden affair, government sued USIS, accusing the firm of pushing through clearances without sufficient investigation, in order to qualify for performance bonuses.

4. _Cost underestimation_: The decision to outsource a service ultimately depends on the cost-benefit analysis. Unfortunately, this analysis often underestimates some cost elements, including those that should be associated with effective contract management and monitoring by government workers. Sometimes, when the service is complex and requires elaborate monitoring and quality control, the expected PSI savings can be eaten up by monitoring costs alone!

Two Other Things To Note About PSI

Policymakers in the DCs need to be also aware of the following two features of PSI projects, which can create adverse effects if not managed proactively:

1. *Denial of flexibility*: A typical PSI project will usually tie government's hands and reduce government's flexibility. Take outsourcing as an example: One of its benefits is that it allows government to specify the desired outcomes, which the private firm is obliged to deliver. The problem arises however, if government should desire down the line, to make some modifications. At that point, a PSI program that is not proactively structured, can put government in helpless position, while empowering the private firm to "make a kill". The ultimate result will be a PSI outcome that is not in the best public interest.

    - Earlier, we looked at the Chicago parking meter agreement, which the city entered into with Messrs Morgan Stanley (MS). The agreement committed the city to compensate MS for any actions the city might take that impaired the revenue inflow from any of the meters, for 75 long years! This seriously tied the city's hands, because it meant that the city could not for example, block any of the roads for street festivals, nor remove any parking meter from the system (for example, for road expansion, or street redesign)! And for a whopping 75 years!

    - Similarly, remember the 2005 concessioning of Nigeria's seaports to private-sector port operators, as highlighted earlier. The widely criticized concessioning arrangement made no provisions for a regulator for the sector! However, following years of outcry from Nigerian port users about the abuse by the port operators, the federal government of President Goodluck Jonathan appointed the Nigerian Shippers Council to become the temporary regulator of the sector. The private port operators refused, and went to court to challenge government. They believed that the agreement tied government's hands from ever appoint a regulator for the ports!

    - In some cases, government oversight bodies have been known to experience problems accessing the operations records of some private firms involved in a PSI program, because the latter can claim concerns about commercial and trade secrets.

2. *Neglect of workforce*: Let us also note that with the growing role of PSI, government may start craving the speed, quality and reliability of the private sector, while allowing the quality of its own workforce to deteriorate.

Chapter 32

32. Leveraging The Potentials of Unsolicited Private Projects Proposals

"Finance is a vital requirement, but often not the determinant factor. A viable project will attract funding, but an unviable project will ultimately fail, no matter how well funded"

(Eng. Mansur Ahmed, Director-General, Nigeria's Infrastructure Concession Regulatory Commission (ICRC), at the CBN Infrastructure Finance Conference, Sheraton Hotel, December 2010)

Topics Covered in This Chapter:

- Introduction To Unsolicited Private Proposals
- Benefits of Unsolicited Private Proposals
- The potential pitfalls of Unsolicited Private Proposals
- How to avoid these potential pitfalls
- Conclusion

Introduction To Unsolicited Private Proposals

This Chapter looks at the issue of unsolicited project proposals (UPPs), the independent projects ideas and proposals that government often receives unsolicited from the private sector. Such proposals can be for any kind of projects – infrastructural projects, social projects, youth programs, and so on. Some of them can involve initial funding partnerships with government, or may even not cost government anything.

When a private party spends its resources to execute an independent project, it will be doing so as an investment, which it expects to recoup in future, usually through fees to those who use the service. For example, if the project has to do with road construction, the private party will typically impose a toll on the road.

Benefits of Unsolicited Private Proposals

A well-articulated policy on UPPs can bring some benefits to DC, including the following:

1. *Enhanced project conceptualisation capacity*: In a typical DC, those in government may not be qualified for the positions they occupy. Tribalism, nepotism and other vices usually influence employment into the public service.

In view of that, a well-articulated policy on UPPs is one tool that the DC can wisely use, to:

    a.   Complement its policymaking capacity with the superior resources that may be available outside government, thus effectively making the private sector an extension of government's available resources for project conceptualisation!

    b.   Increase the speed and diversity of projects conceptualisation in the DC.

    c.   Harness without cost, the ideas, versatility, and expertise of the private sector in conceptualizing, designing, and developing projects. Note that even when government is unable to take immediate advantage of a project idea, officials will still have become sensitized on those ideas and concepts.

2. *Enhanced policymaking capacity*: Such a policy will create the enabling environment (and may even become the starting point) for policymakers to begin to wisely harvest in other ways, the "dispersed" ideas that may be domiciled in the wider society; which will increase citizens participation in governance.

Potential Pitfalls of Unsolicited Private Proposals

As explained by John Hodges (2003, a private sector development specialist at the World Bank), many of the world's most controversial private infrastructure projects (such as the Dabhol Power Plant in India and many independent power generation plants in Indonesia) originated as unsolicited proposals. There is therefore every need to be careful with the management of such proposals.

The pitfalls that are usually associated with UPPs are not necessarily because the projects are unsolicited, but mostly because the process adopted often open the door to corruption and opportunistic behaviors. For example, the greatest source of pitfall is the desperation of the proponents of UPPs to prevent competitive bidding, and instead settle for sole-source negotiations. It is the darkness of such negotiations that facilitates corruption and the pitfalls.

On the other hand, a well-conceived competitive bidding process for UPPs will notably:

1. Create the usual transparency and efficiency gains of well-managed competitive tender processes;

2. Enable government to define its terms in a tender document (note that by contrast, the private firm is likely to define the criteria, in sole-source negotiations);

3. Remove the public doubts that would inevitably be created, if a public project is awarded without competitive bidding, even when carried out in good faith.

4. Give government a ready fall-back option in case of disappointment: For example, even if the original proponent emerges as the preferred bidder after a competitive bidding process, the process would nevertheless have thrown up a "next preferred" bidder, who can take over if the winner should violate the agreed terms, or fail in any other way. This fall-back position will not be immediately available, from a sole-source negotiation.

We can see from these that the potential pitfalls are not necessarily because the concepts are unsolicited, but mostly because the process, if not well managed, can open the door to corruption and opportunistic behaviors.

If therefore a nation can proactively articulate robust guidelines for UPPs, to help keep such doors shut, it can reap the harvests of unsolicited proposals, while avoiding their pitfalls.

How to Avoid These Potential Pitfalls

To help guard against the foregoing pitfalls, let us now review the typical ways that such projects fall into pitfalls, and how a prudent government can possibly respond. Credit for most of the insights brought out here must go to John Hodges (2003) of the World Bank, from whose works most of these insights came.

Now, here are some of the arguments that a proponent can advance for sole-source negotiations, and how government can respond:

1. The proponent can claim that the project involves intellectual property-rights, which may be violated by a competitive bidding process.

    - When there is a real case for intellectual property-rights, any of the following techniques can be used to make the process competitive:

        - Reimbursing the original proponent for its project development costs, and then adopting an open tender process;

        - Using an open tender process, which gives the original proponent some defined advantage; or

        - Even purchasing the project concept from the original proponent, and then holding an open tender for the project.

2. The proponent can claim that the project uses new technologies or techniques not available from other sources. In this case, government's response can be:

    - To start by assessing even the need for that technology, by specifying the expected output of the project (while protecting the original proponent's proprietary rights) and allowing different bidders to propose their own solutions for obtaining the specified output. Those alternative solutions can then be compared with that of the new unsolicited technology.

    - To go ahead and advertise for alternative or substitute technologies (which are almost always available) and compare the cost-effectiveness of the new technology with such alternatives;

    - If the original proponent requested a subsidy, government can ask other bidders to compete based on the minimum subsidy that they will accept for the specified output.

3. Government officials can ask for sole-source negotiations because the project may not be able to attract other bidders (for example, because it is too small, or too remotely located) such that inviting other bidders may not be cost-efficient. Some unsolicited proposals do indeed cleverly target such projects!

   - Even when it is feared that the project may not be able to attract other bidders, it is still better to call for expressions of interest, at least for transparency. If no other firm responds, it will at least be clear that there has been transparency.

   - Also, if the problem is that the project is too small, government can decide to make it more attractive to more bidders, by for example, pooling it together with additional projects or services in the tender.

4. There may be an emergency, whose urgent needs may justify immediate exclusive negotiations with the proponent

   - Rushing into exclusive sole-source negotiations (on the excuse of emergencies) is not advisable. As noted by John Hodges, the experience from several such emergencies is that sole-source negotiations usually end up taking more time than originally expected and often end up delaying the project for longer years

5. Government officials may be confident that the original proponent will win, and so argue that there is no need going into tender process, and incurring the costs it will entail

   - Again, it is still better to call for expressions of interest, notwithstanding this confidence. If the original proponent wins, it will at least be clear that there has been transparency. If another firm wins, then government will have been vindicated in its decision to open it up!

In general, whenever there is a successful argument for sole-source negotiations, the main challenge for government will be to strive to ensure that the transparency and efficiency gains of a well-conceived competitive tender process are not lost – that the winning participant's investment and operating costs are similar whether the project is awarded through competition or sole-source negotiations!

Bibliography

1. Abdulahi: "MINT: Beyond CBN's Takeover", Vanguard Newspapers, March 8, 2005
2. Aberdeen Group: Best Practices in E-Procurement, December 2005
3. Accenture: Be Like a Business, Not Bad for Business; June 2015
4. Accenture: Florida Department of Business and Professional Regulation: Licensing system, 2016
5. Accenture: Meet the public service growth hackers: How regulatory and licensing agencies can embrace digital to drive the economy, 2015
6. Accenture: US citizens are ready, willing—and waiting—for digital government, 2016
7. Acemoglu, D; Johnson, S; & Robinson, J.A: The Colonial Origins of Comparative Development: an Empirical Investigation; American Economic Review, 91 (5), 2001 (see also Acemoglu & James Robinson: The Role of Institutions in Growth & Development)
8. Acemoglu, Daron & Johnson, Simon: Unbundling Institutions, Journal of Political Economy (vol. 113, no. 5) 2005
9. Acemoglu, Daron & Robinson, James A: Why Nations Fail, Profile Books Ltd, London 2012
10. Acemoglu, Daron & Robinson, James: The Role of Institutions in Growth & Development, Review of Economics and Institutions, Vol. 1 – No. 2, Fall 2010
11. Acemoglu, Daron: Understanding Institutions (Based on joint work with Simon Johnson & James Robinson) Lionel Robbins Lectures, London School Economics, Feb.23-25
12. Adams, Isiaka: "Why Nigerians Prefer Cotonou Ports for Vehicle Importation" The Punch February 14, 2004
13. ADB (Asian Development Bank): Results-Based Lending for Programs
14. Ade Ogidan & Ugwu, Enitar: "Govt's Economic reforms are Turning Things Around for the Better, Says Ogbu", The Guardian, February 15, 2005
15. Adegoroye, Goke (on the loyalty of the civil service): see his paper: Public Service Reform For Sustainable Development: The Nigerian Experience, 2006
16. Adeniyi, Olusegun: "As the Elephant Begins to Dance", Thisday Newspapers, February 3, 2005
17. Adeniyi, Olusegun: "No Electric Power Again (NEPA)", Thisday Newspapers, March 3, 2005
18. Adeniyi, Olusegun: Fighting Corruption in Nigeria: The Verdict, Thisdaylive, July 14, 2016
19. Adeniyi, Olusegun: Leadership in a Time of Recession, The Verdict, Thisday July 28, 2016
20. Adetayo, Lekan: Access To President: Buhari's Powerful Aides Bar Ministers, Family, Friends, Punch, February 26, 2017
21. Agabi, Kanu The Powers of Service Please see BPSR (Bureau of Public Service Reforms): NIGERIA Public Service Reform Series #1 (The Vision & Challenges)
22. AGSA (Auditor General of South Africa): Please see the website
23. Aguilera, Rodrigo: Costa Rica: Life after Intel, The Huffington Post, Jul 01, 2014
24. Ahmad, Muhammad: Updated: INEC Resident Commissioner, Wife, Children Killed In "Strange" Fire, Premium Times, April 19, 2018
25. Ahmed, Dr. Mahmud Yayale, CFR (on relationship between Permanent Secretaries & their political heads): Please see BPSR (Bureau of Public Service Reforms): NIGERIA Public Service Reform Series #3 (Driving Reforms)
26. Ahmed, Dr. Mahmud Yayale, CFR: Please see BPSR (Bureau of Public Service Reforms): NIGERIA Public Service Reform Series #3 (Driving Reforms)
27. Ahmed, Dr. Mahmud Yayale, CFR: Please see BPSR (Bureau of Public Service Reforms): NIGERIA Public Service Reform Series #1 (The Vision & Challenges)
28. Ahmed, Dr. Mahmud Yayale, CFR: Support for Innovation, Modernization, & Change in the Civil Service: The Nigerian Experience (An Anniversary Lecture Delivered in Commemoration of the Civil Service Week of the Republic of Ghana & Africa Day of Administration), June 22, 2005
29. Ajayi, Taiwo Eniola, Prof.: please see Olatunji, Bukola: "Educational Planning as Way Forward for an Ailing Sector"
30. Akhigbe, Nathaniel & Dimma, Mabel: Missing $20bn Exposes Nigeria's Weak Auditing System Business Day, Mar 22, 2015
31. Akinwumi, Olayemi Prof: Please see Shala, Daniel: "Not Business as Usual: The Obasanjo Reforms"

32. Alifa, Daniel: Ezekwesili Stoops to Lift Education: The Guardian Newspapers, Tuesday, September 26, 2006

33. Alohan, Juliet: Discos Rejecting Power Allocation Risk License Withdrawal – FG, Leadership newspaper, November 25, 2014

34. Andrews, Matt: Why Institutional Reforms In The Developing World Aren't Working, The Guardian, Friday 8 March 2013

35. Anya, Victor: Between strong institutions and strong individuals, Daily Independent, Feb 13, 2014

36. Arbes, Ross & Bethea, Charles: Songdo, South Korea: City of the Future? Sep 27, 2014

37. Argyropoulos, Christos: Who regulates the regulators? The BMJ, 23 July 2014

38. Arthur, W. Brian: Please see David Rotman

39. Arthur-Worrey, Fola: Does Nigeria Need a New Police Force? Thisday, 24 Dec 2012

40. Asian Development Bank Institute: "*Understanding the Digital Economy: What Is It and How Can It Transform Asia?*" Event | 21 - 22 February 2018 New Delhi, India

41. Assuras, Thalia: How The GI Bill Changed America; CBS News, June 22, 2008

42. Astheimer, Stefan Kip: See Sherman, Erik

43. ASU's P3: See Productivity and Prosperity Project (P3) of the Arizona State University (ASU)

44. Atuanya, Patrick: Employers bemoan regulators seen squeezing business (Nigeria), BusinessDay, Nigeria December 1, 2014

45. Auditor, State of Washington: Who Audits the Auditor? Even the Auditor's Office is audited. Funkhouser, Mark: The Impact That Government Auditing Could Have (and Doesn't) , Governing, August 2015

46. Auditor-General: Constitution Bars Us from Auditing NNPC, The Citizen, March 3, 2014 Joseph Onoja & Abdullah Fagbemi: Why Audit Bill 2015 Should Not Be Signed By The President (1), The Union, August 12, 2015

47. Auriol, Emmanuelle & Picard, Pierre M: *Government Outsourcing: Public Contracting With Private Monopoly*, 24 November 2009

48. Australian Government, Financial Reporting Council (FRC): Monitoring Auditor Independence, Annual report 2011-2012

49. Azemati, Hanna; Belinsky, Michael; Gillette, Ryan; Liebman, Jeffrey; Sellman, Alina; & Wyse, Angela: Social Impact Bonds: Lessons Learned So Far, John F. Kennedy School of Government, Harvard University

50. Ball, Molly The Privatization Backlash, The Atlantic, Apr 23, 2014

51. Barrett, Katherine & Greene, Richard : The Trials and Tribulations of Auditing Government, Governance, January 7, 2016

52. Bay Area Council Economic Institute: New Study: For Every New High-Tech Job, Four More Created, 2015

53. Beattie, Vivien & Fearnley, Stella: Auditor Independence and Non-Audit Services: A Literature Review

54. Bell, Dr. Jon: The strengths and weaknesses of self-regulation

55. Bello, Muhammad: House Moves to Take over Appointment of Auditor-General of the Federation, Thisday, 05 Nov 2014

56. Bello, Remi : please see BusinessNews July 19, 2014

57. Bethel, Sheila Murray: "Making A Difference: 12 Qualities that Make You a Leader", Berkley Books, 1990

58. Better Government Competition: Benchmarking to Make State Government More Efficient, 2006

59. Beyer, Hannah & Fening, Fred: The Impact of Formal Institutions on Global Strategy in Developed vs. Emerging Economies, International Journal of Business and Social Science, Vol. 3 No. 15; August 2012

60. Blakeman, Joseph: Benchmarking: Definitions and Overview, Center for Urban Transportation Studies (CUTS), University of Wisconsin-Milwaukee, June, 2002

61. Bosah, Chinedu: Private Management of Unity Schools – Not the Solution: Adequately Public Funding is Needed, CDWRN, 13 November 2006

62. Boston, Jonathan: Separation of Policy and Operations in Government: the New Zealand experience; In International Governance Network, Policy and Operations. Ottawa: Canadian Center for Management Development; 1996

63. BPSR (Bureau of Public Service Reforms): Generic Guidelines for the Reform of Parastatals: March, 2006

64. BPSR (Bureau of Public Service Reforms): NIGERIA Public Service Reform Series #3 (Driving Reforms), Edited by Dr. Goke Adegoroye: 2005

65. BPSR (Bureau of Public Service Reforms): NIGERIA Public Service Reform Series #2 (Purpose & Propriety in Public Service), Edited by Dr. Goke Adegoroye: 2005

66. BPSR (Bureau of Public Service Reforms): NIGERIA Public Service Reform Series #1 (The Vision & Challenges), Edited by Dr. Goke Adegoroye: 2005

67. BPSR (Bureau of Public Service Reforms): NIGERIA Public Service Reform Series #4 (Organizational Integrity & Strategic Corruption Control): Edited by Dr. Goke Adegoroye: 2005

68. BPSR (Bureau of Public Service Reforms): NIGERIA: Country Case Study on Public Service Reforms: A Presentation by BPSR at the CAPAM In-Country Seminar, August 8-10, 2006

69. Braunfels, Elias: Further Unbundling Institutions, Norwegian School of Economics, September 19, 2016

70. Brice, Leamon: Please see Davidson

71. Brinded, Lianna: Manpower's CEO just gave us an awesome solution to the 'robots taking human jobs' conundrum, Business Insider, Jan. 23, 2016

72. Brooks, David: What Machines Can't Do, The New York Times, Feb 3, 2014

73. Brynjolfsson, Erik & McAfee, Andrew: How To Survive In A Tech-Driven Economy, The Christian Science Monitor, December 12, 2012

74. Bureau of Justice Assistance: "Trial Court Performance Standards & Measurement System Implementation Manual", Series: BJA Monograph, July 1997

75. Business Insider (quoting Geoff Colvin): The Robots May Be Coming To Take Our Jobs — But One Trait Might Keep You Safe, August 19, 2015

76. BusinessNews: Overlapping functions by government agencies affecting businesses – LCCI, July 19, 2014

77. Butkovitz, Alan: Please see Barrett, Katherine & Greene, Richard

78. Byrnes, Nanette: Work in Transition, MIT Technology Review, September 28, 2015

79. Cahyadi, Gundy; Kursten, Barbara; Weiss, Marc; & Yang, Guang: Singapore's Economic Transformation, Global Urban Development, Prague, Czech Republic; June 2004

80. Cannon, Robert: Please see Smith, Aaron & Anderson, Janna

81. Carey. John M. Parchment, Equilibria, and Institutions, Comparative Political Studies, 2000 (See DFID, "Beyond Institutions")

82. Carmel, Erran: The New Software Exporting Nations: Success Factors, American University, Washington D.C., USA, 2003

83. Carrigan, Christopher & Poole, Lindsey: Structuring Regulators: The Effects of Organizational Design on Regulatory Behavior and Performance, Research Paper Prepared for the Penn Program on Regulation's Best-in-Class Regulator Initiative, June, 2015

84. Celis, William 3D: 50 Years Later, the Value of the G.I. Bill Is Questioned; The New York Times Archives; 1994

85. Christensen, Jørgen Grønnegaard & Yesilkagit, Kutsal: Delegation and specialization in regulatory administration: (A comparative analysis of Denmark, Sweden and The Netherlands), Paper prepared for the SOG and Scancor Workshop on Autonomization of the state: From integrated administrative models to single purpose organizations Scancor, Stanford University, April 1-2, 2005

86. Chubb, John E., Moe, Terry M.: "Politics, Markets, & American Schools", The Hoover Institution, 1990

87. Chubb, John E.: "Education: Real Choice", The Hoover Digest, No. 2, 2003

88. Chubb, John E.: "Ignoring The Market", The Hoover Institution, 2003

89. Chubb, John E.: "Within Our Reach: How America Can Educate Every Child", Rowman & Littlefield, 2003

90. Cisco Consulting Services: Please see Lopez Research

91. Clark, Liat: Automation will allow less skilled surgeons to perform complicated procedures, Wired UK, 12 November 12

92. Coburn, Senator Tom: Please see O'Keefe, Ed

93. Cohen , Donald & Farmer, Prof. Stephanie: Why Chicago's Botched Parking Meter Privatization Is Also Bad for the Environment, Next City, June 4, 2014

94. Colvin, Geoff: Business's real problem: Uncertainty, uncertainty, uncertainty, Fortune, August 13, 2012

95.   Colvin, Geoff: Fortune's World's Greatest Leaders: 50 intrepid guides for a messy world, Fortune, March 26, 2015
96.   Colvin, Geoff: Humans are underrated, Fortune, July 23, 2015
97.   Colvin, Geoff: In the future, will there be any work left for people to do? Fortune, June 16, 2014
98.   Colvin, Geoff: Listen up, biz leaders: It's time to rethink everything, September 4, 2012
99.   Colvin, Geoff: Power: A cooling trend, Fortune, December 11, 2007
100.   Colvin, Geoff: Talent is Overrated: What Really Separates World-Class Performers From Everybody Else, 2008
101.   Congressional Quarterly, Structures and Institutions, CQ Press, 2017
102.   Cooper, Mark N. (Dr.): "Reconsidering Electricity Structuring: Do Market Problems Indicate a Short Circuit or a Total Blackout?" Consumer Federation of America; November 2000
103.   Cossin, Didier: Action Needed On Regulating The Regulators, ft.com, September 23, 2012
104.   Craig, William: What Everyone Gets Wrong About Giving to Charity, Fortune, December 20, 2015
105.   Cramton, Roger C.: Regulatory Structure and Regulatory Performance: A Critique of the Ash Council Report, Cornell Law Faculty Publications, 1972
106.   Crowe, Dan; Gash, Tom; Kippin Henry: Beyond Big Contracts Commissioning public services for better outcomes, Calouste Gulbenkian Foundation, Institute For Government
107.   Currey, Kevin: Some Evolving Trends At The World Bank: Lending, Funding, Staffing (Briefing Note), The Ford Foundation, May 2014
108.   Darlington, Lloyd: Please see wikibooks.org
109.   Davidson Launches Open Town Hall, town portal, October 13, 2015 http://www.ci.davidson.nc.us/CivicAlerts.aspx?AID=859
110.   David-West, Tam (Philosophical Essays): See Femi Adesina's PMB's Health: Gloating Is Of No Value; Vanguard newspaper, March 25, 2017
111.   DBIS (UK Department for Business, Innovation and Skills): Better Regulation Framework Manual - Practical Guidance for UK Government Officials, March, 2015
112.   DBIS (UK Department for Business, Innovation and Skills): Policy paper 2010 to 2015 on Government Policy: Business Regulation Updated 8 May 2015
113.   De Leon, Daniel: see Socialist Labor Party (SLP)
114.   Deech, Baroness of Cumnor DBE: Regulating the Regulators, Gresham College, 2012 (see also John Cassar White)
115.   Deech, Baroness: Please see John Cassar White
116.   Deft-Rains Solutions: Smart Cities Internet of Things (IOT) Examples and Applications, Deft-Rains Solutions' ICT Blog
117.   Delaney, Tom: Please see the Economist Intelligence Unit white paper
118.   Deloitte: Regulatory change - It's Not About Ticking The Box, Accessed, December, 2016
119.   DFID: Beyond Institutions. Institutions And Organizations In The Politics And Economics Of Poverty Reduction - A Thematic Synthesis Of Research Evidence, DFID-funded (IPPG) Research Program, September 2010
120.   DFID: Designing and Delivering Payment by Results Programs: A DFID Smart Guide, 2014
121.   Dickey, Megan Rose : How Robots Could Make Their Way Into The Classroom, Business Insider, Feb. 5, 2013
122.   Drucker, Peter: "Innovation and Entrepreneurship", Harper & Row, 1985
123.   Drucker, Peter: "The New Realities", Harper & Row, 1988
124.   Duffrin, Elizabeth: "Where Councils Lost Ground"
125.   Ebegbulem, Simon: World bank to states: Build strong institutions like Lagos, Edo, benefit from our loans, Vanguard on August 23, 2015
126.   Economist Intelligence Unit white paper: The Future Of Higher Education: How Technology Will Shape Learning, 2008
127.   Eggers, William D., Meyers, Max & Niech, Claire: How the Internet of Things Could Transform Public Services, Governing, September 2, 2015
128.   Eichler, Rena & De, Susna: Paying for Performance in Health, Guide to Developing the Blueprint (DRAFT), M AY 2008
129.   Ekaette, Chief U.J. (CFR, mni), (on government's 31 Ministries): Please see BPSR (Bureau of Public Service Reforms): NIGERIA Public Service Reform Series #3 (Driving Reforms)

130. Ekaette, Chief U.J. (CFR, mni): The Imperatives of a Harmonious Working Relationship Amongst The Top Functionaries of Government; an address at the Presidential Retreat on public sector reforms and public/private partnerships for Ministers, Permanent Secretaries, and Organized Private Sector, August 18-20, 2005

131. Ekule, Robert: Please see Akhigbe, Nathaniel & Dimma, Mabel

132. Elliott, Robert K. & Jacobson, Peter D., Audit independence concepts, The CPA Journal 68 no12 30-4+ D '98

133. el-Rufai, Mallam Nasir Ahmad (OFR): Please see BPSR (Bureau of Public Service Reforms): NIGERIA Public Service Reform Series #3 (Driving Reforms)

134. el-Rufai, Mallam Nasir Ahmad (OFR): Reforming Our Dysfunctional Public Service, Thisday, 01 October 2011

135. Eric Schnurer , "When Government Competes Against the Private Sector, Everybody Wins", The Atlantic, March 11, 2015

136. Estepon, Meredith: 5 Ways To Monitor Your Customer Service, Unitiv, Jun 19, 2012

137. Estonia public website, Estonia.eu (Welcome to Estonia)

138. Evans, Phillip & Wurster, Thomas S. : "Blown to Bits: How the New Economics of Information Transforms Strategy"

139. Ezekwesili Oby (Mrs.): on Education budget (please See Daniel Alifa)

140. Fernholz, Tim: Who Regulates the Regulators? The American Prospect, June 19, 2009

141. Financial Conduct Authority: Principles of good regulation, First published 21/04/2016, Updated: 07/07/2016

142. FitzGerald, Gerry J. & Bange, Ray: Policy & Service Delivery -Defining a Regulatory Framework for Paramedics- A Discussion Paper, Journal of Emergency Primary Health Care (JEPHC), Vol.5, Issue 2, 2007

143. Fogel, Georgine K: Economic Institutions In China - Reforms And Transition, Lawrence Technological University

144. Foster, Peter: Who regulates the regulators? Financial Post, October 15, 2014

145. Frost, Robert: Please see Sheila Murray Bethel

146. Fukuyama, Francis: Review of Acemoglu and Robinson on Why Nations Fail, The American Interest, 2012/03/26

147. Fung, Archon: "Accountable Autonomy: Toward Empowered Deliberation in Chicago Schools & Policing", Politics & Society, Vol. 29, No. 1, March 2001

148. Funkhouser, Mark: The Impact That Government Auditing Could Have (and Doesn't), Governing The States & Localities August 2015

149. GAO: Driver's License Security: Federal Leadership Needed to Address Remaining Vulnerabilities, GAO-12-893, Published Sep 21, 2012.

150. GAO: GAO's Forensic Audits and Investigative Service Team, GAO_Watchblog (Official Blog of the U.S. Government Accountability Office) April 24, 2014

151. GAO: US Govt Accountability Office- 2013 Annual Report, GAO-13-279SP: Published: Apr 9, 2013

152. Gartner: Please see Todd Newcomb

153. George Gĩthĩnji: The Role of the Office of the Ombudsman in Kenya, PoliticsKenya, Sep 14, 2016

154. Georgetown University (The Beeck Center for Social Impact & Innovation): FUNDING FOR RESULTS: A Review of Government Outcomes-Based Agreements, November 2014

155. Goldsmith, Stephen, Outsourcing, Insourcing, Rightsourcing, Governing States & Local Governments, 21 October, 2009

156. Goldsmith, Stephen: Us Department Of Labor, Working Together For Public Service: Snapshot: Indianapolis

157. Goldstein, Gordon M: The End of Power From Boardrooms to Battlefields and Churches to States, Why Being In Charge Isn't What It Used, by Moises Naim, Washington Post, March 8, 2013

158. Gomes da Silva Filho, Milton: Improvements In Fraud And Corruption Detection And Prevention In Federal Public Administration, GAO's International Auditor Fellowship Program, 2006

159. Grameen Support Group, Australia: Summary Paper, Mount Colah, NSW 2079 , Australia

160. Graves, Bob : The Soft Infrastructure of Smart Cities, Governing The States & Localities, March 25, 2014

161. Graves, Bob: Can Smart Infrastructure Be Cyber-Secure? Governing The States & Localities, August 26, 2015

162. Gray, Kimi: Please see Osborne David and Gaebler, Ted
163. Greene, Jay P; Greg Forrester, & Marcus A. Winters.: "Apples to Apples: An Evaluation of Charter Schools Serving General Student Population", Education Working paper, Manhattan Institute of Policy Research, July 2003
164. Hall, Peter A. 'The Movement from Keynesianism to Monterarism; Institutional analysis and British economic policy in the 1970s', in Sven Steinmo, Kathleen Thelen and Frank Longstreth (eds.) Structuring Politics. Historical Institutionalizm in Comparative Analysis, Cambridge, Cambridge University Press, 1992 (See DFID, "Beyond Institutions")
165. Hall, Terri, Anti-toll candidates sweep in many key races across Texas , Terri Hall Blog, March 5, 2014
166. Hammer, Michael & Champy, James: "Reengineering the Corporation: A Manifesto for Business Revolution", HarperCollins, 2001
167. Hartley, Jon: Social Impact Bonds Are Going Mainstream, Forbes, Sep 15, 2014
168. Henig, Robin Marantz: Death by Robot, The New York Times Magazine, Jan 9, 2015
169. HMIC: Integrity Matters - An Inspection Of Arrangements To Ensure Integrity And To Provide The Capability To Tackle Corruption In Policing; January 2015
170. Hodges, John: Unsolicited Proposals, The Issues for Private Infrastructure Projects, The World Bank, 2003
171. Hodgson, Geoffrey M: What Are Institutions? Journal Of Economic Issues, Vol. XL No. 1, March 2006
172. HOFA (Hotel Owners Forum Association): Multiple Taxes May Force Nigerian Hotel Proprietors Out Of Business, Premium Times, June 22, 2013
173. Hogan, Timothy: An Overview Of The Knowledge Economy, With A Focus On Arizona, A report from Productivity and Prosperity Project (P3) of the Arizona State University (ASU's P3); An initiative supported by the Office of the University Economist, August 2011
174. Holloway, Josh: eDemocracy @ Weebly: http://edemocracy.weebly.com/why-edemocracy.html
175. Hong Kong Police Force: Ethics And Integrity In The Hong Kong Police Force (from www.police.gov.hk)
176. Hongbo ,WU, in his Foreword to: United Nations E-Government Survey 2014, Department of Economic and Social Affairs, United Nations, New York, 2014
177. Hoskins, Rich: Please see Jahn, Lindsey
178. House of Commons, Public Administration Select Committee: As extracted from BPSR (Bureau of Public Service Reforms): NIGERIA Public Service Reform Series #2 (Page 10)
179. HSBC: Navigating The Digitized Landscape, HSBC Bank Plc; 20 December 2016
180. Hulsink ,Wim, Manuel, Dick & Bouwman, Harry: Clustering In Ict: From Route 128 To Silicon Valley, From DEC To Google, From Hardware To Content; July 2008 https://www.researchgate.net/ [Accessed Jul 09 2018]
181. Hutchcroft, Paul D. & Rocamora, Joel: Strong Demands and Weak Institutions: The Origins and Evolution of the Democratic Deficit in the Philippines, Journal of East Asian Studies, May 2003
182. Hutchins, Robert Maynard (quoted by Thalia Assuras & Khan Academy): The GI Bill, the Veterans & The Colleges; University of Kentucky Press, Lexington; 1974
183. Hutzelman, David: Government as Referee: Who Regulates the Regulators? Master Resource, Oct 14 2011
184. Ibileke, Jethro: Nigeria's Poor Healthcare System Wories Medical Expert; PM News on September 11, 2012, By /Benin
185. IBTC: "Managing Your Retirement Benefits Under the Pension Reform Act 2004" Thisday Newspapers, December 11, 2005
186. IDA Please see International Development Association
187. Igor Novikov: How Does Institutional Environment Affect The Internationalization Of Small Enterprises? Enterprise and the Competitive Environment 2014 Conference, ECE 2014, Brno, Czech Republic 6–7 March 2014,
188. IMF: Please see International Monetary Fund
189. International Development Association (IDA) IDA at Work: Building Strong Institutions for Sustained Results,
190. International Development Association (The World Bank's Fund For The Poorest) IDA at Work: Building Strong Institutions for Sustained Results,
191. International Monetary Fund: World Economic Outlook, 2005 (see also DFID, 2010).

192. International Monetary Fund: Chapter 3: Building Institutions
193. ITU-T Technology Watch Report: Smart Cities Seoul: a case study, February 2013
194. Jacobs, Scott & Coolidge, Jacqueline: Reducing Administrative Barriers To Investment – Lessons Learned, FIAS (a Joint Service of the IFC & World Bank)
195. Jahn, Lindsey (Associate Editor): IBIE Q&A: Baking Automation Rises to the Occasion, Food Manufacturing, Thu, 08/15/2013
196. John Ofikhenua, NERC reads riot act to DISCOs over electricity allocation rejection, The Nation, August 05, 2015
197. Johnson, Carrie: Policing The Police: U.S. Steps Up Enforcement, NPR, June 12, 2011
198. Jorgenson, D: Please see Productivity and Prosperity Project (P3) of the Arizona State University (or ASU's P3)
199. Kahlenberg, Richard D. & Potter Halley: The Original Charter School Vision, New York Times, Aug 30, 2014
200. Katz, Lawrence: Please see David Rotman in How Technology Is Destroying Jobs
201. Kaufmann, Daniel & Mastruzzi, Massimo: Governance Matters IV: Governance Indicators for 1996-2004, World Bank Policy Research Working Paper 3630, June 2005
202. Kaye, Morris: What Are the Advantages of Having an External Audit? Houston Chronicle
203. Khan Academy, a 501(c)(3) non-profit organization; Accessed from their website June, 2018
204. King, Hope: The jobs that are most threatened by technology, CNN Money, August 19, 2015
205. Kohlberg, Jerome: Please see William Celis
206. Kolawole, Simon: "Lessons for our Education System" Thisday Newspapers, October 31, 2005
207. Kolawole, Simon: "Soludo, Banking is no Ludo" Thisday Newspapers, July 17, 2004
208. Kumo, Gimba Ya'u: Please see Newswatch Times of October 1, 2014
209. Lao-tzu: Please see Bethel, Sheila Murray: "Making A Difference: 12 Qualities that Make You a Leader"
210. Laurel Adams: Confusing overlap in government assistance programs, Center for Public Integrity, Updated: May 19, 2014
211. Lawrence, Georgina: Who Regulates The Regulators? CRI Occasional Paper 16, 23 May 2012
212. Lectric Law Library: "Some Background on the Criminal Justice System of Malaysia", www.lectlaw.com
213. Lemieux, Thomas & Card, David: Please see Wikipedia, "Education, earnings, and the 'Canadian GI Bill; Canadian Journal of Economics/Revue canadienne d'économique. 34 (2): 313–344, (2001):
214. Leonid Bershidsky: Envying Estonia's Digital Government, Bloomberg View, Mar 4, 2015
215. Lewis, Abbie : Kenya Launch Online e-procurement System, 21.08.2014
216. Lin, Gloria & Espinoza, Nicole: Electronic Voting Case Studies, Stanford University, 2007
217. Lobo, Rita: Could Songdo be the world's smartest city? World Finance, Tuesday, January 21st, 2014
218. Lohor, Josephine: "Nigeria's Foreign Debt Riddled with Fraud – ICAN" Thisday Newspapers, October 3, 2003
219. Lohr, Steve: Jobs Created and Displaced, June 24, 2010
220. Lopez Research: "An Introduction to the Internet of Things (IoT)", http://www.cisco.com/web/solutions/trends/iot/introduction_to_IoT_november.pdf, November 2013
221. Loucks, Michael K. & Gorman, Alexandra M: Who Regulates The Regulators? Forbes, May 2, 2012
222. Luke Johnson & Ryan Grim: GAO Cannot Audit Federal Government, Cites Department Of Defense Problems, Huffington Post, Jan 19, 2013
223. Lynch, Amy: Please see the Economist Intelligence Unit white paper
224. Mandić, Sofija: Dilemmas About Police Integrity Testing; Pointpulse Magazine, May 25, 2016
225. Manning, Nick; Mukherjee, Ranjana & Gokcekus, Omer: Public officials and their institutional environment: An analytical model for assessing the impact of institutional change on public sector performance
226. Manu, Joseph: How India Became an Outsourcing Magnet, 2016 The New York Times, March 28, 2012

227. Marchessault, Lindsey & Hasan Quamrul : Governance for Development - Pushing the frontier of e-government procurement in Africa with the open contracting standard, World Bank Blog, 11-May-2015

228. Marlowe, Justin: Should Someone Audit Government Auditors? Governing The States & Localities, August 2014

229. Martin Ford: Please see Paul Wiseman

230. Mauldin, John: Here's How Robots Could Change The World By 2025, Business Insider, Aug. 20, 2014

231. Melnitze, Julius: Associates threatened by artificial intelligence, Law Times, 08 December 2014

232. Ménard, Claude & Shirley, Mary M: The Contribution of Douglass North to New Institutional Economics (DRAFT for editors), Cambridge University Press: Cambridge, June 21, 2011

233. MetroNews: NHIS: Reps' probe opens can of worms, MetroNews NG, June 28, 2017

234. Meyers, Max; Niech, Claire & Eggers William D: Anticipate, sense, and respond: Connected government and the Internet of Things, Deloitte University Press, August 28, 2015

235. Mihalopoulosnov, Dan: Company Piles Up Profits From City's Parking Meter Deal, New York Times, 19 November 2009

236. Miller, Claire Cain: Will You Lose Your Job To A Robot? Silicon Valley Is Split The New York Times, Aug. 6, 2014

237. Millot Marc Dean: "What Are Charter Schools? An Introduction to the Concept & the Statutes", A Rand Corporation Report

238. Mills, Mark P: "Saudi Arabia And The Future Of Oil Prices: Look To What Robots Will Do, Not What Trump Tweets"; Forbes, Nov 29, 2018

239. Mokgoro, T.J.: Strategic Issues & Change Management in Reforms: A Presentation at the CAPAM In-Country Seminar, August 8-10, 2006

240. Morgan, Jacob: A Simple Explanation Of 'The Internet Of Things', Forbes, May 13, 2014

241. Muhtar, Dr. Mansur: Please see BPSR (Bureau of Public Service Reforms): NIGERIA Public Service Reform Series #3 (Driving Reforms)

242. Mukherjee , Nivi: Please see Stewart, Philippa

243. Nabli, Mustapha: Institutional Reform for Economic Growth in the Arab Countries; Presented at IMF/AMF High-Level Seminar on Institutions and Economic Growth in the Arab Countries, Abu Dhabi, UAE, December 19-20, 2006

244. Naím, Moisés: "The End of Power: From Boardrooms to Battlefields and Churches to States, Why Being in Charge Isn't What It Used to Be", Amazon Paperback, 11 Mar 2014

245. Naím, Moisés: "Vladimir Putin's ebbing power", FORTUNE, April 1, 2015

246. National Center for State Courts: Please see Bureau of Justice Assistance: "Trial Court Performance Standards & Measurement System Implementation Manual"

247. National Commission on Excellence in Education: "A Nation at Risk" 1983 [Some Extracts only]

248. National Working Group on Prison Reforms & Decongestion: Please see Okenwa, Lilian: "Nigerian Prisons, Still Turning Inmates into Cadavers?"

249. Ndukwe, Dr. (Mrs.) Chinyere & Nwakamma, Michael Chibuzor: Privatization Of Unity Schools In Nigeria: Implications For The Education Sector, Journal of Policy and Development Studies Vol. 9, No. 4, August 2015

250. NERC (riot act): Please see John Ofikhenuaon & Juliet Alohan

251. Newcombe, Tod: A Security Dilemma for Smart Devices, Governing The States & Localities, February 11, 2015

252. Newcombe, Tod Santander: The Smartest Smart City, Governing, May 2014

253. NHIS: "Benefit Package for Participants in the National Health Insurance Scheme (NHIS)" Thisday Newspapers, Monday, August 28, 2006

254. Nick Ryan: Benchmarking And Use Of Targets In Public Sector Organizations, ACCA (last updated 18 Aug 2015)

255. Nickols, Fred: Please see Ahmed, Dr. Mahmud Yayale, CFR: Please see BPSR (Bureau of Public Service Reforms): NIGERIA Public Service Reform Series #1 (The Vision & Challenges)

256. North Douglass C; Wallis, John Joseph; & Weingast, Barry R: Violence and Social Orders A Conceptual Framework for Interpreting Recorded Human History, Cambridge University Press, 2009

257. North, Anna: Don't Be Afraid of Robots, Says Ayanna Howard, The New York Times, January 14, 2015

258. North, Anna: What Happens When Robots Write the Future? The New York Times, August 18, 2014

259. North, Douglass C: Five Propositions About Institutional Change, Washington University, St. Louis

260. North, Douglass C: Institutions, Institutional Change and Economic Performance, Cambridge University Press, October 1990

261. North, Douglass C: Institutions, Organizations And Market Competition Washington University, St. Louis

262. North, James: Outcome-Based Contracting Is On The Up: Who's Doing It, Why, And What You Need To Know About It, 13 May 2014

263. Nwogwugwu, Ijeoma: "Adebayo's Requiem Mass for NITEL (III)", Business Times, March 14-16, 2005

264. O'Toole, James: The Hidden Business Benefits of Regulation, Strategy +Business, April 24, 2014

265. Obama, Barack President [on African Union]: "Remarks by President Obama to the People of Africa", The White House, Office of the Press Secretary, July 28, 2015

266. Obama, Barack President [on strong institutions]: Remarks by the President to the Ghanaian Parliament, The White House, Office of the Press Secretary, July 11, 2009

267. Obama, Barack President [on whistleblowers]: Please see Sanjour, William

268. Obasanjo, Olusegun (at EFCC's 1st Executive Session on corruption (Abuja, August 2005): Please see BPSR (Bureau of Public Service Reforms): NIGERIA Public Service Reform Series #3 (Driving Reforms)

269. OECD (Organization for Economic Co-operation and Development): Industry Self-Regulation: Role And Use In Supporting Consumer Interests;   Directorate For Science, Technology And Innovation Committee On Consumer Policy,   23-Mar-2015

270. OECD: Building More Effective, Accountable & Inclusive Institutions For All, OECD Post-2015 Reflections, Element 6, Paper 1

271. Oehlkers, William J. & DiDonato, Cindy: Will Technology Advance Learning, or Prove a Distraction, Education Week, March 23, 2012

272. Ogbu, Dr. Osita: Please see Ogidan & Ugwu, Enitar: "Govt's Economic reforms are Turning Things Around for the Better, Says Ogbu"

273. Ogundare, Funmi: "Ezekwesili Stresses Need for State-of-the-Art Technologies" Thisday Newspapers, Wednesday September 27, 2006

274. Ogunjimi, L. O. Ajibola , C. A. and Akah, L. U: Sustenance Of Education Sector Reforms In Nigeria Through Adequate Participation By All Stakeholders, International NGO Journal, April 2009

275. Ohai, Chux: Foreign medical trips and legacy of lies; Punch, February 19, 2013

276. O'Keefe, Ed: GAO: Overlapping Government Programs Cost Billions, The Washington Post, February 28, 2012

277. Okenwa, Lilian: "Nigerian Prisons, Still Turning Inmates into Cadavers?" Thisday Newspapers, March 6, 2005

278. Okonji, Emma: "NIPOST Revokes Licenses of Eight Courier Firms", Thisday, 14-December-2015

279. Okonjo-Iweala, Ngozi Dr. (Mrs.): (Update on Nigeria's Economic Reform Agenda) Please see BPSR #3(Driving Reforms)

280. Okonjo-Iweala, Ngozi Dr. (Mrs.): "Budget 2006: Building on Human Infrastructure for Job Creation & Poverty Eradication" Budget Presentation to the National Assembly. The Guardian, Thursday December 8, 2005

281. Okonjo-Iweala, Ngozi Dr. (Mrs.): "Needs and the Future of Nigerian Education" Business Times, March 14-16, 2005

282. Okonjo-Iweala, Ngozi Dr. (Mrs.): "Understanding Nigeria's Debt Situation" Thisday Newspapers, Monday February 28, 2005

283. Okonjo-Iweala, Ngozi Dr. (Mrs.): Budget 2006 Presentation: Please see The Guardian Newspapers, Thursday December 7, 2005

284. Olatunji, Bukola: "Educational Planning as Way Forward for an Ailing Sector", Thisday Newspapers, Wednesday November 30, 2005

285. Oluwagbemiga, Oyerogba Ezekiel, Zaccheaus, Solomon Adeoluwa, Olaleye Michael Olugbenga, & Oluwaseyi, AdesinaTemitope: Stakeholders' Perception of the Independence of Public Sector Auditors in Nigeria, Asian Journal of Finance & Accounting, December 1, 2014

286. Ombudsman Association: About ombudsmen, The role of an ombudsman (from www.ombudsmanassociation.org)
287. O'Neill, Robert J. Jr: Public Services and the Wonders of the Third Week in August, Governing, June 9, 2015
288. Opejobi, Seun: Why We Register Underage Voters – INEC, Daily Post Nigeria, February 15, 2018
289. Orient software: Why Outsourcing to Vietnam
290. Osborne David and Gaebler, Ted: "Reinventing Government", The Penguin Group, 1992
291. Osuntokun, Akin: Ode to The Kaduna Mafia, Thisday 23 May 2012
292. Outsource2India: The Outsourcing History of India
293. Parrado, Salvador & Loeffler, Elke: Collaborative benchmarking in public services: Lessons from the UK for the Brazilian public sector (Product 2), Product II: Versão Preliminary do relatório, Draft report of 31 January 2013
294. Parsons, Q.N, & Robinson, J.A: State Formation and Governance in Botswana; Journal of African Economies, 15 (1), 2006 (see Acemoglu & James Robinson: The Role of Institutions in Growth & Development)
295. Patterson, James T: (quoted by Khan Academy): Grand Expectations: The United States, 1945-1971; Oxford University Press, New York:, 1996
296. Pearlstein, Steven: The federal outsourcing boom and why it's failing Americans, Washington Post, January 31, 2014
297. Philipsen, Klaus: Sane Governance in the Digital City, Sustainable Cities Collective, July 24, 2015
298. Pranevičienė, Birutė & Margevičiūtė, Agnė: Challenges To The Implementation Of Institutional Reform In The Lithuanian General Education System, Baltic Journal Of Law & Politics Volume 8 , Number 1, 2015
299. Pratley, Nils: Who audits the auditors? The Guardian (UK), Wednesday 16 June 2010
300. Premium Times: Nigeria Begins Moves To Teach Maths, Science Subjects In Indigenous Languages, Premium Times, May 31, 2017
301. Prescott, Roberta: Inside Brazil's first smart city, RCR Wireless News, August 18, 2015
302. President Olusegun Obasanjo on our Aviation industry: (Please see Ndubuisi, Francis)
303. Przeworski, Adam, Alvarez, Michael E., Cheibub, Jose Antonio, & Limongi, Fernando: Democracy And Development: Political Institutions And Well-Being In The World, 1950–1990. Cambridge: Cambridge University Press, 2000 (see North Douglass C; Wallis, John Joseph; & Weingast, Barry R)
304. Punch Editorial Board: Nigeria's housing crisis is getting worse, Punch, November 9, 2012
305. Punch newspaper [February 26, 2017, on the Kaduna Mafia]: see Adetayo, Lekan
306. Quora: How do auditing firms get audited? Feb 6, 2015
307. Rahmany, David: But Who will Monitor the Monitor, University of Minnesota, September 6, 2010
308. Rahn, Richard W.: Why do we regulate? The Washington Times, August 10, 2005
309. Rangaswami, JP: Please see Smith, Aaron & Anderson, Janna
310. Reich, Justin: Please see Smith, Aaron & Anderson, Janna
311. Rheingold, Howard: Please see Sperli, Jared
312. Richardson, Charley: How to Monitor the Monitors, Labor Notes, May 18, 2011
313. Riddle, Stewart: The robots are coming for your job! Why digital literacy is so important for the jobs of the future, August 27, 2015
314. Rita Lobo, Could Songdo be the world's smartest city? Infrastructure | Inward Investment Tuesday, January 21st, 2014
315. Roberts, David: "Utilities for dummies, part 2: Why we need competitive electricity markets (with fennec foxes!)", Grist Energy Series, 23 May 2013
316. Rodríguez-Clare, Andrés: Costa Rica's Development Strategy Based On Human Capital And Technology: How It Got There, The Impact Of Intel, And Lessons For Other Countries, Written for the Human Development Report of 2001, UNDP February 2001
317. Roose, Kevin: Robots Are Invading the News Business, and It's Great for Journalists, NY Magazine, July 11, 2014
318. Rothlein, Steve: Conducting Integrity Tests on Law Enforcement Officers, Issues and Recommendations, Legal & Liability Risk Management Institute, April 2010
319. Rotman, David: How Technology Is Destroying Jobs, MIT Technology Review, June 12, 2013

320. Rouse, Margaret & Pratt: *"Definition: Digital Economy"*
https://searchcio.techtarget.com/definition/digital-economy
321. Sahoo, Ms & Nair, CKG: Regulating The Regulators, BusinessLine, July 5, 2015
322. Salvador Parrado & Elke Loeffler: Collaborative benchmarking in public services: Lessons from the UK for the Brazilian public sector (Product 2), Product II: Versão Preliminary do relatório, Draft report of 31 January 2013
323. Sanjour, William: Designed to Fail: Why Regulatory Agencies Don't Work, Independent Science News, May 1, 2012
324. Savedoff, William D: Basic Economics of Results-Based Financing in Health, Social Insight, Bath, Maine USA, June 2010
325. Scheuerell, Frank & Breene, Paul: Best Practice for Audit Committees: Monitoring the Independent Auditor, NACD Directorship March/April 2012
326. Seltzer, Susanna : See www.quora.com (referenced March, 2017)
327. SERVICOM Office: "SERVICOM & The Citizen"
328. Shah, Ritula: Is US Monopoly On The Use Of Soft Power At An End? BBC World Tonight, 19 November 2014
329. Shapiro, Gary: Six Ways to Create Economic Growth, Forbes, Jan 23, 2013
330. Sherman, Erik: 5 White-Collar Jobs Robots Already Have Taken, Fortune, February 25, 2015
331. Shufen, Goh: Please see HSBC
332. Sigurdur Helgason: International Benchmarking Experiences from OECD Countries, A Paper Presented at International Benchmarking Conference, Copenhagen, 20-21 February 1997
333. Singapore Government: Various e-gov publications, including e-Government Governance, eGov 2015 > SingPass, and eGov2015 > OneInbox
334. Singh, N.K. : Regulating the regulators, Livemint, Sep 22 2015
335. Skonnard, Aaron: 5 Top Trends in Education Technology 2015, Inc.com, Feb 3, 2015
336. Smith, Aaron & Anderson, Janna: AI, Robotics, and the Future of Jobs, Pew Research Center on the responses to the 2014 Future of the Internet canvassing, August 6, 2014
337. Socialist Labor Party (SLP): America's Socialist Labor Party: http://www.slp.org/what_is.htm
338. Soko Directory: How the IFMIS e-procurement system works, June 26, 2015
339. SOMO (Center for Research on Multinational Corporations) & Accountability Counsel: The World Bank Inspection Panel, (Pamphlet published by these two agencies)
340. Sperli, Jared: If Schools Don't Change, Robots Will Bring On a 'Permanent Underclass', Panda Whale, Aug 06 2014
341. Spillane, Christopher, Batty, James & Wallace, Paul: *Four Charts That Show Why MTN's Nigerian Fine Matters So Much*; Bloomberg
342. Srivastava, Shishir: India: Islands of prosperity in an ocean of poverty; Poverty News Blog (from Meri News), December 29, 2007
343. State University of New York: The Future of E-Government, The Research Foundation of State University of New York, 2012
344. Stewart, Philippa H: A Technology Revolution In Kenya's Schools, Al Jazeera, 20 Jul 2013
345. Susan Taplinger: The Plain Facts: Why Self-Regulation Works Better Than Government Regulation, Posted May 9th, 2014
346. Tambur, Silver: There's a new self-driving robot on the road – and it's Estonian, Estonian World, November 9, 2015
347. Tencer, Daniel: 12 Jobs You Wouldn't Think Are Threatened By Robots, But Are, The Huffington Post Canada, 12/22/2014
348. The Coaching Group Inc: Enhancing The Growth Process,
349. The Economist: Who audits the auditors? Jun 8, 2000
350. The Economist: Who regulates the regulators? Mar 27, 2008
351. The Foundation for Law, Justice & Society: Economists And Policymakers Ask: Who Regulates The Regulators? Roundtable Of Expert Academics And Policymakers, 18 April 2011
352. The Guardian: "Government and Tax Reforms", Editorial Opinion, March 17, 2005
353. The Guardian: "Nigerians make a community of experts in America", March 11, 2005
354. Thelen, K: How Institutions Evolve. The Political Economy of Skills in Germany, Britain, the United States and Japan, Cambridge, Cambridge University Press, 2004 (see DFID: Beyond Institutions)

355. Tingle, Bryce C. : Regulating The Regulators: Why Canada's Current Regulatory System Works, Financial Post, December 22, 2014
356. TMA Solutions: The Tech Giants Have Moved To Vietnam. Why & Will You Follow Suit? 2015
357. Tobe, Frank: Please see Sherman, Erik
358. Tracy, Brian: The Top Seven Leadership Qualities & Attributes of Great Leaders, Brian Tracy International blog, October 2015
359. Treasury Today: Regulation: Don't Just Tick The Box, Jul 2015
360. Trew, Alex: Contracting Institutions & Development, University of St Andrews, October 18, 2010
361. Troev, Theodor and Petrov, Angel: Bulgaria Is Becoming A Top Outsourcing Destination, ft.com, June 5, 2015
362. Trujillo, John A., "Managed Competition Practices", US Conference of Mayors, 2010 (Assistant Director, Public Works Department)
363. Trujillo, John A., "Managed Competition Practices", US Conference of Mayors, 2010 (Assistant Director, Public Works Department)
364. TUV (The Tenants Union of Victoria): Response to the Inquiry into Victoria's Regulatory Framework Issues Paper, 17 September 2010
365. Ugeh, Patrick: Nigeria: NMA Wants Foreign Medical Trips for Public Officials Restricted; Thisday, 30 January 2013
366. UK's Department for Culture, Media & Sport, Ed Vaizey MP & Innovate UK, £10m Internet of Things competition for UK cities launched, 13 July 2015
367. UNICEF: State of the World's Children (1999) // http://www.unicef.org/sowc99/sowc99a.pdf (see also Pranevičienė & Margevičiūtė)
368. United Nations Committee of Experts on Public Administration: see United Nations: Governance & development Thematic Think Piece
369. United Nations Development Program (UNDP): Institutional Arrangements
370. United Nations E-Government Survey 2014, Department of Economic and Social Affairs, United Nations, New York, 2014
371. United Nations: Governance & development Thematic Think Piece; UN System Task Team on the post-2015 UN Development Agenda
372. Utomi, Pat: Building Enduring Institutions For National Development, The Guardian, Sep 9, 2012
373. Vahtra-Hellat, Anu: 26 countries show interest in Estonia's e-state solutions Estonian World, February 17, 2015
374. Varian, Hal: Please see Smith, Aaron & Anderson, Janna
375. Ventures Africa: Strengthening institutions of governance in Africa, April 6, 2015
376. Verver, John: Continuous Monitoring and Auditing: What is the difference? Protiviti, 2016
377. Veteran Administration (VA, USA) Education and Training: *GI Bill, History and Timeline* - US Government, , November 21, 2013
378. Vietnam Economic Times: Please see Orient software
379. Vock, Daniel C: 7 Ways Self-Driving Cars Could Impact States and Localities, Governing The States & Localities, January 15, 2015
380. Walberg, Herbert J.: "Lifting School Standards", The Hoover Institution, 2005
381. Wallis, John Joseph: Structure and change in economic history: The ideas of Douglass North, VOX CEPR's Policy Portal, 27 November 2015
382. Walters, Jonathan : Policing the Police, Governance, March 31, 2010
383. Webb, Amy: Please see Smith, Aaron & Anderson, Janna
384. Weise, Michelle R & Christensen, Clayton M: Please see Skonnard, Aaron
385. Wentling, Mark: Making Aid Work by Building Strong Institutions, Foreign Service Despatches & Periodic Reports on US Foreign Policy, American Diplomacy Publishers Chapel Hill NC, June 2015
386. White, John Cassar: Regulating the regulators, Times of Malta, Monday, May 23, 2016
387. White, John Cassar: Regulating the regulators, timesofmalta, Monday, May 23, 2016
388. Wiggins, S. and Davis, J: Economic Institutions, IPPG Briefing Paper 3 , 2006 (see DFID: Beyond Institutions)
389. wikibooks.org: The Information Age/Information Knowledge and the New Economy, Accessed April 16, 2016
390. Wikipedia, the free encyclopaedia: *G.I. Bill*; Accessed, June 2018
391. Wikipedia, the free encyclopaedia: Internet of Things, November 2015

392. Wikipedia, the free encyclopedia: Auditor General of Canada
393. Wilson, James O.: "What Government Agencies Do & Why They Do It", Basic Books Inc, 1989
394. Wiseman, Paul: Humans Need Not Apply: A World Where Technology Replaces Workers Christian Science Monitor (Associated Press), January 24, 2013
395. Wood, Adrian: "Telecoms Regulation and Fruit (III)", Business Times, March 17-20, 2005
396. World Bank (PSGB): Better Results from Public Sector Institutions - The World Bank's Approach to Public Sector Management 2011 – 2020, 2012
397. World Bank, Mexico: the federal procurement system saves money for social projects, May 7, 2012
398. World Bank, PPPIRC (Public-Private-Partnership In Infrastructure Resource Center): Regulation of Sectors & Regulatory Issues Impacting PPPs
399. World Bank: Doing Business Report, 2005-2016 & various other years
400. World Bank: Electronic Government Procurement (e-GP), World Bank Draft Strategy, The World Bank Procurement Policy & Services Group, Washington, D.C.; October 2003
401. World Bank: Reforming Public Institutions & Strengthening Governance, A World Bank Strategy, November 2000
402. World Bank: Reforming Public Institutions & Strengthening Governance - A World Bank Strategy, Public Sector Board Poverty Reduction and Economic Management Network, September, 2000
403. World Bank: What is Governance? Arriving at a Common Understanding of "Governance:" , (http://web.worldbank.org/WBSITE/EXTERNAL/COUNTRIES/MENAEXT/EXTMNAREGTOP GOVERNANCE/0,,contentMDK:20513159~pagePK:34004173~piPK:34003707~theSitePK:4970 24,00.html)
404. World Bank: World Development Report, 2000 - 2017
405. World Bank's Strategy For Reforming Public Institutions (see Manning, Nick; Mukherjee, Ranjana & Gokcekus, Omer)
406. Yakubu, Tanimu Mallam: Please see Simire, Michael: "Depository-based Housing Finance System has Fallen Short"
407. Yesufu, Kemi: Reps & Its Investigation Into N351bn Health Insurance Payment; The Sun, July 4, 2017
408. Yost, Dave: Performance Audits, Ohio Auditor-gov
409. Zairi, M. & Leonard, P: Please see Blakeman, Joseph

Index